S0-APM-036

Cram101 Textbook Outlines to accompany:

International Business: The Challenge of Global Competition

Donald Ball, 12th Edition

A Cram101 Inc. publication (c) 2010.

PRACTICE EXAMS.

Get all of the self-teaching practice exams for each chapter of this textbook at **www.Cram101.com** and ace the tests. Here is an example:

Chapter 1

International Business: The Challenge of Global Competition
Donald Ball, 12th Edition,
All Material Written and Prepared by Cram101

I WANT A BETTER GRADE. Items 1 - 50 of 100.

1 _________ is a term used to collectively describe topics relating to the operations of firms with interests in multiple countries. Such firms are sometimes called multinational corporations . Well known MNCs include fast food companies McDonald's and Yum Brands, vehicle manufacturers such as General Motors and Toyota, consumer electronics companies like Samsung, LG and Sony, and energy companies such as ExxonMobil and BP.

- International business
- I Am Canadian
- I learned it by watching you
- I Love the World

2 _________ is a term that has different meanings. For example, in 1952, Alfred Kroeber and Clyde Kluckhohn compiled a list of 164 definitions of _________ in _________ A Critical Review of Concepts and Definitions. However, the word _________ is most commonly used in three basic senses:

· excellence of taste in the fine arts and humanities, also known as high _________
· an integrated pattern of human knowledge, belief, and behavior that depends upon the capacity for symbolic thought and social learning
· the set of shared attitudes, values, goals, and practices that characterizes an institution, organization or group.

When the concept first emerged in eighteenth- and nineteenth-century Europe, it connoted a process of cultivation or improvement, as in agri _________ or horti _________ . In the nineteenth century, it came to refer first to the betterment or refinement of the individual, especially through education, and then to the fulfillment of

With Cram101.com online, you also have access to extensive reference material.

You will nail those essays and papers. Here is an example from a Cram101 Biology text:

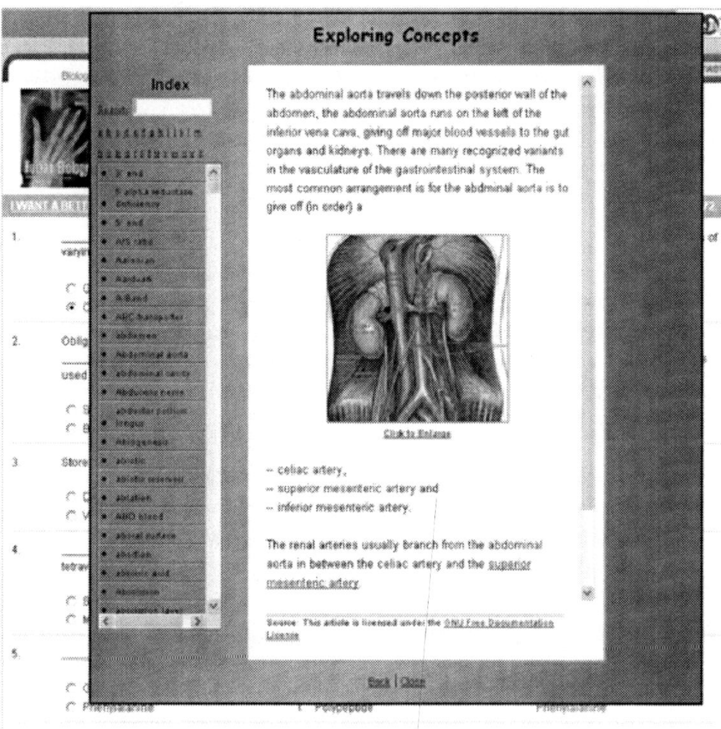

Visit **www.Cram101.com**, click Sign Up at the top of the screen, and enter DK73DW8064 in the promo code box on the registration screen. Access to www.Cram101.com is normally $9.95 per month, but because you have purchased this book, your access fee is only $4.95 per month, cancel at any time. Sign up and stop highlighting textbooks forever.

Learning System

Cram101 Textbook Outlines is a learning system. The notes in this book are the highlights of your textbook, you will never have to highlight a book again.

How to use this book. Take this book to class, it is your notebook for the lecture. The notes and highlights on the left hand side of the pages follow the outline and order of the textbook. All you have to do is follow along while your instructor presents the lecture. Circle the items emphasized in class and add other important information on the right side. With Cram101 Textbook Outlines you'll spend less time writing and more time listening. Learning becomes more efficient.

Cram101.com Online

Increase your studying efficiency by using Cram101.com's practice tests and online reference material. It is the perfect complement to Cram101 Textbook Outlines. Use self-teaching matching tests or simulate in-class testing with comprehensive multiple choice tests, or simply use Cram's true and false tests for quick review. Cram101.com even allows you to enter your in-class notes for an integrated studying format combining the textbook notes with your class notes.

Visit **www.Cram101.com**, click Sign Up at the top of the screen, and enter **DK73DW8064** in the promo code box on the registration screen. Access to www.Cram101.com is normally $9.95 per month, but because you have purchased this book, your access fee is only $4.95 per month. Sign up and stop highlighting textbooks forever.

 ISBN(s): 9781428891463.

International Business: The Challenge of Global Competition
Donald Ball, 12th

CONTENTS

International business

International business is a term used to collectively describe topics relating to the operations of firms with interests in multiple countries. Such firms are sometimes called multinational corporations . Well known MNCs include fast food companies McDonald's and Yum Brands, vehicle manufacturers such as General Motors and Toyota, consumer electronics companies like Samsung, LG and Sony, and energy companies such as ExxonMobil and BP.

Culture

Culture is a term that has different meanings. For example, in 1952, Alfred Kroeber and Clyde Kluckhohn compiled a list of 164 definitions of culture in culture A Critical Review of Concepts and Definitions. However, the word culture is most commonly used in three basic senses:

· excellence of taste in the fine arts and humanities, also known as high culture
· an integrated pattern of human knowledge, belief, and behavior that depends upon the capacity for symbolic thought and social learning
· the set of shared attitudes, values, goals, and practices that characterizes an institution, organization or group.

When the concept first emerged in eighteenth- and nineteenth-century Europe, it connoted a process of cultivation or improvement, as in agri culture or horti culture . In the nineteenth century, it came to refer first to the betterment or refinement of the individual, especially through education, and then to the fulfillment of national aspirations or ideals.

Expert witnesses

An expert witness or professional witness is a witness, who by virtue of education, training, skill is believed to have knowledge in a particular subject beyond that of the average person, sufficient that others may officially (and legally) rely upon the witness's specialized (scientific, technical or other) opinion about an evidence or fact issue within the scope of their expertise, referred to as the expert opinion, as an assistance to the fact-finder. Expert witnesses may also deliver expert evidence about facts from the domain of their expertise. At times, their testimony may be rebutted with a learned treatise, sometimes to the detriment of their reputations.

Function cost analysis

Function cost analysis is the a method of technical and economic research of the systems for purpose to optimize a parity between system's consumer functions or properties and expenses to achieve those functions or properties.

This methodology for continuous perfection of production, industrial technologies, organizational structures was developed by Juryj Sobolev in 1948 at the 'Perm telephone factory'

· 1948 Juryj Sobolev - the first success in application of a method analysis at the 'Perm telephone factory' .
· 1949 - the first application for the invention as result of use of the new method.

Today in economically developed countries practically each enterprise or the company use methodology of the kind of functional-cost analysis as a practice of the quality management, most full satisfying to principles of standards of series ISO 9000.

· Interest of consumer not in products itself, but the advantage which it will receive from its usage.
· The consumer aspires to reduce his expenses
· Functions needed by consumer can be executed in the various ways, and, hence, with various efficiency and expenses.

Among possible alternatives of realization of functions exist such in which the parity of quality and the price is the optimal for the consumer.

The goal of Function cost analysis is achievement of the highest consumer satisfaction of production at simultaneous decrease in all kinds of industrial expenses Classical Function cost analysis has three English synonyms - Value Engineering, Value Management, Value Analysis.

Export

In economics, an export is any good or commodity, transported from one country to another country in a legitimate fashion, typically for use in trade. export goods or services are provided to foreign consumers by domestic producers. export is an important part of international trade.

Globalization

Globalization in its literal sense is the process of transformation of local or regional phenomena into global ones. It can be described as a process by which the people of the world are unified into a single society and function together.

This process is a combination of economic, technological, sociocultural and political forces.

Characteristic

Characteristic has several particular meanings:

· in mathematics

- · Euler characteristic
- · method of characteristic s (partial differential equations)

· in physics and engineering

· any characteristic curve that shows the relationship between certain input- and output parameters, e.g.
· an I-V or current-voltage characteristic is the current in a circuit as a function of the applied voltage
· Receiver-Operator characteristic
· in navigation, the characteristic pattern of a lighted beacon.
· in fiction

· in Dungeons ' Dragons, characteristic is another name for ability score .

Report

In writing, a report is a document characterized by information or other content reflective of inquiry or investigation, which is tailored to the context of a given situation and audience. The purpose of report s is usually to inform. However, report s may include persuasive elements, such as recommendations, suggestions, or other motivating conclusions that indicate possible future actions the report reader might take.

United Nations

The United Nations is an international organization whose stated aims are to facilitate cooperation in international law, international security, economic development, social progress, human rights and achieving world peace. The United Nations was founded in 1945 after World War II to replace the League of Nations, to stop wars between countries and to provide a platform for dialogue.

There are currently 192 member states, including nearly every recognized independent state in the world.

Market

A Market is any one of a variety of different systems, institutions, procedures, social relations and infrastructures whereby persons trade, and goods and services are exchanged, forming part of the economy. It is an arrangement that allows buyers and sellers to exchange things. Market s vary in size, range, geographic scale, location, types and variety of human communities, as well as the types of goods and services traded.

Ownership

Ownership is the state or fact of exclusive rights and control over property, which may be an object, land/real estate, or some other kind of property (like government-granted monopolies collectively referred to as intellectual property.) It is embodied in an Ownership right also referred to as title.

Ownership is the key building block in the development of the capitalist socio-economic system.

United Nations Conference on Trade and Development

The United Nations Conference on Trade and Development was established in 1964 as a permanent intergovernmental body. It is the principal organ of the United Nations General Assembly dealing with trade, investment and development issues.

The organization's goals are to 'maximize the trade, investment and development opportunities of developing countries and assist them in their efforts to integrate into the world economy on an equitable basis.' (from official website.)

Fair Trade

Fair trade is an organized social movement and market-based approach that aims to help producers in developing countries and promote sustainability. The movement advocates the payment of a fair price as well as social and environmental standards in areas related to the production of a wide variety of goods. It focuses in particular on exports from developing countries to developed countries, most notably handicrafts, coffee, cocoa, sugar, tea, bananas, honey, cotton, wine, fresh fruit, chocolate and flowers.

Mercantilism

Mercantilism is an economic theory that holds that the prosperity of a nation is dependent upon its supply of capital, and that the global volume of international trade is 'unchangeable.' Economic assets or capital, are represented by bullion (gold, silver, and trade value) held by the state, which is best increased through a positive balance of trade with other nations (exports minus imports.) Mercantilism suggests that the ruling government should advance these goals by playing a protectionist role in the economy; by encouraging exports and discouraging imports, notably through the use of tariffs and subsidies.

Mercantilism was the dominant school of thought throughout the early modern period (from the 16th to the 18th century.)

Direct investment

Foreign Direct investment in its classic form is defined as a company from one country making a physical investment into building a factory in another country. It is the establishment of an enterprise by a foreigner. Its definition can be extended to include investments made to acquire lasting interest in enterprises operating outside of the economy of the investor.

Foreign direct investment

Foreign direct investment in its classic form is defined as a company from one country making a physical investment into building a factory in another country. It is the establishment of an enterprise by a foreigner. Its definition can be extended to include investments made to acquire lasting interest in enterprises operating outside of the economy of the investor.

Advertising

Advertising is a form of communication that typically attempts to persuade potential customers to purchase or to consume more of a particular brand of product or service. 'While now central to the contemporary global economy and the reproduction of global production networks, it is only quite recently that Advertising has been more than a marginal influence on patterns of sales and production. The formation of modern Advertising was intimately bound up with the emergence of new forms of monopoly capitalism around the end of the 19th and beginning of the 20th century as one element in corporate strategies to create, organize and where possible control markets, especially for mass produced consumer goods.

Business

A business is a legally recognized organization designed to provide goods and/or services to consumers. business es are predominant in capitalist economies, most being privately owned and formed to earn profit that will increase the wealth of its owners and grow the business itself. The owners and operators of a business have as one of their main objectives the receipt or generation of a financial return in exchange for work and acceptance of risk.

Cable	A cable is two or more wires or ropes running side by side and bonded, twisted or braided together to form a single assembly. In mechanics, cable s are used for lifting and hauling; in electricity they are used to carry electrical currents. An optical cable contains one or more optical fibers in a protective jacket that supports the fibers.
Economic	An economy (or 'the economy') is the realized Economic system of a country or other area. It includes the production, exchange, distribution, and consumption of goods and services of that area. The study of different types and examples of economies is the subject of Economic systems.
Economic globalization	Economic globalization can be defined as the process of increasing economic integration between two countries, leading to the emergence of a global marketplace or a single world market. Depending on the paradigm, globalization can be viewed as both a positive and a negative phenomenon. Whilst Economic globalization has been occurring for the last several thousand years (since the emergence of trans-national trade), it has begun to occur at an increased rate over the last 20-30 years.
Free Trade	Free trade is a type of trade policy that allows traders to act and transact without interference from government. Thus, the policy permits trading partners mutual gains from trade, with goods and services produced according to the theory of comparative advantage. Under a Free trade policy, prices are a reflection of true supply and demand, and are the sole determinant of resource allocation.
North American Free Trade Agreement	The North American Free Trade Agreement is a trilateral trade bloc in North America created by the governments of the United States, Canada, and Mexico. It superseded the Canada-United States Free Trade Agreement between the US and Canada. Following diplomatic negotiations dating back to 1990 between the three nations, the leaders met in San Antonio, Texas on December 17, 1992 to sign North American Free Trade Agreement.
Privatization	Privatization is the incidence or process of transferring ownership of a business, enterprise, agency or public service from the public sector (government) to the private sector (business.) In a broader sense, Privatization refers to transfer of any government function to the private sector including governmental functions like revenue collection and law enforcement. The term 'Privatization' also has been used to describe two unrelated transactions.
Satellite	In the context of spaceflight, a satellite is an object which has been placed into orbit by human endeavor. Such objects are sometimes called artificial satellite s to distinguish them from natural satellite s such as the Moon. The first artificial satellite Sputnik 1, was launched by the Soviet Union in 1957.
Consumer	Consumer is a broad label that refers to any individuals or households that use goods and services generated within the economy. The concept of a Consumer is used in different contexts, so that the usage and significance of the term may vary. A Consumer is a person who uses any product or service.
Consumer goods	Consumer goods are final goods specifically intended for the mass market. For instance, consumer goods do not include investment assets, like precious antiques, even though these antiques are final goods.

Manufactured goods are goods that have been processed by way of machinery.

Global reach

Global Reach is a business initiative to increase the access between a company and their current and potential customers through the use of the Internet. The Internet allows the company to market themselves and attract new customers to their website where they can provide product information and better customer service. Customers can place orders electronically, therefore reducing expensive long distant phone calls and postage costs of placing orders, while saving time on behalf of the customer and company.

Good

A good is an object whose consumption increases the utility of the consumer, for which the quantity demanded exceeds the quantity supplied at zero price. Goods are usually modeled as having diminishing marginal utility. The first individual purchase has high utility; the second has less.

Set TSP

In combinatorial optimization, the set TSP group TSP, One-of-a-set TSP, Multiple Choice TSP or Covering Salesman Problem, is a generalization of the Traveling salesman problem, whereby it is required to find a shortest tour in a graph which visits all specified disjoint subsets of the vertices of a graph. The ordinary TSP is a special case of the set TSP when all subsets to be visited are singletons. Therefore the set TSP is also NP-hard.

Organization

An organization is a social arrangement which pursues collective goals, which controls its own performance, and which has a boundary separating it from its environment. The word itself is derived from the Greek word á½„ργανον (organon [itself derived from the better-known word á¼"ργον ergon - work; deed - > ergonomics, etc]) meaning tool. The term is used in both daily and scientific English in multiple ways.

World Trade Organization

The World Trade Organization is an international organization designed to supervise and liberalize international trade. The World Trade Organization came into being on 1 January 1995, and is the successor to the General Agreement on Tariffs and Trade (GATT), which was created in 1947, and continued to operate for almost five decades as a de facto international organization.

The World Trade Organization deals with the rules of trade between nations at a near-global level; it is responsible for negotiating and implementing new trade agreements, and is in charge of policing member countries' adherence to all the World Trade Organization agreements, signed by the majority of the world's trading nations and ratified in their parliaments.

Cost

In economics, business, retail, and accounting, a cost is the value of money that has been used up to produce something, and hence is not available for use anymore. In economics, a cost is an alternative that is given up as a result of a decision. In business, the cost may be one of acquisition, in which case the amount of money expended to acquire it is counted as cost.

Economies of scale

Economies of scale in microeconomics, are the cost advantages that a business obtains due to expansion. They are factors that cause a producer's average cost per unit to fall as scale is increased. Economies of scale is a long run concept and refers to reductions in unit cost as the size of a facility, or scale, increases.

Internet	The Internet is a global network of interconnected computers, enabling users to share information along multiple channels. Typically, a computer that connects to the Internet can access information from a vast array of available servers and other computers by moving information from them to the computer's local memory. The same connection allows that computer to send information to servers on the network; that information is in turn accessed and potentially modified by a variety of other interconnected computers.
Mercosur	MERCOSUR or Mercosul is a Regional Trade Agreement among Argentina, Brazil, Paraguay and Uruguay founded in 1991 by the Treaty of Asunción, which was later amended and updated by the 1994 Treaty of Ouro Preto. Its purpose is to promote free trade and the fluid movement of goods, people, and currency. MERCOSUR origins trace back to 1985 when Presidents Raúl Alfonsín of Argentina and José Sarney of Brazil signed the Argentina-Brazil Integration and Economics Cooperation Program or PICE .
Absenteeism	Absenteeism is a habitual pattern of absence from a duty or obligation. Frequent absence from the workplace may be indicative of poor morale or of sick building syndrome. However, many employers have implemented absence policies which make no distinction between absences for genuine illness and absence for inappropriate reasons.
Purchasing	Purchasing refers to a business or organization attempting to acquire goods or services to accomplish the goals of the enterprise. Though there are several organizations that attempt to set standards in the Purchasing process, processes can vary greatly between organizations. Typically the word 'Purchasing' is not used interchangeably with the word 'procurement', since procurement typically includes Expediting, Supplier Quality, and Traffic and Logistics (T'L) in addition to Purchasing.
Purchasing power	Purchasing power is the number of goods/services that can be purchased with a unit of currency. For example, if you had taken one dollar to a store in the 1950s, you would have been able to buy a greater number of items than you would today, indicating that you would have had a greater purchasing power in the 1950s. Currency can be either a commodity money, like gold or silver, or fiat currency like US dollars which are the world reserve currency.
Purchasing power parity	The Purchasing power parity theory uses the long-term equilibrium exchange rate of two currencies to equalize their purchasing power. Developed by Gustav Cassel in 1918, it is based on the law of one price: the theory states that, in ideally efficient markets, identical goods should have only one price. This purchasing power SEM rate equalizes the purchasing power of different currencies in their home countries for a given basket of goods.
Asset	In business and accounting, asset s are economic resources owned by business or company. Anything tangible or intangible that one possesses, usually considered as applicable to the payment of one's debts is considered an asset Simplistically stated, asset s are things of value that can be readily converted into cash.
International trade	International trade is exchange of capital, goods, and services across international borders or territories. In most countries, it represents a significant share of gross domestic product (GDP.) While International trade has been present throughout much of history , its economic, social, and political importance has been on the rise in recent centuries.

Merchandise	Merchandising refers to the methods, practices and operations conducted to promote and sustain certain categories of commercial activity. The term is understood to have different specific meanings depending on the context. merchandise is a sale goods at a store In marketing, one of the definitions of merchandising is the practice in which the brand or image from one product or service is used to sell another.
Mergers and Acquisitions	The phrase Mergers and Acquisitions refers to the aspect of corporate strategy, corporate finance and management dealing with the buying, selling and combining of different companies that can aid, finance, or help a growing company in a given industry grow rapidly without having to create another business entity. An acquisition, also known as a takeover or a buyout, is the buying of one company (the 'target') by another. An acquisition may be friendly or hostile.
Mergers	The phrase mergers and acquisitions refers to the aspect of corporate strategy, corporate finance and management dealing with the buying, selling and combining of different companies that can aid, finance, or help a growing company in a given industry grow rapidly without having to create another business entity. An acquisition, also known as a takeover or a buyout, is the buying of one company (the 'target') by another. An acquisition may be friendly or hostile.
Comparative advertising	Comparative advertising is an advertisement in which a particular product specifically mentions a competitor by name for the express purpose of showing why the competitor is inferior to the product naming it. This should not be confused with parody advertisements, where a fictional product is being advertised for the purpose of poking fun at the particular advertisement, nor should it be confused with the use of a coined brand name for the purpose of comparing the product without actually naming an actual competitor. ('Wikipedia tastes better and is less filling than the Encyclopedia Galactica.') In the 1980s, during what has been referred to as the cola wars, soft-drink manufacturer Pepsi ran a series of advertisements where people, caught on hidden camera, in a blind taste test, chose Pepsi over rival Coca-Cola.
United States	The United States of America (commonly referred to as the United States the U.S., the United States A, or America) is a federal constitutional republic comprising fifty states and a federal district. The country is situated mostly in central North America, where its 48 contiguous states and Washington, D.C., the capital district, lie between the Pacific and Atlantic Oceans, bordered by Canada to the north and Mexico to the south. The state of Alaska is in the northwest of the continent, with Canada to its east and Russia to the west across the Bering Strait.
Acquisition	The phrase mergers and acquisitions refers to the aspect of corporate strategy, corporate finance and management dealing with the buying, selling and combining of different companies that can aid, finance, or help a growing company in a given industry grow rapidly without having to create another business entity. An Acquisition, also known as a takeover or a buyout, is the buying of one company (the 'target') by another. An Acquisition may be friendly or hostile.
Affiliate	In the broadcasting industry (especially in North America), a network Affiliate is a local broadcaster which carries some or all of the programme line-up of a television or radio network, but is owned by a company other than the owner of the network. This distinguishes such a station from an owned-and-operated station (O'O), which is owned by its parent network.

	In the United States, Federal Communications Commission (FCC) regulations limit the number of network-owned stations as a percentage of total market size.
Discrimination	Discrimination toward or against a person of a certain group is the treatment or consideration based on class or category rather than individual merit. It can be behavior promoting a certain group (e.g. affirmative action), or it can be negative behavior directed against a certain group (e.g. redlining.) Racial discrimination differentiates between individuals on the basis of real and perceived racial differences, and has been official government policy in several countries, such as South Africa in the apartheid era, and the USA.
Gross domestic product	The Gross domestic product or gross domestic income (GDI), a basic measure of an economy's economic performance, is the market value of all final goods and services produced within the borders of a nation in a year. Gross domestic product can be defined in three ways, all of which are conceptually identical. First, it is equal to the total expenditures for all final goods and services produced within the country in a stipulated period of time (usually a 365-day year.)
Electronic Commerce	Electronic commerce, commonly known as e-commerce or eCommerce, consists of the buying and selling of products or services over electronic systems such as the Internet and other computer networks. The amount of trade conducted electronically has grown extraordinarily with wide-spread Internet usage. A wide variety of commerce is conducted in this way, spurring and drawing on innovations in electronic funds transfer, supply chain management, Internet marketing, online transaction processing, electronic data interchange (EDI), inventory management systems, and automated data collection systems.
Microsoft	Microsoft Corporation (NASDAQ: MSFT, HKEX: 4338) is an United States-based multinational computer technology corporation that develops, manufactures, licenses, and supports a wide range of software products for computing devices. Headquartered in Redmond, Washington, USA, its most profitable products are the Microsoft Windows operating system and the Microsoft Office suite of productivity software. The company was founded to develop and sell BASIC interpreters for the Altair 8800.
Adam Smith	Adam Smith was a Scottish moral philosopher and a pioneer of political economy. One of the key figures of the Scottish Enlightenment, Smith is the author of The Theory of Moral Sentiments and An Inquiry into the Nature and Causes of the Wealth of Nations. The latter, usually abbreviated as The Wealth of Nations, is considered his magnum opus and the first modern work of economics.
Child labour	Child labour refers to the employment of children at regular and sustained labour. This practice is considered exploitative by many international organizations and is illegal in many countries. Child labour was utilized to varying extents through most of history, but entered public dispute with the beginning of universal schooling, with changes in working conditions during industrialization, and with the emergence of the concepts of workers' and children's rights.
Theory of the firm	The Theory of the firm consists of a number of economic theories which describe the nature of the firm, company including its existence, its behaviour, and its relationship with the market.

In simplified terms, the Theory of the firm aims to answer these questions:

- Existence - why do firms emerge, why are not all transactions in the economy mediated over the market?
- Boundaries - why the boundary between firms and the market is located exactly there? Which transactions are performed internally and which are negotiated on the market?
- Organization - why are firms structured in such specific way? What is the interplay of formal and informal relationships?

The First World War period saw a change of emphasis in economic theory away from industry-level analysis which mainly included analysing markets to analysis at the level of the firm, as it became increasingly clear that perfect competition was no longer an adequate model of how firms behaved. Economic theory till then had focussed on trying to understand markets alone and there had been little study on understanding why firms or organisations exist. Market are mainly guided by prices as illustrated by vegetable markets where a buyer is free to switch sellers in an exchange.

Economic development

Economic development is the development of economic wealth of countries or regions for the well-being of their inhabitants. It is the process by which a nation improves the economic, political, and social well being of its people. From a policy perspective, Economic development can be defined as efforts that seek to improve the economic well-being and quality of life for a community by creating and/or retaining jobs and supporting or growing incomes and the tax base.

International Finance

International finance is the branch of economics that studies the dynamics of exchange rates, foreign investment, and how these affect international trade. It also studies international projects, international investments and capital flows, and trade deficits. It includes the study of futures, options and currency swaps.

Job creation

Job creation programs are programs or projects undertaken by a government of a nation in order to assist unemployed members of the population in seeking employment. They are especially common during time of high unemployment. They may either concentrate on macroeconomic policy in order to increase the supply of jobs, or create more efficient means to pair employment seekers to their prospective employers .

Procter ' Gamble

Procter is a surname, and may also refer to:

- Bryan Waller Procter (pseud. Barry Cornwall), English poet
- Goodwin Procter, American law firm
- Procter ' Gamble, consumer products multinational .

Expectancy

Expectancy theory is about the mental processes regarding choice, or choosing. It explains the processes that an individual undergoes to make choices. In organizational behavior study, expectancy theory is a motivation theory first proposed by Victor Vroom of the Yale School of Management.

Government Procurement

Government procurement or public procurement, is the procurement of goods and services on behalf of a public authority, such as a government agency. With 10 to 15% of GDP in developed countries, and up to 20% in developing countries, Government procurement accounts for a substantial part of the global economy.

	To prevent fraud, waste, corruption or local protectionism, the law of most countries regulates Government procurement more or less closely.
Economic inequality	Economic inequality comprises all disparities in the distribution of economic assets and income. The term typically refers to inequality among individuals and groups within a society, but can also refer to inequality among countries. Economic inequality generally refers to equality of outcome, and is related to the idea of equality of opportunity.
International Monetary Fund	The International Monetary Fund is an international organization that oversees the global financial system by following the macroeconomic policies of its member countries, in particular those with an impact on exchange rates and the balance of payments. It is an organization formed to stabilize international exchange rates and facilitate development. It also offers financial and technical assistance to its members, making it an international lender of last resort.
Monetary	Monetary policy is the process by which the government, central bank (ii) availability of money, and (iii) cost of money or rate of interest, in order to attain a set of objectives oriented towards the growth and stability of the economy. monetary theory provides insight into how to craft optimal monetary policy. monetary policy is referred to as either being an expansionary policy where an expansionary policy increases the total supply of money in the economy, and a contractionary policy decreases the total money supply.
Triple bottom line	The Triple bottom line captures an expanded spectrum of values and criteria for measuring organizational success: economic, ecological and social. With the ratification of the United Nations and ICLEI Triple bottom line standard for urban and community accounting in early 2007, this became the dominant approach to public sector full cost accounting. Similar UN standards apply to natural capital and human capital measurement to assist in measurements required by Triple bottom line, e.g. the ecoBudget standard for reporting ecological footprint.
Challenge	Challenge is a United Kingdom digital TV channel owned by Virgin Media Television. It was originally called The Family Channel from 1 September 1993 to 31 January 1997 but it was later re-branded as challenge TV from 1 February 1997. On 20 May 2002 the channel was re-named again but this time it was just challenge? and 30 June 2003 the question mark was removed to leave the challenge name in its place.
Embargo	An Embargo is the prohibition of commerce and trade with a certain country, in order to isolate it and to put its government into a difficult internal situation, given that the effects of the Embargo are often able to make its economy suffer from the initiative. It is similar to a blockade, as in 'el bloqueo' or the American blockade on Cuba. Embargo s generally attempt to pressure weaker adversaries to do what the abarcading country wishes.
Failure	Failure refers to the state or condition of not meeting a desirable or intended objective, and may be viewed as the opposite of success. Product failure ranges from failure to sell the product to fracture of the product, in the worst cases leading to personal injury, the province of forensic engineering. The criteria for failure are heavily dependent on context of use, and may be relative to a particular observer or belief system.
Numerary	Numerary is a civil designation for persons who are incorporated in a fixed or permanent way to a society or group: regular member of the working staff, permanent staff distinguished from a super Numerary . The term Numerary and its counterpart, 'super Numerary ,' originated in Spanish and Latin American academy and government; it is now also used in countries all over the world, such as France, the U.S., England, Italy, etc.

There are Numerary members of surgical organizations, of universities, of gastronomical associations, etc.

Economic integration

Economic integration is a term used to describe how different aspects between economies are integrated. The basics of this theory were written by the Hungarian Economist Béla Balassa in the 1960s. As economic integration increases, the barriers of trade between markets diminishes.

Job migration

Job migration is a term that has gained widespread use in the recent years and although it means relocation of jobs from one geographical area to another, it has come to symbolize the migration or relocation of jobs to other countries.

In most situations jobs are moved from one location to another, or to multiple other locations, because of changes in one or many of the following: supply and demand for products and services, business conditions, labor markets, government policies, political reasons, competition, environmental conditions, local business costs, technological obsolescence, outsourcing, higher productivity, etc.

Job migration usually leads to rise in unemployment often accompanied by a difficult transition to new jobs and new locations requiring new training and lowered living standards, although not for everyone.

Kraft Foods

Kraft Foods Inc. (NYSE: Kraft Foods T) is the largest food and beverage company headquartered in the United States and the second largest in the world (after Nestlé SA.)

Kraft is headquartered in Northfield, Illinois, USA, a Chicago suburb.

Pollution

Pollution is the introduction of contaminants into an environment that causes instability, disorder, harm or discomfort to the ecosystem i.e. physical systems or living organisms . Pollution can take the form of chemical substances, or energy, such as noise, heat, or light energy. Pollutants, the elements of Pollution, can be foreign substances or energies, or naturally occurring; when naturally occurring, they are considered contaminants when they exceed natural levels.

Race to the bottom

A Race to the bottom usually refers to an individual entity seeking a more favorable outcome at the expense of other entities by upsetting an equilibrium to their own favor, only to cause an inevitable retaliation by the other individuals to rebalance the equilibrium, resulting in all participants having an overall less favorable outcome. For example, people may have a tendency to buy increasingly larger, heavier, and often more expensive cars because the additional weight can help make the car safer in a collision with a smaller, lighter car. Thus, to keep up with the average vehicle weight for safety's sake, drivers must buy heavier, more expensive, less efficient cars while safety on the whole does not improve compared to when the average vehicle was lighter.

Competitive

Competitive ness is a comparative concept of the ability and performance of a firm, sub-sector or country to sell and supply goods and/or services in a given market. Although widely used in economics and business management, the usefulness of the concept, particularly in the context of national competitive ness, is vigorously disputed by economists, such as Paul Krugman .

The term may also be applied to markets, where it is used to refer to the extent to which the market structure may be regarded as perfectly competitive

External

In economics, an external ity or spillover of an economic transaction is an impact on a party that is not directly involved in the transaction. In such a case, prices do not reflect the full costs or benefits in production or consumption of a product or service. A positive impact is called an external benefit, while a negative impact is called an external cost.

Variable	Variables are used in open sentences. For instance, in the formula x + 1 = 5, x is a variable which represents an 'unknown' number. Variables are often represented by letters of the Roman alphabet, or those of other alphabets, such as Greek, and use other special symbols.
Cuba	The Republic of Cuba) is an island country in the Caribbean. It consists of the island of Cuba, the Isla de la Juventud, and several archipelagos. Havana is the largest city in Cuba and the country's capital.
Control	Control is one of the managerial functions like planning, organizing, staffing and directing. It is an important function because it helps to check the errors and to take the corrective action so that deviation from standards are minimized and stated goals of the organization are achieved in desired manner.According to modern concepts, Control is a foreseeing action whereas earlier concept of Control was used only when errors were detected. Control in management means setting standards, measuring actual performance and taking corrective action.
Foreign ownership	Foreign ownership refers to the complete or majority ownership/control of a business or resource in a country by individuals who are not citizens of that country, or by companies whose headquarters are not in that country.
Decision making	Decision making can be regarded as an outcome of mental processes (cognitive process) leading to the selection of a course of action among several alternatives. Every decision making process produces a final choice. The output can be an action or an opinion of choice.
Expatriate	An expatriate is a person temporarily or permanently residing in a country and culture other than that of the person's upbringing or legal residence. The word comes from the Latin ex and patria (country, fatherland.) The term is sometimes used in the context of Westerners living in non-Western countries, although it is also used to describe Westerners living in other Western countries, such as U.S. citizens living in the United Kingdom, or Britons living in Spain.
World Bank	The World Bank is an international financial institution that provides financial and technical assistance to developing countries for development programs (e.g. bridges, roads, schools, etc.) with the stated goal of reducing poverty. The World Bank differs from the World Bank Group, in that the World Bank comprises only two institutions: · International Bank for Reconstruction and Development (IBRD) · International Development Association (IDA) Whereas the latter incorporates these two in addition to three more: · International Finance Corporation (IFC) · Multilateral Investment Guarantee Agency (MIGA) · International Centre for Settlement of Investment Disputes (ICSID) John Maynard Keynes (right) represented the UK at the conference, and Harry Dexter White represented the US. The World Bank was created following the ratification of the United Nations Monetary and Financial Conference of the Bretton Woods agreement. The concept was originally conceived in July 1944 at the United Nations Monetary and Financial Conference.

Facing	Facing,, is a common tool in the retail industry to create the look of a perfectly stocked store by pulling all of the products on a display or shelf to the front, as well as downstacking all the canned and stacked items. It is also done to keep the store appearing neat and organized. The workers who face commonly have jobs doing other things in the store such as customer service, stocking shelves, daytime cleaning, bagging and carryouts, etc.
Extortion	'Extortion', outwresting property or services from a person, entity through coercion. Refraining from doing harm is sometimes euphemistically called protection. Extortion is commonly practiced by organized crime groups.
Business marketing	Business marketing is the practice of individuals including commercial businesses, governments and institutions, facilitating the sale of their products or services to other companies or organizations that in turn resell them, use them as components in products or services they offer Business marketing is also called business-to-Business marketing for short. (Note that while marketing to government entities shares some of the same dynamics of organizational marketing, B2G Marketing is meaningfully different.)
Business model	A business model is a framework for creating economic, social, and/or other forms of value. The term business model is thus used for a broad range of informal and formal descriptions to represent core aspects of a business, including purpose, offerings, strategies, infrastructure, organizational structures, trading practices, and operational processes and policies. In the most basic sense, a business model is the method of doing business by which a company can sustain itself -- that is, generate revenue.
Project management	Project management is the discipline of planning, organizing and managing resources to bring about the successful completion of specific project goals and objectives. It is often closely related to and sometimes conflated with Program management. A project is a finite endeavor--having specific start and completion dates--undertaken to meet particular goals and objectives, usually to bring about beneficial change or added value.
Exchange rate	In finance, the Exchange rate s between two currencies specifies how much one currency is worth in terms of the other. It is the value of a foreign nation's currency in terms of the home nation's currency. For example an Exchange rate of 95 Japanese yen to the United States dollar means that JPY 95 is worth the same as USD 1.
International Chamber of Commerce	The International Chamber of Commerce is a non-profit, private international organization that works to promote and support global trade and globalization. It serves as an advocate of some world businesses in the global economy, in the interests of economic growth, job creation, and prosperity. As a global business organization, made up of member states, it helps the development of global outlooks on business matters.
Internships	An intern is one who works in a temporary position with an emphasis on on-the-job training rather than merely employment, making it similar to an apprenticeship. Interns are usually college or university students, but they can also be high school students or post graduate adults seeking skills for a new career. Student Internships provide opportunities for students to gain experience in their field, determine if they have an interest in a particular career, create a network of contacts, or gain school credit.

Intern	An Intern is one who works in a temporary position with an emphasis on on-the-job training rather than merely employment, making it similar to an apprenticeship. Intern s are usually college or university students, but they can also be high school students or post graduate adults seeking skills for a new career. Student Intern ships provide opportunities for students to gain experience in their field, determine if they have an interest in a particular career, create a network of contacts, or gain school credit.
Price	Price in economics and business is the result of an exchange and from that trade we assign a numerical monetary value to a good, service or asset. If I trade 4 apples for an orange, the price of an orange is 4 - apples. Inversely, the price of an apple is 1/4 oranges.
Cultural identity	Cultural identity is the identity of a group or culture, or of an individual as far as one is influenced by one's belonging to a group or culture. Cultural identity is similar to and has overlaps with, but is not synonymous with, identity politics. There are modern questions of culture that are transferred into questions of identity.
Population	In biology, a Population , is the collection of inter-breeding organisms of a particular species; in sociology, a collection of human beings. Individuals within a Population share a factor may be reduced by statistical means, but such a generalization may be too vague to imply anything. Demography is used extensively in marketing, which relates to economic units, such as retailers, to potential customers.

Department of Commerce	The United States Department of Commerce is the Cabinet department of the United States government concerned with promoting economic growth. It was originally created as the United States Department of Commerce and Labor on February 14, 1903. It was subsequently renamed to the Department of Commerce on March 4, 1913, and its bureaus and agencies specializing in labor were transferred to the new Department of Labor.
Foreign direct investment	Foreign direct investment in its classic form is defined as a company from one country making a physical investment into building a factory in another country. It is the establishment of an enterprise by a foreigner. Its definition can be extended to include investments made to acquire lasting interest in enterprises operating outside of the economy of the investor.
Kraft Foods	Kraft Foods Inc. (NYSE: Kraft Foods T) is the largest food and beverage company headquartered in the United States and the second largest in the world (after Nestlé SA.) Kraft is headquartered in Northfield, Illinois, USA, a Chicago suburb.
United States	The United States of America (commonly referred to as the United States the U.S., the United States A, or America) is a federal constitutional republic comprising fifty states and a federal district. The country is situated mostly in central North America, where its 48 contiguous states and Washington, D.C., the capital district, lie between the Pacific and Atlantic Oceans, bordered by Canada to the north and Mexico to the south. The state of Alaska is in the northwest of the continent, with Canada to its east and Russia to the west across the Bering Strait.
International trade	International trade is exchange of capital, goods, and services across international borders or territories. In most countries, it represents a significant share of gross domestic product (GDP.) While International trade has been present throughout much of history , its economic, social, and political importance has been on the rise in recent centuries.
Job interview	A Job interview is a process in which a potential employee is evaluated by an employer for prospective employment in their company, organization and was established in the late 16th century. A Job interview typically precedes the hiring decision, and is used to evaluate the candidate. The interview is usually preceded by the evaluation of submitted résumés from interested candidates, then selecting a small number of candidates for interviews.
Fair Trade	Fair trade is an organized social movement and market-based approach that aims to help producers in developing countries and promote sustainability. The movement advocates the payment of a fair price as well as social and environmental standards in areas related to the production of a wide variety of goods. It focuses in particular on exports from developing countries to developed countries, most notably handicrafts, coffee, cocoa, sugar, tea, bananas, honey, cotton, wine, fresh fruit, chocolate and flowers.
Business	A business is a legally recognized organization designed to provide goods and/or services to consumers. business es are predominant in capitalist economies, most being privately owned and formed to earn profit that will increase the wealth of its owners and grow the business itself. The owners and operators of a business have as one of their main objectives the receipt or generation of a financial return in exchange for work and acceptance of risk.
Base	Bases may be the plural form of:

· base
· Basis
Bases may also refer to:

· Bases (fashion), a military style of dress adopted by the chivalry of the sixteenth century. .

Census Bureau

The United States Census Bureau is the government agency that is responsible for the United States Census. It also gathers other national demographic and economic data.

English

English is a West Germanic language that originated in Anglo Saxon England. As a result of the military, economic, scientific, political and cultural influence of the British Empire during the 18th, 19th and 20th centuries and of the United States since the late 19th century, it has become the lingua franca in many parts of the world. It is used extensively as a second language and as an official language in Commonwealth countries and many international organizations.

International Trade Administration

The International Trade Administration is an agency in the United States Department of Commerce that promotes United States exports of nonagricultural U.S. services and goods.

The International Trade Administration's stated goals are to

- Provide practical information to help Americans select markets and products.
- Ensure that Americans have access to international markets as required by the U.S. trade agreements.
- Safeguard Americans from unfair competition from dumped and subsidized imports.

International Trade Administration consists of four sub-units. These are: Import Administration (IA), Market Access and Compliance (MAC), Manufacturing and Services (MAS) and the US Commercial Service (USCS.)

The International Trade Administration was created on January 2, 1980 and is headed by the Under Secretary of Commerce for International Trade.

Merchandise

Merchandising refers to the methods, practices and operations conducted to promote and sustain certain categories of commercial activity. The term is understood to have different specific meanings depending on the context. merchandise is a sale goods at a store

In marketing, one of the definitions of merchandising is the practice in which the brand or image from one product or service is used to sell another.

Comparative advertising

Comparative advertising is an advertisement in which a particular product specifically mentions a competitor by name for the express purpose of showing why the competitor is inferior to the product naming it.

This should not be confused with parody advertisements, where a fictional product is being advertised for the purpose of poking fun at the particular advertisement, nor should it be confused with the use of a coined brand name for the purpose of comparing the product without actually naming an actual competitor. ('Wikipedia tastes better and is less filling than the Encyclopedia Galactica.')

In the 1980s, during what has been referred to as the cola wars, soft-drink manufacturer Pepsi ran a series of advertisements where people, caught on hidden camera, in a blind taste test, chose Pepsi over rival Coca-Cola.

Test market

A test market in the field of business and marketing, is a geographic region or demographic group used to gauge the viability of a product or service in the mass market prior to a wide scale roll-out. The criteria used to judge the acceptability of a test market region or group include:

· a population that is demographically similar to the proposed target market; and
· relative isolation from densely populated media markets so that advertising to the test audience can be efficient and economical.

The test market ideally aims to duplicate 'everything' - promotion and distribution as well as `product' - on a smaller scale. The technique replicates, typically in one area, what is planned to occur in a national launch; and the results are very carefully monitored, so that they can be extrapolated to projected national results. The `area' may be any one of the following:

· Television area
internet online test

· Test town
· Residential neighborhood
· Test site

A number of decisions have to be taken about any test market

· Which test market
· What is to be tested?
· How long a test?
· What are the success criteria?

The simple go or no-go decision, together with the related reduction of risk, is normally the main justification for the expense of test market s. At the same time, however, such test market s can be used to test specific elements of a new product's marketing mix; possibly the version of the product itself, the promotional message and media spend, the distribution channels and the price.

Discrimination

Discrimination toward or against a person of a certain group is the treatment or consideration based on class or category rather than individual merit. It can be behavior promoting a certain group (e.g. affirmative action), or it can be negative behavior directed against a certain group (e.g. redlining.)

Racial discrimination differentiates between individuals on the basis of real and perceived racial differences, and has been official government policy in several countries, such as South Africa in the apartheid era, and the USA.

Export

In economics, an export is any good or commodity, transported from one country to another country in a legitimate fashion, typically for use in trade. export goods or services are provided to foreign consumers by domestic producers. export is an important part of international trade.

Sourcing

In business, the term word Sourcing refers to a number of procurement practices, aimed at finding, evaluating and engaging suppliers of goods and services:

· Global Sourcing a procurement strategy aimed at exploiting global efficiencies in production
· Strategic Sourcing a component of supply chain management, for improving and re-evaluating purchasing activities
- · Co Sourcing a type of auditing service

· Low-cost country Sourcing a procurement strategy for acquiring materials from countries with lower labour and production costs in order to cut operating expenses
· Corporate Sourcing a supply chain, purchasing/procurement, and inventory function
· Second-tier Sourcing a practice of rewarding suppliers for attempting to achieve minority-owned business spending goals of their customer
· Net Sourcing , a practice of utilizing an established group of businesses, individuals, or hardware ' software applications to streamline or initiate procurement practices by tapping in to and working through a third party provider
· Inverted Sourcing a price volatility reduction strategy usually conducted by procurement or supply-chain person by which the value of an organization's waste-stream is maximized by actively seeking out the highest price possible from a range of potential buyers exploiting price trends and other market factors
· Multi Sourcing , a strategy that treats a given function, such as IT, as a portfolio of activities, some of which should be outsourced and others of which should be performed by internal staff.
· Crowd Sourcing , using an undefined, generally large group of people or community in the form of an open call to perform a task

In journalism, it can also refer to:

· Journalism Sourcing the practice of identifying a person or publication that gives information
· Single Sourcing the reuse of content in publishing

In computing, it can refer to:

· Open Sourcing the act of releasing previously proprietary software under an open source/free software license
· Power Sourcing equipment, network devices that will provide power in a Power over Ethernet (PoE) setup .

Organization

An organization is a social arrangement which pursues collective goals, which controls its own performance, and which has a boundary separating it from its environment. The word itself is derived from the Greek word á½„ργανον (organon [itself derived from the better-known word á¼"ργον ergon - work; deed - > ergonomics, etc]) meaning tool. The term is used in both daily and scientific English in multiple ways.

World Trade Organization

The World Trade Organization is an international organization designed to supervise and liberalize international trade. The World Trade Organization came into being on 1 January 1995, and is the successor to the General Agreement on Tariffs and Trade (GATT), which was created in 1947, and continued to operate for almost five decades as a de facto international organization.

The World Trade Organization deals with the rules of trade between nations at a near-global level; it is responsible for negotiating and implementing new trade agreements, and is in charge of policing member countries' adherence to all the World Trade Organization agreements, signed by the majority of the world's trading nations and ratified in their parliaments.

Embargo

An Embargo is the prohibition of commerce and trade with a certain country, in order to isolate it and to put its government into a difficult internal situation, given that the effects of the Embargo are often able to make its economy suffer from the initiative. It is similar to a blockade, as in 'el bloqueo' or the American blockade on Cuba.

Embargo s generally attempt to pressure weaker adversaries to do what the abarcading country wishes.

Statistics

Statistics is a mathematical science pertaining to the collection, analysis, interpretation or explanation, and presentation of data. It also provides tools for prediction and forecasting based on data. It is applicable to a wide variety of academic disciplines, from the natural and social sciences to the humanities, government and business.

Procter ' Gamble

Procter is a surname, and may also refer to:

· Bryan Waller Procter (pseud. Barry Cornwall), English poet
· Goodwin Procter, American law firm
· Procter ' Gamble, consumer products multinational .

Import

An import is any good (e.g. a commodity) or service brought into one country from another country in a legitimate fashion, typically for use in trade.It is a good that is brought in from another country for sale. import goods or services are provided to domestic consumers by foreign producers. An import in the receiving country is an export to the sending country.

Manufacturing

Manufacturing is the application of tools and a processing medium to the transformation of raw materials into finished goods for sale. This effort includes all intermediate processes required for the production and integration of a product's components. Some industries, like semiconductor and steel manufacturers use the term fabrication instead.

Function cost analysis

Function cost analysis is the a method of technical and economic research of the systems for purpose to optimize a parity between system's consumer functions or properties and expenses to achieve those functions or properties.

This methodology for continuous perfection of production, industrial technologies, organizational structures was developed by Juryj Sobolev in 1948 at the 'Perm telephone factory'

· 1948 Juryj Sobolev - the first success in application of a method analysis at the 'Perm telephone factory' .
· 1949 - the first application for the invention as result of use of the new method.

Today in economically developed countries practically each enterprise or the company use methodology of the kind of functional-cost analysis as a practice of the quality management, most full satisfying to principles of standards of series ISO 9000.

· Interest of consumer not in products itself, but the advantage which it will receive from its usage.
· The consumer aspires to reduce his expenses
· Functions needed by consumer can be executed in the various ways, and, hence, with various efficiency and expenses.

Among possible alternatives of realization of functions exist such in which the parity of quality and the price is the optimal for the consumer.

The goal of Function cost analysis is achievement of the highest consumer satisfaction of production at simultaneous decrease in all kinds of industrial expenses Classical Function cost analysis has three English synonyms - Value Engineering, Value Management, Value Analysis.

Value added	Value added refers to the additional value of a commodity over the cost of commodities used to produce it from the previous stage of production. An example is the price of gasoline at the pump over the price of the oil in it. In national accounts used in macroeconomics, it refers to the contribution of the factors of production, i.e., land, labor, and capital goods, to raising the value of a product and corresponds to the incomes received by the owners of these factors.
Cost	In economics, business, retail, and accounting, a cost is the value of money that has been used up to produce something, and hence is not available for use anymore. In economics, a cost is an alternative that is given up as a result of a decision. In business, the cost may be one of acquisition, in which case the amount of money expended to acquire it is counted as cost.
Customer	A customer also client, buyer or purchaser is usually used to refer to a current or potential buyer or user of the products of an individual or organization, mostly called the supplier or seller. This is typically through purchasing or renting goods or services. However in certain contexts the term customer also includes by extension anyone who uses or experiences the services of another.
Developed country	The term developed country is used to describe countries that have a high level of development according to some criteria. Which criteria, and which countries are classified as being developed, is a contentious issue and there is fierce debate about this. Economic criteria have tended to dominate discussions.
Organizational structure	An organizational structure is a mostly hierarchical concept of subordination of entities that collaborate and contribute to serve one common aim. Organizations are a variant of clustered entities. The structure of an organization is usually set up in many a styles, dependent on their objectives and ambience.
Population ageing	Population ageing occurs when the median age of a country or region rises. With the exception of 18 countries termed by the United Nations 'demographic outliers' this process is taking place in every country and region across the globe. Population ageing is constituted by a shift in the distribution of a country's population towards greater ages.
Demand	In economics, Demand is the desire to own something and the ability to pay for it. The term Demand signifies the ability or the willingness to buy a particular commodity at a given point of time . .
Business marketing	Business marketing is the practice of individuals including commercial businesses, governments and institutions, facilitating the sale of their products or services to other companies or organizations that in turn resell them, use them as components in products or services they offer Business marketing is also called business-to-Business marketing for short. (Note that while marketing to government entities shares some of the same dynamics of organizational marketing, B2G Marketing is meaningfully different.)
Skilled worker	A Skilled worker is any worker who has some special skill, knowledge, or (usually acquired) ability in his work. A Skilled worker may have attended a college, university or technical school. Or, a Skilled worker may have learned his skills on the job.

Free Trade	Free trade is a type of trade policy that allows traders to act and transact without interference from government. Thus, the policy permits trading partners mutual gains from trade, with goods and services produced according to the theory of comparative advantage. Under a Free trade policy, prices are a reflection of true supply and demand, and are the sole determinant of resource allocation.
North American Free Trade Agreement	The North American Free Trade Agreement is a trilateral trade bloc in North America created by the governments of the United States, Canada, and Mexico. It superseded the Canada-United States Free Trade Agreement between the US and Canada. Following diplomatic negotiations dating back to 1990 between the three nations, the leaders met in San Antonio, Texas on December 17, 1992 to sign North American Free Trade Agreement.
International Monetary Fund	The International Monetary Fund is an international organization that oversees the global financial system by following the macroeconomic policies of its member countries, in particular those with an impact on exchange rates and the balance of payments. It is an organization formed to stabilize international exchange rates and facilitate development. It also offers financial and technical assistance to its members, making it an international lender of last resort.
Monetary	Monetary policy is the process by which the government, central bank (ii) availability of money, and (iii) cost of money or rate of interest, in order to attain a set of objectives oriented towards the growth and stability of the economy. monetary theory provides insight into how to craft optimal monetary policy. monetary policy is referred to as either being an expansionary policy where an expansionary policy increases the total supply of money in the economy, and a contractionary policy decreases the total money supply.
Challenge	Challenge is a United Kingdom digital TV channel owned by Virgin Media Television. It was originally called The Family Channel from 1 September 1993 to 31 January 1997 but it was later re-branded as challenge TV from 1 February 1997. On 20 May 2002 the channel was re-named again but this time it was just challenge? and 30 June 2003 the question mark was removed to leave the challenge name in its place.
Good	A good is an object whose consumption increases the utility of the consumer, for which the quantity demanded exceeds the quantity supplied at zero price. Goods are usually modeled as having diminishing marginal utility. The first individual purchase has high utility; the second has less.
Direct investment	Foreign Direct investment in its classic form is defined as a company from one country making a physical investment into building a factory in another country. It is the establishment of an enterprise by a foreigner. Its definition can be extended to include investments made to acquire lasting interest in enterprises operating outside of the economy of the investor.
Portfolio investment	In economics and finance, Portfolio investment represents passive holdings of securities such as foreign stocks, bonds, or other financial assets, none of which entails active management or control of the securities' issuer by the investor; where such control exists, it is known as foreign direct investment. Generally, this means the investor holds less than 10% of the total shares or less than the amount needed to hold the majority vote. Some examples of Portfolio investment are:

· purchase of shares in a foreign company.
· purchase of bonds issued by a foreign government.
· acquisition of assets in a foreign country.

Factors affecting international Portfolio investment:

· tax rates on interest or dividends (investors will normally prefer countries where the tax rates are relatively low)
· interest rates (money tends to flow to countries with high interest rates)
· exchange rates (foreign investors may be attracted if the local currency is expected to strengthen)

Portfolio investment is part of the capital account on the balance of payments statistics.

Foreign ownership

Foreign ownership refers to the complete or majority ownership/control of a business or resource in a country by individuals who are not citizens of that country, or by companies whose headquarters are not in that country.

Asset

In business and accounting, asset s are economic resources owned by business or company. Anything tangible or intangible that one possesses, usually considered as applicable to the payment of one's debts is considered an asset Simplistically stated, asset s are things of value that can be readily converted into cash.

Affiliate

In the broadcasting industry (especially in North America), a network Affiliate is a local broadcaster which carries some or all of the programme line-up of a television or radio network, but is owned by a company other than the owner of the network. This distinguishes such a station from an owned-and-operated station (O'O), which is owned by its parent network.

In the United States, Federal Communications Commission (FCC) regulations limit the number of network-owned stations as a percentage of total market size.

Investment

Investment or investing is a term with several closely-related meanings in business management, finance and economics, related to saving or deferring consumption. Investing is the active redirecting resources from being consumed today so that they may create benefits in the future; the use of assets to earn income or profit.

An Investment is the choice by the individual to risk his savings with the hope of gain.

Investor

An Investor is any party that makes an investment.

The term has taken on a specific meaning in finance to describe the particular types of people and companies that regularly purchase equity or debt securities for financial gain in exchange for funding an expanding company. Less frequently, the term is applied to parties who purchase real estate, currency, commodity derivatives, personal property, or other assets.

Set TSP

In combinatorial optimization, the set TSP group TSP, One-of-a-set TSP, Multiple Choice TSP or Covering Salesman Problem, is a generalization of the Traveling salesman problem, whereby it is required to find a shortest tour in a graph which visits all specified disjoint subsets of the vertices of a graph. The ordinary TSP is a special case of the set TSP when all subsets to be visited are singletons. Therefore the set TSP is also NP-hard.

Net worth	In business, net worth is the total liabilities minus total outside assets of an individual or a company. For a company, this is called shareholders' preference and may be referred to as book value. net worth is stated as at a particular year in time.
Tariff	A Tariff is a duty imposed on goods when they are moved across a political boundary. They are usually associated with protectionism, the economic policy of restraining trade between nations. For political reasons, Tariff s are usually imposed on imported goods, although they may also be imposed on exported goods.
Residual capacity	The residual capacity of an edge is $c_f(u,v) = c(u,v) - f(u,v)$. This defines a residual network denoted $G_f(V, E_f)$, giving the amount of available capacity. See that there can be an edge from u to v in the residual network, even though there is no edge from u to v in the original network.
Characteristic	Characteristic has several particular meanings: · in mathematics • · Euler characteristic • · method of characteristic s (partial differential equations) · in physics and engineering · any characteristic curve that shows the relationship between certain input- and output parameters, e.g. · an I-V or current-voltage characteristic is the current in a circuit as a function of the applied voltage · Receiver-Operator characteristic · in navigation, the characteristic pattern of a lighted beacon. · in fiction · in Dungeons ' Dragons, characteristic is another name for ability score .
Economic	An economy (or 'the economy') is the realized Economic system of a country or other area. It includes the production, exchange, distribution, and consumption of goods and services of that area. The study of different types and examples of economies is the subject of Economic systems.
Economic development	Economic development is the development of economic wealth of countries or regions for the well-being of their inhabitants. It is the process by which a nation improves the economic, political, and social well being of its people. From a policy perspective, Economic development can be defined as efforts that seek to improve the economic well-being and quality of life for a community by creating and/or retaining jobs and supporting or growing incomes and the tax base.
United Nations	The United Nations is an international organization whose stated aims are to facilitate cooperation in international law, international security, economic development, social progress, human rights and achieving world peace. The United Nations was founded in 1945 after World War II to replace the League of Nations, to stop wars between countries and to provide a platform for dialogue.

	There are currently 192 member states, including nearly every recognized independent state in the world.
United Nations Conference on Trade and Development	The United Nations Conference on Trade and Development was established in 1964 as a permanent intergovernmental body. It is the principal organ of the United Nations General Assembly dealing with trade, investment and development issues. The organization's goals are to 'maximize the trade, investment and development opportunities of developing countries and assist them in their efforts to integrate into the world economy on an equitable basis.' (from official website.)
Theory of the firm	The Theory of the firm consists of a number of economic theories which describe the nature of the firm, company including its existence, its behaviour, and its relationship with the market. In simplified terms, the Theory of the firm aims to answer these questions: · Existence - why do firms emerge, why are not all transactions in the economy mediated over the market? · Boundaries - why the boundary between firms and the market is located exactly there? Which transactions are performed internally and which are negotiated on the market? · Organization - why are firms structured in such specific way? What is the interplay of formal and informal relationships? The First World War period saw a change of emphasis in economic theory away from industry-level analysis which mainly included analysing markets to analysis at the level of the firm, as it became increasingly clear that perfect competition was no longer an adequate model of how firms behaved. Economic theory till then had focussed on trying to understand markets alone and there had been little study on understanding why firms or organisations exist. Market are mainly guided by prices as illustrated by vegetable markets where a buyer is free to switch sellers in an exchange.
Gross domestic product	The Gross domestic product or gross domestic income (GDI), a basic measure of an economy's economic performance, is the market value of all final goods and services produced within the borders of a nation in a year. Gross domestic product can be defined in three ways, all of which are conceptually identical. First, it is equal to the total expenditures for all final goods and services produced within the country in a stipulated period of time (usually a 365-day year.)
Human	A human is a member of a species of bipedal primates in the family Hominidae . DNA and fossil evidence indicates that modern human s originated in east Africa about 200,000 years ago. When compared to other animals and primates, human s have a highly developed brain, capable of abstract reasoning, language, introspection and problem solving.
International Finance	International finance is the branch of economics that studies the dynamics of exchange rates, foreign investment, and how these affect international trade. It also studies international projects, international investments and capital flows, and trade deficits. It includes the study of futures, options and currency swaps.

Internet

The Internet is a global network of interconnected computers, enabling users to share information along multiple channels. Typically, a computer that connects to the Internet can access information from a vast array of available servers and other computers by moving information from them to the computer's local memory. The same connection allows that computer to send information to servers on the network; that information is in turn accessed and potentially modified by a variety of other interconnected computers.

Market

A Market is any one of a variety of different systems, institutions, procedures, social relations and infrastructures whereby persons trade, and goods and services are exchanged, forming part of the economy. It is an arrangement that allows buyers and sellers to exchange things. Market s vary in size, range, geographic scale, location, types and variety of human communities, as well as the types of goods and services traded.

Profit

A profit , in the law of real property, is a nonpossessory interest in land similar to the better-known easement, which gives the holder the right to take natural resources such as petroleum, minerals, timber, and wild game from the land of another. Indeed, because of the necessity of allowing access to the land so that resources may be gathered, every profit contains an implied easement for the owner of the profit to enter the other party's land for the purpose of collecting the resources permitted by the profit.

Like an easement, profits can be created expressly by an agreement between the property owner and the owner of the profit, or by prescription, where the owner of the profit has made 'open and notorious' use of the land for a continuous and uninterrupted statutory period.

Report

In writing, a report is a document characterized by information or other content reflective of inquiry or investigation, which is tailored to the context of a given situation and audience. The purpose of report s is usually to inform. However, report s may include persuasive elements, such as recommendations, suggestions, or other motivating conclusions that indicate possible future actions the report reader might take.

Globalization

Globalization in its literal sense is the process of transformation of local or regional phenomena into global ones. It can be described as a process by which the people of the world are unified into a single society and function together.

This process is a combination of economic, technological, sociocultural and political forces.

Failure

Failure refers to the state or condition of not meeting a desirable or intended objective, and may be viewed as the opposite of success. Product failure ranges from failure to sell the product to fracture of the product, in the worst cases leading to personal injury, the province of forensic engineering.

The criteria for failure are heavily dependent on context of use, and may be relative to a particular observer or belief system.

Two-phase locking

In databases and transaction processing, Two-phase locking, (2PL) is a concurrency control locking protocol which guarantees serializability. It is also the name of the resulting class (set) of transaction schedules. Using locks that block processes, 2PL may be subject to deadlocks that result from the mutual blocking of two transactions or more.

Peer Review

Peer review is the process of subjecting an author's scholarly work, research, or ideas to the scrutiny of others who are experts in the same field. peer review requires a community of experts in a given field, who are qualified and able to perform impartial review. Impartial review, especially of work in less narrowly defined or inter-disciplinary fields, may be difficult to accomplish; and the significance of an idea may never be widely appreciated among its contemporaries.

Cost of goods sold

In financial accounting, Cost of goods sold or cost of sales includes the direct costs attributable to the production of the goods sold by a company. This amount includes the materials cost used in creating the goods along with the direct labor costs used to produce the good. It excludes indirect expenses such as distribution costs and sales force costs.

Offshoring

Offshoring describes the relocation by a company of a business process from one country to another -- typically an operational process, such as manufacturing such as accounting. Even state governments employ Offshoring.

The term is in use in several distinct but closely related ways.

Incentive

In economics and sociology, an Incentive is any factor (financial or non-financial) that enables or motivates a particular course of action, or counts as a reason for preferring one choice to the alternatives. It is an expectation that encourages people to behave in a certain way. Since human beings are purposeful creatures, the study of Incentive structures is central to the study of all economic activity (both in terms of individual decision-making and in terms of co-operation and competition within a larger institutional structure.)

Free trade zone

A Free trade zone or export processing zone (EPZ) is one or more special areas of a country where some normal trade barriers such as tariffs and quotas are eliminated and bureaucratic requirements are lowered in hopes of attracting new business and foreign investments. It is a a region where a group of countries has agreed to reduce or eliminate trade barriers. They can be defined as labor intensive manufacturing centers that involve the import of raw materials or components and the export of factory products.

Maquiladora

A Maquiladora or maquila is a factory that imports materials and equipment on a duty-free and tariff-free basis for assembly or manufacturing and then re-exports the assembled product, usually back to the originating country. A maquila is also referred to as a 'twin plant', or 'in-bond' industry. Nearly half a million Mexicans are employed in Maquiladora s.

Standardization

Standardization or standardisation is the process of developing and agreeing upon technical standards. A standard is a document that establishes uniform engineering or technical specifications, criteria, methods, processes, or practices. Some standards are mandatory while others are voluntary.

Marketing

Marketing is defined by the American Marketing Association as the activity, set of institutions, and processes for creating, communicating, delivering, and exchanging offerings that have value for customers, clients, partners, and society at large. The term developed from the original meaning which referred literally to going to market, as in shopping, or going to a market to sell goods or services.

Marketing practice tends to be seen as a creative industry, which includes advertising, distribution and selling.

Balance of payments

In economics, the Balance of payments, (or Balance of payments) measures the payments that flow between any individual country and all other countries. It is used to summarize all international economic transactions for that country during a specific time period, usually a year. The Balance of payments is determined by the country's exports and imports of goods, services, and financial capital, as well as financial transfers.

Downstream

Downstream in manufacturing refers to processes that occur later on in a production sequence or production line.

Viewing a company 'from order to cash' might have high-level processes such as Marketing, Sales, Order Entry, Manufacturing, Packaging, Shipping, Invoicing. Each of these could be deconstructed into many sub-processes and supporting processes.

Exchange rate

In finance, the Exchange rate s between two currencies specifies how much one currency is worth in terms of the other. It is the value of a foreign nation's currency in terms of the home nation's currency. For example an Exchange rate of 95 Japanese yen to the United States dollar means that JPY 95 is worth the same as USD 1.

Geography

Geography is the study of the Earth and its lands, features, inhabitants, and phenomena. A literal translation would be 'to describe or write about the Earth'. The first person to use the word 'Geography' was Eratosthenes .

Global strategy

Global strategy as defined in business terms is an organization's strategic guide to globalization. A sound Global strategy should address these questions: what must be (versus what is) the extent of market presence in the world's major markets? How to build the necessary global presence? What must be (versus what is) the optimal locations around the world for the various value chain activities? How to run global presence into global competitive advantage?

Academic research on Global strategy came of age during the 1980s, including work by Michael Porter and Christopher Bartlett ' Sumantra Ghoshal. Among the forces perceived to bring about the globalization of competition were convergence in economic systems and technological change, especially in information technology, that facilitated and required the coordination of a multinational firm's strategy on a worldwide scale.

Protectionism

Protectionism is the economic policy of restraining trade between nations, through methods such as tariffs on imported goods, restrictive quotas, and a variety of other restrictive government regulations designed to discourage imports, and prevent foreign take-over of local markets and companies. This policy is closely aligned with anti-globalization, and contrasts with free trade, where government barriers to trade are kept to a minimum. The term is mostly used in the context of economics, where Protectionism refers to policies or doctrines which 'protect' businesses and workers within a country by restricting or regulating trade with foreign nations.

Raw material

A raw material is something that is acted upon or used by or by human labour or industry, for use as a building material to create some product or structure. Often the term is used to denote material that came from nature and is in an unprocessed or minimally processed state. Iron ore, logs, and crude oil, would be examples.

Acquisition

The phrase mergers and acquisitions refers to the aspect of corporate strategy, corporate finance and management dealing with the buying, selling and combining of different companies that can aid, finance, or help a growing company in a given industry grow rapidly without having to create another business entity.

An Acquisition, also known as a takeover or a buyout, is the buying of one company (the 'target') by another. An Acquisition may be friendly or hostile.

Distribution

Distribution is one of the four elements of marketing mix. An organization or set of organizations (go-betweens) involved in the process of making a product or service available for use or consumption by a consumer or business user.

The other three parts of the marketing mix are product, pricing, and promotion.

Diversification	Diversification in finance is a risk management technique, related to hedging, that mixes a wide variety of investments within a portfolio. It is the spreading out investments to reduce risks. Because the fluctuations of a single security have less impact on a diverse portfolio, Diversification minimizes the risk from any one investment.
International business	International business is a term used to collectively describe topics relating to the operations of firms with interests in multiple countries. Such firms are sometimes called multinational corporations . Well known MNCs include fast food companies McDonald's and Yum Brands, vehicle manufacturers such as General Motors and Toyota, consumer electronics companies like Samsung, LG and Sony, and energy companies such as ExxonMobil and BP.
Advertising	Advertising is a form of communication that typically attempts to persuade potential customers to purchase or to consume more of a particular brand of product or service. 'While now central to the contemporary global economy and the reproduction of global production networks, it is only quite recently that Advertising has been more than a marginal influence on patterns of sales and production. The formation of modern Advertising was intimately bound up with the emergence of new forms of monopoly capitalism around the end of the 19th and beginning of the 20th century as one element in corporate strategies to create, organize and where possible control markets, especially for mass produced consumer goods.
Culture	Culture is a term that has different meanings. For example, in 1952, Alfred Kroeber and Clyde Kluckhohn compiled a list of 164 definitions of culture in culture A Critical Review of Concepts and Definitions. However, the word culture is most commonly used in three basic senses: · excellence of taste in the fine arts and humanities, also known as high culture · an integrated pattern of human knowledge, belief, and behavior that depends upon the capacity for symbolic thought and social learning · the set of shared attitudes, values, goals, and practices that characterizes an institution, organization or group. When the concept first emerged in eighteenth- and nineteenth-century Europe, it connoted a process of cultivation or improvement, as in agri culture or horti culture . In the nineteenth century, it came to refer first to the betterment or refinement of the individual, especially through education, and then to the fulfillment of national aspirations or ideals.
Expatriate	An expatriate is a person temporarily or permanently residing in a country and culture other than that of the person's upbringing or legal residence. The word comes from the Latin ex and patria (country, fatherland.) The term is sometimes used in the context of Westerners living in non-Western countries, although it is also used to describe Westerners living in other Western countries, such as U.S. citizens living in the United Kingdom, or Britons living in Spain.
Skill	A skill is the learned capacity to carry out pre-determined results often with the minimum outlay of time, energy, or both. skill s can often be divided into domain-general and domain-specific skill s. For example, in the domain of work, some general skill s would include time management, teamwork and leadership, self motivation and others, whereas domain-specific skill s would be useful only for a certain job.
Numerary	Numerary is a civil designation for persons who are incorporated in a fixed or permanent way to a society or group: regular member of the working staff, permanent staff distinguished from a super Numerary . The term Numerary and its counterpart, 'super Numerary ,' originated in Spanish and Latin American academy and government; it is now also used in countries all over the world, such as France, the U.S., England, Italy, etc.

There are Numerary members of surgical organizations, of universities, of gastronomical associations, etc.

Emerging markets

The term Emerging markets is used to describe a nation's social or business activity in the process of rapid growth and industrialization. Currently, there are approximately 28 Emerging markets in the world, with the economies of China and India considered to be two of the largest. According to The Economist many people find the term dated, but a new term has yet to gain much traction.

Liquidity

Market Liquidity is a business, economics or investment term that refers to an asset's ability to be easily converted through an act of buying or selling without causing a significant movement in the price and with minimum loss of value. Money, or cash on hand, is the most liquid asset. An act of exchange of a less liquid asset with a more liquid asset is called liquidation.

Risk

Risk is a concept that denotes the precise probability of specific eventualities. Technically, the notion of Risk is independent from the notion of value and, as such, eventualities may have both beneficial and adverse consequences. However, in general usage the convention is to focus only on potential negative impact to some characteristic of value that may arise from a future event.

Economic
An economy (or 'the economy') is the realized Economic system of a country or other area. It includes the production, exchange, distribution, and consumption of goods and services of that area. The study of different types and examples of economies is the subject of Economic systems.

Free market
A free market is a theoretical term that economists use to describe a market which is free from government intervention (i.e. no regulation, no subsidization, no single monetary system and no governmental monopolies.) In a free market, property rights are voluntarily exchanged at a price arranged solely by the mutual consent of sellers and buyers. By definition, buyers and sellers do not coerce each other, in the sense that they obtain each other's property without the use of physical force, threat of physical force, or fraud, nor is the coerced by a third party (such as by government via transfer payments) and they engage in trade simply because they both consent and believe that it is a good enough choice.

Import
An import is any good (e.g. a commodity) or service brought into one country from another country in a legitimate fashion, typically for use in trade.It is a good that is brought in from another country for sale. import goods or services are provided to domestic consumers by foreign producers. An import in the receiving country is an export to the sending country.

United States
The United States of America (commonly referred to as the United States the U.S., the United States A, or America) is a federal constitutional republic comprising fifty states and a federal district. The country is situated mostly in central North America, where its 48 contiguous states and Washington, D.C., the capital district, lie between the Pacific and Atlantic Oceans, bordered by Canada to the north and Mexico to the south. The state of Alaska is in the northwest of the continent, with Canada to its east and Russia to the west across the Bering Strait.

Direct investment
Foreign Direct investment in its classic form is defined as a company from one country making a physical investment into building a factory in another country. It is the establishment of an enterprise by a foreigner. Its definition can be extended to include investments made to acquire lasting interest in enterprises operating outside of the economy of the investor.

Foreign direct investment
Foreign direct investment in its classic form is defined as a company from one country making a physical investment into building a factory in another country. It is the establishment of an enterprise by a foreigner. Its definition can be extended to include investments made to acquire lasting interest in enterprises operating outside of the economy of the investor.

Need
A need is something that is necessary for humans to live a healthy life. need s are distinguished from wants because a deficiency would cause a clear negative outcome, such as dysfunction or death. need s can be objective and physical, such as food and water, or they can be subjective and psychological, such as the need for self-esteem.

Comparative
In grammar, the comparative is the form of an adjective or adverb which denotes the degree or grade by which a person, thing and is used in this context with a subordinating conjunction, such as than, as...as, etc.

The structure of a comparative in English consists normally of the positive form of the adjective or adverb, plus the suffix -er e.g. 'he is taller than his father is', or 'the village is less picturesque than the town nearby'.

Comparative advantage	In economics, Comparative advantage refers to the ability of a person or a country to produce a particular good at a lower marginal cost and opportunity cost than another person or country. It is the ability to produce a product most efficiently given all the other products that could be produced. It can be contrasted with absolute advantage which refers to the ability of a person or a country to produce a particular good at a lower absolute cost than another.
International trade	International trade is exchange of capital, goods, and services across international borders or territories. In most countries, it represents a significant share of gross domestic product (GDP.) While International trade has been present throughout much of history , its economic, social, and political importance has been on the rise in recent centuries.
Mercosur	MERCOSUR or Mercosul is a Regional Trade Agreement among Argentina, Brazil, Paraguay and Uruguay founded in 1991 by the Treaty of Asunción, which was later amended and updated by the 1994 Treaty of Ouro Preto. Its purpose is to promote free trade and the fluid movement of goods, people, and currency. MERCOSUR origins trace back to 1985 when Presidents Raúl Alfonsín of Argentina and José Sarney of Brazil signed the Argentina-Brazil Integration and Economics Cooperation Program or PICE .
Absolute advantage	In economics, Absolute advantage refers to the ability of a party to produce a good service using fewer real resources than another entity, producing the same good service.. A party has an Absolute advantage when using the same input as another party, it can produce a greater output. Since Absolute advantage is determined by a simple comparison of labor productivities, it is possible for a party to have no Absolute advantage in anything.
Job interview	A Job interview is a process in which a potential employee is evaluated by an employer for prospective employment in their company, organization and was established in the late 16th century. A Job interview typically precedes the hiring decision, and is used to evaluate the candidate. The interview is usually preceded by the evaluation of submitted résumés from interested candidates, then selecting a small number of candidates for interviews.
Exchange rate	In finance, the Exchange rate s between two currencies specifies how much one currency is worth in terms of the other. It is the value of a foreign nation's currency in terms of the home nation's currency. For example an Exchange rate of 95 Japanese yen to the United States dollar means that JPY 95 is worth the same as USD 1.
Export	In economics, an export is any good or commodity, transported from one country to another country in a legitimate fashion, typically for use in trade. export goods or services are provided to foreign consumers by domestic producers. export is an important part of international trade.
Fair Trade	Fair trade is an organized social movement and market-based approach that aims to help producers in developing countries and promote sustainability. The movement advocates the payment of a fair price as well as social and environmental standards in areas related to the production of a wide variety of goods. It focuses in particular on exports from developing countries to developed countries, most notably handicrafts, coffee, cocoa, sugar, tea, bananas, honey, cotton, wine, fresh fruit, chocolate and flowers.

Mercantilism

Mercantilism is an economic theory that holds that the prosperity of a nation is dependent upon its supply of capital, and that the global volume of international trade is 'unchangeable.' Economic assets or capital, are represented by bullion (gold, silver, and trade value) held by the state, which is best increased through a positive balance of trade with other nations (exports minus imports.) Mercantilism suggests that the ruling government should advance these goals by playing a protectionist role in the economy; by encouraging exports and discouraging imports, notably through the use of tariffs and subsidies.

Mercantilism was the dominant school of thought throughout the early modern period (from the 16th to the 18th century.)

Net worth

In business, net worth is the total liabilities minus total outside assets of an individual or a company. For a company, this is called shareholders' preference and may be referred to as book value. net worth is stated as at a particular year in time.

Control

Control is one of the managerial functions like planning, organizing, staffing and directing. It is an important function because it helps to check the errors and to take the corrective action so that deviation from standards are minimized and stated goals of the organization are achieved in desired manner.According to modern concepts, Control is a foreseeing action whereas earlier concept of Control was used only when errors were detected. Control in management means setting standards, measuring actual performance and taking corrective action.

Devaluation

Devaluation is a reduction in the value of a currency with respect to other monetary units. In common modern usage, it specifically implies an official lowering of the value of a country's currency within a fixed exchange rate system, by which the monetary authority formally sets a new fixed rate with respect to a foreign reference currency. In contrast, depreciation is used for the unofficial decrease in the exchange rate in a floating exchange rate system.

Embargo

An Embargo is the prohibition of commerce and trade with a certain country, in order to isolate it and to put its government into a difficult internal situation, given that the effects of the Embargo are often able to make its economy suffer from the initiative. It is similar to a blockade, as in 'el bloqueo' or the American blockade on Cuba.

Embargo s generally attempt to pressure weaker adversaries to do what the abarcading country wishes.

Foreign exchange controls

Foreign exchange controls are various forms of controls imposed by a government on the purchase/sale of foreign currencies by residents or on the purchase/sale of local currency by nonresidents.

Common Foreign exchange controls include:

· Banning the use of foreign currency within the country
· Banning locals from possessing foreign currency
· Restricting currency exchange to government-approved exchangers
· Fixed exchange rates
· Restrictions on the amount of currency that may be imported or exported

Countries with Foreign exchange controls are also known as 'Article 14 countries,' after the provision in the International Monetary Fund agreement allowing exchange controls for transitional economies. Such controls used to be common in most countries, particularly poorer ones, until the 1990s when free trade and globalization started a trend towards economic liberalization. Today, countries which still impose exchange controls are the exception rather than the rule.

Statistics

Statistics is a mathematical science pertaining to the collection, analysis, interpretation or explanation, and presentation of data. It also provides tools for prediction and forecasting based on data. It is applicable to a wide variety of academic disciplines, from the natural and social sciences to the humanities, government and business.

Zero-sum

In game theory and economic theory, Zero-sum describes a situation in which a participant's gain or loss is exactly balanced by the losses or gains of the other participant(s.) If the total gains of the participants are added up, and the total losses are subtracted, they will sum to zero. Zero-sum can be thought of more generally as constant sum where the benefits and losses to all players sum to the same value of money and pride and dignity.

Adam Smith

Adam Smith was a Scottish moral philosopher and a pioneer of political economy. One of the key figures of the Scottish Enlightenment, Smith is the author of The Theory of Moral Sentiments and An Inquiry into the Nature and Causes of the Wealth of Nations. The latter, usually abbreviated as The Wealth of Nations, is considered his magnum opus and the first modern work of economics.

Free trade

Free trade is a type of trade policy that allows traders to act and transact without interference from government. Thus, the policy permits trading partners mutual gains from trade, with goods and services produced according to the theory of comparative advantage.

Under a Free trade policy, prices are a reflection of true supply and demand, and are the sole determinant of resource allocation.

Terms of trade

In international economics and international trade, Terms of trade is the relative prices of a country's export to import. 'Terms of trade' are sometimes used as a proxy for the relative social welfare of a country, but this heuristic is technically questionable and should be used with extreme caution. An improvement in a nation's Terms of trade is good for that country in the sense that it has to pay less for the products it imports.

Factor endowment

In economics a country's Factor endowment is commonly understood as the amount of land, labor, capital, and entrepreneurship that a country possesses and can exploit for manufacturing. Countries with a large endowment of resources tend to be more prosperous than those with a small endowment, all other things being equal. The development of sound institutions to access and equitably distribute these resources, however, is necessary in order for a country to obtain the greatest benefit from its Factor endowment.

Investment

Investment or investing is a term with several closely-related meanings in business management, finance and economics, related to saving or deferring consumption. Investing is the active redirecting resources from being consumed today so that they may create benefits in the future; the use of assets to earn income or profit.

An Investment is the choice by the individual to risk his savings with the hope of gain.

Labor intensity

Labor intensity is the relative proportion of labor (compared to capital) used in a process. The term 'labor intensive' can be used when proposing the amount of work that is assigned to each worker/employee (labor), emphasizing on the skill involved in the respective line of work.

Minimum wage

A Minimum wage is the lowest hourly, daily or monthly wage that employers may legally pay to employees or workers. Equivalently, it is the lowest wage at which workers may sell their labor. Although Minimum wage laws are in effect in a great many jurisdictions, there are differences of opinion about the benefits and drawbacks of a Minimum wage.

Cost	In economics, business, retail, and accounting, a cost is the value of money that has been used up to produce something, and hence is not available for use anymore. In economics, a cost is an alternative that is given up as a result of a decision. In business, the cost may be one of acquisition, in which case the amount of money expended to acquire it is counted as cost.
Labor intensive	Labor intensity is the relative proportion of labor (compared to capital) used in a process. The term 'Labor intensive' can be used when proposing the amount of work that is assigned to each worker/employee (labor), emphasizing on the skill involved in the respective line of work.
Price	Price in economics and business is the result of an exchange and from that trade we assign a numerical monetary value to a good, service or asset. If I trade 4 apples for an orange, the price of an orange is 4 - apples. Inversely, the price of an apple is 1/4 oranges.
Labor force	In economics, the people in the Labor force are the suppliers of labor. The Labor force is all the nonmilitary people who are employed or unemployed. In 2005, the worldwide Labor force was over 3 billion people.
Offshoring	Offshoring describes the relocation by a company of a business process from one country to another -- typically an operational process, such as manufacturing such as accounting. Even state governments employ Offshoring. The term is in use in several distinct but closely related ways.
Outsourcing	Outsourcing is subcontracting a process, such as product design or manufacturing, to a third-party company. The decision to outsource is often made in the interest of lowering cost or making better use of time and energy costs, redirecting or conserving energy directed at the competencies of a particular business, or to make more efficient use of land, labor, capital, (information) technology and resources. outsourcing became part of the business lexicon during the 1980s.
Comparative advertising	Comparative advertising is an advertisement in which a particular product specifically mentions a competitor by name for the express purpose of showing why the competitor is inferior to the product naming it. This should not be confused with parody advertisements, where a fictional product is being advertised for the purpose of poking fun at the particular advertisement, nor should it be confused with the use of a coined brand name for the purpose of comparing the product without actually naming an actual competitor. ('Wikipedia tastes better and is less filling than the Encyclopedia Galactica.') In the 1980s, during what has been referred to as the cola wars, soft-drink manufacturer Pepsi ran a series of advertisements where people, caught on hidden camera, in a blind taste test, chose Pepsi over rival Coca-Cola.
Design	Design is used both as a noun and a verb. The term is often tied to the various applied arts and engineering As a verb, 'to design' refers to the process of originating and developing a plan for a product, structure, system, or component with intention.
Industry	An Industry is the manufacturing of a good or service within a category. Although Industry is a broad term for any kind of economic production, in economics and urban planning Industry is a synonym for the secondary sector, which is a type of economic activity involved in the manufacturing of raw materials into goods and products.

There are four key industrial economic sectors: the primary sector, largely raw material extraction industries such as mining and farming; the secondary sector, involving refining, construction, and manufacturing; the tertiary sector, which deals with services (such as law and medicine) and distribution of manufactured goods; and the quaternary sector, a relatively new type of knowledge Industry focusing on technological research, design and development such as computer programming, and biochemistry.

Unemployment

Unemployment occurs when a person is available to work and seeking work but currently without work. The prevalence of Unemployment is usually measured using the Unemployment rate, which is defined as the percentage of those in the labor force who are unemployed. The Unemployment rate is also used in economic studies and economic indexes such as the United States' Conference Board's Index of Leading Indicators as a measure of the state of the macroeconomics.

Business

A business is a legally recognized organization designed to provide goods and/or services to consumers. business es are predominant in capitalist economies, most being privately owned and formed to earn profit that will increase the wealth of its owners and grow the business itself. The owners and operators of a business have as one of their main objectives the receipt or generation of a financial return in exchange for work and acceptance of risk.

Business model

A business model is a framework for creating economic, social, and/or other forms of value. The term business model is thus used for a broad range of informal and formal descriptions to represent core aspects of a business, including purpose, offerings, strategies, infrastructure, organizational structures, trading practices, and operational processes and policies.

In the most basic sense, a business model is the method of doing business by which a company can sustain itself -- that is, generate revenue.

Wage

A Wage is a compensation, usually financial, received by a worker in exchange for their labor.

Compensation in terms of Wage s is given to worker and compensation in terms of salary is given to employees. Compensation is a monetary benefits given to employees in returns of the services provided by them.

Paradox

A Paradox is a statement or group of statements that leads to a contradiction or a situation which defies intuition; or, it can be an apparent contradiction that actually expresses a non-dual truth (cf. Koan, Catuskoti.) Typically, either the statements in question do not really imply the contradiction, the puzzling result is not really a contradiction, or the premises themselves are not all really true or cannot all be true together.

Big Mac index

The Big Mac Index is published by The Economist as an informal way of measuring the purchasing power parity (PPP) between two currencies and provides a test of the extent to which market exchange rates result in goods costing the same in different countries. It 'seeks to make exchange-rate theory a bit more digestible'.

Demand

In economics, Demand is the desire to own something and the ability to pay for it. The term Demand signifies the ability or the willingness to buy a particular commodity at a given point of time .

Money	Money is anything that is generally accepted as payment for goods and services and repayment of debts. The main uses of Money are as a medium of exchange, a unit of account, and a store of value. Some authors explicitly require Money to be a standard of deferred payment.
Argentina	Argentina, officially the Argentine Republic , is a country in South America, constituted as a federation of 23 provinces and an autonomous city, Buenos Aires. It is the second largest country in South America and eighth in the world by land area and the largest among Spanish-speaking nations, though Mexico, Colombia and Spain are more populous. Its continental area is 2,766,890 km^2 , between the Andes mountain range in the west and the southern Atlantic Ocean in the east and south.
Inflation	In economics, Inflation is a rise in the general level of prices of goods and services in an economy over a period of time. The term 'Inflation' once referred to increases in the money supply (monetary Inflation); however, economic debates about the relationship between money supply and price levels have led to its primary use today in describing price Inflation. Inflation can also be described as a decline in the real value of money--a loss of purchasing power in the medium of exchange which is also the monetary unit of account.
Manufacturing	Manufacturing is the application of tools and a processing medium to the transformation of raw materials into finished goods for sale. This effort includes all intermediate processes required for the production and integration of a product's components. Some industries, like semiconductor and steel manufacturers use the term fabrication instead.
Per capita income	Per capita income means how much each individual receives, in monetary terms, of the yearly income generated in the country. This is what each citizen is to receive if the yearly national income is divided equally among everyone. per capita income is usually reported in units of currency per year (e.g. US$20,000 per year.)
Product differentiation	In marketing, Product differentiation is the process of distinguishing the differences of a product or offering from others, to make it more attractive to a particular target market. This involves differentiating it from competitors' products as well as one's own product offerings. Differentiation is a source of competitive advantage.
Standardization	Standardization or standardisation is the process of developing and agreeing upon technical standards. A standard is a document that establishes uniform engineering or technical specifications, criteria, methods, processes, or practices. Some standards are mandatory while others are voluntary.
Tariff	A Tariff is a duty imposed on goods when they are moved across a political boundary. They are usually associated with protectionism, the economic policy of restraining trade between nations. For political reasons, Tariff s are usually imposed on imported goods, although they may also be imposed on exported goods.
Product life cycle	Product life cycle Management is the succession of strategies used by management as a product goes through its product life cycle. The conditions in which a product is sold changes over time and must be managed as it moves through its succession of stages. The product life cycle goes through many phases, involves many professional disciplines, and requires many skills, tools and processes.

Free trade zone

A Free trade zone or export processing zone (EPZ) is one or more special areas of a country where some normal trade barriers such as tariffs and quotas are eliminated and bureaucratic requirements are lowered in hopes of attracting new business and foreign investments. It is a a region where a group of countries has agreed to reduce or eliminate trade barriers. They can be defined as labor intensive manufacturing centers that involve the import of raw materials or components and the export of factory products.

Theory of the firm

The Theory of the firm consists of a number of economic theories which describe the nature of the firm, company including its existence, its behaviour, and its relationship with the market.

In simplified terms, the Theory of the firm aims to answer these questions:

· Existence - why do firms emerge, why are not all transactions in the economy mediated over the market?
· Boundaries - why the boundary between firms and the market is located exactly there? Which transactions are performed internally and which are negotiated on the market?
· Organization - why are firms structured in such specific way? What is the interplay of formal and informal relationships?

The First World War period saw a change of emphasis in economic theory away from industry-level analysis which mainly included analysing markets to analysis at the level of the firm, as it became increasingly clear that perfect competition was no longer an adequate model of how firms behaved. Economic theory till then had focussed on trying to understand markets alone and there had been little study on understanding why firms or organisations exist. Market are mainly guided by prices as illustrated by vegetable markets where a buyer is free to switch sellers in an exchange.

International Finance

International finance is the branch of economics that studies the dynamics of exchange rates, foreign investment, and how these affect international trade. It also studies international projects, international investments and capital flows, and trade deficits. It includes the study of futures, options and currency swaps.

World Bank

The World Bank is an international financial institution that provides financial and technical assistance to developing countries for development programs (e.g. bridges, roads, schools, etc.) with the stated goal of reducing poverty.

The World Bank differs from the World Bank Group, in that the World Bank comprises only two institutions:

· International Bank for Reconstruction and Development (IBRD)
· International Development Association (IDA)

Whereas the latter incorporates these two in addition to three more:

· International Finance Corporation (IFC)
· Multilateral Investment Guarantee Agency (MIGA)
· International Centre for Settlement of Investment Disputes (ICSID) John Maynard Keynes (right) represented the UK at the conference, and Harry Dexter White represented the US.

The World Bank was created following the ratification of the United Nations Monetary and Financial Conference of the Bretton Woods agreement. The concept was originally conceived in July 1944 at the United Nations Monetary and Financial Conference.

Economies of scale

Economies of scale in microeconomics, are the cost advantages that a business obtains due to expansion. They are factors that cause a producer's average cost per unit to fall as scale is increased. Economies of scale is a long run concept and refers to reductions in unit cost as the size of a facility, or scale, increases.

Expert witnesses

An expert witness or professional witness is a witness, who by virtue of education, training, skill is believed to have knowledge in a particular subject beyond that of the average person, sufficient that others may officially (and legally) rely upon the witness's specialized (scientific, technical or other) opinion about an evidence or fact issue within the scope of their expertise, referred to as the expert opinion, as an assistance to the fact-finder. Expert witnesses may also deliver expert evidence about facts from the domain of their expertise. At times, their testimony may be rebutted with a learned treatise, sometimes to the detriment of their reputations.

Experience curve

Models of the learning curve effect and the closely related Experience curve effect express the relationship between equations for experience and efficiency or between efficiency gains and investment in the effort.

The Experience curve effect is broader in scope than the learning curve effect encompassing far more than just labor time. It states that the more often a task is performed the lower will be the cost of doing it. The task can be the production of any good or service. Each time cumulative volume doubles, value added costs (including administration, marketing, distribution, and manufacturing) fall by a constant and predictable percentage.

Fixed costs

In economics, Fixed costs are business expenses that are not dependent on the activities of the business They tend to be time-related, such as salaries or rents being paid per month. This is in contrast to variable costs, which are volume-related (and are paid per quantity.)

In management accounting, Fixed costs are defined as expenses that do not change in proportion to the activity of a business, within the relevant period or scale of production.

Imperfect competition

In economic theory, Imperfect competition is the competitive situation in any market where the conditions necessary for perfect competition are not satisfied. It is a market structure that does not meet the conditions of perfect competition.

Forms of Imperfect competition include:

· Monopoly, in which there is only one seller of a good.
· Oligopoly, in which there is a small number of sellers.
· Monopolistic competition, in which there are many sellers producing highly differentiated goods.
· Monopsony, in which there is only one buyer of a good.
· Oligopsony, in which there is a small number of buyers.

There may also be Imperfect competition in markets due to buyers or sellers lacking information about prices and the goods being traded.

There may also be Imperfect competition due to a time lag in a market.

Learning

Learning is acquiring new knowledge, behaviors, skills, values, preferences or understanding, and may involve synthesizing different types of information. The ability to learn is possessed by humans, animals and some machines. Progress over time tends to follow learning curves.

Learning curve

The term Learning curve refers to a graphical representation of the changing rate of learning (in the average person) for a given activity or tool. Typically, the increase in retention of information is sharpest after the initial attempts, and then gradually evens out, meaning that less and less new information is retained after each repetition.

The Learning curve can also represent at a glance the initial difficulty of learning something and, to an extent, how much there is to learn after initial familiarity.

Market

A Market is any one of a variety of different systems, institutions, procedures, social relations and infrastructures whereby persons trade, and goods and services are exchanged, forming part of the economy. It is an arrangement that allows buyers and sellers to exchange things. Market s vary in size, range, geographic scale, location, types and variety of human communities, as well as the types of goods and services traded.

Market share

Market share, in strategic management and marketing, is the percentage or proportion of the total available market or market segment that is being serviced by a company. It can be expressed as a company's sales revenue (from that market) divided by the total sales revenue available in that market. It can also be expressed as a company's unit sales volume (in a market) divided by the total volume of units sold in that market.

Globalization

Globalization in its literal sense is the process of transformation of local or regional phenomena into global ones. It can be described as a process by which the people of the world are unified into a single society and function together.

This process is a combination of economic, technological, sociocultural and political forces.

Factors of production

In economics, Factors of production are the resources employed to produce goods and services. They facilitate production but do not become part of the product (as with raw materials) or significantly transformed by the production process (as with fuel used to power machinery.) To 19th century economists, the Factors of production were land (natural resources, gifts from nature), labor (the ability to work), and capital goods (human-made tools and equipment.)

Perfect competition

In neoclassical economics and microeconomics, Perfect competition describes a market in which there are many small firms, all producing homogeneous goods. In the short term, such markets are productively inefficient as output will not occur where mc is equal to ac, but allocatively efficient, as output under Perfect competition will always occur where mc is equal to mr, and therefore where mc equals ar. However, in the long term, such markets are both allocatively and productively efficient.

Monopolistic advantage theory

The monopolistic advantage theory is an approach in international business which explain why firms can compete in foreign settings against indigenous competitors.

It is frequently associated with the seminal contribution of Stephen Hymer. Hymer was puzzled by the inability of the prevailing neo-classical theories of international trade and international finance (portfolio capital investment) to explain the foreign activities of firms.

Modern portfolio theory

Modern portfolio theory proposes how rational investors will use diversification to optimize their portfolios, and how a risky asset should be priced. The basic concepts of the theory are Markowitz diversification, the efficient frontier, capital asset pricing model, the alpha and beta coefficients, the Capital Market Line and the Securities Market Line.

Modern portfolio theory models an asset's return as a random variable, and models a portfolio as a weighted combination of assets so that the return of a portfolio is the weighted combination of the assets' returns.

Set TSP

In combinatorial optimization, the set TSP group TSP, One-of-a-set TSP, Multiple Choice TSP or Covering Salesman Problem, is a generalization of the Traveling salesman problem, whereby it is required to find a shortest tour in a graph which visits all specified disjoint subsets of the vertices of a graph. The ordinary TSP is a special case of the set TSP when all subsets to be visited are singletons. Therefore the set TSP is also NP-hard.

Economic stability

Economic stability refers to an absence of excessive fluctuations in the macroeconomy. An economy with fairly constant output growth and low and stable inflation would be considered economically stable. An economy with frequent large recessions, a pronounced business cycle, very high or variable inflation, or frequent financial crises would be considered economically unstable.

Internationalization

Internationalization has been viewed as a process of increasing involvement of enterprises in international markets, although there is no agreed definition of Internationalization or international entrepreneurship. There are several Internationalization theories which try to explain why there are international activities.

Adam Smith claimed that a country should specialise in, and export, commodities in which it had an absolute advantage.

Ownership

Ownership is the state or fact of exclusive rights and control over property, which may be an object, land/real estate, or some other kind of property (like government-granted monopolies collectively referred to as intellectual property.) It is embodied in an Ownership right also referred to as title.

Ownership is the key building block in the development of the capitalist socio-economic system.

Customer

A customer also client, buyer or purchaser is usually used to refer to a current or potential buyer or user of the products of an individual or organization, mostly called the supplier or seller. This is typically through purchasing or renting goods or services. However in certain contexts the term customer also includes by extension anyone who uses or experiences the services of another.

Swap

In finance, a Swap is a derivative in which two counterparties agree to exchange one stream of cash flow against another stream. These streams are called the legs of the Swap.

The cash flows are calculated over a notional principal amount, which is usually not exchanged between counterparties.

Brazil

Brazil, officially the Federative Republic of Brazil (Portuguese: >Rep>ública Federativa do Brasil) Â·), is a country in South America. It is the fifth largest country by geographical area, occupying nearly half of South America, the fifth most populous country, and the fourth most populous democracy in the world. Bounded by the Atlantic Ocean on the east, Brazil has a coastline of over 7,491 kilometers (4,655 mi.)

English

English is a West Germanic language that originated in Anglo-Saxon England. As a result of the military, economic, scientific, political and cultural influence of the British Empire during the 18th, 19th and 20th centuries and of the United States since the late 19th century, it has become the lingua franca in many parts of the world. It is used extensively as a second language and as an official language in Commonwealth countries and many international organizations.

Cultural identity

Cultural identity is the identity of a group or culture, or of an individual as far as one is influenced by one's belonging to a group or culture. Cultural identity is similar to and has overlaps with, but is not synonymous with, identity politics.

There are modern questions of culture that are transferred into questions of identity.

International business	International business is a term used to collectively describe topics relating to the operations of firms with interests in multiple countries. Such firms are sometimes called multinational corporations . Well known MNCs include fast food companies McDonald's and Yum Brands, vehicle manufacturers such as General Motors and Toyota, consumer electronics companies like Samsung, LG and Sony, and energy companies such as ExxonMobil and BP.
Culture	Culture is a term that has different meanings. For example, in 1952, Alfred Kroeber and Clyde Kluckhohn compiled a list of 164 definitions of culture in culture A Critical Review of Concepts and Definitions. However, the word culture is most commonly used in three basic senses: · excellence of taste in the fine arts and humanities, also known as high culture · an integrated pattern of human knowledge, belief, and behavior that depends upon the capacity for symbolic thought and social learning · the set of shared attitudes, values, goals, and practices that characterizes an institution, organization or group. When the concept first emerged in eighteenth- and nineteenth-century Europe, it connoted a process of cultivation or improvement, as in agri culture or horti culture . In the nineteenth century, it came to refer first to the betterment or refinement of the individual, especially through education, and then to the fulfillment of national aspirations or ideals.
Skill	A skill is the learned capacity to carry out pre-determined results often with the minimum outlay of time, energy, or both. skill s can often be divided into domain-general and domain-specific skill s. For example, in the domain of work, some general skill s would include time management, teamwork and leadership, self motivation and others, whereas domain-specific skill s would be useful only for a certain job.
Resources	Human beings are also considered to be Resources because they have the ability to change raw materials into valuable Resources. The term Human Resources can also be defined as the skills, energies, talents, abilities and knowledge that are used for the production of goods or the rendering of services. While taking into account human beings as Resources, the following things have to be kept in mind: · The size of the population · The capabilities of the individuals in that population Many Resources cannot be consumed in their original form. They have to be processed in order to change them into more usable commodities.
Information technology outsourcing	Information Technology Outsourcing or Information Technology Outsourcing is a company's outsourcing of computer or Internet related work, such as programming, to other companies. It is used in reference to Business Process Outsourcing or BPO, which is the outsourcing of the work that does not require much of technical skills. The reasons for IT outsourcing are: lack of resource,cost reduction, etc.

Global Compact	The United Nations Global Compact is an United Nations initiative to encourage businesses worldwide to adopt sustainable and socially responsible policies, and to report on their implementation. The Global Compact is a principle based framework for businesses, stating ten principles in the areas of human rights, labour, the environment and anti-corruption. Under the Global Compact, companies are brought together with UN agencies, labour groups and civil society.
Goal	A Goal or objective is a projected state of affairs that a person or a system plans or intends to achieve--a personal or organizational desired end-point in some sort of assumed development. Many people endeavor to reach Goal s within a finite time by setting deadlines. A desire or an intention becomes a Goal if and only if one activates an action for achieving it
United Nations	The United Nations is an international organization whose stated aims are to facilitate cooperation in international law, international security, economic development, social progress, human rights and achieving world peace. The United Nations was founded in 1945 after World War II to replace the League of Nations, to stop wars between countries and to provide a platform for dialogue. There are currently 192 member states, including nearly every recognized independent state in the world.
Economic	An economy (or 'the economy') is the realized Economic system of a country or other area. It includes the production, exchange, distribution, and consumption of goods and services of that area. The study of different types and examples of economies is the subject of Economic systems.
English	English is a West Germanic language that originated in Anglo-Saxon England. As a result of the military, economic, scientific, political and cultural influence of the British Empire during the 18th, 19th and 20th centuries and of the United States since the late 19th century, it has become the lingua franca in many parts of the world. It is used extensively as a second language and as an official language in Commonwealth countries and many international organizations.
International Monetary Fund	The International Monetary Fund is an international organization that oversees the global financial system by following the macroeconomic policies of its member countries, in particular those with an impact on exchange rates and the balance of payments. It is an organization formed to stabilize international exchange rates and facilitate development. It also offers financial and technical assistance to its members, making it an international lender of last resort.
International Organization for Standardization	The International Organization for Standardization, widely known as ISO , is an international-standard-setting body composed of representatives from various national standards organizations. Founded on 23 February 1947, the organization promulgates worldwide proprietary industrial and commercial standards. It is headquartered in Geneva, Switzerland.
Monetary	Monetary policy is the process by which the government, central bank (ii) availability of money, and (iii) cost of money or rate of interest, in order to attain a set of objectives oriented towards the growth and stability of the economy. monetary theory provides insight into how to craft optimal monetary policy. monetary policy is referred to as either being an expansionary policy where an expansionary policy increases the total supply of money in the economy, and a contractionary policy decreases the total money supply.

Organization	An organization is a social arrangement which pursues collective goals, which controls its own performance, and which has a boundary separating it from its environment. The word itself is derived from the Greek word á½„ργανον (organon [itself derived from the better-known word á¼"ργον ergon - work; deed - > ergonomics, etc]) meaning tool. The term is used in both daily and scientific English in multiple ways.
World Trade Organization	The World Trade Organization is an international organization designed to supervise and liberalize international trade. The World Trade Organization came into being on 1 January 1995, and is the successor to the General Agreement on Tariffs and Trade (GATT), which was created in 1947, and continued to operate for almost five decades as a de facto international organization. The World Trade Organization deals with the rules of trade between nations at a near-global level; it is responsible for negotiating and implementing new trade agreements, and is in charge of policing member countries' adherence to all the World Trade Organization agreements, signed by the majority of the world's trading nations and ratified in their parliaments.
Characteristic	Characteristic has several particular meanings: · in mathematics • · Euler characteristic • · method of characteristic s (partial differential equations) · in physics and engineering · any characteristic curve that shows the relationship between certain input- and output parameters, e.g. · an I-V or current-voltage characteristic is the current in a circuit as a function of the applied voltage · Receiver-Operator characteristic · in navigation, the characteristic pattern of a lighted beacon. · in fiction · in Dungeons ' Dragons, characteristic is another name for ability score .
Extortion	'Extortion', outwresting property or services from a person, entity through coercion. Refraining from doing harm is sometimes euphemistically called protection. Extortion is commonly practiced by organized crime groups.
Cognitive	Cognition is the scientific term for 'the process of thought.' Its usage varies in different ways in accord with different disciplines: For example, in psychology and cognitive science it refers to an information processing view of an individual's psychological functions. Other interpretations of the meaning of cognition link it to the development of concepts; individual minds, groups, organizations, and even larger coalitions of entities, can be modelled as 'societies' (Society of Mind), which cooperate to form concepts. The autonomous elements of each 'society' would have the opportunity to demonstrate emergent behavior in the face of some crisis or opportunity.

Supplier	A 'supply chain is the system of organizations, people, technology, activities, information and resources involved in moving a product or service from supplier to customer. Supply chain activities transform natural resources, raw materials and components into a finished product that is delivered to the end customer. In sophisticated supply chain systems, used products may re-enter the supply chain at any point where residual value is recyclable.
United States	The United States of America (commonly referred to as the United States the U.S., the United States A, or America) is a federal constitutional republic comprising fifty states and a federal district. The country is situated mostly in central North America, where its 48 contiguous states and Washington, D.C., the capital district, lie between the Pacific and Atlantic Oceans, bordered by Canada to the north and Mexico to the south. The state of Alaska is in the northwest of the continent, with Canada to its east and Russia to the west across the Bering Strait.
Game	A Game is a structured activity, usually undertaken for enjoyment and sometimes used as an educational tool. Game s are distinct from work, which is usually carried out for remuneration, and from art, which is more concerned with the expression of ideas. However, the distinction is not clear-cut, and many Game s are also considered to be work (such as professional players of spectator sports/ Game s) or art (such as jigsaw puzzles or Game s involving an artistic layout such as Mah-jongg solitaire.)
Image	An Image is an artifact that has a similar appearance to some subject--usually a physical object or a person. Image s may be two-dimensional, such as a photograph, screen display, and as well as a three-dimensional, such as a statue. They may be captured by optical devices--such as cameras, mirrors, lenses, telescopes, microscopes, etc.
Set TSP	In combinatorial optimization, the set TSP group TSP, One-of-a-set TSP, Multiple Choice TSP or Covering Salesman Problem, is a generalization of the Traveling salesman problem, whereby it is required to find a shortest tour in a graph which visits all specified disjoint subsets of the vertices of a graph. The ordinary TSP is a special case of the set TSP when all subsets to be visited are singletons. Therefore the set TSP is also NP-hard.
International trade	International trade is exchange of capital, goods, and services across international borders or territories. In most countries, it represents a significant share of gross domestic product (GDP.) While International trade has been present throughout much of history , its economic, social, and political importance has been on the rise in recent centuries.
International business	International business is a term used to collectively describe topics relating to the operations of firms with interests in multiple countries. Such firms are sometimes called multinational corporations . Well known MNCs include fast food companies McDonald's and Yum Brands, vehicle manufacturers such as General Motors and Toyota, consumer electronics companies like Samsung, LG and Sony, and energy companies such as ExxonMobil and BP.
World Bank	The World Bank is an international financial institution that provides financial and technical assistance to developing countries for development programs (e.g. bridges, roads, schools, etc.) with the stated goal of reducing poverty. The World Bank differs from the World Bank Group, in that the World Bank comprises only two institutions: · International Bank for Reconstruction and Development (IBRD) · International Development Association (IDA) Whereas the latter incorporates these two in addition to three more:

· International Finance Corporation (IFC)
· Multilateral Investment Guarantee Agency (MIGA)
· International Centre for Settlement of Investment Disputes (ICSID) John Maynard Keynes (right) represented the UK at the conference, and Harry Dexter White represented the US.

The World Bank was created following the ratification of the United Nations Monetary and Financial Conference of the Bretton Woods agreement. The concept was originally conceived in July 1944 at the United Nations Monetary and Financial Conference.

Culture

Culture is a term that has different meanings. For example, in 1952, Alfred Kroeber and Clyde Kluckhohn compiled a list of 164 definitions of culture in culture A Critical Review of Concepts and Definitions. However, the word culture is most commonly used in three basic senses:

· excellence of taste in the fine arts and humanities, also known as high culture
· an integrated pattern of human knowledge, belief, and behavior that depends upon the capacity for symbolic thought and social learning
· the set of shared attitudes, values, goals, and practices that characterizes an institution, organization or group.

When the concept first emerged in eighteenth- and nineteenth-century Europe, it connoted a process of cultivation or improvement, as in agri culture or horti culture . In the nineteenth century, it came to refer first to the betterment or refinement of the individual, especially through education, and then to the fulfillment of national aspirations or ideals.

Manufacturing

Manufacturing is the application of tools and a processing medium to the transformation of raw materials into finished goods for sale. This effort includes all intermediate processes required for the production and integration of a product's components. Some industries, like semiconductor and steel manufacturers use the term fabrication instead.

Business marketing

Business marketing is the practice of individuals including commercial businesses, governments and institutions, facilitating the sale of their products or services to other companies or organizations that in turn resell them, use them as components in products or services they offer Business marketing is also called business-to-Business marketing for short. (Note that while marketing to government entities shares some of the same dynamics of organizational marketing, B2G Marketing is meaningfully different.)

Business

A business is a legally recognized organization designed to provide goods and/or services to consumers. business es are predominant in capitalist economies, most being privately owned and formed to earn profit that will increase the wealth of its owners and grow the business itself. The owners and operators of a business have as one of their main objectives the receipt or generation of a financial return in exchange for work and acceptance of risk.

Electronic Business

Electronic business, commonly referred to as 'eBusiness' or 'e-Business', may be defined as the utilization of information and communication technologies (ICT) in support of all the activities of business. Commerce constitutes the exchange of products and services between businesses, groups and individuals and hence can be seen as one of the essential activities of any business. Hence, electronic commerce or eCommerce focuses on the use of ICT to enable the external activities and relationships of the business with individuals, groups and other businesses .

International Court of Justice	The International Court of Justice is the primary judicial organ of the United Nations. It is based in the Peace Palace in The Hague, Netherlands. Its main functions are to settle legal disputes submitted to it by states and to give advisory opinions on legal questions submitted to it by duly authorized international organs, agencies, and the UN General Assembly.
Kyoto Protocol	The Kyoto Protocol is a protocol to the United Nations Framework Convention on Climate Change (UNFCCC or FCCC), an international environmental treaty which was produced with the goal of achieving 'stabilization of greenhouse gas concentrations in the atmosphere at a level that would prevent dangerous anthropogenic interference with the climate system.' The Kyoto Protocol establishes legally binding commitments for the reduction of four greenhouse gases (carbon dioxide, methane, nitrous oxide, sulphur hexafluoride), and two groups of gases (hydrofluorocarbons and perfluorocarbons) produced by 'Annex I' (industrialized) nations, as well as general commitments for all member countries. As of January 2009, 183 parties have ratified the protocol, which was initially have been adopted for use on 11 December 1997 in Kyoto, Japan and which entered into force on 16 February 2005. Under Kyoto, industrialized countries agreed to reduce their collective GHG emissions by 5.2% compared to the year 1990.
Numerary	Numerary is a civil designation for persons who are incorporated in a fixed or permanent way to a society or group: regular member of the working staff, permanent staff distinguished from a super Numerary . The term Numerary and its counterpart, 'super Numerary ,' originated in Spanish and Latin American academy and government; it is now also used in countries all over the world, such as France, the U.S., England, Italy, etc. There are Numerary members of surgical organizations, of universities, of gastronomical associations, etc.
Control	Control is one of the managerial functions like planning, organizing, staffing and directing. It is an important function because it helps to check the errors and to take the corrective action so that deviation from standards are minimized and stated goals of the organization are achieved in desired manner.According to modern concepts, Control is a foreseeing action whereas earlier concept of Control was used only when errors were detected. Control in management means setting standards, measuring actual performance and taking corrective action.
Kraft Foods	Kraft Foods Inc. (NYSE: Kraft Foods T) is the largest food and beverage company headquartered in the United States and the second largest in the world (after Nestlé SA.) Kraft is headquartered in Northfield, Illinois, USA, a Chicago suburb.
Job interview	A Job interview is a process in which a potential employee is evaluated by an employer for prospective employment in their company, organization and was established in the late 16th century. A Job interview typically precedes the hiring decision, and is used to evaluate the candidate. The interview is usually preceded by the evaluation of submitted résumés from interested candidates, then selecting a small number of candidates for interviews.
Relevance	Relevance is a term used to describe how pertinent, connected, or applicable something is to a given matter. A thing is relevant if it serves as a means to a given purpose. Imagine a patient suffering a well-defined disease such as scurvy caused by lack of vitamin C. The relevant medical treatment for him would be doses of tablets containing vitamin C (ascorbic acid.)

Good	A good is an object whose consumption increases the utility of the consumer, for which the quantity demanded exceeds the quantity supplied at zero price. Goods are usually modeled as having diminishing marginal utility. The first individual purchase has high utility; the second has less.
Human	A human is a member of a species of bipedal primates in the family Hominidae . DNA and fossil evidence indicates that modern human s originated in east Africa about 200,000 years ago. When compared to other animals and primates, human s have a highly developed brain, capable of abstract reasoning, language, introspection and problem solving.
Human Rights	Human rights refer to the 'basic rights and freedoms to which all humans are entitled.' Examples of rights and freedoms which have come to be commonly thought of as human rights include civil and political rights, such as the right to life and liberty, freedom of expression, and equality before the law; and economic, social and cultural rights, including the right to participate in culture, the right to food, the right to work, and the right to education. The earliest sign of human rights has been found on the Cyrus Cylinder written during the reign of Cyrus the Great of Persia/Iran. The history of human rights dates back thousands of years and is judged based upon religious, cultural, philosophical and legal developments throughout the years.
International Trade Law	International trade law includes the appropriate rules and customs for handling trade between countries or between private companies across borders. Over the past twenty years, it has become one of the fastest growing areas of international law. International trade law should be distinguished from the broader field of international economic law.
United Nations Commission on International Trade Law	The United Nations Commission on International Trade Law was established by the United Nations General Assembly by its Resolution 2205 (XXI) of 17 December 1966 'to promote the progressive harmonization and unification of international trade law. UNCITRAL carries out its work at annual sessions held alternately in New York City and Vienna. When world trade began to expand dramatically in the 1960s, national governments began to realize the need for a global set of standards and rules to harmonize national and regional regulations, which until then governed international trade.
Big Mac index	The Big Mac Index is published by The Economist as an informal way of measuring the purchasing power parity (PPP) between two currencies and provides a test of the extent to which market exchange rates result in goods costing the same in different countries. It 'seeks to make exchange-rate theory a bit more digestible'.
Bretton Woods system	The Bretton Woods system of monetary management established the rules for commercial and financial relations among the world's major industrial states in the mid 20th Century. The Bretton Woods system was the first example of a fully negotiated monetary order intended to govern monetary relations among independent nation-states. Preparing to rebuild the international economic system as World War II was still raging, 730 delegates from all 44 Allied nations gathered at the Mount Washington Hotel in Bretton Woods, New Hampshire, United States, for the United Nations Monetary and Financial Conference.

Eurozone

The eurozone is a currency union of 16 European Union (EU) states which have adopted the euro as their sole legal tender. It currently consists of Austria, Belgium, Cyprus, Finland, France, Germany, Greece, Ireland, Italy, Luxembourg, Malta, the Netherlands, Portugal, Slovakia, Slovenia and Spain. Eight other states are obliged to adopt the zone once they fulfill the strict entry criteria.

Gold standard

The Gold standard is a monetary system in which a region's common medium of exchange are paper notes that are normally freely convertible into pre-set, fixed quantities of gold. The Gold standard is not currently used by any government, having been replaced completely by fiat currency. Gold certificates were used as paper currency in the United States from 1882 to 1933, these certificates were freely convertable into gold coins.

The use of paper money, convertible into gold, to replace gold coins, originated in China in the 9th century CE.

International Bank for Reconstruction and Development

The International Bank for Reconstruction and Development is institutions that comprise the World Bank Group. The IBRD is an international organization whose original mission was to finance the reconstruction of nations devastated by World War II. Now, its mission has expanded to fight poverty by means of financing states.

Par value

Par value, in finance and accounting, means stated value or face value. From this comes the expressions at par (at the par value), over par (over par value) and under par (under par value.)

The term 'par value' has several meanings depending on context and geography.

Challenge

Challenge is a United Kingdom digital TV channel owned by Virgin Media Television. It was originally called The Family Channel from 1 September 1993 to 31 January 1997 but it was later re-branded as challenge TV from 1 February 1997. On 20 May 2002 the channel was re-named again but this time it was just challenge? and 30 June 2003 the question mark was removed to leave the challenge name in its place.

Exchange rate

In finance, the Exchange rate s between two currencies specifies how much one currency is worth in terms of the other. It is the value of a foreign nation's currency in terms of the home nation's currency. For example an Exchange rate of 95 Japanese yen to the United States dollar means that JPY 95 is worth the same as USD 1.

Mercantilism

Mercantilism is an economic theory that holds that the prosperity of a nation is dependent upon its supply of capital, and that the global volume of international trade is 'unchangeable.' Economic assets or capital, are represented by bullion (gold, silver, and trade value) held by the state, which is best increased through a positive balance of trade with other nations (exports minus imports.) Mercantilism suggests that the ruling government should advance these goals by playing a protectionist role in the economy; by encouraging exports and discouraging imports, notably through the use of tariffs and subsidies.

Mercantilism was the dominant school of thought throughout the early modern period (from the 16th to the 18th century.)

Brazil

Brazil, officially the Federative Republic of Brazil (Portuguese: >Rep>ública Federativa do Brasil) Â·), is a country in South America. It is the fifth largest country by geographical area, occupying nearly half of South America, the fifth most populous country, and the fourth most populous democracy in the world. Bounded by the Atlantic Ocean on the east, Brazil has a coastline of over 7,491 kilometers (4,655 mi.)

Protectionism

Protectionism is the economic policy of restraining trade between nations, through methods such as tariffs on imported goods, restrictive quotas, and a variety of other restrictive government regulations designed to discourage imports, and prevent foreign take-over of local markets and companies. This policy is closely aligned with anti-globalization, and contrasts with free trade, where government barriers to trade are kept to a minimum. The term is mostly used in the context of economics, where Protectionism refers to policies or doctrines which 'protect' businesses and workers within a country by restricting or regulating trade with foreign nations.

Job description

A Job description is a list of the general tasks and responsibilities of a position. Typically, it also includes to whom the position reports, specifications such as the qualifications needed by the person in the job, salary range for the position, etc. A Job description is usually developed by conducting a job analysis, which includes examining the tasks and sequences of tasks necessary to perform the job.

Chief brand officer

A Chief brand officer is a relatively new executive level position at a corporation, company, organization typically reporting directly to the CEO or board of directors. The Chief brand officer is responsible for a brand's image, experience, and promise, and propagating it throughout all aspects of the company. The brand officer oversees marketing, advertising, design, public relations and customer service departments.

Theory of the firm

The Theory of the firm consists of a number of economic theories which describe the nature of the firm, company including its existence, its behaviour, and its relationship with the market.

In simplified terms, the Theory of the firm aims to answer these questions:

· Existence - why do firms emerge, why are not all transactions in the economy mediated over the market?
· Boundaries - why the boundary between firms and the market is located exactly there? Which transactions are performed internally and which are negotiated on the market?
· Organization - why are firms structured in such specific way? What is the interplay of formal and informal relationships?

The First World War period saw a change of emphasis in economic theory away from industry-level analysis which mainly included analysing markets to analysis at the level of the firm, as it became increasingly clear that perfect competition was no longer an adequate model of how firms behaved. Economic theory till then had focussed on trying to understand markets alone and there had been little study on understanding why firms or organisations exist. Market are mainly guided by prices as illustrated by vegetable markets where a buyer is free to switch sellers in an exchange.

Dispute

Controversy is a state of prolonged public dispute or debate usually concerning a matter of opinion. The term originates circa 1384 from Latin controversia, as a composite of controversus - 'turned in an opposite direction,' from contra - 'against' - and vertere - to turn, or versus , hence, 'to turn against.'

Benford's law of controversy, as expressed by science-fiction author Gregory Benford in 1980, states: 'Passion is inversely proportional to the amount of real (true) information available.' In other words, the more untruths the more controversy there is, and the more truths the less controversy there is.

A controversy is always the result of either ignorance (lack of sufficient true information), misinformation, misunderstandings, half-truths, distortions, bias or prejudice, deliberate lies or fabrications (disinformation), opposed underlying motives or purposes (sometimes masked or hidden), or a combination of these factors.

Economic Development	Economic development is the development of economic wealth of countries or regions for the well-being of their inhabitants. It is the process by which a nation improves the economic, political, and social well being of its people. From a policy perspective, Economic development can be defined as efforts that seek to improve the economic well-being and quality of life for a community by creating and/or retaining jobs and supporting or growing incomes and the tax base.
Entrepreneur	An entrepreneur is a person who has possession of an enterprise and assumes significant accountability for the inherent risks and the outcome. It is an ambitious leader who combines land, labor, and capital to create and market new goods or services. The term is a loanword from French and was first defined by the Irish economist Richard Cantillon.
Guarantee	The act of becoming a surety is also called a Guarantee. Traditionally a Guarantee was distinguished from a surety in that the surety's liability was joint and primary with the principal, whereas the guaranty's liability was ancillary and derivative, but many jurisdictions have abolished this distinction
International Finance	International finance is the branch of economics that studies the dynamics of exchange rates, foreign investment, and how these affect international trade. It also studies international projects, international investments and capital flows, and trade deficits. It includes the study of futures, options and currency swaps.
Investment	Investment or investing is a term with several closely-related meanings in business management, finance and economics, related to saving or deferring consumption. Investing is the active redirecting resources from being consumed today so that they may create benefits in the future; the use of assets to earn income or profit. An Investment is the choice by the individual to risk his savings with the hope of gain.
Direct investment	Foreign Direct investment in its classic form is defined as a company from one country making a physical investment into building a factory in another country. It is the establishment of an enterprise by a foreigner. Its definition can be extended to include investments made to acquire lasting interest in enterprises operating outside of the economy of the investor.
Foreign direct investment	Foreign direct investment in its classic form is defined as a company from one country making a physical investment into building a factory in another country. It is the establishment of an enterprise by a foreigner. Its definition can be extended to include investments made to acquire lasting interest in enterprises operating outside of the economy of the investor.
Sector	In the context of computer disk storage, a sector is a subdivision of a track (Figure 1, item A) on a magnetic disk or optical disc. Each sector stores a fixed amount of data. The typical formatting of these media provides space for 512 bytes (for magnetic disks) or 2048 bytes (for optical discs) of user-accessible data per sector.
Embargo	An Embargo is the prohibition of commerce and trade with a certain country, in order to isolate it and to put its government into a difficult internal situation, given that the effects of the Embargo are often able to make its economy suffer from the initiative. It is similar to a blockade, as in 'el bloqueo' or the American blockade on Cuba. Embargo s generally attempt to pressure weaker adversaries to do what the abarcading country wishes.

General Agreement on Tariffs and Trade

The General Agreement on Tariffs and Trade was the outcome of the failure of negotiating governments to create the International Trade Organization (ITO.) GATT was formed in 1947 and lasted until 1994, when it was replaced by the World Trade Organization. The Bretton Woods Conference had introduced the idea for an organization to regulate trade as part of a larger plan for economic recovery after World War II.

Government Procurement

Government procurement or public procurement, is the procurement of goods and services on behalf of a public authority, such as a government agency. With 10 to 15% of GDP in developed countries, and up to 20% in developing countries, Government procurement accounts for a substantial part of the global economy.

To prevent fraud, waste, corruption or local protectionism, the law of most countries regulates Government procurement more or less closely.

Tariff

A Tariff is a duty imposed on goods when they are moved across a political boundary. They are usually associated with protectionism, the economic policy of restraining trade between nations. For political reasons, Tariff s are usually imposed on imported goods, although they may also be imposed on exported goods.

Predictability

Predictability is the degree to which a correct prediction or forecast of a system's state can be made either qualitatively or quantitatively. Although the second law of thermodynamics can tell us about the equilibrium state that a system will evolve to, and steady states in dissipative systems can sometimes be predicted, there exists no general rule to predict the time evolution of systems far from equilibrium, e.g. chaotic systems, if they do not approach some kind of equilibrium. Their predictability usually deteriorates with time.

Smoot-Hawley Tariff Act

The Smoot-Hawley Tariff Act was an act signed into law on June 17, 1930, that raised U.S. tariffs on over 20,000 imported goods to record levels. In the United States 1,028 economists signed a petition against this legislation, and after it was passed, many countries retaliated with their own increased tariffs on U.S. goods, and American exports and imports were reduced by more than half.

Transparency

A high degree of market Transparency can result in disintermediation due to the buyer's increased knowledge of supply pricing.

Transparency is important since it is one of the theoretical conditions required for a free market to be efficient.

Price Transparency can, however, lead to higher prices, if it makes sellers reluctant to give steep discounts to certain buyers, or if it facilitates collusion.

Discrimination

Discrimination toward or against a person of a certain group is the treatment or consideration based on class or category rather than individual merit. It can be behavior promoting a certain group (e.g. affirmative action), or it can be negative behavior directed against a certain group (e.g. redlining.)

Racial discrimination differentiates between individuals on the basis of real and perceived racial differences, and has been official government policy in several countries, such as South Africa in the apartheid era, and the USA.

Globalization

Globalization in its literal sense is the process of transformation of local or regional phenomena into global ones. It can be described as a process by which the people of the world are unified into a single society and function together.

This process is a combination of economic, technological, sociocultural and political forces.

Statistics	Statistics is a mathematical science pertaining to the collection, analysis, interpretation or explanation, and presentation of data. It also provides tools for prediction and forecasting based on data. It is applicable to a wide variety of academic disciplines, from the natural and social sciences to the humanities, government and business.
Intellectual property	Intellectual property are legal property rights over creations of the mind, both artistic and commercial, and the corresponding fields of law. Under intellectual property law, owners are granted certain exclusive rights to a variety of intangible assets, such as musical, literary, and artistic works; ideas, discoveries and inventions; and words, phrases, symbols, and designs. Common types of intellectual property include copyrights, trademarks, patents, industrial design rights and trade secrets.
Litigation	The conduct of a lawsuit is called Litigation. Rules of criminal or civil procedure govern the conduct of a lawsuit in the common law adversarial system of dispute resolution. Procedural rules are additionally constrained/informed by separate statutory laws, case law, and constitutional provisions that define the rights of the parties to a lawsuit , though the rules will generally reflect this legal context on their face.
Population	In biology, a Population , is the collection of inter-breeding organisms of a particular species; in sociology, a collection of human beings. Individuals within a Population share a factor may be reduced by statistical means, but such a generalization may be too vague to imply anything. Demography is used extensively in marketing, which relates to economic units, such as retailers, to potential customers.
Labor force	In economics, the people in the Labor force are the suppliers of labor. The Labor force is all the nonmilitary people who are employed or unemployed. In 2005, the worldwide Labor force was over 3 billion people.
Piracy	Piracy is a war-like act committed by a non-state actor, especially robbery or criminal violence committed at sea, on water, or sometimes on shore. It does not normally include crimes on board a vessel among passengers or crew. The term has been used to refer to raids across land borders by non-state actors.
Unemployment	Unemployment occurs when a person is available to work and seeking work but currently without work. The prevalence of Unemployment is usually measured using the Unemployment rate, which is defined as the percentage of those in the labor force who are unemployed. The Unemployment rate is also used in economic studies and economic indexes such as the United States' Conference Board's Index of Leading Indicators as a measure of the state of the macroeconomics.
Industry	An Industry is the manufacturing of a good or service within a category. Although Industry is a broad term for any kind of economic production, in economics and urban planning Industry is a synonym for the secondary sector, which is a type of economic activity involved in the manufacturing of raw materials into goods and products. There are four key industrial economic sectors: the primary sector, largely raw material extraction industries such as mining and farming; the secondary sector, involving refining, construction, and manufacturing; the tertiary sector, which deals with services (such as law and medicine) and distribution of manufactured goods; and the quaternary sector, a relatively new type of knowledge Industry focusing on technological research, design and development such as computer programming, and biochemistry.
Infringement	Infringement, when used alone, has several possible meanings in the English language.

In a legal context, an infringement refers to the violation of a law or a right. This includes intellectual property infringements such as:

· copyright infringement
· patent infringement
· trademark infringement
· civel building infringement .

Patent

A patent is a set of exclusive rights granted by a state to an inventor or his assignee for a limited period of time in exchange for a disclosure of an invention.

The procedure for granting patent s, the requirements placed on the patent ee and the extent of the exclusive rights vary widely between countries according to national laws and international agreements. Typically, however, a patent application must include one or more claims defining the invention which must be new, inventive, and useful or industrially applicable.

Patent infringement

Patent infringement is the commission of a prohibited act with respect to a patented invention without permission from the patent holder. Permission may typically be granted in the form of a licence. The definition of patent infringement may vary by jurisdiction, but it typically includes using or selling the patented invention.

Report

In writing, a report is a document characterized by information or other content reflective of inquiry or investigation, which is tailored to the context of a given situation and audience. The purpose of report s is usually to inform. However, report s may include persuasive elements, such as recommendations, suggestions, or other motivating conclusions that indicate possible future actions the report reader might take.

Free Trade

Free trade is a type of trade policy that allows traders to act and transact without interference from government. Thus, the policy permits trading partners mutual gains from trade, with goods and services produced according to the theory of comparative advantage.

Under a Free trade policy, prices are a reflection of true supply and demand, and are the sole determinant of resource allocation.

Mercosur

MERCOSUR or Mercosul is a Regional Trade Agreement among Argentina, Brazil, Paraguay and Uruguay founded in 1991 by the Treaty of Asunción, which was later amended and updated by the 1994 Treaty of Ouro Preto. Its purpose is to promote free trade and the fluid movement of goods, people, and currency.

MERCOSUR origins trace back to 1985 when Presidents Raúl Alfonsín of Argentina and José Sarney of Brazil signed the Argentina-Brazil Integration and Economics Cooperation Program or PICE .

North American Free Trade Agreement

The North American Free Trade Agreement is a trilateral trade bloc in North America created by the governments of the United States, Canada, and Mexico. It superseded the Canada-United States Free Trade Agreement between the US and Canada.

Following diplomatic negotiations dating back to 1990 between the three nations, the leaders met in San Antonio, Texas on December 17, 1992 to sign North American Free Trade Agreement.

Cooperative	A cooperative is defined by the International Co-operative Alliance's Statement on the Co-operative Identity as an autonomous association of persons united voluntarily to meet their common economic, social, and cultural needs and aspirations through a jointly-owned and democratically-controlled enterprise. It is a business organization owned and operated by a group of individuals for their mutual benefit. A cooperative may also be defined as a business owned and controlled equally by the people who use its services or who work at it.
Security agreement	A security agreement is the contract that governs the relationship between the parties to a secured transaction (ie, the lender and the borrower A written security agreement needs a description of the collateral, must be authenticated by the borrower (ie, signed), and must use words showing an intent to create a security interest
Bribery	Bribery, a form of pecuniary corruption, is an act implying money or gift given that alters the behaviour of the recipient. bribery constitutes a crime and is defined by Black's Law Dictionary as the offering, giving, receiving, or soliciting of any item of value to influence the actions of an official or other person in discharge of a public or legal duty. The bribe is the gift bestowed to influence the recipient's conduct.
Congress	A Congress is a formal meeting of representatives from different countries (or by extension constituent states), or independent organizations (such as different trade unions.) The term Congress was chosen for the United States Congress to emphasize the status of each state represented there as a self-governing unit. Subsequently to the use of Congress by the US legislature, the term has been adopted by many states within unions, and by unitary nation-states in the Americas, to refer to their legislatures.
Petroleum industry	The Petroleum industry includes the global processes of exploration, extraction, refining, transporting (often by oil tankers and pipelines), and marketing petroleum products. The largest volume products of the industry are fuel oil and gasoline (petrol.) Petroleum is also the raw material for many chemical products, including pharmaceuticals, solvents, fertilizers, pesticides, and plastics.
Price	Price in economics and business is the result of an exchange and from that trade we assign a numerical monetary value to a good, service or asset. If I trade 4 apples for an orange, the price of an orange is 4 - apples. Inversely, the price of an apple is 1/4 oranges.
Korea	Korea (Hangul: í•œêµ or ì¡°ì„) is a civilization and formerly unified nation currently divided into two states. Located on the Korea n Peninsula, it borders China to the northwest, Russia to the northeast, and is separated from Japan to the east by the Korea Strait.
Money	Money is anything that is generally accepted as payment for goods and services and repayment of debts. The main uses of Money are as a medium of exchange, a unit of account, and a store of value. Some authors explicitly require Money to be a standard of deferred payment.
Money Laundering	Money laundering is the practice of disguising illegally obtained funds so that they seem legal. It is a crime in many jurisdictions with varying definitions. It is a key operation of the underground economy.

Task Force

A Task force is a temporary unit or formation established to work on a single defined task or activity. Originally introduced by the United States Navy, the term has now caught on for general usage and is a standard part of NATO terminology. Many non-military organizations now create ' Task force s' or task groups for temporary activities that might have once been performed by ad hoc committees.

Consumer

Consumer is a broad label that refers to any individuals or households that use goods and services generated within the economy. The concept of a Consumer is used in different contexts, so that the usage and significance of the term may vary.

A Consumer is a person who uses any product or service.

Share

In business and finance, a share of stock (also referred to as equity share) means a share of ownership in a corporation (company.) In the plural, stocks is often used as a synonym for shares especially in the United States, but it is less commonly used that way outside of North America.

In the United Kingdom, South Africa, and Australia, stock can also refer to completely different financial instruments such as government bonds or, less commonly, to all kinds of marketable securities.

Skilled worker

A Skilled worker is any worker who has some special skill, knowledge, or (usually acquired) ability in his work. A Skilled worker may have attended a college, university or technical school. Or, a Skilled worker may have learned his skills on the job.

Topics

In microeconomics, industrial organization is the field which describes the behavior of firms in the marketplace with regard to production, pricing, employment and other decisions. Topics in this field range from classical issues such as opportunity cost to neoclassical concepts such as factors of production.

· Production theory basics

· production efficiency
· factors of production
· total, average, and marginal product curves
· marginal productivity
· isoquants ' isocosts
· the marginal rate of technical substitution
· Economic rent

· classical factor rents
· Paretian factor rents
· Production possibility frontier

· what products are possible given a set of resources
· the trade-off between producing one product rather than another
· the marginal rate of transformation
· Production function

· inputs
· diminishing returns to inputs
· the stages of production
· shifts in a production function
· Cost theory

· the different types of costs

· opportunity cost
· accounting cost or historical costs
· transaction cost
· sunk cost
· marginal cost
· the isocost line
· Cost-of-production theory of value
· Long-run cost and production functions

· long-run average cost
· long-run production function and efficiency
· returns to scale and isoclines
· minimum efficient scale
· plant capacity
· Economies of density
· Economies of scale

· the efficiency consequences of increasing or decreasing the level of production
· Economies of scope

· the efficiency consequences of increasing or decreasing the number of different types of products produced, promoted, and distributed
· Optimum factor allocation

· output elasticity of factor costs
· marginal revenue product
· marginal resource cost
· Pricing

· various aspects of the pricing decision
· Transfer pricing

· selling within a multi-divisional company
· Joint product pricing

· price setting when two products are linked
· Price discrimination

· different prices to different buyers
· types of price discrimination
· yield management
· Price skimming

· price discrimination over time
· Two part tariffs

· charging a price composed of two parts, usually an initial fee and an ongoing fee
· Price points

· the effects of a non-linear demand curve on pricing
· Cost-plus pricing

· a markup is applied to a cost term in order to calculate price
· cost-plus pricing with elasticity considerations
· cost plus pricing is often used along with break even analysis
· Rate of return pricing

· calculate price based on the required rate of return on investment, or rate of return on sales
· Profit maximization

· determining the optimum price and quantity
· the totals approach
· marginal approach of production .

Free trade area

Free trade area is a designated group of countries that have agreed to eliminate tariffs, quotas and preferences on most (if not all) goods and services traded between them. It can be considered the second stage of economic integration. Countries choose this kind of economic integration form if their economical structures are complementary.

Customs

Customs is an authority or agency in a country responsible for collecting and safeguarding customs duties and for controlling the flow of goods including animals, personal effects and hazardous items in and out of a country. Depending on local legislation and regulations, the import or export of some goods may be restricted or forbidden, and the customs agency enforces these rules. The customs agency may be different from the immigration authority, which monitors persons who leave or enter the country, checking for appropriate documentation, apprehending people wanted by international arrest warrants, and impeding the entry of others deemed dangerous to the country.

Customs union

A Customs union is a free trade area with a common external tariff. The participant countries set up common external trade policy, but in some cases they use different import quotas. Common competition policy is also helpful to avoid competition deficiency.

Economic integration	Economic integration is a term used to describe how different aspects between economies are integrated. The basics of this theory were written by the Hungarian Economist Béla Balassa in the 1960s. As economic integration increases, the barriers of trade between markets diminishes.
Procter ' Gamble	Procter is a surname, and may also refer to: · Bryan Waller Procter (pseud. Barry Cornwall), English poet · Goodwin Procter, American law firm · Procter ' Gamble, consumer products multinational .
Common market	A common market is a customs union with common policies on product regulation, and freedom of movement of the factors of production (capital and labour) and of enterprise. The goal is that the movement of capital, labour, goods, and services between the members is as easy as within them. This is the fourth stage of economic integration.
Central Bank	A central bank, reserve bank, or monetary authority is the entity responsible for the monetary policy of a country or of a group of member states. It is a bank that can lend money to other banks in times of need. Its primary responsibility is to maintain the stability of the national currency and money supply, but more active duties include controlling subsidized-loan interest rates, and acting as a lender of last resort to the banking sector during times of financial crisis (private banks often being integral to the national financial system.)
Copyright	Copyright is a form of intellectual property which gives the creator of an original work exclusive rights for a certain time period in relation to that work, including its publication, distribution and adaptation; after which time the work is said to enter the public domain. Copyright applies to any expressible form of an idea or information that is substantive and discrete. Some jurisdictions also recognize 'moral rights' of the creator of a work, such as the right to be credited for the work.
Economic growth	Economic growth is the increase in the amount of the goods and services produced by an economy over time and is dependent on an increase in the creation of money. Growth is conventionally measured as the percent rate of increase in real gross domestic product, or real GDP. GDP is usually calculated in real terms, i.e.
Original	Original ity is the aspect of created or invented works by as being new or novel, and thus can be distinguished from reproductions, clones, forgeries, or derivative works. An original work is one not received from others nor one copied based on the work of others. The term ' original ity' is often applied as a compliment to the creativity of artists, writers, and thinkers.
Demographic	Demographic or Demographic data refers to selected population characteristics as used in government, marketing or opinion research, or the Demographic profiles used in such research. Note the distinction from the term 'demography' Commonly-used Demographic include race, age, income, disabilities, mobility (in terms of travel time to work or number of vehicles available), educational attainment, home ownership, employment status, and even location.

Gross domestic product

The Gross domestic product or gross domestic income (GDI), a basic measure of an economy's economic performance, is the market value of all final goods and services produced within the borders of a nation in a year. Gross domestic product can be defined in three ways, all of which are conceptually identical. First, it is equal to the total expenditures for all final goods and services produced within the country in a stipulated period of time (usually a 365-day year.)

Merchandise

Merchandising refers to the methods, practices and operations conducted to promote and sustain certain categories of commercial activity. The term is understood to have different specific meanings depending on the context. merchandise is a sale goods at a store

In marketing, one of the definitions of merchandising is the practice in which the brand or image from one product or service is used to sell another.

Distribution

Distribution is one of the four elements of marketing mix. An organization or set of organizations (go-betweens) involved in the process of making a product or service available for use or consumption by a consumer or business user.

The other three parts of the marketing mix are product, pricing, and promotion.

Export

In economics, an export is any good or commodity, transported from one country to another country in a legitimate fashion, typically for use in trade. export goods or services are provided to foreign consumers by domestic producers. export is an important part of international trade.

Fee

A Fee is the price one pays as remuneration for services, especially the honorarium paid to a doctor, lawyer, consultant, or other member of a learned profession. Fee s usually allow for overhead, wages, costs, and markup.

Traditionally, professionals in Great Britain received a Fee in contradistinction to a payment, salary, or wage, and would often use guineas rather than pounds as units of account.

Long-run

In economic models, the long-run time frame assumes no fixed factors of production. Firms can enter or leave the marketplace, and the cost (and availability) of land, labor, raw materials, and capital goods can be assumed to vary. In contrast, in the short-run time frame, certain factors are assumed to be fixed, because there is not sufficient time for them to change.

Free Trade Area of the Americas

The Free Trade Area of the Americas , Portuguese: Área de Livre Comércio das Américas (ALCA), Dutch: Vrijhandelszone van de Amerika's) was a proposed agreement to eliminate or reduce the trade barriers among all countries in the Americas but Cuba. In the latest round of negotiations, trade ministers from 34 nations met in Miami, Florida, United States, in November 2003 to discuss the proposal. The proposed agreement was an extension of the North American Free Trade Agreement (NAFTA) between Canada, Mexico and the United States.

Facing

Facing,, is a common tool in the retail industry to create the look of a perfectly stocked store by pulling all of the products on a display or shelf to the front, as well as downstacking all the canned and stacked items. It is also done to keep the store appearing neat and organized.

The workers who face commonly have jobs doing other things in the store such as customer service, stocking shelves, daytime cleaning, bagging and carryouts, etc.

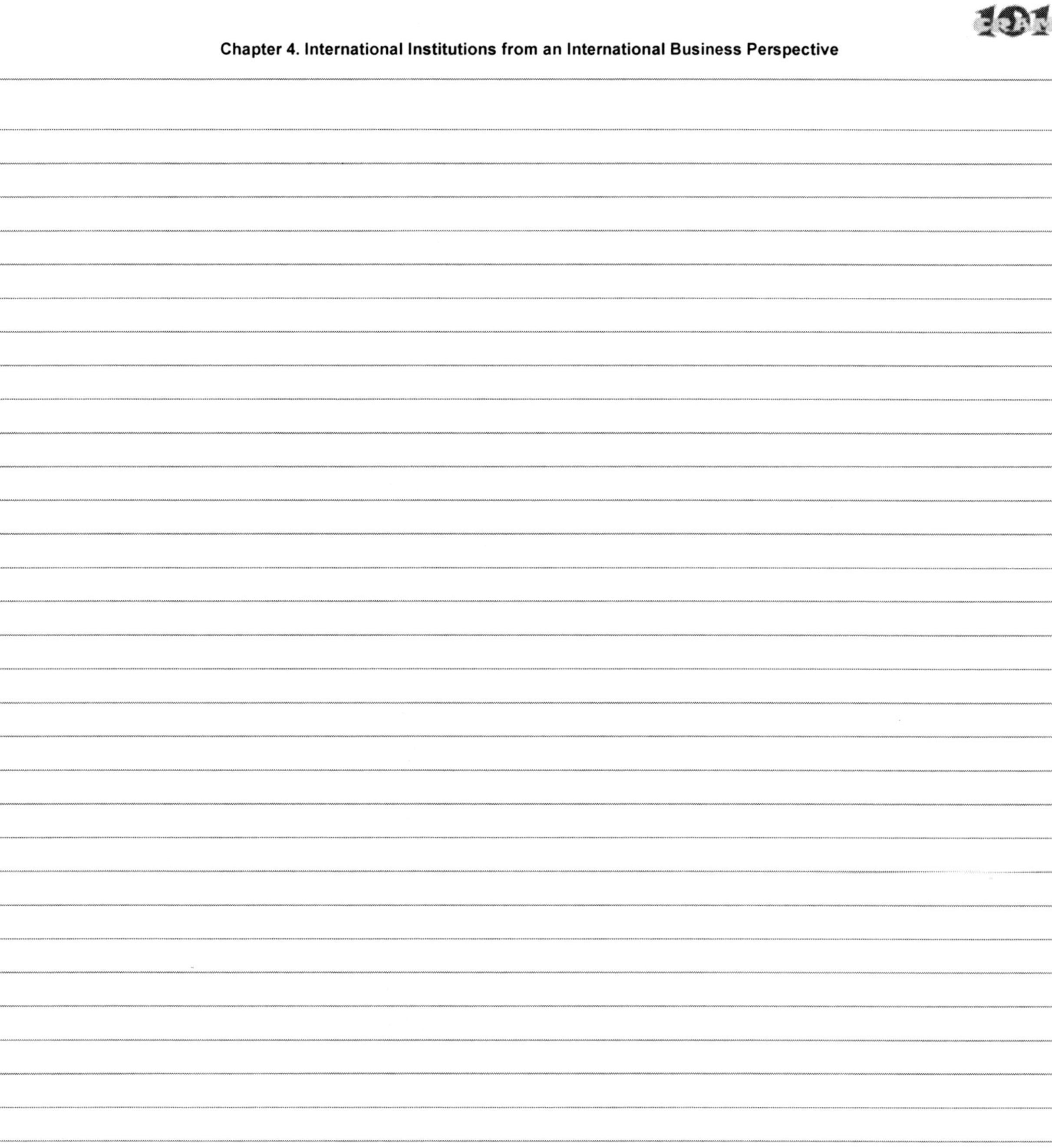

Common Market for Eastern and Southern Africa	The Common Market for Eastern and Southern Africa, is a preferential trading area with nineteen member states stretching from Libya to Zimbabwe. COMESA formed in December 1994, replacing a Preferential Trade Area which had existed since 1981. Nine of the member states formed a free trade area in 2000 (Djibouti, Egypt, Kenya, Madagascar, Malawi, Mauritius, Sudan, Zambia and Zimbabwe), with Rwanda and Burundi joining the FTA in 2004 and the Comoros and Libya in 2006.
Southern African Development Community	The Southern African Development Community is an inter-governmental organization headquartered in Gaborone, Botswana. Its goal is to further socio-economic cooperation and integration as well as political and security cooperation among 15 southern African states. It complements the role of the African Union.
Asia-Pacific	Asia-Pacific or APAC is that part of the world in or near the Western Pacific Ocean. The area includes much of East Asia, Southeast Asia, Australasia and Oceania.) Sometimes the term Asia-Pacific includes South Asia, though India and its neighbours are on or near the Indian Ocean rather than the Pacific Ocean.
Asia-Pacific Economic Cooperation	Asia-Pacific Economic Cooperation is a forum for 21 Pacific Rim countries (styled 'member economies') to cooperate on regional trade and investment liberalisation and facilitation. APEC's objective is to enhance economic growth and prosperity in the region and to strengthen the Asia-Pacific community. Members account for approximately 40% of the world's population, approximately 54% of world GDP and about 44% of world trade.
Internal Market	An Internal market operates inside an organizations or set of organizations which have decoupled internal components. Each component trades its services and interfaces with the others. Often a set of government or government-funded set of organizations will operate an Internal market.
Maastricht Treaty	The Maastricht Treaty was signed on 7 February 1992 in Maastricht, the Netherlands after final negotiations on 9 December 1991 between the members of the European Community and entered into force on 1 November 1993 during the Delors Commission. It created the European Union and led to the creation of the euro. The Maastricht Treaty has been amended to a degree by later treaties.
Steel	Steel is an alloy consisting mostly of iron, with a carbon content between 0.2% and 2.14% by weight (C:110-10Fe), depending on grade. Carbon is the most cost-effective alloying material for iron, but various other alloying elements are used such as manganese, chromium, vanadium, and tungsten. Carbon and other elements act as a hardening agent, preventing dislocations in the iron atom crystal lattice from sliding past one another.
Population size	In population genetics and population ecology, population size is the number of individual organisms in a population. The effective population size (N_e) is defined as 'the number of breeding individuals in an idealized population that would show the same amount of dispersion of allele frequencies under random genetic drift or the same amount of inbreeding as the population under consideration.' N_e is usually less than N (the absolute population size) and this has important applications in conservation genetics. Small population size results in increased genetic drift.

Euro	The Euro (â,¬) is the official currency of 16 of the 27 member states of the Euro pean Union (EU.) The states, known collectively as the Euro zone, are Austria, Belgium, Cyprus, Finland, France, Germany, Greece, Ireland, Italy, Luxembourg, Malta, the Netherlands, Portugal, Slovakia, Slovenia, and Spain. The currency is also used in a further five Euro pean countries, with and without formal agreements and is consequently used daily by some 327 million Euro peans.
Monetary Union	An economic and Monetary union is a single market with a common currency. It is to be distinguished from a mere currency union , which does not involve a single market. This is the fifth stage of economic integration.
Foreign policy	A country's foreign policy is a set of goals outlining how the country will interact with other countries economically, politically, socially and militarily, and to a lesser extent, how the country will interact with non-state actors. The aforementioned interaction is evaluated and monitored in attempts to maximize benefits of multilateral international cooperation. Foreign policies are designed to help protect a country's national interests, national security, ideological goals, and economic prosperity.
Labeling	Labeling- Identifies the product or brand; describe several things about the product - who made it, when it was made, where it was made, its content, how is it to be use and how to use it safely.
Competition Commission	The Competition Commission is an non-departmental public body body responsible for investigating mergers, markets and other inquiries related to regulated industries under United Kingdom competition law. It is under the Department for Business, Enterprise and Regulatory Reform (formerly the Department for of Trade and Industry.) The Competition Commission replaced the Monopolies and Mergers Commission on 1 April 1999.
Investment Bank	An investment bank is a financial institution that raises capital, trades in securities and manages corporate mergers and acquisitions. investment bank s profit from companies and governments by raising money through issuing and selling securities in the capital markets (both equity, debt) and insuring bonds (e.g. selling credit default swaps), as well as providing advice on transactions such as mergers and acquisitions. To perform these services in the United States, an adviser must be a licensed broker-dealer, and is subject to SEC (FINRA) regulation see SEC. Until the late 1980s, the United States maintained a separation between investment bank ing and commercial banks.
Mergers and Acquisitions	The phrase Mergers and Acquisitions refers to the aspect of corporate strategy, corporate finance and management dealing with the buying, selling and combining of different companies that can aid, finance, or help a growing company in a given industry grow rapidly without having to create another business entity. An acquisition, also known as a takeover or a buyout, is the buying of one company (the 'target') by another. An acquisition may be friendly or hostile.
Mergers	The phrase mergers and acquisitions refers to the aspect of corporate strategy, corporate finance and management dealing with the buying, selling and combining of different companies that can aid, finance, or help a growing company in a given industry grow rapidly without having to create another business entity. An acquisition, also known as a takeover or a buyout, is the buying of one company (the 'target') by another. An acquisition may be friendly or hostile.

Microsoft

Microsoft Corporation (NASDAQ: MSFT, HKEX: 4338) is an United States-based multinational computer technology corporation that develops, manufactures, licenses, and supports a wide range of software products for computing devices. Headquartered in Redmond, Washington, USA, its most profitable products are the Microsoft Windows operating system and the Microsoft Office suite of productivity software.

The company was founded to develop and sell BASIC interpreters for the Altair 8800.

Acquisition

The phrase mergers and acquisitions refers to the aspect of corporate strategy, corporate finance and management dealing with the buying, selling and combining of different companies that can aid, finance, or help a growing company in a given industry grow rapidly without having to create another business entity.

An Acquisition, also known as a takeover or a buyout, is the buying of one company (the 'target') by another. An Acquisition may be friendly or hostile.

Regulation

Regulation refers to 'controlling human or societal behaviour by rules or restrictions.' Regulation can take many forms: legal restrictions promulgated by a government authority, self-Regulation, social Regulation, co-Regulation and market Regulation. One can consider Regulation as actions of conduct imposing sanctions (such as a fine.) This action of administrative law, or implementing regulatory law, may be contrasted with statutory or case law.

Trust

In common law legal systems, a trust is an arrangement whereby property (including real, tangible and intangible) is managed by one person (or persons, or organizations) for the benefit of another. A trust is created by a settlor, who entrusts some or all of his or her property to people of his choice (the trustees.) The trustees hold legal title to the trust property (or trust corpus), but they are obliged to hold the property for the benefit of one or more individuals or organizations (the beneficiary, a.k.a. cestui que use or cestui que trust), usually specified by the settlor, who hold equitable title.

Cultural identity

Cultural identity is the identity of a group or culture, or of an individual as far as one is influenced by one's belonging to a group or culture. Cultural identity is similar to and has overlaps with, but is not synonymous with, identity politics.

There are modern questions of culture that are transferred into questions of identity.

Resources

Human beings are also considered to be Resources because they have the ability to change raw materials into valuable Resources. The term Human Resources can also be defined as the skills, energies, talents, abilities and knowledge that are used for the production of goods or the rendering of services. While taking into account human beings as Resources, the following things have to be kept in mind:

· The size of the population
· The capabilities of the individuals in that population

Many Resources cannot be consumed in their original form. They have to be processed in order to change them into more usable commodities.

International business | International business is a term used to collectively describe topics relating to the operations of firms with interests in multiple countries. Such firms are sometimes called multinational corporations . Well known MNCs include fast food companies McDonald's and Yum Brands, vehicle manufacturers such as General Motors and Toyota, consumer electronics companies like Samsung, LG and Sony, and energy companies such as ExxonMobil and BP.

Trust | In common law legal systems, a trust is an arrangement whereby property (including real, tangible and intangible) is managed by one person (or persons, or organizations) for the benefit of another. A trust is created by a settlor, who entrusts some or all of his or her property to people of his choice (the trustees.) The trustees hold legal title to the trust property (or trust corpus), but they are obliged to hold the property for the benefit of one or more individuals or organizations (the beneficiary, a.k.a. cestui que use or cestui que trust), usually specified by the settlor, who hold equitable title.

United States | The United States of America (commonly referred to as the United States the U.S., the United States A, or America) is a federal constitutional republic comprising fifty states and a federal district. The country is situated mostly in central North America, where its 48 contiguous states and Washington, D.C., the capital district, lie between the Pacific and Atlantic Oceans, bordered by Canada to the north and Mexico to the south. The state of Alaska is in the northwest of the continent, with Canada to its east and Russia to the west across the Bering Strait.

Culture | Culture is a term that has different meanings. For example, in 1952, Alfred Kroeber and Clyde Kluckhohn compiled a list of 164 definitions of culture in culture A Critical Review of Concepts and Definitions. However, the word culture is most commonly used in three basic senses:

· excellence of taste in the fine arts and humanities, also known as high culture
· an integrated pattern of human knowledge, belief, and behavior that depends upon the capacity for symbolic thought and social learning
· the set of shared attitudes, values, goals, and practices that characterizes an institution, organization or group.

When the concept first emerged in eighteenth- and nineteenth-century Europe, it connoted a process of cultivation or improvement, as in agri culture or horti culture . In the nineteenth century, it came to refer first to the betterment or refinement of the individual, especially through education, and then to the fulfillment of national aspirations or ideals.

Learning | Learning is acquiring new knowledge, behaviors, skills, values, preferences or understanding, and may involve synthesizing different types of information. The ability to learn is possessed by humans, animals and some machines. Progress over time tends to follow learning curves.

Advertising | Advertising is a form of communication that typically attempts to persuade potential customers to purchase or to consume more of a particular brand of product or service. 'While now central to the contemporary global economy and the reproduction of global production networks, it is only quite recently that Advertising has been more than a marginal influence on patterns of sales and production. The formation of modern Advertising was intimately bound up with the emergence of new forms of monopoly capitalism around the end of the 19th and beginning of the 20th century as one element in corporate strategies to create, organize and where possible control markets, especially for mass produced consumer goods.

Business

A business is a legally recognized organization designed to provide goods and/or services to consumers. business es are predominant in capitalist economies, most being privately owned and formed to earn profit that will increase the wealth of its owners and grow the business itself. The owners and operators of a business have as one of their main objectives the receipt or generation of a financial return in exchange for work and acceptance of risk.

Marketing

Marketing is defined by the American Marketing Association as the activity, set of institutions, and processes for creating, communicating, delivering, and exchanging offerings that have value for customers, clients, partners, and society at large. The term developed from the original meaning which referred literally to going to market, as in shopping, or going to a market to sell goods or services.

Marketing practice tends to be seen as a creative industry, which includes advertising, distribution and selling.

Procter ' Gamble

Procter is a surname, and may also refer to:

· Bryan Waller Procter (pseud. Barry Cornwall), English poet
· Goodwin Procter, American law firm
· Procter ' Gamble, consumer products multinational .

Consumer

Consumer is a broad label that refers to any individuals or households that use goods and services generated within the economy. The concept of a Consumer is used in different contexts, so that the usage and significance of the term may vary.

A Consumer is a person who uses any product or service.

Consumer goods

Consumer goods are final goods specifically intended for the mass market. For instance, consumer goods do not include investment assets, like precious antiques, even though these antiques are final goods.

Manufactured goods are goods that have been processed by way of machinery.

Cultural identity

Cultural identity is the identity of a group or culture, or of an individual as far as one is influenced by one's belonging to a group or culture. Cultural identity is similar to and has overlaps with, but is not synonymous with, identity politics.

There are modern questions of culture that are transferred into questions of identity.

Good

A good is an object whose consumption increases the utility of the consumer, for which the quantity demanded exceeds the quantity supplied at zero price. Goods are usually modeled as having diminishing marginal utility. The first individual purchase has high utility; the second has less.

Planning

Planning in organizations and public policy is both the organizational process of creating and maintaining a plan; and the psychological process of thinking about the activities required to create a desired goal on some scale. As such, it is a fundamental property of intelligent behavior. This thought process is essential to the creation and refinement of a plan, or integration of it with other plans, that is, it combines forecasting of developments with the preparation of scenarios of how to react to them.

Failure

Failure refers to the state or condition of not meeting a desirable or intended objective, and may be viewed as the opposite of success. Product failure ranges from failure to sell the product to fracture of the product, in the worst cases leading to personal injury, the province of forensic engineering.

The criteria for failure are heavily dependent on context of use, and may be relative to a particular observer or belief system.

Manufacturing	Manufacturing is the application of tools and a processing medium to the transformation of raw materials into finished goods for sale. This effort includes all intermediate processes required for the production and integration of a product's components. Some industries, like semiconductor and steel manufacturers use the term fabrication instead.
Standardization	Standardization or standardisation is the process of developing and agreeing upon technical standards. A standard is a document that establishes uniform engineering or technical specifications, criteria, methods, processes, or practices. Some standards are mandatory while others are voluntary.
Job description	A Job description is a list of the general tasks and responsibilities of a position. Typically, it also includes to whom the position reports, specifications such as the qualifications needed by the person in the job, salary range for the position, etc. A Job description is usually developed by conducting a job analysis, which includes examining the tasks and sequences of tasks necessary to perform the job.
Human	A human is a member of a species of bipedal primates in the family Hominidae . DNA and fossil evidence indicates that modern human s originated in east Africa about 200,000 years ago. When compared to other animals and primates, human s have a highly developed brain, capable of abstract reasoning, language, introspection and problem solving.
Human resource management	Human resource management is the strategic and coherent approach to the management of an organisation's most valued assets - the people working there who individually and collectively contribute to the achievement of the objectives of the business. The terms 'Human resource management' and 'human resources' (HR) have largely replaced the term 'personnel management' as a description of the processes involved in managing people in organizations. In simple sense, Human resource management means employing people, developing their resources, utilizing, maintaining and compensating their services in tune with the job and organizational requirement.
Set TSP	In combinatorial optimization, the set TSP group TSP, One-of-a-set TSP, Multiple Choice TSP or Covering Salesman Problem, is a generalization of the Traveling salesman problem, whereby it is required to find a shortest tour in a graph which visits all specified disjoint subsets of the vertices of a graph. The ordinary TSP is a special case of the set TSP when all subsets to be visited are singletons. Therefore the set TSP is also NP-hard.
Kraft Foods	Kraft Foods Inc. (NYSE: Kraft Foods T) is the largest food and beverage company headquartered in the United States and the second largest in the world (after Nestlé SA.) Kraft is headquartered in Northfield, Illinois, USA, a Chicago suburb.
Numerary	Numerary is a civil designation for persons who are incorporated in a fixed or permanent way to a society or group: regular member of the working staff, permanent staff distinguished from a super Numerary . The term Numerary and its counterpart, 'super Numerary ,' originated in Spanish and Latin American academy and government; it is now also used in countries all over the world, such as France, the U.S., England, Italy, etc. There are Numerary members of surgical organizations, of universities, of gastronomical associations, etc.

Vertical slice

A Vertical slice, sometimes abbreviated to Vertical slice, is a type of milestone, benchmark with emphasis on demonstrating progress across all components of a project. It could be considered a project management buzzword, and may have originated in the games industry.

Expatriate

An expatriate is a person temporarily or permanently residing in a country and culture other than that of the person's upbringing or legal residence. The word comes from the Latin ex and patria (country, fatherland.)

The term is sometimes used in the context of Westerners living in non-Western countries, although it is also used to describe Westerners living in other Western countries, such as U.S. citizens living in the United Kingdom, or Britons living in Spain.

Overtime

Overtime is the amount of time someone works beyond normal working hours. Normal hours may be determined in several ways:

· by custom (what is considered healthy or reasonable by society),
· by practices of a given trade or profession,
· by legislation,
· by agreement between employers and workers or their representatives.

Most nations have Overtime laws designed to dissuade or prevent employers from forcing their employees to work excessively long hours. These laws may take into account other considerations than the humanitarian, such as increasing the overall level of employment in the economy. One common approach to regulating Overtime is to require employers to pay workers at a higher hourly rate for Overtime work.

Foreign direct investment

Foreign direct investment in its classic form is defined as a company from one country making a physical investment into building a factory in another country. It is the establishment of an enterprise by a foreigner. Its definition can be extended to include investments made to acquire lasting interest in enterprises operating outside of the economy of the investor.

Protestant work ethic

The Protestant work ethic, sometimes called the Puritan Work Ethic, is a sociological, theoretical concept. It is based upon the notion that the Calvinist emphasis on the necessity for hard work is proponent of a person's calling and worldly success is a sign of personal salvation. It is argued that Protestants beginning with Martin Luther had reconceptualised worldly work as a duty which benefits both the individual and society as a whole.

Work ethic

Work ethic is a set of values based on hard work and diligence. It is also a belief in the moral benefit of work and its ability to enhance character. An example would be the Protestant Work ethic.

Characteristic

Characteristic has several particular meanings:

· in mathematics
- · Euler characteristic
- · method of characteristic s (partial differential equations)

· in physics and engineering

· any characteristic curve that shows the relationship between certain input- and output parameters, e.g.
· an I-V or current-voltage characteristic is the current in a circuit as a function of the applied voltage
· Receiver-Operator characteristic
· in navigation, the characteristic pattern of a lighted beacon.
· in fiction

· in Dungeons ' Dragons, characteristic is another name for ability score .

Cost

In economics, business, retail, and accounting, a cost is the value of money that has been used up to produce something, and hence is not available for use anymore. In economics, a cost is an alternative that is given up as a result of a decision. In business, the cost may be one of acquisition, in which case the amount of money expended to acquire it is counted as cost.

Prestige

Prestige is a word commonly used to describe reputation or esteem, though it has three somewhat related meanings that, to some degree, may be contradictory. Which meaning applies depends on the historical context and the person using the word.

Originally, Prestige referred to pomposity, which was taken as a sign of poor taste.

Trend analysis

The term 'trend analysis' refers to the concept of collecting information and attempting to spot a pattern in the information. In some fields of study, the term 'trend analysis' has more formally-defined meanings.

In project management trend analysis is a mathematical technique that uses historical results to predict future outcome.

Jihad

Jihad , an Islamic term, is a religious duty of Muslims. In Arabic, the word jihÄ d is a noun meaning 'struggle.' Jihad appears frequently in the Qur'an and common usage as the idiomatic expression 'striving in the way of Allah '. A person engaged in Jihad is called a mujahid, the plural is mujahideen.

Dispute

Controversy is a state of prolonged public dispute or debate usually concerning a matter of opinion. The term originates circa 1384 from Latin controversia, as a composite of controversus - 'turned in an opposite direction,' from contra - 'against' - and vertere - to turn, or versus , hence, 'to turn against.'

Benford's law of controversy, as expressed by science-fiction author Gregory Benford in 1980, states: 'Passion is inversely proportional to the amount of real (true) information available.' In other words, the more untruths the more controversy there is, and the more truths the less controversy there is.

A controversy is always the result of either ignorance (lack of sufficient true information), misinformation, misunderstandings, half-truths, distortions, bias or prejudice, deliberate lies or fabrications (disinformation), opposed underlying motives or purposes (sometimes masked or hidden), or a combination of these factors.

Goal

A Goal or objective is a projected state of affairs that a person or a system plans or intends to achieve--a personal or organizational desired end-point in some sort of assumed development. Many people endeavor to reach Goal s within a finite time by setting deadlines.

A desire or an intention becomes a Goal if and only if one activates an action for achieving it

Market	A Market is any one of a variety of different systems, institutions, procedures, social relations and infrastructures whereby persons trade, and goods and services are exchanged, forming part of the economy. It is an arrangement that allows buyers and sellers to exchange things. Market s vary in size, range, geographic scale, location, types and variety of human communities, as well as the types of goods and services traded.
Minority	A Minority or digger group is a sociological group that does not constitute a politically dominant voting majority of the total population of a given society. A sociological Minority is not necessarily a numerical Minority -- it may include any group that is subnormal with respect to a dominant group in terms of social status, education, employment, wealth and political power. To avoid confusion, some writers prefer the terms 'subordinate group' and 'dominant group' rather than 'Minority' and 'majority', respectively.
Division of labour	Division of labour or specialization is the specialization of cooperative labour in specific, circumscribed tasks and roles, intended to increase the productivity of labour. Historically the growth of a more and more complex Division of labour is closely associated with the growth of total output and trade, the rise of capitalism, and of the complexity of industrialization processes. Later, the Division of labour reached the level of a scientifically-based management practice with the time and motion studies associated with Taylorism.
Knowledge management	Knowledge management comprises a range of practices used in an organisation to identify, create, represent, distribute and enable adoption of insights and experiences. Such insights and experiences comprise knowledge, either embodied in individuals or embedded in organisational processes or practice. An established discipline since 1991 , knowledge management includes courses taught in the fields of business administration, information systems, management, and library and information sciences .
Leverage	In finance, leverage or leveraging refers to the use of debt to supplement investment. Companies usually leverage to increase returns to stock, as this practice can maximize gains (and losses.) The easy but high-risk increases in stock prices due to leveraging at US banks has been blamed for the unusually high rate of pay for top executives during the recent banking crisis, since gains in stock are often rewarded regardless of method.
Automation	Automation is the use of control systems (such as numerical control, programmable logic control, and other industrial control systems), in concert with other applications of information technology (such as computer-aided technologies [CAD, CAM, CAx]), to control industrial machinery and processes, reducing the need for human intervention. In the scope of industrialization, Automation is a step beyond mechanization. Whereas mechanization provided human operators with machinery to assist them with the physical requirements of work, Automation greatly reduces the need for human sensory and mental requirements as well.
Internet	The Internet is a global network of interconnected computers, enabling users to share information along multiple channels. Typically, a computer that connects to the Internet can access information from a vast array of available servers and other computers by moving information from them to the computer's local memory. The same connection allows that computer to send information to servers on the network; that information is in turn accessed and potentially modified by a variety of other interconnected computers.
Labor intensity	Labor intensity is the relative proportion of labor (compared to capital) used in a process. The term 'labor intensive' can be used when proposing the amount of work that is assigned to each worker/employee (labor), emphasizing on the skill involved in the respective line of work.

Unemployment	Unemployment occurs when a person is available to work and seeking work but currently without work. The prevalence of Unemployment is usually measured using the Unemployment rate, which is defined as the percentage of those in the labor force who are unemployed. The Unemployment rate is also used in economic studies and economic indexes such as the United States' Conference Board's Index of Leading Indicators as a measure of the state of the macroeconomics.
English	English is a West Germanic language that originated in Anglo-Saxon England. As a result of the military, economic, scientific, political and cultural influence of the British Empire during the 18th, 19th and 20th centuries and of the United States since the late 19th century, it has become the lingua franca in many parts of the world. It is used extensively as a second language and as an official language in Commonwealth countries and many international organizations.
Capital structure	In finance, Capital structure refers to the way a corporation finances its assets through some combination of equity, debt, or hybrid securities. A firm's Capital structure is then the composition or 'structure' of its liabilities. For example, a firm that sells $20 billion in equity and $80 billion in debt is said to be 20% equity-financed and 80% debt-financed.
Bribery	Bribery, a form of pecuniary corruption, is an act implying money or gift given that alters the behaviour of the recipient. bribery constitutes a crime and is defined by Black's Law Dictionary as the offering, giving, receiving, or soliciting of any item of value to influence the actions of an official or other person in discharge of a public or legal duty. The bribe is the gift bestowed to influence the recipient's conduct.
Extortion	'Extortion', outwresting property or services from a person, entity through coercion. Refraining from doing harm is sometimes euphemistically called protection. Extortion is commonly practiced by organized crime groups.
Fair Trade	Fair trade is an organized social movement and market-based approach that aims to help producers in developing countries and promote sustainability. The movement advocates the payment of a fair price as well as social and environmental standards in areas related to the production of a wide variety of goods. It focuses in particular on exports from developing countries to developed countries, most notably handicrafts, coffee, cocoa, sugar, tea, bananas, honey, cotton, wine, fresh fruit, chocolate and flowers.
Gift economy	In the social sciences, a Gift economy is a society where valuable goods and services are regularly given without any explicit agreement for immediate or future rewards (i.e. there is no visible quid pro quo). Ideally, simultaneous or recurring giving serves to circulate and redistribute valuables within the community. The organization of a Gift economy stands in contrast to a barter economy or a market economy.
Transparency	A high degree of market Transparency can result in disintermediation due to the buyer's increased knowledge of supply pricing. Transparency is important since it is one of the theoretical conditions required for a free market to be efficient. Price Transparency can, however, lead to higher prices, if it makes sellers reluctant to give steep discounts to certain buyers, or if it facilitates collusion.

Bribe	Bribe ry, a form of pecuniary corruption, is an act implying money or gift given that alters the behaviour of the recipient. bribe ry constitutes a crime and is defined by Black's Law Dictionary as the offering, giving, receiving, or soliciting of any item of value to influence the actions of an official or other person in discharge of a public or legal duty. The bribe is the gift bestowed to influence the recipient's conduct.
Organization	An organization is a social arrangement which pursues collective goals, which controls its own performance, and which has a boundary separating it from its environment. The word itself is derived from the Greek word á½„ργανον (organon [itself derived from the better-known word á¼"ργον ergon - work; deed - > ergonomics, etc]) meaning tool. The term is used in both daily and scientific English in multiple ways.
World Trade Organization	The World Trade Organization is an international organization designed to supervise and liberalize international trade. The World Trade Organization came into being on 1 January 1995, and is the successor to the General Agreement on Tariffs and Trade (GATT), which was created in 1947, and continued to operate for almost five decades as a de facto international organization. The World Trade Organization deals with the rules of trade between nations at a near-global level; it is responsible for negotiating and implementing new trade agreements, and is in charge of policing member countries' adherence to all the World Trade Organization agreements, signed by the majority of the world's trading nations and ratified in their parliaments.
Collectivism	Collectivism is a term used to describe any moral, political that stresses human interdependence and the importance of a collective, rather than the importance of separate individuals. Collectivists focus on community and society, and seek to give priority to group goals over individual goals. The philosophical underpinnings of collectivism are for some related to holism or organicism - the view that the whole is greater than the sum of its parts/pieces.
Entrepreneur	An entrepreneur is a person who has possession of an enterprise and assumes significant accountability for the inherent risks and the outcome. It is an ambitious leader who combines land, labor, and capital to create and market new goods or services. The term is a loanword from French and was first defined by the Irish economist Richard Cantillon.
Entrepreneurial mindset	An Entrepreneurial mindset is described by a conglomerate of meta-physical dispositions meant to cause the innovative and energetic practice to identify or create an opportunity and take action aimed at realizing it. The philosophical themes - existentialism, axiology, pragmatism, ethics - are thereby understood to be strange attractors influencing the construction of the entity's persona as well as the concrete practices of the entity Figure 1:Conceptual Model of Philosophical Components of an Entrepreneurial mindset Important for entrepreneurship is the 'creative mindset' that helps entrepreneurs to create new ideas and bring these to the market in a way appropriate to create value for an external audience.
Entrepreneurship	Entrepreneurship according to Onuoha (2007) is the practice of starting new organizations or revitalizing mature organizations, particularly new businesses generally in response to identified opportunities. Entrepreneurship is often a difficult undertaking, as a vast majority of new businesses fail. Entrepreneurial activities are substantially different depending on the type of organization that is being started.

Individualism	Individualism is the moral stance, political philosophy, or social outlook that stresses independence and self-reliance. Individualists promote the exercise of one's goals and desires, while opposing most external interference upon one's choices, whether by society, or any other group or institution. individualism is opposed to collectivism, which stress that communal, community, group, societal, or national goals should take priority over individual goals.
Self-employment	Self-employment is where a person works for themselves rather than someone else or a company that they do not own. To be self-employed, an individual is normally highly skilled in a trade or has a niche product or service for their local community. With the creation of the Internet the ability for an individual to become self-employed has increased dramatically.
Uncertainty	Uncertainty is a term used in subtly different ways in a number of fields, including philosophy, physics, statistics, economics, finance, insurance, psychology, sociology, engineering, and information science. It applies to predictions of future events, to physical measurements already made, or to the unknown. In his seminal work Risk, Uncertainty, and Profit University of Chicago economist Frank Knight (1921) established the important distinction between risk and Uncertainty: 'Uncertainty must be taken in a sense radically distinct from the familiar notion of risk, from which it has never been properly separated....
Gerard Hendrik Hofstede	Gerard Hendrik Hofstede is an influential Dutch writer on the interactions between national cultures and organizational cultures, and is an author of several books including Culture's Consequences and Cultures and Organizations, Software of the Mind, co-authored by his son Gert Jan Hofstede. Hofstede's study demonstrated that there are national and regional cultural groupings that affect the behaviour of societies and organizations, and that are very persistent across time. He has found five dimensions of culture in his study of national work related values: · Low vs. High Power Distance - the extent to which the less powerful members of institutions and organizations expect and accept that power is distributed unequally. Low power distance (e.g. Austria, Australia, Denmark, New Zealand) expect and accept power relations that are more consultative or democratic. People relate to one another more as equals regardless of formal positions. Subordinates are more comfortable with and demand the right to contribute to and critique the decision making of those in power. In High power distance countries , less powerful accept power relations that are more autocratic and paternalistic. Subordinates acknowledge the power of others simply based on where they are situated in certain formal, hierarchical positions. As such, the Power Distance Index Hofstede defines does not reflect an objective difference in power distribution, but rather the way people perceive power differences. In Europe, Power Distance tends to be lower in Northern countries and higher in Southern and Eastern parts. There seems to be an admittedly disputable correlation with predominant religions. · Individualism vs. collectivism - individualism is contrasted with collectivism, and refers to the extent to which people are expected to stand up for themselves and to choose their own affiliations, or alternatively act predominantly as a member of a life-long group or organization. Latin American cultures rank among the most collectivist in this category, while Anglo countries such as the U.S.A., Great Britain and Australia are the most individualistic cultures.

Etiquette	Etiquette is a code of behavior that influences expectations for social behavior according to contemporary conventional norms within a society, social class, or group. Rules of Etiquette are usually unwritten, but aspects of Etiquette have been codified from time to time. Rules of Etiquette encompass most aspects of social interaction in any society, though the term itself is not commonly used.

Switzerland

Switzerland in Western Europe with an area of 41,285 km^2. Switzerland is a federal republic consisting of 26 states, called cantons. Bern is the seat of the federal authorities, while the country's economic centres are its three global cities, Geneva, Basel and especially Zürich.

Competitive

Competitive ness is a comparative concept of the ability and performance of a firm, sub-sector or country to sell and supply goods and/or services in a given market. Although widely used in economics and business management, the usefulness of the concept, particularly in the context of national competitive ness, is vigorously disputed by economists, such as Paul Krugman .

The term may also be applied to markets, where it is used to refer to the extent to which the market structure may be regarded as perfectly competitive

Competitive advantage

Competitive advantage is, in very basic words, a position a firm occupies against its competitors.

According to Michael Porter, the three methods for creating a sustainable Competitive advantage are through:

1. Cost leadership - Cost advantage occurs when a firm delivers the same services as its competitors but at a lower cost;

2.

Asset

In business and accounting, asset s are economic resources owned by business or company. Anything tangible or intangible that one possesses, usually considered as applicable to the payment of one's debts is considered an asset Simplistically stated, asset s are things of value that can be readily converted into cash.

Factors of production

In economics, Factors of production are the resources employed to produce goods and services. They facilitate production but do not become part of the product (as with raw materials) or significantly transformed by the production process (as with fuel used to power machinery.) To 19th century economists, the Factors of production were land (natural resources, gifts from nature), labor (the ability to work), and capital goods (human-made tools and equipment.)

Natural resource

Natural resource s (economically referred to as land or raw materials) occur naturally within environments that exist relatively undisturbed by mankind, in a natural form. A Natural resource is often characterized by amounts of biodiversity existent in various ecosystems.

Natural resource s are derived from the environment.

Resources

Human beings are also considered to be Resources because they have the ability to change raw materials into valuable Resources. The term Human Resources can also be defined as the skills, energies, talents, abilities and knowledge that are used for the production of goods or the rendering of services. While taking into account human beings as Resources, the following things have to be kept in mind:

· The size of the population
· The capabilities of the individuals in that population

Many Resources cannot be consumed in their original form. They have to be processed in order to change them into more usable commodities.

Manufacturing	Manufacturing is the application of tools and a processing medium to the transformation of raw materials into finished goods for sale. This effort includes all intermediate processes required for the production and integration of a product's components. Some industries, like semiconductor and steel manufacturers use the term fabrication instead.
Standardization	Standardization or standardisation is the process of developing and agreeing upon technical standards. A standard is a document that establishes uniform engineering or technical specifications, criteria, methods, processes, or practices. Some standards are mandatory while others are voluntary.
United States	The United States of America (commonly referred to as the United States the U.S., the United States A, or America) is a federal constitutional republic comprising fifty states and a federal district. The country is situated mostly in central North America, where its 48 contiguous states and Washington, D.C., the capital district, lie between the Pacific and Atlantic Oceans, bordered by Canada to the north and Mexico to the south. The state of Alaska is in the northwest of the continent, with Canada to its east and Russia to the west across the Bering Strait.
Direct investment	Foreign Direct investment in its classic form is defined as a company from one country making a physical investment into building a factory in another country. It is the establishment of an enterprise by a foreigner. Its definition can be extended to include investments made to acquire lasting interest in enterprises operating outside of the economy of the investor.
Embargo	An Embargo is the prohibition of commerce and trade with a certain country, in order to isolate it and to put its government into a difficult internal situation, given that the effects of the Embargo are often able to make its economy suffer from the initiative. It is similar to a blockade, as in 'el bloqueo' or the American blockade on Cuba. Embargo s generally attempt to pressure weaker adversaries to do what the abarcading country wishes.
Foreign direct investment	Foreign direct investment in its classic form is defined as a company from one country making a physical investment into building a factory in another country. It is the establishment of an enterprise by a foreigner. Its definition can be extended to include investments made to acquire lasting interest in enterprises operating outside of the economy of the investor.
Individualism	Individualism is the moral stance, political philosophy, or social outlook that stresses independence and self-reliance. Individualists promote the exercise of one's goals and desires, while opposing most external interference upon one's choices, whether by society, or any other group or institution. individualism is opposed to collectivism, which stress that communal, community, group, societal, or national goals should take priority over individual goals.
Collectivism	Collectivism is a term used to describe any moral, political that stresses human interdependence and the importance of a collective, rather than the importance of separate individuals. Collectivists focus on community and society, and seek to give priority to group goals over individual goals. The philosophical underpinnings of collectivism are for some related to holism or organicism - the view that the whole is greater than the sum of its parts/pieces.

Triple bottom line

The Triple bottom line captures an expanded spectrum of values and criteria for measuring organizational success: economic, ecological and social. With the ratification of the United Nations and ICLEI Triple bottom line standard for urban and community accounting in early 2007, this became the dominant approach to public sector full cost accounting. Similar UN standards apply to natural capital and human capital measurement to assist in measurements required by Triple bottom line, e.g. the ecoBudget standard for reporting ecological footprint.

Range

In descriptive statistics, the Range is the length of the smallest interval which contains all the data. It is calculated by subtracting the smallest observation (sample minimum) from the greatest (sample maximum) and provides an indication of statistical dispersion.

It is measured in the same units as the data.

English

English is a West Germanic language that originated in Anglo-Saxon England. As a result of the military, economic, scientific, political and cultural influence of the British Empire during the 18th, 19th and 20th centuries and of the United States since the late 19th century, it has become the lingua franca in many parts of the world. It is used extensively as a second language and as an official language in Commonwealth countries and many international organizations.

Characteristic

Characteristic has several particular meanings:

· in mathematics

- · Euler characteristic
- · method of characteristic s (partial differential equations)

· in physics and engineering

· any characteristic curve that shows the relationship between certain input- and output parameters, e.g.
· an I-V or current-voltage characteristic is the current in a circuit as a function of the applied voltage
· Receiver-Operator characteristic
· in navigation, the characteristic pattern of a lighted beacon.
· in fiction

· in Dungeons ' Dragons, characteristic is another name for ability score .

Brazil

Brazil, officially the Federative Republic of Brazil (Portuguese: >Rep>ública Federativa do Brasil) Â·), is a country in South America. It is the fifth largest country by geographical area, occupying nearly half of South America, the fifth most populous country, and the fourth most populous democracy in the world. Bounded by the Atlantic Ocean on the east, Brazil has a coastline of over 7,491 kilometers (4,655 mi.)

TRIPs

The Agreement on Trade Related Aspects of Intellectual Property Rights (TRIPs) is an international agreement administered by the World Trade Organization (WTO) that sets down minimum standards for many forms of intellectual property (IP) regulation. It was negotiated at the end of the Uruguay Round of the General Agreement on Tariffs and Trade (GATT) in 1994.

Specifically, TRIPs contains requirements that nations' laws must meet for: copyright rights, including the rights of performers, producers of sound recordings and broadcasting organizations; geographical indications, including appellations of origin; industrial designs; integrated circuit layout-designs; patents; monopolies for the developers of new plant varieties; trademarks; trade dress; and undisclosed or confidential information.

Population

In biology, a Population , is the collection of inter-breeding organisms of a particular species; in sociology, a collection of human beings. Individuals within a Population share a factor may be reduced by statistical means, but such a generalization may be too vague to imply anything. Demography is used extensively in marketing, which relates to economic units, such as retailers, to potential customers.

Industry

An Industry is the manufacturing of a good or service within a category. Although Industry is a broad term for any kind of economic production, in economics and urban planning Industry is a synonym for the secondary sector, which is a type of economic activity involved in the manufacturing of raw materials into goods and products.

There are four key industrial economic sectors: the primary sector, largely raw material extraction industries such as mining and farming; the secondary sector, involving refining, construction, and manufacturing; the tertiary sector, which deals with services (such as law and medicine) and distribution of manufactured goods; and the quaternary sector, a relatively new type of knowledge Industry focusing on technological research, design and development such as computer programming, and biochemistry.

International Trade

International trade is exchange of capital, goods, and services across international borders or territories. In most countries, it represents a significant share of gross domestic product (GDP.) While International trade has been present throughout much of history , its economic, social, and political importance has been on the rise in recent centuries.

Dispute

Controversy is a state of prolonged public dispute or debate usually concerning a matter of opinion. The term originates circa 1384 from Latin controversia, as a composite of controversus - 'turned in an opposite direction,' from contra - 'against' - and vertere - to turn, or versus , hence, 'to turn against.'

Benford's law of controversy, as expressed by science-fiction author Gregory Benford in 1980, states: 'Passion is inversely proportional to the amount of real (true) information available.' In other words, the more untruths the more controversy there is, and the more truths the less controversy there is.

A controversy is always the result of either ignorance (lack of sufficient true information), misinformation, misunderstandings, half-truths, distortions, bias or prejudice, deliberate lies or fabrications (disinformation), opposed underlying motives or purposes (sometimes masked or hidden), or a combination of these factors.

Distribution

Distribution is one of the four elements of marketing mix. An organization or set of organizations (go-betweens) involved in the process of making a product or service available for use or consumption by a consumer or business user.

The other three parts of the marketing mix are product, pricing, and promotion.

Export

In economics, an export is any good or commodity, transported from one country to another country in a legitimate fashion, typically for use in trade. export goods or services are provided to foreign consumers by domestic producers. export is an important part of international trade.

Containerization	Containerization is a system of intermodal freight transport using standard intermodal containers that are standardised by the International Organization for Standardization (ISO.) These can be loaded and sealed intact onto container ships, railroad cars, planes, and trucks.
International Monetary Fund	The International Monetary Fund is an international organization that oversees the global financial system by following the macroeconomic policies of its member countries, in particular those with an impact on exchange rates and the balance of payments. It is an organization formed to stabilize international exchange rates and facilitate development. It also offers financial and technical assistance to its members, making it an international lender of last resort.
Monetary	Monetary policy is the process by which the government, central bank (ii) availability of money, and (iii) cost of money or rate of interest, in order to attain a set of objectives oriented towards the growth and stability of the economy. monetary theory provides insight into how to craft optimal monetary policy. monetary policy is referred to as either being an expansionary policy where an expansionary policy increases the total supply of money in the economy, and a contractionary policy decreases the total money supply.
Tariff	A Tariff is a duty imposed on goods when they are moved across a political boundary. They are usually associated with protectionism, the economic policy of restraining trade between nations. For political reasons, Tariff s are usually imposed on imported goods, although they may also be imposed on exported goods.
Challenge	Challenge is a United Kingdom digital TV channel owned by Virgin Media Television. It was originally called The Family Channel from 1 September 1993 to 31 January 1997 but it was later re-branded as challenge TV from 1 February 1997. On 20 May 2002 the channel was re-named again but this time it was just challenge? and 30 June 2003 the question mark was removed to leave the challenge name in its place.
Set TSP	In combinatorial optimization, the set TSP group TSP, One-of-a-set TSP, Multiple Choice TSP or Covering Salesman Problem, is a generalization of the Traveling salesman problem, whereby it is required to find a shortest tour in a graph which visits all specified disjoint subsets of the vertices of a graph. The ordinary TSP is a special case of the set TSP when all subsets to be visited are singletons. Therefore the set TSP is also NP-hard.
Economic	An economy (or 'the economy') is the realized Economic system of a country or other area. It includes the production, exchange, distribution, and consumption of goods and services of that area. The study of different types and examples of economies is the subject of Economic systems.
Economic development	Economic development is the development of economic wealth of countries or regions for the well-being of their inhabitants. It is the process by which a nation improves the economic, political, and social well being of its people. From a policy perspective, Economic development can be defined as efforts that seek to improve the economic well-being and quality of life for a community by creating and/or retaining jobs and supporting or growing incomes and the tax base.
International business	International business is a term used to collectively describe topics relating to the operations of firms with interests in multiple countries. Such firms are sometimes called multinational corporations . Well known MNCs include fast food companies McDonald's and Yum Brands, vehicle manufacturers such as General Motors and Toyota, consumer electronics companies like Samsung, LG and Sony, and energy companies such as ExxonMobil and BP.

Culture	Culture is a term that has different meanings. For example, in 1952, Alfred Kroeber and Clyde Kluckhohn compiled a list of 164 definitions of culture in culture A Critical Review of Concepts and Definitions. However, the word culture is most commonly used in three basic senses: · excellence of taste in the fine arts and humanities, also known as high culture · an integrated pattern of human knowledge, belief, and behavior that depends upon the capacity for symbolic thought and social learning · the set of shared attitudes, values, goals, and practices that characterizes an institution, organization or group. When the concept first emerged in eighteenth- and nineteenth-century Europe, it connoted a process of cultivation or improvement, as in agri culture or horti culture . In the nineteenth century, it came to refer first to the betterment or refinement of the individual, especially through education, and then to the fulfillment of national aspirations or ideals.
Failure	Failure refers to the state or condition of not meeting a desirable or intended objective, and may be viewed as the opposite of success. Product failure ranges from failure to sell the product to fracture of the product, in the worst cases leading to personal injury, the province of forensic engineering. The criteria for failure are heavily dependent on context of use, and may be relative to a particular observer or belief system.
Chief brand officer	A Chief brand officer is a relatively new executive level position at a corporation, company, organization typically reporting directly to the CEO or board of directors. The Chief brand officer is responsible for a brand's image, experience, and promise, and propagating it throughout all aspects of the company. The brand officer oversees marketing, advertising, design, public relations and customer service departments.
Procter ' Gamble	Procter is a surname, and may also refer to: · Bryan Waller Procter (pseud. Barry Cornwall), English poet · Goodwin Procter, American law firm · Procter ' Gamble, consumer products multinational .
Report	In writing, a report is a document characterized by information or other content reflective of inquiry or investigation, which is tailored to the context of a given situation and audience. The purpose of report s is usually to inform. However, report s may include persuasive elements, such as recommendations, suggestions, or other motivating conclusions that indicate possible future actions the report reader might take.
Organization	An organization is a social arrangement which pursues collective goals, which controls its own performance, and which has a boundary separating it from its environment. The word itself is derived from the Greek word á½„ργανον (organon [itself derived from the better-known word á¼"ργον ergon - work; deed - > ergonomics, etc]) meaning tool. The term is used in both daily and scientific English in multiple ways.
Escalation	Escalation is the phenomenon of something getting more intense step by step, for example a quarrel, or, notably, military presence and nuclear armament during the Cold War. (Compare to escalator, a device that lifts something to a higher level.) The term is often said to be originally coined by Herman Kahn in his 1965 work On Escalation.

Price	Price in economics and business is the result of an exchange and from that trade we assign a numerical monetary value to a good, service or asset. If I trade 4 apples for an orange, the price of an orange is 4 - apples. Inversely, the price of an apple is 1/4 oranges.
Investment	Investment or investing is a term with several closely-related meanings in business management, finance and economics, related to saving or deferring consumption. Investing is the active redirecting resources from being consumed today so that they may create benefits in the future; the use of assets to earn income or profit. An Investment is the choice by the individual to risk his savings with the hope of gain.
Investment risk	Depending on the nature of the investment, the type of Investment risk will vary. A common concern with any investment is that you may lose the money you invest - your capital. This risk is therefore often referred to as 'capital risk.' If the assets you invest in are held in another currency there is a risk that currency movements alone may affect the value.
Globalization	Globalization in its literal sense is the process of transformation of local or regional phenomena into global ones. It can be described as a process by which the people of the world are unified into a single society and function together. This process is a combination of economic, technological, sociocultural and political forces.
Consumer	Consumer is a broad label that refers to any individuals or households that use goods and services generated within the economy. The concept of a Consumer is used in different contexts, so that the usage and significance of the term may vary. A Consumer is a person who uses any product or service.
Consumer price index	A Consumer Price Index is a measure of the average price of consumer goods and services purchased by households. It is a price index determined by measuring the price of a standard group of goods meant to represent the typical market basket of a typical urban consumer. Related, but different, terms are the Consumer Price Index, the RPI, and the RPIX used in the United Kingdom.
Fair Trade	Fair trade is an organized social movement and market-based approach that aims to help producers in developing countries and promote sustainability. The movement advocates the payment of a fair price as well as social and environmental standards in areas related to the production of a wide variety of goods. It focuses in particular on exports from developing countries to developed countries, most notably handicrafts, coffee, cocoa, sugar, tea, bananas, honey, cotton, wine, fresh fruit, chocolate and flowers.
Kraft Foods	Kraft Foods Inc. (NYSE: Kraft Foods T) is the largest food and beverage company headquartered in the United States and the second largest in the world (after Nestlé SA.) Kraft is headquartered in Northfield, Illinois, USA, a Chicago suburb.

Kyoto Protocol

The Kyoto Protocol is a protocol to the United Nations Framework Convention on Climate Change (UNFCCC or FCCC), an international environmental treaty which was produced with the goal of achieving 'stabilization of greenhouse gas concentrations in the atmosphere at a level that would prevent dangerous anthropogenic interference with the climate system.' The Kyoto Protocol establishes legally binding commitments for the reduction of four greenhouse gases (carbon dioxide, methane, nitrous oxide, sulphur hexafluoride), and two groups of gases (hydrofluorocarbons and perfluorocarbons) produced by 'Annex I' (industrialized) nations, as well as general commitments for all member countries. As of January 2009, 183 parties have ratified the protocol, which was initially have been adopted for use on 11 December 1997 in Kyoto, Japan and which entered into force on 16 February 2005. Under Kyoto, industrialized countries agreed to reduce their collective GHG emissions by 5.2% compared to the year 1990.

United Nations

The United Nations is an international organization whose stated aims are to facilitate cooperation in international law, international security, economic development, social progress, human rights and achieving world peace. The United Nations was founded in 1945 after World War II to replace the League of Nations, to stop wars between countries and to provide a platform for dialogue.

There are currently 192 member states, including nearly every recognized independent state in the world.

United Nations Framework Convention on Climate Change

The United Nations Framework Convention on Climate Change is an international environmental treaty produced at the United Nations Conference on Environment and Development (UNCED), informally known as the Earth Summit, held in Rio de Janeiro from 3 to 14 June 1992. The treaty is aimed at stabilizing greenhouse gas concentrations in the atmosphere at a level that would prevent dangerous anthropogenic interference with the climate system.

The treaty as originally framed set no mandatory limits on greenhouse gas emissions for individual nations and contained no enforcement provisions; it is therefore considered legally non-binding.

Wage

A Wage is a compensation, usually financial, received by a worker in exchange for their labor.

Compensation in terms of Wage s is given to worker and compensation in terms of salary is given to employees. Compensation is a monetary benefits given to employees in returns of the services provided by them.

Share

In business and finance, a share of stock (also referred to as equity share) means a share of ownership in a corporation (company.) In the plural, stocks is often used as a synonym for shares especially in the United States, but it is less commonly used that way outside of North America.

In the United Kingdom, South Africa, and Australia, stock can also refer to completely different financial instruments such as government bonds or, less commonly, to all kinds of marketable securities.

Sustainability

Sustainability, in general terms, is the ability to maintain balance of a certain process or state in any system. It is now most frequently used in connection with biological and human systems. In an ecological context, sustainability can be defined as the ability of an ecosystem to maintain ecological processes, functions, biodiversity and productivity into the future.

Clean Air Act

A Clean Air Act describes one of a number of pieces of legislation relating to the reduction of smog and air pollution in general. The use by governments to enforce clean air standards has contributed to an improvement in human health and longer life spans. Critics argue it has also sapped corporate profits and contributed to outsourcing, while defenders counter that improved environmental air quality has generated more jobs than it has eliminated.

Clean Water Act	The Clean Water Act is the primary federal law in the United States governing water pollution. Commonly abbreviated as the Clean Water Act, the act established the symbolic goals of eliminating releases to water of high amounts of toxic substances, eliminating additional water pollution by 1985, and ensuring that surface waters would meet standards necessary for human sports and recreation by 1983. The principal body of law currently in effect is based on the Federal Water Pollution Control Amendments of 1972, which significantly expanded and strengthened earlier legislation.
Control	Control is one of the managerial functions like planning, organizing, staffing and directing. It is an important function because it helps to check the errors and to take the corrective action so that deviation from standards are minimized and stated goals of the organization are achieved in desired manner.According to modern concepts, Control is a foreseeing action whereas earlier concept of Control was used only when errors were detected. Control in management means setting standards, measuring actual performance and taking corrective action.
Environmental Protection	Environmental protection is a practice of protecting the environment, on individual, organisational or governmental level, for the benefit of the natural environment and (or) humans. Due to the pressures of population and technology the biophysical environment is being degraded, sometimes permanently. This has been recognised and governments began placing restraints on activities that caused environmental degradation.
Environmental Protection Agency	The U.S. Environmental Protection Agency is an agency of the federal government of the United States charged to regulate chemicals and protect human health by safeguarding the natural environment: air, water, and land. The Environmental Protection Agency was proposed by President Richard Nixon and began operation on December 2, 1970, when its establishment was passed by Congress, and signed into law by President Nixon, and has since been chiefly responsible for the environmental policy of the United States. It is led by its Administrator, who is appointed by the President of the United States.
National Environmental Policy Act	The National Environmental Policy Act is a United States environmental law that was signed into law on January 1, 1970 by U.S. President Richard Nixon. The law established a U.S. national policy promoting the enhancement of the environment and also established the President's Council on Environmental Quality (CEQ.) But National Environmental Policy Act's most significant effect was to set up procedural requirements for all federal government agencies to prepare Environmental Assessments (EAs) and Environmental Impact Statements (EISs.)
Policy	A Policy is typically described as a deliberate plan of action to guide decisions and achieve rational outcome(s.) However, the term may also be used to denote what is actually done, even though it is unplanned. The term may apply to government, private sector organizations and groups, and individuals.
Precautionary principle	The Precautionary principle is a moral and political principle which states that if an action or policy might cause severe or irreversible harm to the public or to the environment, in the absence of a scientific consensus that harm would not ensue, the burden of proof falls on those who would advocate taking the action. The principle implies that there is a responsibility to intervene and protect the public from exposure to harm where scientific investigation discovers a plausible risk in the course of having screened for other suspected causes. The protections that mitigate suspected risks can be relaxed only if further scientific findings emerge that more robustly support an alternative explanation.

Texas	Texas is a state in the South Central United States, nicknamed the Lone Star State. It is bordered by Mexico to the south, New Mexico to the west, Oklahoma to the north, Arkansas to the northeast, and Louisiana to the east. Texas is the second largest U.S. state in both area and population, with an area of 268,820 square miles (696,200 km^2), and with a growing population of 24.6 million residents.
World Trade Organization	The World Trade Organization is an international organization designed to supervise and liberalize international trade. The World Trade Organization came into being on 1 January 1995, and is the successor to the General Agreement on Tariffs and Trade (GATT), which was created in 1947, and continued to operate for almost five decades as a de facto international organization. The World Trade Organization deals with the rules of trade between nations at a near-global level; it is responsible for negotiating and implementing new trade agreements, and is in charge of policing member countries' adherence to all the World Trade Organization agreements, signed by the majority of the world's trading nations and ratified in their parliaments.
Environmental law	Environmental law is a complex and interlocking body of statutes, common law, treaties, conventions, regulations and policies which, very broadly, operate to regulate the interaction of humanity and the rest of the biophysical or natural environment, toward the purpose of reducing or minimizing the impacts of human activity, both on the natural environment for its own sake, and on humanity itself. Environmental law draws from and is influenced by principles of environmentalism, including ecology, conservation, stewardship, responsibility and sustainability. From an economic perspective it can be understood as concerned with the prevention of present and future externalities.
Regulation	Regulation refers to 'controlling human or societal behaviour by rules or restrictions.' Regulation can take many forms: legal restrictions promulgated by a government authority, self-Regulation, social Regulation, co-Regulation and market Regulation. One can consider Regulation as actions of conduct imposing sanctions (such as a fine.) This action of administrative law, or implementing regulatory law, may be contrasted with statutory or case law.
Developed country	The term developed country is used to describe countries that have a high level of development according to some criteria. Which criteria, and which countries are classified as being developed, is a contentious issue and there is fierce debate about this. Economic criteria have tended to dominate discussions.
Interdependence	Interdependence is a dynamic of being mutually and physically responsible to and sharing a common set of principles with others. This concept differs distinctly from 'dependence' in that an interdependent relationship implies that all participants are emotionally, economically, ecologically and or morally 'interdependent.' Some people advocate freedom or independence as a sort of ultimate good; others do the same with devotion to one's family, community, or society. Interdependence recognizes the truth in each position and weaves them together.
Sustainable business	Sustainable business is enterprise that has no negative impact on the global or local environment, community, society Sustainable business es have progressive environmental and human rights policies. A Sustainable business is any organization that participates in environmentally-friendly or green activities to ensure that all processes, products, and manufacturing activities adequately address current environmental concerns while maintaining a profit.
Population ageing	Population ageing occurs when the median age of a country or region rises. With the exception of 18 countries termed by the United Nations 'demographic outliers' this process is taking place in every country and region across the globe.

Population ageing is constituted by a shift in the distribution of a country's population towards greater ages.

Function cost analysis

Function cost analysis is the a method of technical and economic research of the systems for purpose to optimize a parity between system's consumer functions or properties and expenses to achieve those functions or properties.

This methodology for continuous perfection of production, industrial technologies, organizational structures was developed by Juryj Sobolev in 1948 at the 'Perm telephone factory'

· 1948 Juryj Sobolev - the first success in application of a method analysis at the 'Perm telephone factory' .
· 1949 - the first application for the invention as result of use of the new method.

Today in economically developed countries practically each enterprise or the company use methodology of the kind of functional-cost analysis as a practice of the quality management, most full satisfying to principles of standards of series ISO 9000.

· Interest of consumer not in products itself, but the advantage which it will receive from its usage.
· The consumer aspires to reduce his expenses
· Functions needed by consumer can be executed in the various ways, and, hence, with various efficiency and expenses. Among possible alternatives of realization of functions exist such in which the parity of quality and the price is the optimal for the consumer.

The goal of Function cost analysis is achievement of the highest consumer satisfaction of production at simultaneous decrease in all kinds of industrial expenses Classical Function cost analysis has three English synonyms - Value Engineering, Value Management, Value Analysis.

Equity

Equity is the name given to the set of legal principles, in jurisdictions following the English common law tradition, which supplement strict rules of law where their application would operate harshly.

As noted below, a historic criticism of Equity as it developed was that it had no fixed rules of its own, with the Lord Chancellor from time to time judging in the main according to his own conscience. As time went on the rules of Equity did lose much of their flexibility, and from the 17th century onwards Equity was rapidly consolidated into a system of precedents much like its common-law cousin.

Stakeholder theory

The stakeholder theory is a theory of organizational management and business ethics that addresses morals and values in managing an organization. It was originally detailed by R. Edward Freeman in the book Strategic Management: A Stakeholder Approach, and identifies and models the groups which are stakeholders of a corporation, and both describes and recommends methods by which management can give due regard to the interests of those groups.

Sustainable Development

Sustainable development is a pattern of resource use that aims to meet human needs while preserving the environment so that these needs can be met not only in the present, but in the indefinite future. The term was used by the Brundtland Commission which coined what has become the most often-quoted definition of sustainable development as development that 'meets the needs of the present without compromising the ability of future generations to meet their own needs.'

sustainable development is the way in which developing nations undergoing the process of industrialisation will avoid becoming like current industralised carbon intensive nations with high level of emissions.

	sustainable development ties together concern for the carrying capacity of natural systems with the social challenges facing humanity.
Geography	Geography is the study of the Earth and its lands, features, inhabitants, and phenomena. A literal translation would be 'to describe or write about the Earth'. The first person to use the word 'Geography' was Eratosthenes .
Big Mac index	The Big Mac Index is published by The Economist as an informal way of measuring the purchasing power parity (PPP) between two currencies and provides a test of the extent to which market exchange rates result in goods costing the same in different countries. It 'seeks to make exchange-rate theory a bit more digestible'.
Trend analysis	The term 'trend analysis' refers to the concept of collecting information and attempting to spot a pattern in the information. In some fields of study, the term 'trend analysis' has more formally-defined meanings. In project management trend analysis is a mathematical technique that uses historical results to predict future outcome.
Green Job	A Green job according to the United Nations Environment Program, 'work in agricultural, manufacturing, research and development, administrative, and service activities that contribute substantially to preserving or restoring environmental quality. Specifically, but not exclusively, this includes jobs that help to protect ecosystems and biodiversity; reduce energy, materials, and water consumption through highefficiency strategies; de-carbonize the economy; and minimize or altogether avoid generation of all forms of waste and pollution.' In 2007 the United Nations Environment Programme, the International Labor Organization, and the International Trade Union Confederation jointly launched the Green job s Initiative. The International Employers Organization joined the Initiative in 2008.

English	English is a West Germanic language that originated in Anglo-Saxon England. As a result of the military, economic, scientific, political and cultural influence of the British Empire during the 18th, 19th and 20th centuries and of the United States since the late 19th century, it has become the lingua franca in many parts of the world. It is used extensively as a second language and as an official language in Commonwealth countries and many international organizations.
Population	In biology, a Population , is the collection of inter-breeding organisms of a particular species; in sociology, a collection of human beings. Individuals within a Population share a factor may be reduced by statistical means, but such a generalization may be too vague to imply anything. Demography is used extensively in marketing, which relates to economic units, such as retailers, to potential customers.
Procter ' Gamble	Procter is a surname, and may also refer to: · Bryan Waller Procter (pseud. Barry Cornwall), English poet · Goodwin Procter, American law firm · Procter ' Gamble, consumer products multinational .
Distribution	Distribution is one of the four elements of marketing mix. An organization or set of organizations (go-betweens) involved in the process of making a product or service available for use or consumption by a consumer or business user. The other three parts of the marketing mix are product, pricing, and promotion.
Economic	An economy (or 'the economy') is the realized Economic system of a country or other area. It includes the production, exchange, distribution, and consumption of goods and services of that area. The study of different types and examples of economies is the subject of Economic systems.
Competitive	Competitive ness is a comparative concept of the ability and performance of a firm, sub-sector or country to sell and supply goods and/or services in a given market. Although widely used in economics and business management, the usefulness of the concept, particularly in the context of national competitive ness, is vigorously disputed by economists, such as Paul Krugman . The term may also be applied to markets, where it is used to refer to the extent to which the market structure may be regarded as perfectly competitive
Gross domestic product	The Gross domestic product or gross domestic income (GDI), a basic measure of an economy's economic performance, is the market value of all final goods and services produced within the borders of a nation in a year. Gross domestic product can be defined in three ways, all of which are conceptually identical. First, it is equal to the total expenditures for all final goods and services produced within the country in a stipulated period of time (usually a 365-day year.)
Market	A Market is any one of a variety of different systems, institutions, procedures, social relations and infrastructures whereby persons trade, and goods and services are exchanged, forming part of the economy. It is an arrangement that allows buyers and sellers to exchange things. Market s vary in size, range, geographic scale, location, types and variety of human communities, as well as the types of goods and services traded.
Characteristic	Characteristic has several particular meanings: · in mathematics

- · Euler characteristic
- · method of characteristic s (partial differential equations)

· in physics and engineering

· any characteristic curve that shows the relationship between certain input- and output parameters, e.g.
· an I-V or current-voltage characteristic is the current in a circuit as a function of the applied voltage
· Receiver-Operator characteristic
· in navigation, the characteristic pattern of a lighted beacon.
· in fiction

· in Dungeons ' Dragons, characteristic is another name for ability score .

Globalization

Globalization in its literal sense is the process of transformation of local or regional phenomena into global ones. It can be described as a process by which the people of the world are unified into a single society and function together.

This process is a combination of economic, technological, sociocultural and political forces.

Inflation

In economics, Inflation is a rise in the general level of prices of goods and services in an economy over a period of time. The term 'Inflation' once referred to increases in the money supply (monetary Inflation); however, economic debates about the relationship between money supply and price levels have led to its primary use today in describing price Inflation. Inflation can also be described as a decline in the real value of money--a loss of purchasing power in the medium of exchange which is also the monetary unit of account.

Extortion

'Extortion', outwresting property or services from a person, entity through coercion. Refraining from doing harm is sometimes euphemistically called protection. Extortion is commonly practiced by organized crime groups.

Manufacturing

Manufacturing is the application of tools and a processing medium to the transformation of raw materials into finished goods for sale. This effort includes all intermediate processes required for the production and integration of a product's components. Some industries, like semiconductor and steel manufacturers use the term fabrication instead.

Swap

In finance, a Swap is a derivative in which two counterparties agree to exchange one stream of cash flow against another stream. These streams are called the legs of the Swap.

The cash flows are calculated over a notional principal amount, which is usually not exchanged between counterparties.

Developed country

The term developed country is used to describe countries that have a high level of development according to some criteria. Which criteria, and which countries are classified as being developed, is a contentious issue and there is fierce debate about this. Economic criteria have tended to dominate discussions.

Economic development

Economic development is the development of economic wealth of countries or regions for the well-being of their inhabitants. It is the process by which a nation improves the economic, political, and social well being of its people. From a policy perspective, Economic development can be defined as efforts that seek to improve the economic well-being and quality of life for a community by creating and/or retaining jobs and supporting or growing incomes and the tax base.

Emerging markets	The term Emerging markets is used to describe a nation's social or business activity in the process of rapid growth and industrialization. Currently, there are approximately 28 Emerging markets in the world, with the economies of China and India considered to be two of the largest. According to The Economist many people find the term dated, but a new term has yet to gain much traction.
United Nations	The United Nations is an international organization whose stated aims are to facilitate cooperation in international law, international security, economic development, social progress, human rights and achieving world peace. The United Nations was founded in 1945 after World War II to replace the League of Nations, to stop wars between countries and to provide a platform for dialogue. There are currently 192 member states, including nearly every recognized independent state in the world.
Population ageing	Population ageing occurs when the median age of a country or region rises. With the exception of 18 countries termed by the United Nations 'demographic outliers' this process is taking place in every country and region across the globe. Population ageing is constituted by a shift in the distribution of a country's population towards greater ages.
Direct investment	Foreign Direct investment in its classic form is defined as a company from one country making a physical investment into building a factory in another country. It is the establishment of an enterprise by a foreigner. Its definition can be extended to include investments made to acquire lasting interest in enterprises operating outside of the economy of the investor.
Foreign direct investment	Foreign direct investment in its classic form is defined as a company from one country making a physical investment into building a factory in another country. It is the establishment of an enterprise by a foreigner. Its definition can be extended to include investments made to acquire lasting interest in enterprises operating outside of the economy of the investor.
Purchasing	Purchasing refers to a business or organization attempting to acquire goods or services to accomplish the goals of the enterprise. Though there are several organizations that attempt to set standards in the Purchasing process, processes can vary greatly between organizations. Typically the word 'Purchasing' is not used interchangeably with the word 'procurement', since procurement typically includes Expediting, Supplier Quality, and Traffic and Logistics (T'L) in addition to Purchasing.
Purchasing power	Purchasing power is the number of goods/services that can be purchased with a unit of currency. For example, if you had taken one dollar to a store in the 1950s, you would have been able to buy a greater number of items than you would today, indicating that you would have had a greater purchasing power in the 1950s. Currency can be either a commodity money, like gold or silver, or fiat currency like US dollars which are the world reserve currency.
Purchasing power parity	The Purchasing power parity theory uses the long-term equilibrium exchange rate of two currencies to equalize their purchasing power. Developed by Gustav Cassel in 1918, it is based on the law of one price: the theory states that, in ideally efficient markets, identical goods should have only one price. This purchasing power SEM rate equalizes the purchasing power of different currencies in their home countries for a given basket of goods.

Underground economy	The Underground economy or black market is a market where all commerce is conducted without regard to taxation, law or regulations of trade. The term is also often known as the underdog, shadow economy, black economy, parallel economy or phantom trades. In modern societies the Underground economy covers a vast array of activities.
Range	In descriptive statistics, the Range is the length of the smallest interval which contains all the data. It is calculated by subtracting the smallest observation (sample minimum) from the greatest (sample maximum) and provides an indication of statistical dispersion. It is measured in the same units as the data.
Big Mac index	The Big Mac Index is published by The Economist as an informal way of measuring the purchasing power parity (PPP) between two currencies and provides a test of the extent to which market exchange rates result in goods costing the same in different countries. It 'seeks to make exchange-rate theory a bit more digestible'.
Black market	The underground economy or Black market is a market where all commerce is conducted without regard to taxation, law or regulations of trade. The term is also often known as the underdog, shadow economy, black economy, parallel economy or phantom trades. In modern societies the underground economy covers a vast array of activities.
International Monetary Fund	The International Monetary Fund is an international organization that oversees the global financial system by following the macroeconomic policies of its member countries, in particular those with an impact on exchange rates and the balance of payments. It is an organization formed to stabilize international exchange rates and facilitate development. It also offers financial and technical assistance to its members, making it an international lender of last resort.
Monetary	Monetary policy is the process by which the government, central bank (ii) availability of money, and (iii) cost of money or rate of interest, in order to attain a set of objectives oriented towards the growth and stability of the economy. monetary theory provides insight into how to craft optimal monetary policy. monetary policy is referred to as either being an expansionary policy where an expansionary policy increases the total supply of money in the economy, and a contractionary policy decreases the total money supply.
Trend analysis	The term 'trend analysis' refers to the concept of collecting information and attempting to spot a pattern in the information. In some fields of study, the term 'trend analysis' has more formally-defined meanings. In project management trend analysis is a mathematical technique that uses historical results to predict future outcome.
United States	The United States of America (commonly referred to as the United States the U.S., the United States A, or America) is a federal constitutional republic comprising fifty states and a federal district. The country is situated mostly in central North America, where its 48 contiguous states and Washington, D.C., the capital district, lie between the Pacific and Atlantic Oceans, bordered by Canada to the north and Mexico to the south. The state of Alaska is in the northwest of the continent, with Canada to its east and Russia to the west across the Bering Strait.

Challenge

Challenge is a United Kingdom digital TV channel owned by Virgin Media Television. It was originally called The Family Channel from 1 September 1993 to 31 January 1997 but it was later re-branded as challenge TV from 1 February 1997. On 20 May 2002 the channel was re-named again but this time it was just challenge? and 30 June 2003 the question mark was removed to leave the challenge name in its place.

Income distribution

In economics, Income distribution is how a nation's total economy is distributed among its population. .Income distribution has always been a central concern of economic theory and economic policy. Classical economists such as Adam Smith, Thomas Malthus and David Ricardo were mainly concerned with factor Income distribution, that is, the distribution of income between the main factors of production, land, labour and capital.

Report

In writing, a report is a document characterized by information or other content reflective of inquiry or investigation, which is tailored to the context of a given situation and audience. The purpose of report s is usually to inform. However, report s may include persuasive elements, such as recommendations, suggestions, or other motivating conclusions that indicate possible future actions the report reader might take.

Numerary

Numerary is a civil designation for persons who are incorporated in a fixed or permanent way to a society or group: regular member of the working staff, permanent staff distinguished from a super Numerary .

The term Numerary and its counterpart, 'super Numerary ,' originated in Spanish and Latin American academy and government; it is now also used in countries all over the world, such as France, the U.S., England, Italy, etc.

There are Numerary members of surgical organizations, of universities, of gastronomical associations, etc.

Chief brand officer

A Chief brand officer is a relatively new executive level position at a corporation, company, organization typically reporting directly to the CEO or board of directors. The Chief brand officer is responsible for a brand's image, experience, and promise, and propagating it throughout all aspects of the company. The brand officer oversees marketing, advertising, design, public relations and customer service departments.

Discretionary income

Discretionary income is income after subtracting taxes and normal expenses (such as rent or mortgage and food) to maintain a certain standard of living. It is the amount of an individual's income available for spending after the essentials (such as food, clothing, and shelter) have been taken care of:

discretionary income = Gross income - taxes - necessities

Despite the formal definitions above, disposable income is commonly used to denote discretionary income. The meaning should therefore be interpreted from context.

Disposable income

Disposable income is gross income minus income tax on that income.

Discretionary income is income after subtracting taxes and normal expenses (such as rent or mortgage and food) to maintain a certain standard of living. It is the amount of an individual's income available for spending after the essentials (such as food, clothing, and shelter) have been taken care of:

Discretionary income = Gross income - taxes - necessities

Despite the formal definitions above, disposable income is commonly used to denote Discretionary income.

Export

In economics, an export is any good or commodity, transported from one country to another country in a legitimate fashion, typically for use in trade. export goods or services are provided to foreign consumers by domestic producers. export is an important part of international trade.

Industry

An Industry is the manufacturing of a good or service within a category. Although Industry is a broad term for any kind of economic production, in economics and urban planning Industry is a synonym for the secondary sector, which is a type of economic activity involved in the manufacturing of raw materials into goods and products.

There are four key industrial economic sectors: the primary sector, largely raw material extraction industries such as mining and farming; the secondary sector, involving refining, construction, and manufacturing; the tertiary sector, which deals with services (such as law and medicine) and distribution of manufactured goods; and the quaternary sector, a relatively new type of knowledge Industry focusing on technological research, design and development such as computer programming, and biochemistry.

Containerization

Containerization is a system of intermodal freight transport using standard intermodal containers that are standardised by the International Organization for Standardization (ISO.) These can be loaded and sealed intact onto container ships, railroad cars, planes, and trucks.

Cost

In economics, business, retail, and accounting, a cost is the value of money that has been used up to produce something, and hence is not available for use anymore. In economics, a cost is an alternative that is given up as a result of a decision. In business, the cost may be one of acquisition, in which case the amount of money expended to acquire it is counted as cost.

International trade

International trade is exchange of capital, goods, and services across international borders or territories. In most countries, it represents a significant share of gross domestic product (GDP.) While International trade has been present throughout much of history , its economic, social, and political importance has been on the rise in recent centuries.

Business

A business is a legally recognized organization designed to provide goods and/or services to consumers. business es are predominant in capitalist economies, most being privately owned and formed to earn profit that will increase the wealth of its owners and grow the business itself. The owners and operators of a business have as one of their main objectives the receipt or generation of a financial return in exchange for work and acceptance of risk.

Internet

The Internet is a global network of interconnected computers, enabling users to share information along multiple channels. Typically, a computer that connects to the Internet can access information from a vast array of available servers and other computers by moving information from them to the computer's local memory. The same connection allows that computer to send information to servers on the network; that information is in turn accessed and potentially modified by a variety of other interconnected computers.

Mobile phone

A mobile phone or mobile is a long-range, electronic device used for mobile telecommunications over a cellular network of specialized base stations known as cell sites. In addition to the standard voice function, current mobile phone s may support many additional services, and accessories, such as SMS for text messaging, email, packet switching for access to the Internet, gaming, Bluetooth, infrared, camera with video recorder and MMS for sending and receiving photos and video, mobile phone 3 player, radio and GPS. Most current mobile phone s connect to a cellular network consisting of switching points and base stations owned by a mobile network operator

As opposed to a radio telephone, a mobile phone offers full duplex communication, automatised calling to and paging from a public switched telephone network, and handoff /handover during a phone call when the user moves from one cell to another.

Telephone

The telephone is a telecommunications device that transmits and receives sound, most commonly the human voice. It is one of the most common household appliances in the developed world, and has long been considered indispensable to business, industry and government. The word telephone has been adapted to many languages and is widely recognized around the world.

Advertising

Advertising is a form of communication that typically attempts to persuade potential customers to purchase or to consume more of a particular brand of product or service. 'While now central to the contemporary global economy and the reproduction of global production networks, it is only quite recently that Advertising has been more than a marginal influence on patterns of sales and production. The formation of modern Advertising was intimately bound up with the emergence of new forms of monopoly capitalism around the end of the 19th and beginning of the 20th century as one element in corporate strategies to create, organize and where possible control markets, especially for mass produced consumer goods.

Fair Trade

Fair trade is an organized social movement and market-based approach that aims to help producers in developing countries and promote sustainability. The movement advocates the payment of a fair price as well as social and environmental standards in areas related to the production of a wide variety of goods. It focuses in particular on exports from developing countries to developed countries, most notably handicrafts, coffee, cocoa, sugar, tea, bananas, honey, cotton, wine, fresh fruit, chocolate and flowers.

Kraft Foods

Kraft Foods Inc. (NYSE: Kraft Foods T) is the largest food and beverage company headquartered in the United States and the second largest in the world (after Nestlé SA.)

Kraft is headquartered in Northfield, Illinois, USA, a Chicago suburb.

Tariff

A Tariff is a duty imposed on goods when they are moved across a political boundary. They are usually associated with protectionism, the economic policy of restraining trade between nations. For political reasons, Tariff s are usually imposed on imported goods, although they may also be imposed on exported goods.

Theory of the firm

The Theory of the firm consists of a number of economic theories which describe the nature of the firm, company including its existence, its behaviour, and its relationship with the market.

In simplified terms, the Theory of the firm aims to answer these questions:

· Existence - why do firms emerge, why are not all transactions in the economy mediated over the market?
· Boundaries - why the boundary between firms and the market is located exactly there? Which transactions are performed internally and which are negotiated on the market?
· Organization - why are firms structured in such specific way? What is the interplay of formal and informal relationships?

The First World War period saw a change of emphasis in economic theory away from industry-level analysis which mainly included analysing markets to analysis at the level of the firm, as it became increasingly clear that perfect competition was no longer an adequate model of how firms behaved. Economic theory till then had focussed on trying to understand markets alone and there had been little study on understanding why firms or organisations exist. Market are mainly guided by prices as illustrated by vegetable markets where a buyer is free to switch sellers in an exchange.

International Finance

International finance is the branch of economics that studies the dynamics of exchange rates, foreign investment, and how these affect international trade. It also studies international projects, international investments and capital flows, and trade deficits. It includes the study of futures, options and currency swaps.

Wage

A Wage is a compensation, usually financial, received by a worker in exchange for their labor.

Compensation in terms of Wage s is given to worker and compensation in terms of salary is given to employees. Compensation is a monetary benefits given to employees in returns of the services provided by them.

Exchange rate

In finance, the Exchange rate s between two currencies specifies how much one currency is worth in terms of the other. It is the value of a foreign nation's currency in terms of the home nation's currency. For example an Exchange rate of 95 Japanese yen to the United States dollar means that JPY 95 is worth the same as USD 1.

Import

An import is any good (e.g. a commodity) or service brought into one country from another country in a legitimate fashion, typically for use in trade.It is a good that is brought in from another country for sale. import goods or services are provided to domestic consumers by foreign producers. An import in the receiving country is an export to the sending country.

Price

Price in economics and business is the result of an exchange and from that trade we assign a numerical monetary value to a good, service or asset. If I trade 4 apples for an orange, the price of an orange is 4 - apples. Inversely, the price of an apple is 1/4 oranges.

Control

Control is one of the managerial functions like planning, organizing, staffing and directing. It is an important function because it helps to check the errors and to take the corrective action so that deviation from standards are minimized and stated goals of the organization are achieved in desired manner.According to modern concepts, Control is a foreseeing action whereas earlier concept of Control was used only when errors were detected. Control in management means setting standards, measuring actual performance and taking corrective action.

Debtor

In economics a debtor is an entity that owes a debt to someone else. The entity may be an individual, a firm, a government, a company or other legal person. The counterparty is called a creditor.

Human

A human is a member of a species of bipedal primates in the family Hominidae . DNA and fossil evidence indicates that modern human s originated in east Africa about 200,000 years ago. When compared to other animals and primates, human s have a highly developed brain, capable of abstract reasoning, language, introspection and problem solving.

Human capital

Human capital refers to the stock of skills and knowledge embodied in the ability to perform labor so as to produce economic value. It is the skills and knowledge gained by a worker through education and experience. Many early economic theories refer to it simply as labor, one of three factors of production, and consider it to be a fungible resource -- homogeneous and easily interchangeable.

Investment

Investment or investing is a term with several closely-related meanings in business management, finance and economics, related to saving or deferring consumption. Investing is the active redirecting resources from being consumed today so that they may create benefits in the future; the use of assets to earn income or profit.

An Investment is the choice by the individual to risk his savings with the hope of gain.

Need

A need is something that is necessary for humans to live a healthy life. need s are distinguished from wants because a deficiency would cause a clear negative outcome, such as dysfunction or death. need s can be objective and physical, such as food and water, or they can be subjective and psychological, such as the need for self-esteem.

Expectancy

Expectancy theory is about the mental processes regarding choice, or choosing. It explains the processes that an individual undergoes to make choices. In organizational behavior study, expectancy theory is a motivation theory first proposed by Victor Vroom of the Yale School of Management.

Demographic

Demographic or Demographic data refers to selected population characteristics as used in government, marketing or opinion research, or the Demographic profiles used in such research. Note the distinction from the term 'demography' Commonly-used Demographic include race, age, income, disabilities, mobility (in terms of travel time to work or number of vehicles available), educational attainment, home ownership, employment status, and even location.

Organization

An organization is a social arrangement which pursues collective goals, which controls its own performance, and which has a boundary separating it from its environment. The word itself is derived from the Greek word á½„ργανον (organon [itself derived from the better-known word á¼”ργον ergon - work; deed - > ergonomics, etc]) meaning tool. The term is used in both daily and scientific English in multiple ways.

Population size

In population genetics and population ecology, population size is the number of individual organisms in a population.

The effective population size (N_e) is defined as 'the number of breeding individuals in an idealized population that would show the same amount of dispersion of allele frequencies under random genetic drift or the same amount of inbreeding as the population under consideration.' N_e is usually less than N (the absolute population size) and this has important applications in conservation genetics.

Small population size results in increased genetic drift.

Planning

Planning in organizations and public policy is both the organizational process of creating and maintaining a plan; and the psychological process of thinking about the activities required to create a desired goal on some scale. As such, it is a fundamental property of intelligent behavior. This thought process is essential to the creation and refinement of a plan, or integration of it with other plans, that is, it combines forecasting of developments with the preparation of scenarios of how to react to them.

Internal Market

An Internal market operates inside an organizations or set of organizations which have decoupled internal components. Each component trades its services and interfaces with the others. Often a set of government or government-funded set of organizations will operate an Internal market.

Population growth

Population growth is the change in population over time, and can be quantified as the change in the number of individuals in a population using 'per unit time' for measurement. The term Population growth can technically refer to any species, but almost always refers to humans, and it is often used informally for the more specific demographic term Population growth rate , and is often used to refer specifically to the growth of the population of the world.

Simple models of Population growth include the Malthusian Growth Model and the logistic model.

Capital structure

In finance, Capital structure refers to the way a corporation finances its assets through some combination of equity, debt, or hybrid securities. A firm's Capital structure is then the composition or 'structure' of its liabilities. For example, a firm that sells $20 billion in equity and $80 billion in debt is said to be 20% equity-financed and 80% debt-financed.

Job migration

Job migration is a term that has gained widespread use in the recent years and although it means relocation of jobs from one geographical area to another, it has come to symbolize the migration or relocation of jobs to other countries.

In most situations jobs are moved from one location to another, or to multiple other locations, because of changes in one or many of the following: supply and demand for products and services, business conditions, labor markets, government policies, political reasons, competition, environmental conditions, local business costs, technological obsolescence, outsourcing, higher productivity, etc.

Job migration usually leads to rise in unemployment often accompanied by a difficult transition to new jobs and new locations requiring new training and lowered living standards, although not for everyone.

Retirement

Retirement is the point where a person stops employment completely. A person may also semi-retire and keep some sort of Retirement job, out of choice rather than necessity. This usually happens upon reaching a determined age, when physical conditions don't allow the person to work any more (by illness or accident), or even for personal choice (usually in the presence of an adequate pension or personal savings.)

Set TSP

In combinatorial optimization, the set TSP group TSP, One-of-a-set TSP, Multiple Choice TSP or Covering Salesman Problem, is a generalization of the Traveling salesman problem, whereby it is required to find a shortest tour in a graph which visits all specified disjoint subsets of the vertices of a graph. The ordinary TSP is a special case of the set TSP when all subsets to be visited are singletons. Therefore the set TSP is also NP-hard.

Labor force

In economics, the people in the Labor force are the suppliers of labor. The Labor force is all the nonmilitary people who are employed or unemployed. In 2005, the worldwide Labor force was over 3 billion people.

Advertising Age

Advertising Age is a magazine, delivering news, analysis and data on marketing and media. The magazine was started as a broadsheet newspaper in Chicago in 1930. Today, its content appears in a print weekly distributed around the world and on many electronic platforms, including: AdAge.com, daily e-mail newsletters called Ad Age Daily, Ad Age's Mediaworks and Ad Age Digital; weekly newsletters such as Madison ' Vine (about branded entertainment) and Ad Age China; podcasts called Why It Matters and various videos.

Promotional mix

There are four main aspects of a Promotional mix. These are:

1 Advertising- Any paid presentation and promotion of ideas, goods, or services by an identified sponsor. Examples: Print ads, radio, television, billboard, direct mail, brochures and catalogs, signs, in-store displays, posters, motion pictures, Web pages, banner ads, and emails.

Cost of living

Cost of living is the cost of maintaining a certain standard of living. Changes in the Cost of living over time are often operationalized in a Cost of living index. Cost of living calculations are also used to compare the cost of maintaining a certain standard of living in different geographic areas.

Comparative advertising

Comparative advertising is an advertisement in which a particular product specifically mentions a competitor by name for the express purpose of showing why the competitor is inferior to the product naming it.

This should not be confused with parody advertisements, where a fictional product is being advertised for the purpose of poking fun at the particular advertisement, nor should it be confused with the use of a coined brand name for the purpose of comparing the product without actually naming an actual competitor. ('Wikipedia tastes better and is less filling than the Encyclopedia Galactica.')

In the 1980s, during what has been referred to as the cola wars, soft-drink manufacturer Pepsi ran a series of advertisements where people, caught on hidden camera, in a blind taste test, chose Pepsi over rival Coca-Cola.

Smuggling

Smuggling is the clandestine transportation of goods or persons past a point where prohibited, such as out of a building, into a prison in violation of the law or other rules.

There are various motivations to smuggle, most, but not all, of which are financial. These include the participation in illegal trade, such as drugs, illegal immigration or emigration, tax evasion, providing contraband to a prison inmate, or the theft of the items being smuggled.

Rebranding

Rebranding is the process by which a product or service developed with one brand, company or product line affiliation is marketed or distributed with a different identity. This may involve radical changes to the brand's logo, brand name, image, marketing strategy, and advertising themes. These changes are typically aimed at the repositioning of the brand/company, usually in an attempt to distance itself from certain negative connotations of the previous branding, or to move the brand upmarket.

Expropriation

Expropriation refers to confiscation of private property with the stated purpose of establishing social equality.

Unlike eminent domain, Expropriation takes place beyond the common law legal systems and refers to socially-motivated confiscations of any property rather than to taking away the real estate. Just compensation to owners is given.

Gross national product

A variety of measures of national income and output are used in economics to estimate total economic activity in a country or region, including gross domestic product (GDP), Gross national product , and net national income (NNI.)

Gross national product is defined as the 'value of all (final) goods and services produced in a country in one year by the nationals, plus income earned by its citizens abroad,

Fixed asset

Fixed asset plant, and equipment, is a term used in accountancy for assets and property which cannot easily be converted into cash. This can be compared with current assets such as cash or bank accounts, which are described as liquid assets. In most cases, only tangible assets are referred to as fixed.

Takeovers

Takeovers in the UK (meaning acquisitions of public companies only) are governed by the City Code on Takeovers and Mergers, also known as the 'City Code' or 'Takeover Code'. The rules for a takeover, can be found what is primarily known as 'The Blue Book'. The Code used to be a non-statutory set of rules that was controlled by City institutions on a theoretically voluntary basis.

Regulation

Regulation refers to 'controlling human or societal behaviour by rules or restrictions.' Regulation can take many forms: legal restrictions promulgated by a government authority, self-Regulation, social Regulation, co-Regulation and market Regulation. One can consider Regulation as actions of conduct imposing sanctions (such as a fine.) This action of administrative law, or implementing regulatory law, may be contrasted with statutory or case law.

Control

Control is one of the managerial functions like planning, organizing, staffing and directing. It is an important function because it helps to check the errors and to take the corrective action so that deviation from standards are minimized and stated goals of the organization are achieved in desired manner.According to modern concepts, Control is a foreseeing action whereas earlier concept of Control was used only when errors were detected. Control in management means setting standards, measuring actual performance and taking corrective action.

Foreign exchange controls

Foreign exchange controls are various forms of controls imposed by a government on the purchase/sale of foreign currencies by residents or on the purchase/sale of local currency by nonresidents.

Common Foreign exchange controls include:

· Banning the use of foreign currency within the country
· Banning locals from possessing foreign currency
· Restricting currency exchange to government-approved exchangers
· Fixed exchange rates
· Restrictions on the amount of currency that may be imported or exported

Countries with Foreign exchange controls are also known as 'Article 14 countries,' after the provision in the International Monetary Fund agreement allowing exchange controls for transitional economies. Such controls used to be common in most countries, particularly poorer ones, until the 1990s when free trade and globalization started a trend towards economic liberalization. Today, countries which still impose exchange controls are the exception rather than the rule.

Planning

Planning in organizations and public policy is both the organizational process of creating and maintaining a plan; and the psychological process of thinking about the activities required to create a desired goal on some scale. As such, it is a fundamental property of intelligent behavior. This thought process is essential to the creation and refinement of a plan, or integration of it with other plans, that is, it combines forecasting of developments with the preparation of scenarios of how to react to them.

Co-determination

Co-determination is a practice whereby the employees have a role in management of a company. The word is a somewhat clumsy and literal translation from the German word Mitbestimmung. Co-determination rights are different in different legal environments.

Corporatism

Corporatism is a system of economic, political, and social organization where social groups or interest groups, such as business, ethnic, farmer, labour, military are joined together under a common governing jurisdiction to try to achieve societal harmony and promote coordinated development. Corporatism is based on the sociological concept of functionalism.

The word 'Corporatism' is derived from the Latin word for body, corpus.

Foreign direct investment

Foreign direct investment in its classic form is defined as a company from one country making a physical investment into building a factory in another country. It is the establishment of an enterprise by a foreigner. Its definition can be extended to include investments made to acquire lasting interest in enterprises operating outside of the economy of the investor.

Kraft Foods

Kraft Foods Inc. (NYSE: Kraft Foods T) is the largest food and beverage company headquartered in the United States and the second largest in the world (after Nestlé SA.)

Kraft is headquartered in Northfield, Illinois, USA, a Chicago suburb.

Business

A business is a legally recognized organization designed to provide goods and/or services to consumers. business es are predominant in capitalist economies, most being privately owned and formed to earn profit that will increase the wealth of its owners and grow the business itself. The owners and operators of a business have as one of their main objectives the receipt or generation of a financial return in exchange for work and acceptance of risk.

Nationalization

Nationalization, is the act of taking an industry or assets into the public ownership of a national government or state. Nationalization usually refers to private assets, but may also mean assets owned by lower levels of government, such as municipalities, being state operated or owned by the state. The opposite of Nationalization is usually privatization or de-nationalisation, but may also be municipalization.

United States

The United States of America (commonly referred to as the United States the U.S., the United States A, or America) is a federal constitutional republic comprising fifty states and a federal district. The country is situated mostly in central North America, where its 48 contiguous states and Washington, D.C., the capital district, lie between the Pacific and Atlantic Oceans, bordered by Canada to the north and Mexico to the south. The state of Alaska is in the northwest of the continent, with Canada to its east and Russia to the west across the Bering Strait.

Job interview

A Job interview is a process in which a potential employee is evaluated by an employer for prospective employment in their company, organization and was established in the late 16th century.

A Job interview typically precedes the hiring decision, and is used to evaluate the candidate. The interview is usually preceded by the evaluation of submitted résumés from interested candidates, then selecting a small number of candidates for interviews.

Globalization

Globalization in its literal sense is the process of transformation of local or regional phenomena into global ones. It can be described as a process by which the people of the world are unified into a single society and function together.

This process is a combination of economic, technological, sociocultural and political forces.

Objective may also refer to:

The word objective may also refer to:

· Objective (military), the achievement of a final set of actions within a given military operation
· Objective pronoun, a noun as the target of a verb
· Objective (optics), an element in a camera or microscope
· Objective Corporation, a software company
· Objectivity (philosophy) (opposed to subjectivity)
· Objective (goal), a projected state of affairs that a person or a system plans or intends to achieve .

Ownership

Ownership is the state or fact of exclusive rights and control over property, which may be an object, land/real estate, or some other kind of property (like government-granted monopolies collectively referred to as intellectual property.) It is embodied in an Ownership right also referred to as title.

Ownership is the key building block in the development of the capitalist socio-economic system.

Unfair competition

Unfair competition in commercial law can refer to any of various distinct areas of law which may give rise to distinct criminal offences and civil causes of action:

· Matters pertaining to antitrust law, known in the European Union as competition law.
· Unfair business practices such as fraud, misrepresentation, tortious interference, and unconscionable contracts and business practices. In the European Union, each member state must regulate unfair business practices in accordance with the principles laid down in the Unfair Commercial Practices Directive, subject to transitional periods. (.

Privatization

Privatization is the incidence or process of transferring ownership of a business, enterprise, agency or public service from the public sector (government) to the private sector (business.) In a broader sense, Privatization refers to transfer of any government function to the private sector including governmental functions like revenue collection and law enforcement.

The term 'Privatization' also has been used to describe two unrelated transactions.

Comparative advertising

Comparative advertising is an advertisement in which a particular product specifically mentions a competitor by name for the express purpose of showing why the competitor is inferior to the product naming it.

This should not be confused with parody advertisements, where a fictional product is being advertised for the purpose of poking fun at the particular advertisement, nor should it be confused with the use of a coined brand name for the purpose of comparing the product without actually naming an actual competitor. ('Wikipedia tastes better and is less filling than the Encyclopedia Galactica.')

In the 1980s, during what has been referred to as the cola wars, soft-drink manufacturer Pepsi ran a series of advertisements where people, caught on hidden camera, in a blind taste test, chose Pepsi over rival Coca-Cola.

Magazine

Magazine s, periodicals, glossies or serials are publications, generally published on a regular schedule, containing a variety of articles, generally financed by advertising, by a purchase price, by pre-paid magazine subscriptions, or all three. magazine s can be distributed through the mail; through sales by newsstands, bookstores or other vendors; or through free distribution at selected pick up locations.

The various elements that contribute to the production of magazine s vary wildly.

Mozambique

Mozambique, officially the Republic of Mozambique , is a country in southeastern Africa bordered by the Indian Ocean to the east, Tanzania to the north, Malawi and Zambia to the northwest, Zimbabwe to the west and Swaziland and South Africa to the southwest. It was explored by Vasco da Gama in 1498 and colonized by Portugal in 1505. By 1510, the Portuguese had virtual control of all of the former Swahili sultanates on the east African coast.

Unemployment

Unemployment occurs when a person is available to work and seeking work but currently without work. The prevalence of Unemployment is usually measured using the Unemployment rate, which is defined as the percentage of those in the labor force who are unemployed. The Unemployment rate is also used in economic studies and economic indexes such as the United States' Conference Board's Index of Leading Indicators as a measure of the state of the macroeconomics.

Industry

An Industry is the manufacturing of a good or service within a category. Although Industry is a broad term for any kind of economic production, in economics and urban planning Industry is a synonym for the secondary sector, which is a type of economic activity involved in the manufacturing of raw materials into goods and products.

There are four key industrial economic sectors: the primary sector, largely raw material extraction industries such as mining and farming; the secondary sector, involving refining, construction, and manufacturing; the tertiary sector, which deals with services (such as law and medicine) and distribution of manufactured goods; and the quaternary sector, a relatively new type of knowledge Industry focusing on technological research, design and development such as computer programming, and biochemistry.

Capital structure

In finance, Capital structure refers to the way a corporation finances its assets through some combination of equity, debt, or hybrid securities. A firm's Capital structure is then the composition or 'structure' of its liabilities. For example, a firm that sells $20 billion in equity and $80 billion in debt is said to be 20% equity-financed and 80% debt-financed.

Numerary

Numerary is a civil designation for persons who are incorporated in a fixed or permanent way to a society or group: regular member of the working staff, permanent staff distinguished from a super Numerary .

The term Numerary and its counterpart, 'super Numerary ,' originated in Spanish and Latin American academy and government; it is now also used in countries all over the world, such as France, the U.S., England, Italy, etc. There are Numerary members of surgical organizations, of universities, of gastronomical associations, etc.

Organization

An organization is a social arrangement which pursues collective goals, which controls its own performance, and which has a boundary separating it from its environment. The word itself is derived from the Greek word á½„ργανον (organon [itself derived from the better-known word á¼"ργον ergon - work; deed - > ergonomics, etc]) meaning tool. The term is used in both daily and scientific English in multiple ways.

World Trade Organization

The World Trade Organization is an international organization designed to supervise and liberalize international trade. The World Trade Organization came into being on 1 January 1995, and is the successor to the General Agreement on Tariffs and Trade (GATT), which was created in 1947, and continued to operate for almost five decades as a de facto international organization.

The World Trade Organization deals with the rules of trade between nations at a near-global level; it is responsible for negotiating and implementing new trade agreements, and is in charge of policing member countries' adherence to all the World Trade Organization agreements, signed by the majority of the world's trading nations and ratified in their parliaments.

Inflation

In economics, Inflation is a rise in the general level of prices of goods and services in an economy over a period of time. The term 'Inflation' once referred to increases in the money supply (monetary Inflation); however, economic debates about the relationship between money supply and price levels have led to its primary use today in describing price Inflation. Inflation can also be described as a decline in the real value of money--a loss of purchasing power in the medium of exchange which is also the monetary unit of account.

Country risk

Country risk refers to the likelihood that changes in the business environment adversely affect operating profits or the value of assets in a specific country. For example, financial factors such as currency controls, devaluation or regulatory changes, or stability factors such as mass riots, civil war and other potential events contribute to companies' operational risks. This term is also sometimes referred to as political risk, however Country risk is a more general term, which generally only refers to risks affecting all companies operating within a particular country.

Risk assessment

Risk assessment is a step in a risk management process. Risk assessment is the determination of quantitative or qualitative value of risk related to a concrete situation and a recognized threat (also called hazard.) Quantitative Risk assessment requires calculations of two components of risk: R, the magnitude of the potential loss L, and the probability p that the loss will occur.

Risk

Risk is a concept that denotes the precise probability of specific eventualities. Technically, the notion of Risk is independent from the notion of value and, as such, eventualities may have both beneficial and adverse consequences. However, in general usage the convention is to focus only on potential negative impact to some characteristic of value that may arise from a future event.

Economic

An economy (or 'the economy') is the realized Economic system of a country or other area. It includes the production, exchange, distribution, and consumption of goods and services of that area. The study of different types and examples of economies is the subject of Economic systems.

Economic sanctions	Economic sanctions are domestic penalties applied by one country (or group of countries) on another for a variety of reasons. Economic sanctions include, but are not limited to, tariffs, trade barriers, import duties, and import or export quotas. Economic sanctions are frequently retaliatory in nature.
Infant industry argument	The infant industry argument is an economic reason for protectionism. The crux of the argument is that nascent industries often do not have the economies of scale that their older competitors from other countries may have, and thus need to be protected until they can attain similar economies of scale. It was first used by Alexander Hamilton in 1790 and later by Friedrich List, in 1841, to support protection for German manufacturing against British industry.
Protectionism	Protectionism is the economic policy of restraining trade between nations, through methods such as tariffs on imported goods, restrictive quotas, and a variety of other restrictive government regulations designed to discourage imports, and prevent foreign take-over of local markets and companies. This policy is closely aligned with anti-globalization, and contrasts with free trade, where government barriers to trade are kept to a minimum. The term is mostly used in the context of economics, where Protectionism refers to policies or doctrines which 'protect' businesses and workers within a country by restricting or regulating trade with foreign nations.
Tariff	A Tariff is a duty imposed on goods when they are moved across a political boundary. They are usually associated with protectionism, the economic policy of restraining trade between nations. For political reasons, Tariff s are usually imposed on imported goods, although they may also be imposed on exported goods.
Ad valorem	An Ad valorem tax is a tax based on the value of real estate or personal property. It is more common than the opposite, a specific duty, or a tax based on the quantity of an item regardless of price. An Ad valorem tax is typically imposed at the time of a transaction), but it may be imposed on an annual basis (real or personal property tax) or in connection with another significant event (inheritance tax, surrendering citizenship, or tariffs.)
Import	An import is any good (e.g. a commodity) or service brought into one country from another country in a legitimate fashion, typically for use in trade.It is a good that is brought in from another country for sale. import goods or services are provided to domestic consumers by foreign producers. An import in the receiving country is an export to the sending country.
Dumping	In economics, 'dumping' can refer to any kind of predatory pricing. However, the word is now generally used only in the context of international trade law, where dumping is defined as the act of a manufacturer in one country exporting a product to another country at a price which is either below the price it charges in its home market or is below its costs of production. The term has a negative connotation, but advocates of free markets see 'dumping' as beneficial for consumers and believe that protectionism to prevent it would have net negative consequences.
Fair Trade	Fair trade is an organized social movement and market-based approach that aims to help producers in developing countries and promote sustainability. The movement advocates the payment of a fair price as well as social and environmental standards in areas related to the production of a wide variety of goods. It focuses in particular on exports from developing countries to developed countries, most notably handicrafts, coffee, cocoa, sugar, tea, bananas, honey, cotton, wine, fresh fruit, chocolate and flowers.

International Trade	International trade is exchange of capital, goods, and services across international borders or territories. In most countries, it represents a significant share of gross domestic product (GDP.) While International trade has been present throughout much of history , its economic, social, and political importance has been on the rise in recent centuries.
International Trade Commission	The United States International Trade Commission is an independent, non-partisan, quasi-judicial, federal agency of the United States that provides trade expertise to both the legislative and executive branches. Further, the agency determines the impact of imports on U.S. industries and directs actions against certain unfair trade practices, such as dumping, patent, trademark, and copyright infringement. The US International Trade Commission was established by the U.S. Congress in 1916 as the U.S. Tariff Commission (the Trade Act of 1974 changed its name to the U.S. International Trade Commission , the agency has broad investigative powers on matters of trade.
Social dumping	'Social dumping' is a term (with a negative connotation) that is used to describe a temporary or transitory movement of labour, whereby employers use workers from one country or area in another country or area where the cost of labour is usually more expensive, thus saving money and potentially increasing profit. There is a controversy around whether Social dumping takes advantage of an EU directive on internal markets: the Bolkestein directive. In the UK, circa February 2009, this is an issue that has become a political 'hot potato'.
Kyoto Protocol	The Kyoto Protocol is a protocol to the United Nations Framework Convention on Climate Change (UNFCCC or FCCC), an international environmental treaty which was produced with the goal of achieving 'stabilization of greenhouse gas concentrations in the atmosphere at a level that would prevent dangerous anthropogenic interference with the climate system.' The Kyoto Protocol establishes legally binding commitments for the reduction of four greenhouse gases (carbon dioxide, methane, nitrous oxide, sulphur hexafluoride), and two groups of gases (hydrofluorocarbons and perfluorocarbons) produced by 'Annex I' (industrialized) nations, as well as general commitments for all member countries. As of January 2009, 183 parties have ratified the protocol, which was initially have been adopted for use on 11 December 1997 in Kyoto, Japan and which entered into force on 16 February 2005. Under Kyoto, industrialized countries agreed to reduce their collective GHG emissions by 5.2% compared to the year 1990.
Trend analysis	The term 'trend analysis' refers to the concept of collecting information and attempting to spot a pattern in the information. In some fields of study, the term 'trend analysis' has more formally-defined meanings. In project management trend analysis is a mathematical technique that uses historical results to predict future outcome.
Function cost analysis	Function cost analysis is the a method of technical and economic research of the systems for purpose to optimize a parity between system's consumer functions or properties and expenses to achieve those functions or properties. This methodology for continuous perfection of production, industrial technologies, organizational structures was developed by Juryj Sobolev in 1948 at the 'Perm telephone factory' · 1948 Juryj Sobolev - the first success in application of a method analysis at the 'Perm telephone factory' . · 1949 - the first application for the invention as result of use of the new method.

Today in economically developed countries practically each enterprise or the company use methodology of the kind of functional-cost analysis as a practice of the quality management, most full satisfying to principles of standards of series ISO 9000.

· Interest of consumer not in products itself, but the advantage which it will receive from its usage.
· The consumer aspires to reduce his expenses
· Functions needed by consumer can be executed in the various ways, and, hence, with various efficiency and expenses. Among possible alternatives of realization of functions exist such in which the parity of quality and the price is the optimal for the consumer.

The goal of Function cost analysis is achievement of the highest consumer satisfaction of production at simultaneous decrease in all kinds of industrial expenses Classical Function cost analysis has three English synonyms - Value Engineering, Value Management, Value Analysis.

Agricultural subsidy

An agricultural subsidy is a governmental subsidy paid to farmers and agribusinesses to supplement their income, manage the supply of agricultural commodities, and influence the cost and supply of such commodities. Examples of such commodities include wheat, feed grains (grain used as fodder, such as maize, sorghum, barley, and oats), cotton, milk, rice, peanuts, sugar, tobacco, and oilseeds such as soybeans.

The European Union use agricultural subsidies to encourage self-sufficiency.

Theory of the firm

The Theory of the firm consists of a number of economic theories which describe the nature of the firm, company including its existence, its behaviour, and its relationship with the market.

In simplified terms, the Theory of the firm aims to answer these questions:

· Existence - why do firms emerge, why are not all transactions in the economy mediated over the market?
· Boundaries - why the boundary between firms and the market is located exactly there? Which transactions are performed internally and which are negotiated on the market?
· Organization - why are firms structured in such specific way? What is the interplay of formal and informal relationships?

The First World War period saw a change of emphasis in economic theory away from industry-level analysis which mainly included analysing markets to analysis at the level of the firm, as it became increasingly clear that perfect competition was no longer an adequate model of how firms behaved. Economic theory till then had focussed on trying to understand markets alone and there had been little study on understanding why firms or organisations exist. Market are mainly guided by prices as illustrated by vegetable markets where a buyer is free to switch sellers in an exchange.

Countervailing duties

Countervailing duties are duties imposed under WTO Rules to neutralize the negative effects of other duties. They are imposed when a foreign country subsidizes its exports, hurting domestic producers in the importing country

Developed country

The term developed country is used to describe countries that have a high level of development according to some criteria. Which criteria, and which countries are classified as being developed, is a contentious issue and there is fierce debate about this. Economic criteria have tended to dominate discussions.

International Finance	International finance is the branch of economics that studies the dynamics of exchange rates, foreign investment, and how these affect international trade. It also studies international projects, international investments and capital flows, and trade deficits. It includes the study of futures, options and currency swaps.
Population ageing	Population ageing occurs when the median age of a country or region rises. With the exception of 18 countries termed by the United Nations 'demographic outliers' this process is taking place in every country and region across the globe. Population ageing is constituted by a shift in the distribution of a country's population towards greater ages.
Consumer	Consumer is a broad label that refers to any individuals or households that use goods and services generated within the economy. The concept of a Consumer is used in different contexts, so that the usage and significance of the term may vary. A Consumer is a person who uses any product or service.
Free Trade	Free trade is a type of trade policy that allows traders to act and transact without interference from government. Thus, the policy permits trading partners mutual gains from trade, with goods and services produced according to the theory of comparative advantage. Under a Free trade policy, prices are a reflection of true supply and demand, and are the sole determinant of resource allocation.
Lobbying	Lobbying is the practice of influencing decisions made by government. It includes all attempts to influence legislators and officials, whether by other legislators, constituents or organized groups. A lobbyist is a person who tries to influence legislation on behalf of a special interest or a member of a lobby.
North American Free Trade Agreement	The North American Free Trade Agreement is a trilateral trade bloc in North America created by the governments of the United States, Canada, and Mexico. It superseded the Canada-United States Free Trade Agreement between the US and Canada. Following diplomatic negotiations dating back to 1990 between the three nations, the leaders met in San Antonio, Texas on December 17, 1992 to sign North American Free Trade Agreement.
Price	Price in economics and business is the result of an exchange and from that trade we assign a numerical monetary value to a good, service or asset. If I trade 4 apples for an orange, the price of an orange is 4 - apples. Inversely, the price of an apple is 1/4 oranges.
Report	In writing, a report is a document characterized by information or other content reflective of inquiry or investigation, which is tailored to the context of a given situation and audience. The purpose of report s is usually to inform. However, report s may include persuasive elements, such as recommendations, suggestions, or other motivating conclusions that indicate possible future actions the report reader might take.
Cost	In economics, business, retail, and accounting, a cost is the value of money that has been used up to produce something, and hence is not available for use anymore. In economics, a cost is an alternative that is given up as a result of a decision. In business, the cost may be one of acquisition, in which case the amount of money expended to acquire it is counted as cost.

Customs | Customs is an authority or agency in a country responsible for collecting and safeguarding customs duties and for controlling the flow of goods including animals, personal effects and hazardous items in and out of a country. Depending on local legislation and regulations, the import or export of some goods may be restricted or forbidden, and the customs agency enforces these rules. The customs agency may be different from the immigration authority, which monitors persons who leave or enter the country, checking for appropriate documentation, apprehending people wanted by international arrest warrants, and impeding the entry of others deemed dangerous to the country.

Smoot-Hawley Tariff Act | The Smoot-Hawley Tariff Act was an act signed into law on June 17, 1930, that raised U.S. tariffs on over 20,000 imported goods to record levels. In the United States 1,028 economists signed a petition against this legislation, and after it was passed, many countries retaliated with their own increased tariffs on U.S. goods, and American exports and imports were reduced by more than half.

Variable | Variables are used in open sentences. For instance, in the formula x + 1 = 5, x is a variable which represents an 'unknown' number. Variables are often represented by letters of the Roman alphabet, or those of other alphabets, such as Greek, and use other special symbols.

Embargo | An Embargo is the prohibition of commerce and trade with a certain country, in order to isolate it and to put its government into a difficult internal situation, given that the effects of the Embargo are often able to make its economy suffer from the initiative. It is similar to a blockade, as in 'el bloqueo' or the American blockade on Cuba.

Embargo s generally attempt to pressure weaker adversaries to do what the abarcading country wishes.

Market | A Market is any one of a variety of different systems, institutions, procedures, social relations and infrastructures whereby persons trade, and goods and services are exchanged, forming part of the economy. It is an arrangement that allows buyers and sellers to exchange things. Market s vary in size, range, geographic scale, location, types and variety of human communities, as well as the types of goods and services traded.

Quantitative | A quantitative attribute is one that exists in a range of magnitudes, and can therefore be measured. Measurements of any particular quantitative property are expressed as a specific quantity, referred to as a unit, multiplied by a number. Examples of physical quantities are distance, mass, and time.

Certification | Certification refers to the confirmation of certain characteristics of an object, person, or organization. This confirmation is often, but not always, provided by some form of external review, education, or assessment. One of the most common types of Certification in modern society is professional Certification, where a person is certified as being able to competently complete a job or task, usually by the passing of an examination.

Export | In economics, an export is any good or commodity, transported from one country to another country in a legitimate fashion, typically for use in trade. export goods or services are provided to foreign consumers by domestic producers. export is an important part of international trade.

Import quota | An Import quota is a type of protectionist trade restriction that sets a physical limit on the quantity of a good that can be imported into a country in a given period of time. Quotas, like other trade restrictions, are used to benefit the producers of a good in a domestic economy at the expense of all consumers of the good in that economy.

Critics say quotas often lead to corruption (bribes to get a quota allocation), smuggling (circumventing a quota), and higher prices for consumers.

Marketing

Marketing is defined by the American Marketing Association as the activity, set of institutions, and processes for creating, communicating, delivering, and exchanging offerings that have value for customers, clients, partners, and society at large. The term developed from the original meaning which referred literally to going to market, as in shopping, or going to a market to sell goods or services.

Marketing practice tends to be seen as a creative industry, which includes advertising, distribution and selling.

Statistics

Statistics is a mathematical science pertaining to the collection, analysis, interpretation or explanation, and presentation of data. It also provides tools for prediction and forecasting based on data. It is applicable to a wide variety of academic disciplines, from the natural and social sciences to the humanities, government and business.

Buy American Act

The Buy American Act passed in 1933 by Congress and signed by President Hoover, required the United States government to prefer U.S.-made products in its purchases. Other pieces of Federal legislation extend similar requirement to third-party purchases that utilize Federal funds, such as highway and transit programs.

General Agreement on Tariffs and Trade

The General Agreement on Tariffs and Trade was the outcome of the failure of negotiating governments to create the International Trade Organization (ITO.) GATT was formed in 1947 and lasted until 1994, when it was replaced by the World Trade Organization. The Bretton Woods Conference had introduced the idea for an organization to regulate trade as part of a larger plan for economic recovery after World War II.

Government Procurement

Government procurement or public procurement, is the procurement of goods and services on behalf of a public authority, such as a government agency. With 10 to 15% of GDP in developed countries, and up to 20% in developing countries, Government procurement accounts for a substantial part of the global economy.

To prevent fraud, waste, corruption or local protectionism, the law of most countries regulates Government procurement more or less closely.

Discrimination

Discrimination toward or against a person of a certain group is the treatment or consideration based on class or category rather than individual merit. It can be behavior promoting a certain group (e.g. affirmative action), or it can be negative behavior directed against a certain group (e.g. redlining.)

Racial discrimination differentiates between individuals on the basis of real and perceived racial differences, and has been official government policy in several countries, such as South Africa in the apartheid era, and the USA.

Labeling

Labeling- Identifies the product or brand; describe several things about the product - who made it, when it was made, where it was made, its content, how is it to be use and how to use it safely.

English

English is a West Germanic language that originated in Anglo-Saxon England. As a result of the military, economic, scientific, political and cultural influence of the British Empire during the 18th, 19th and 20th centuries and of the United States since the late 19th century, it has become the lingua franca in many parts of the world. It is used extensively as a second language and as an official language in Commonwealth countries and many international organizations.

Global sourcing

Global sourcing is a term used to describe practice of sourcing from the global market for goods and services across geopolitical boundaries. Global sourcing often aims to exploit global efficiencies in the delivery of a product or service. These efficiencies include low cost skilled labor, low cost raw material and other economic factors like tax breaks and low trade tariffs.

Trade barrier

A trade barrier is a general term that describes any government policy or regulation that restricts international trade. The barriers can take many forms, including the following terms that include many restrictions in international trade within multiple countries that import and export any items of trade.

· Import duty
· Import licenses
· Export licenses
· Import quotas
· Tariffs
· Subsidies
· Non-tariff barriers to trade
· Voluntary Export Restraints
· Local Content Requirements
· Embargo

Most trade barriers work on the same principle: the imposition of some sort of cost on trade that raises the price of the traded products. If two or more nations repeatedly use trade barriers against each other, then a trade war results.

Second Life

Second Life is a virtual world developed by Linden Lab that launched on June 23, 2003 and is accessible via the Internet. A free client program called the Second Life Viewer enables its users, called Residents, to interact with each other through avatars. Residents can explore, meet other residents, socialize, participate in individual and group activities, and create and trade virtual property and services with one another, or travel throughout the world, which residents refer to as the grid.

EURO

The Euro (â‚¬) is the official currency of 16 of the 27 member states of the Euro pean Union (EU.) The states, known collectively as the Euro zone, are Austria, Belgium, Cyprus, Finland, France, Germany, Greece, Ireland, Italy, Luxembourg, Malta, the Netherlands, Portugal, Slovakia, Slovenia, and Spain. The currency is also used in a further five Euro pean countries, with and without formal agreements and is consequently used daily by some 327 million Euro peans.

Foreign Policy

A country's foreign policy is a set of goals outlining how the country will interact with other countries economically, politically, socially and militarily, and to a lesser extent, how the country will interact with non-state actors. The aforementioned interaction is evaluated and monitored in attempts to maximize benefits of multilateral international cooperation. Foreign policies are designed to help protect a country's national interests, national security, ideological goals, and economic prosperity.

Political risk

Political risk is a type of risk faced by investors, corporations, and governments. It is a risk that can be understood and managed with proper aforethought and investment.

Broadly, Political risk refers to the complications businesses and governments may face as a result of what are commonly referred to as political decisions--or 'any political change that alters the expected outcome and value of a given economic action by changing the probability of achieving business objectives.' .

Child labour

Child labour refers to the employment of children at regular and sustained labour. This practice is considered exploitative by many international organizations and is illegal in many countries. Child labour was utilized to varying extents through most of history, but entered public dispute with the beginning of universal schooling, with changes in working conditions during industrialization, and with the emergence of the concepts of workers' and children's rights.

Labor Rights

Labor rights or workers' rights are a group of legal rights and claimed human rights having to do with labor relations between workers and their employers, usually obtained under labor and employment law. In general, these rights' debates have to do with negotiating workers' pay, benefits, and safe working conditions. One of the most central of these 'rights' is the right to unionize.

Business marketing

Business marketing is the practice of individuals including commercial businesses, governments and institutions, facilitating the sale of their products or services to other companies or organizations that in turn resell them, use them as components in products or services they offer Business marketing is also called business-to-Business marketing for short. (Note that while marketing to government entities shares some of the same dynamics of organizational marketing, B2G Marketing is meaningfully different.)

Set TSP

In combinatorial optimization, the set TSP group TSP, One-of-a-set TSP, Multiple Choice TSP or Covering Salesman Problem, is a generalization of the Traveling salesman problem, whereby it is required to find a shortest tour in a graph which visits all specified disjoint subsets of the vertices of a graph. The ordinary TSP is a special case of the set TSP when all subsets to be visited are singletons. Therefore the set TSP is also NP-hard.

Appropriation	Appropriation is the act of taking possession of or assigning purpose to properties or ideas and is important in many topics, including: · Appropriation in relation to the spread of knowledge · Appropriation (art) · Appropriation (music) in reference to the re-use and proliferation of different types of music · Appropriation (economics) origination of human ownership of previously unowned natural resources such as land · Appropriation (law) as a component of government spending · Cultural Appropriation is the borrowing, or theft, of an element of cultural expression of one group by another. · The tort of Appropriation is one form of invasion of privacy. .
Constitution	A Constitution is set of rules for government -- often codified as a written document -- that establishes principles of an autonomous political entity. In the case of countries, this term refers specifically to a national Constitution defining the fundamental political principles, and establishing the structure, procedures, powers and duties, of a government. By limiting the government's own reach, most Constitution s guarantee certain rights to the people.
Export	In economics, an export is any good or commodity, transported from one country to another country in a legitimate fashion, typically for use in trade. export goods or services are provided to foreign consumers by domestic producers. export is an important part of international trade.
Supremacy Clause	The Supremacy clause is a clause in the United States Constitution, article VI, paragraph 2. The clause establishes the Constitution, Federal Statutes, and U.S. treaties as 'the supreme law of the land'. The text establishes these as the highest form of law in the American legal system, mandating that state judges uphold them, even if state laws or constitutions conflict.
Supreme Court	A supreme court is in some jurisdictions the highest judicial body within that jurisdiction's court system, whose rulings are not subject to further review by another court. The designations for such courts differ among jurisdictions. Courts of last resort typically function primarily as appellate courts, hearing appeals from the lower trial courts or intermediate-level appellate courts.
United States	The United States of America (commonly referred to as the United States the U.S., the United States A, or America) is a federal constitutional republic comprising fifty states and a federal district. The country is situated mostly in central North America, where its 48 contiguous states and Washington, D.C., the capital district, lie between the Pacific and Atlantic Oceans, bordered by Canada to the north and Mexico to the south. The state of Alaska is in the northwest of the continent, with Canada to its east and Russia to the west across the Bering Strait.
Set TSP	In combinatorial optimization, the set TSP group TSP, One-of-a-set TSP, Multiple Choice TSP or Covering Salesman Problem, is a generalization of the Traveling salesman problem, whereby it is required to find a shortest tour in a graph which visits all specified disjoint subsets of the vertices of a graph. The ordinary TSP is a special case of the set TSP when all subsets to be visited are singletons. Therefore the set TSP is also NP-hard.

Covenant

Title covenants serve as guarantees to the recipient of property, ensuring that the recipient receives what he or she bargained for. The English covenants of title, sometimes included in deeds to real property, are that the grantor is lawfully seized (in fee simple) of the property, (2) that the grantor has the right to convey the property to the grantee, (3) that the property is conveyed without encumbrances (this Covenant is frequently modified to allow for certain encumbrances), (4) that the grantor has done no act to encumber the property, (5) that the grantee shall have quiet possession of the property, and (6) that the grantor will execute such further assurances of the land as may be requisite (Nos. 3 and 4, which overlap significantly, are sometimes treated as one item.)

International law

International law is the term commonly used for referring to the system of implicit and explicit agreements that bind together nation-states in adherence to recognized values and standards. It differs from other legal systems in that it primarily concerns states rather than private citizens. However, the term 'International law' can refer to three distinct legal disciplines:

· Public International law, which governs the relationship between states and international organizations.it includes the following specific legal field such as the law of treaty, law of sea, international criminal law and the international humanitarian law.
· Private International law, or conflict of laws, which addresses the questions of (1) in which legal jurisdiction may a case be heard; and (2) the law concerning which jurisdiction(s) apply to the issues in the case.
· Supranational law or the law of supranational organizations, which concerns at present regional agreements where the special distinguishing quality is that laws of nation states are held inapplicable when conflicting with a supranational legal system.

The two traditional branches of the field are:

· jus gentium -- law of nations
· jus inter gentes -- agreements among nations .

Conflict of laws

Conflict of laws is that branch of international law and intranational interstate law that regulates all lawsuits involving a 'foreign' law element where different judgments will result depending on which jurisdiction's laws are applied as the lex causae.

In civil law systems, private international law is a branch of the internal legal system dealing with the determination of which state law is applicable to situations crossing over the borders of one particular state and involving a 'foreign element' (élément d'extranéité), (collisions of law, Conflict of laws.) Lato sensu (at large) it also includes international civil procedure and international commercial arbitration (collisions of jurisdiction, conflict of jurisdictions), as well as citizenship law (which strictly speaking is part of public law.)

Minutes

Minutes also known as protocols, are the instant written record of a meeting or hearing. They often give an overview of the structure of the meeting, starting with a list of those present, a statement of the various issues before the participants, and each of their responses thereto. They are often created at the moment of the hearing by a typist or court recorder at the meeting, who may record the meeting in shorthand, and then prepare the minutes and issue them to the participants afterwards.

United Nations

The United Nations is an international organization whose stated aims are to facilitate cooperation in international law, international security, economic development, social progress, human rights and achieving world peace. The United Nations was founded in 1945 after World War II to replace the League of Nations, to stop wars between countries and to provide a platform for dialogue.

There are currently 192 member states, including nearly every recognized independent state in the world.

Antitrust

Competition law, known in the United States as antitrust law, has three main elements:

· prohibiting agreements or practices that restrict free trading and competition between business entities. This includes in particular the repression of cartels.
· banning abusive behavior by a firm dominating a market, or anti-competitive practices that tend to lead to such a dominant position. Practices controlled in this way may include predatory pricing, tying, price gouging, refusal to deal, and many others.
· supervising the mergers and acquisitions of large corporations, including some joint ventures. Transactions that are considered to threaten the competitive process can be prohibited altogether, or approved subject to 'remedies' such as an obligation to divest part of the merged business or to offer licenses or access to facilities to enable other businesses to continue competing.

The substance and practice of competition law varies from jurisdiction to jurisdiction. Protecting the interests of consumers (consumer welfare) and ensuring that entrepreneurs have an opportunity to compete in the market economy are often treated as important objectives. Competition law is closely connected with law on deregulation of access to markets, state aids and subsidies, the privatization of state owned assets and the establishment of independent sector regulators. In recent decades, competition law has been viewed as a way to provide better public services.

Antitrust law

Competition law, known in the United States as Antitrust law, has three main elements:

· prohibiting agreements or practices that restrict free trading and competition between business entities. This includes in particular the repression of cartels.
· banning abusive behaviour by a firm dominating a market, or anti-competitive practices that tend to lead to such a dominant position. Practices controlled in this way may include predatory pricing, tying, price gouging, refusal to deal, and many others.
· supervising the mergers and acquisitions of large corporations, including some joint ventures. Transactions that are considered to threaten the competitive process can be prohibited altogether, or approved subject to 'remedies' such as an obligation to divest part of the merged business or to offer licences or access to facilities to enable other businesses to continue competing.

The substance and practice of competition law varies from jurisdiction to jurisdiction. Protecting the interests of consumers (consumer welfare) and ensuring that entrepreneurs have an opportunity to compete in the market economy are often treated as important objectives. Competition law is closely connected with law on deregulation of access to markets, state aids and subsidies, the privatisation of state owned assets and the establishment of independent sector regulators. In recent decades, competition law has been viewed as a way to provide better public services.

Competition law

Competition law, known in the United States as antitrust law, has three main elements:

· prohibiting agreements or practices that restrict free trading and competition between business entities. This includes in particular the repression of cartels.
· banning abusive behaviour by a firm dominating a market, or anti-competitive practices that tend to lead to such a dominant position. Practices controlled in this way may include predatory pricing, tying, price gouging, refusal to deal, and many others.
· supervising the mergers and acquisitions of large corporations, including some joint ventures. Transactions that are considered to threaten the competitive process can be prohibited altogether, or approved subject to 'remedies' such as an obligation to divest part of the merged business or to offer licences or access to facilities to enable other businesses to continue competing.

The substance and practice of Competition law varies from jurisdiction to jurisdiction. Protecting the interests of consumers (consumer welfare) and ensuring that entrepreneurs have an opportunity to compete in the market economy are often treated as important objectives. Competition law is closely connected with law on deregulation of access to markets, state aids and subsidies, the privatisation of state owned assets and the establishment of independent sector regulators. In recent decades, Competition law has been viewed as a way to provide better public services.

Dispute

Controversy is a state of prolonged public dispute or debate usually concerning a matter of opinion. The term originates circa 1384 from Latin controversia, as a composite of controversus - 'turned in an opposite direction,' from contra - 'against' - and vertere - to turn, or versus , hence, 'to turn against.'

Benford's law of controversy, as expressed by science-fiction author Gregory Benford in 1980, states: 'Passion is inversely proportional to the amount of real (true) information available.' In other words, the more untruths the more controversy there is, and the more truths the less controversy there is.

A controversy is always the result of either ignorance (lack of sufficient true information), misinformation, misunderstandings, half-truths, distortions, bias or prejudice, deliberate lies or fabrications (disinformation), opposed underlying motives or purposes (sometimes masked or hidden), or a combination of these factors.

Dispute resolution

Dispute resolution is the process of resolving disputes between parties.

Methods of Dispute resolution include:

· lawsuits (litigation)
· arbitration
· collaborative law
· mediation
· conciliation
· many types of negotiation
· facilitation

One could theoretically include violence or even war as part of this spectrum, but Dispute resolution practitioners do not usually do so; violence rarely ends disputes effectively, and indeed, often only escalates them. Some individuals, notably Joseph Stalin, have stated that all problems emanate from man, and absent man, no problems ensue. Hence, violence could theoretically end disputes, but alongside it, life.

International Court of Justice	The International Court of Justice is the primary judicial organ of the United Nations. It is based in the Peace Palace in The Hague, Netherlands. Its main functions are to settle legal disputes submitted to it by states and to give advisory opinions on legal questions submitted to it by duly authorized international organs, agencies, and the UN General Assembly.
Jurisdiction	Jurisdiction is the practical authority granted to a formally constituted legal body or to a political leader to deal with and make pronouncements on legal matters and, by implication, to administer justice within a defined area of responsibility. Alternatively, jurisdiction is the authority given to a legal body, or to a political leader to adjudicate and enforce legal matters. jurisdiction draws its substance from public international law, conflict of laws, constitutional law and the powers of the executive and legislative branches of government to allocate resources to best serve the needs of its native society.
Litigation	The conduct of a lawsuit is called Litigation. Rules of criminal or civil procedure govern the conduct of a lawsuit in the common law adversarial system of dispute resolution. Procedural rules are additionally constrained/informed by separate statutory laws, case law, and constitutional provisions that define the rights of the parties to a lawsuit , though the rules will generally reflect this legal context on their face.
Tariff	A Tariff is a duty imposed on goods when they are moved across a political boundary. They are usually associated with protectionism, the economic policy of restraining trade between nations. For political reasons, Tariff s are usually imposed on imported goods, although they may also be imposed on exported goods.
Arbitration	Arbitration, a form of alternative dispute resolution (ADR), is a legal technique for the resolution of disputes outside the courts, wherein the parties to a dispute refer it to one or more persons (the 'arbitrators', 'arbiters' or 'arbitral tribunal'), by whose decision (the 'award') they agree to be bound. It is a settlement technique in which a third party reviews the case and imposes a decision that is legally binding for both sides. Other forms of ADR include mediation (a form of settlement negotiation facilitated by a neutral third party) and non-binding resolution by experts.
Two-phase locking	In databases and transaction processing, Two-phase locking, (2PL) is a concurrency control locking protocol which guarantees serializability. It is also the name of the resulting class (set) of transaction schedules. Using locks that block processes, 2PL may be subject to deadlocks that result from the mutual blocking of two transactions or more.
Arbitration Award	An Arbitration award (or arbitral award) is a determination on the merits by an arbitration tribunal in an arbitration, and is analogous to a judgment in a court of law. It is referred to as an 'award' even where all of the claimant's claims fail (and thus no money needs to be paid by either party), or the award is of a non-monetary nature. Although Arbitration award s are characteristically an award of damages against a party, tribunals usually have a range of remedies that can form a part of the award.
Business	A business is a legally recognized organization designed to provide goods and/or services to consumers. business es are predominant in capitalist economies, most being privately owned and formed to earn profit that will increase the wealth of its owners and grow the business itself. The owners and operators of a business have as one of their main objectives the receipt or generation of a financial return in exchange for work and acceptance of risk.

Good	A good is an object whose consumption increases the utility of the consumer, for which the quantity demanded exceeds the quantity supplied at zero price. Goods are usually modeled as having diminishing marginal utility. The first individual purchase has high utility; the second has less.
Incoterms	Incoterms or international commercial terms are a series of international sales terms widely used throughout the world. They are used to divide transaction costs and responsibilities between buyer and seller and reflect state-of-the-art transportation practices. They closely correspond to the U.N. Convention on Contracts for the International Sale of Goods.
Intellectual Property	Intellectual property are legal property rights over creations of the mind, both artistic and commercial, and the corresponding fields of law. Under intellectual property law, owners are granted certain exclusive rights to a variety of intangible assets, such as musical, literary, and artistic works; ideas, discoveries and inventions; and words, phrases, symbols, and designs. Common types of intellectual property include copyrights, trademarks, patents, industrial design rights and trade secrets.
International Chamber of Commerce	The International Chamber of Commerce is a non-profit, private international organization that works to promote and support global trade and globalization. It serves as an advocate of some world businesses in the global economy, in the interests of economic growth, job creation, and prosperity. As a global business organization, made up of member states, it helps the development of global outlooks on business matters.
International Trade	International trade is exchange of capital, goods, and services across international borders or territories. In most countries, it represents a significant share of gross domestic product (GDP.) While International trade has been present throughout much of history , its economic, social, and political importance has been on the rise in recent centuries.
International Trade Law	International trade law includes the appropriate rules and customs for handling trade between countries or between private companies across borders. Over the past twenty years, it has become one of the fastest growing areas of international law. International trade law should be distinguished from the broader field of international economic law.
Investment	Investment or investing is a term with several closely-related meanings in business management, finance and economics, related to saving or deferring consumption. Investing is the active redirecting resources from being consumed today so that they may create benefits in the future; the use of assets to earn income or profit. An Investment is the choice by the individual to risk his savings with the hope of gain.
Mediation	Mediation, a form of alternative dispute resolution (ADR) or 'appropriate dispute resolution', aims to assist two (or more) disputants in reaching an agreement. The parties themselves determine the conditions of any settlements reached-- rather than accepting something imposed by a third party. The disputes may involve (as parties) states, organizations, communities, individuals or other representatives with a vested interest in the outcome.

Organization

An organization is a social arrangement which pursues collective goals, which controls its own performance, and which has a boundary separating it from its environment. The word itself is derived from the Greek word á½„ργανον (organon [itself derived from the better-known word á¼"ργον ergon - work; deed - > ergonomics, etc]) meaning tool. The term is used in both daily and scientific English in multiple ways.

Sale of Goods

The sale of goods Act 1979 (c.54) is an Act of the Parliament of the United Kingdom which regulates contracts in which goods are sold and bought. The Act consolidates the sale of goods Act 1893 and subsequent legislation, which in turn consolidated the previous common law.

The sale of goods Act performs several functions.

United Nations Commission on International Trade Law

The United Nations Commission on International Trade Law was established by the United Nations General Assembly by its Resolution 2205 (XXI) of 17 December 1966 'to promote the progressive harmonization and unification of international trade law.

UNCITRAL carries out its work at annual sessions held alternately in New York City and Vienna.

When world trade began to expand dramatically in the 1960s, national governments began to realize the need for a global set of standards and rules to harmonize national and regional regulations, which until then governed international trade.

World Intellectual Property Organization

The World Intellectual Property Organization is one of the 16 specialized agencies of the United Nations. World Intellectual Property Organization was created in 1967 'to encourage creative activity, to promote the protection of intellectual property throughout the world'.

World Intellectual Property Organization currently has 184 member states, administers 24 international treaties, and is headquartered in Geneva, Switzerland.

Business marketing

Business marketing is the practice of individuals including commercial businesses, governments and institutions, facilitating the sale of their products or services to other companies or organizations that in turn resell them, use them as components in products or services they offer Business marketing is also called business-to-Business marketing for short. (Note that while marketing to government entities shares some of the same dynamics of organizational marketing, B2G Marketing is meaningfully different.)

Copyright

Copyright is a form of intellectual property which gives the creator of an original work exclusive rights for a certain time period in relation to that work, including its publication, distribution and adaptation; after which time the work is said to enter the public domain. Copyright applies to any expressible form of an idea or information that is substantive and discrete. Some jurisdictions also recognize 'moral rights' of the creator of a work, such as the right to be credited for the work.

Patent

A patent is a set of exclusive rights granted by a state to an inventor or his assignee for a limited period of time in exchange for a disclosure of an invention.

The procedure for granting patent s, the requirements placed on the patent ee and the extent of the exclusive rights vary widely between countries according to national laws and international agreements. Typically, however, a patent application must include one or more claims defining the invention which must be new, inventive, and useful or industrially applicable.

Trade name

A Trade name is the name which a business trades under for commercial purposes, although its registered, legal name, used for contracts and other formal situations, may be another. Pharmaceuticals also have Trade name s, often dissimilar to their chemical names

Trading names are sometimes registered as trademarks or are regarded as brands.

Trade secret

A trade secret is a formula, practice, process, design, instrument, pattern by which a business can obtain an economic advantage over competitors or customers. In some jurisdictions, such secrets are referred to as 'confidential information' or 'classified information'.

The precise language by which a trade secret is defined varies by jurisdiction (as do the particular types of information that are subject to trade secret protection.)

Trademark

A Trademark or trade mark is a distinctive sign or indicator used by an individual, business organization and to distinguish its products or services from those of other entities.

A Trademark is designated by the following symbols:

· â„¢ (for an unregistered Trademark that is, a mark used to promote or brand goods);
· â„ (for an unregistered service mark, that is, a mark used to promote or brand services); and
· Â® (for a registered Trademark)

A Trademark is a type of intellectual property, and typically a name, word, phrase, logo, symbol, design, image, or a combination of these elements. There is also a range of non-conventional Trademark s comprising marks which do not fall into these standard categories.

The owner of a registered Trademark may commence legal proceedings for Trademark infringement to prevent unauthorized use of that Trademark

World Trade Organization

The World Trade Organization is an international organization designed to supervise and liberalize international trade. The World Trade Organization came into being on 1 January 1995, and is the successor to the General Agreement on Tariffs and Trade (GATT), which was created in 1947, and continued to operate for almost five decades as a de facto international organization.

The World Trade Organization deals with the rules of trade between nations at a near-global level; it is responsible for negotiating and implementing new trade agreements, and is in charge of policing member countries' adherence to all the World Trade Organization agreements, signed by the majority of the world's trading nations and ratified in their parliaments.

Industry

An Industry is the manufacturing of a good or service within a category. Although Industry is a broad term for any kind of economic production, in economics and urban planning Industry is a synonym for the secondary sector, which is a type of economic activity involved in the manufacturing of raw materials into goods and products.

There are four key industrial economic sectors: the primary sector, largely raw material extraction industries such as mining and farming; the secondary sector, involving refining, construction, and manufacturing; the tertiary sector, which deals with services (such as law and medicine) and distribution of manufactured goods; and the quaternary sector, a relatively new type of knowledge Industry focusing on technological research, design and development such as computer programming, and biochemistry.

Civil law

Civil law, as opposed to criminal law, refers to that branch of law dealing with disputes between individuals and/or organizations, in which compensation may be awarded to the victim. For instance, if a car crash victim claims damages against the driver for loss or injury sustained in an accident, this will be a Civil law case.

In the common law, Civil law refers to area of laws and justice that affect the legal status of individuals.

Common law

Common law refers to law and the corresponding legal system developed through decisions of courts and similar tribunals (called case law), rather than through legislative statutes or executive action.

Common law is law created and refined by judges: a decision in a currently pending legal case depends on decisions in previous cases and affects the law to be applied in future cases. When there is no authoritative statement of the law, judges have the authority and duty to make law by creating precedent.

Internal Market

An Internal market operates inside an organizations or set of organizations which have decoupled internal components. Each component trades its services and interfaces with the others. Often a set of government or government-funded set of organizations will operate an Internal market.

Bankruptcy

Bankruptcy is a legally declared inability or impairment of ability of an individual or organization to pay its creditors. Creditors may file a Bankruptcy petition against a debtor ('involuntary Bankruptcy') in an effort to recoup a portion of what they are owed or initiate a restructuring. In the majority of cases, however, Bankruptcy is initiated by the debtor (a 'voluntary Bankruptcy' that is filed by the insolvent individual or organization.)

International Organization for Standardization

The International Organization for Standardization, widely known as ISO , is an international-standard-setting body composed of representatives from various national standards organizations. Founded on 23 February 1947, the organization promulgates worldwide proprietary industrial and commercial standards. It is headquartered in Geneva, Switzerland.

Redistribution

In economics, redistribution is the transfer of income, wealth or property from some individuals to others.

One premise of redistribution is that money should be distributed to benefit the poorer members of society, and that the rich have an obligation to assist the poor, thus creating a more financially egalitarian society. Another argument is that the rich exploit the poor or otherwise gain unfair benefits.

Standardization

Standardization or standardisation is the process of developing and agreeing upon technical standards. A standard is a document that establishes uniform engineering or technical specifications, criteria, methods, processes, or practices. Some standards are mandatory while others are voluntary.

Double taxation

Double taxation is the imposition of two or more taxes on the same income (in the case of income taxes), asset (in the case of capital taxes), or financial transaction (in the case of sales taxes.) It refers to two distinct situations:

· taxation of dividend income without relief or credit for taxes paid by the company paying the dividend on the income from which the dividend is paid. This arises in the so-called 'classical' system of corporate taxation, used in the United States.
· taxation by two or more countries of the same income, asset or transaction, for example income paid by an entity of one country to a resident of a different country. The double liability is often mitigated by tax treaties between countries.

It is not unusual for a business or individual who is resident in one country to make a taxable gain (earnings, profits) in another. This person may find that he is obliged by domestic laws to pay tax on that gain locally and pay again in the country in which the gain was made. Since this is inequitable, many nations make bilateral Double taxation agreements with each other.

Comparative advertising

Comparative advertising is an advertisement in which a particular product specifically mentions a competitor by name for the express purpose of showing why the competitor is inferior to the product naming it.

This should not be confused with parody advertisements, where a fictional product is being advertised for the purpose of poking fun at the particular advertisement, nor should it be confused with the use of a coined brand name for the purpose of comparing the product without actually naming an actual competitor. ('Wikipedia tastes better and is less filling than the Encyclopedia Galactica.')

In the 1980s, during what has been referred to as the cola wars, soft-drink manufacturer Pepsi ran a series of advertisements where people, caught on hidden camera, in a blind taste test, chose Pepsi over rival Coca-Cola.

Capital structure

In finance, Capital structure refers to the way a corporation finances its assets through some combination of equity, debt, or hybrid securities. A firm's Capital structure is then the composition or 'structure' of its liabilities. For example, a firm that sells $20 billion in equity and $80 billion in debt is said to be 20% equity-financed and 80% debt-financed.

Control

Control is one of the managerial functions like planning, organizing, staffing and directing. It is an important function because it helps to check the errors and to take the corrective action so that deviation from standards are minimized and stated goals of the organization are achieved in desired manner.According to modern concepts, Control is a foreseeing action whereas earlier concept of Control was used only when errors were detected. Control in management means setting standards, measuring actual performance and taking corrective action.

Foreign exchange controls

Foreign exchange controls are various forms of controls imposed by a government on the purchase/sale of foreign currencies by residents or on the purchase/sale of local currency by nonresidents.

Common Foreign exchange controls include:

· Banning the use of foreign currency within the country
· Banning locals from possessing foreign currency
· Restricting currency exchange to government-approved exchangers
· Fixed exchange rates
· Restrictions on the amount of currency that may be imported or exported

Countries with Foreign exchange controls are also known as 'Article 14 countries,' after the provision in the International Monetary Fund agreement allowing exchange controls for transitional economies. Such controls used to be common in most countries, particularly poorer ones, until the 1990s when free trade and globalization started a trend towards economic liberalization. Today, countries which still impose exchange controls are the exception rather than the rule.

Incentive

In economics and sociology, an Incentive is any factor (financial or non-financial) that enables or motivates a particular course of action, or counts as a reason for preferring one choice to the alternatives. It is an expectation that encourages people to behave in a certain way. Since human beings are purposeful creatures, the study of Incentive structures is central to the study of all economic activity (both in terms of individual decision-making and in terms of co-operation and competition within a larger institutional structure.)

Regulation

Regulation refers to 'controlling human or societal behaviour by rules or restrictions.' Regulation can take many forms: legal restrictions promulgated by a government authority, self-Regulation, social Regulation, co-Regulation and market Regulation. One can consider Regulation as actions of conduct imposing sanctions (such as a fine.) This action of administrative law, or implementing regulatory law, may be contrasted with statutory or case law.

Bribery

Bribery, a form of pecuniary corruption, is an act implying money or gift given that alters the behaviour of the recipient. bribery constitutes a crime and is defined by Black's Law Dictionary as the offering, giving, receiving, or soliciting of any item of value to influence the actions of an official or other person in discharge of a public or legal duty. The bribe is the gift bestowed to influence the recipient's conduct.

Electronic commerce

Electronic commerce, commonly known as e-commerce or eCommerce, consists of the buying and selling of products or services over electronic systems such as the Internet and other computer networks. The amount of trade conducted electronically has grown extraordinarily with wide-spread Internet usage. A wide variety of commerce is conducted in this way, spurring and drawing on innovations in electronic funds transfer, supply chain management, Internet marketing, online transaction processing, electronic data interchange (EDI), inventory management systems, and automated data collection systems.

International business

International business is a term used to collectively describe topics relating to the operations of firms with interests in multiple countries. Such firms are sometimes called multinational corporations . Well known MNCs include fast food companies McDonald's and Yum Brands, vehicle manufacturers such as General Motors and Toyota, consumer electronics companies like Samsung, LG and Sony, and energy companies such as ExxonMobil and BP.

Culture

Culture is a term that has different meanings. For example, in 1952, Alfred Kroeber and Clyde Kluckhohn compiled a list of 164 definitions of culture in culture A Critical Review of Concepts and Definitions. However, the word culture is most commonly used in three basic senses:

· excellence of taste in the fine arts and humanities, also known as high culture
· an integrated pattern of human knowledge, belief, and behavior that depends upon the capacity for symbolic thought and social learning
· the set of shared attitudes, values, goals, and practices that characterizes an institution, organization or group.

When the concept first emerged in eighteenth- and nineteenth-century Europe, it connoted a process of cultivation or improvement, as in agri culture or horti culture . In the nineteenth century, it came to refer first to the betterment or refinement of the individual, especially through education, and then to the fulfillment of national aspirations or ideals.

Numerary

Numerary is a civil designation for persons who are incorporated in a fixed or permanent way to a society or group: regular member of the working staff, permanent staff distinguished from a super Numerary .

The term Numerary and its counterpart, 'super Numerary ,' originated in Spanish and Latin American academy and government; it is now also used in countries all over the world, such as France, the U.S., England, Italy, etc.

There are Numerary members of surgical organizations, of universities, of gastronomical associations, etc.

Federal Maritime Commission

The Federal Maritime Commission is an independent federal agency, based in Washington D.C., responsible for the regulation of oceanborne transportation in the foreign commerce of the U.S.

The Federal Maritime Commission:

· Regulates certain activities of international shipping lines (called 'ocean common carriers'), marine terminals operators, and ocean transportation intermediaries (OTIs) who operate in the U.S. foreign commerce

· Oversees the financial responsibility of cruise ship lines and other passenger ship operators, to ensure they have the resources to pay compensation for personal injuries or non-performance

· Monitors the laws and practices of foreign governments which could have a discriminatory or otherwise adverse impact on the U.S. shipping industry and U.S. maritime trade, and administers bilateral trade sanctions to persuade foreign governments to remove adverse conditions

· Enforces special regulatory requirements applicable to shipping lines owned or controlled by foreign governments (so-called 'controlled carriers')

· Reviews and regulates agreements between shipping lines and/or marine terminals (which enjoy statutory immunity from the antitrust laws) and service contracts between shipping lines and their customers

· Licenses and regulates ocean transportation intermediaries in the U.S., and ensures all maintain evidence of financial responsibility. These intermediaries include freight forwarders, who make bookings and process paperwork for shipper customers (roughly analogous to a travel agent for freight), and 'non-vessel-operating common carriers', who act as resellers of space on shipping lines' vessels.

The Federal Maritime Commission was established as an independent regulatory agency by Reorganization Plan No.

Market

A Market is any one of a variety of different systems, institutions, procedures, social relations and infrastructures whereby persons trade, and goods and services are exchanged, forming part of the economy. It is an arrangement that allows buyers and sellers to exchange things. Market s vary in size, range, geographic scale, location, types and variety of human communities, as well as the types of goods and services traded.

Fair Trade

Fair trade is an organized social movement and market-based approach that aims to help producers in developing countries and promote sustainability. The movement advocates the payment of a fair price as well as social and environmental standards in areas related to the production of a wide variety of goods. It focuses in particular on exports from developing countries to developed countries, most notably handicrafts, coffee, cocoa, sugar, tea, bananas, honey, cotton, wine, fresh fruit, chocolate and flowers.

Microsoft

Microsoft Corporation (NASDAQ: MSFT, HKEX: 4338) is an United States-based multinational computer technology corporation that develops, manufactures, licenses, and supports a wide range of software products for computing devices. Headquartered in Redmond, Washington, USA, its most profitable products are the Microsoft Windows operating system and the Microsoft Office suite of productivity software.

The company was founded to develop and sell BASIC interpreters for the Altair 8800.

Policy

A Policy is typically described as a deliberate plan of action to guide decisions and achieve rational outcome(s.) However, the term may also be used to denote what is actually done, even though it is unplanned.

The term may apply to government, private sector organizations and groups, and individuals.

Product liability

Product liability is the area of law in which manufacturers, distributors, suppliers, retailers, and others who make products available to the public are held responsible for the injuries those products cause.

In the United States, the claims most commonly associated with product liability are negligence, strict liability, breach of warranty, and various consumer protection claims. The majority of product liability laws are determined at the state level and vary widely from state to state.

Protectionism

Protectionism is the economic policy of restraining trade between nations, through methods such as tariffs on imported goods, restrictive quotas, and a variety of other restrictive government regulations designed to discourage imports, and prevent foreign take-over of local markets and companies. This policy is closely aligned with anti-globalization, and contrasts with free trade, where government barriers to trade are kept to a minimum. The term is mostly used in the context of economics, where Protectionism refers to policies or doctrines which 'protect' businesses and workers within a country by restricting or regulating trade with foreign nations.

Tort

Tort law is a body of law that addresses, and provides remedies for, civil wrongs not arising out of contractual obligations. A person who suffers legal damages may be able to use Tort law to receive compensation from someone who is legally responsible, or 'liable,' for those injuries. Generally speaking, Tort law defines what constitutes a legal injury and establishes the circumstances under which one person may be held liable for another's injury.

Trade barrier

A trade barrier is a general term that describes any government policy or regulation that restricts international trade. The barriers can take many forms, including the following terms that include many restrictions in international trade within multiple countries that import and export any items of trade.

· Import duty
· Import licenses
· Export licenses
· Import quotas
· Tariffs
· Subsidies
· Non-tariff barriers to trade
· Voluntary Export Restraints
· Local Content Requirements
· Embargo

Most trade barriers work on the same principle: the imposition of some sort of cost on trade that raises the price of the traded products. If two or more nations repeatedly use trade barriers against each other, then a trade war results.

Strict liability

Strict liability makes a person responsible for the damage and loss caused by his/her acts and omissions regardless of culpability .) Strict liability is important in torts (especially product liability), corporations law, and criminal law. For analysis of the pros and cons of Strict liability as applied to product liability, the most important Strict liability regime, see product liability.

Second Life

Second Life is a virtual world developed by Linden Lab that launched on June 23, 2003 and is accessible via the Internet. A free client program called the Second Life Viewer enables its users, called Residents, to interact with each other through avatars. Residents can explore, meet other residents, socialize, participate in individual and group activities, and create and trade virtual property and services with one another, or travel throughout the world, which residents refer to as the grid.

Kraft Foods

Kraft Foods Inc. (NYSE: Kraft Foods T) is the largest food and beverage company headquartered in the United States and the second largest in the world (after Nestlé SA.)

Kraft is headquartered in Northfield, Illinois, USA, a Chicago suburb.

Uncertainty	Uncertainty is a term used in subtly different ways in a number of fields, including philosophy, physics, statistics, economics, finance, insurance, psychology, sociology, engineering, and information science. It applies to predictions of future events, to physical measurements already made, or to the unknown. In his seminal work Risk, Uncertainty, and Profit University of Chicago economist Frank Knight (1921) established the important distinction between risk and Uncertainty: 'Uncertainty must be taken in a sense radically distinct from the familiar notion of risk, from which it has never been properly separated....
Bribe	Bribe ry, a form of pecuniary corruption, is an act implying money or gift given that alters the behaviour of the recipient. bribe ry constitutes a crime and is defined by Black's Law Dictionary as the offering, giving, receiving, or soliciting of any item of value to influence the actions of an official or other person in discharge of a public or legal duty. The bribe is the gift bestowed to influence the recipient's conduct.
Bribe payers index	Bribe Payers Index is a measure of how willing a nation appears to comply with demands for corrupt business practices. The first Bribe Payers Index was published by Transparency International on October 26, 1999. The Bribe Payers Index is a ranking of 22 of the leading exporting countries according to the propensity of firms with headquarters within their borders to bribe when operating abroad.
Corporate governance	Corporate governance is the set of processes, customs, policies, laws, and institutions affecting the way a corporation (or company) is directed, administered or controlled. Corporate governance also includes the relationships among the many stakeholders involved and the goals for which the corporation is governed. The principal stakeholders are the shareholders/members, management, and the board of directors.
Corporate scandal	A Corporate scandal is a scandal involving allegations of unethical behavior by people acting within or on behalf of a corporation. A Corporate scandal sometimes involves accounting fraud of some sort. A wave of such scandals swept United States companies in 2002
Financial Accounting Standards Board	The Financial Accounting Standards Board is a private, not-for-profit organization whose primary purpose is to develop generally accepted accounting principles (GAAP) within the United States in the public's interest. The Securities and Exchange Commission (SEC) designated the Financial Accounting Standards Board as the organization responsible for setting accounting standards for public companies in the U.S. It was created in 1973, replacing the Committee on Accounting Procedure (CAP) and the Accounting Principles Board (APB) of the American Institute of Certified Public Accountants (AICPA.) The Financial Accounting Standards Board's mission is 'to establish and improve standards of financial accounting and reporting for the guidance and education of the public, including issuers, auditors, and users of financial information.' To achieve this, Financial Accounting Standards Board has five goals:

· Improve the usefulness of financial reporting by focusing on the primary characteristics of relevance and reliability, and on the qualities of comparability and consistency.
· Keep standards current to reflect changes in methods of doing business and in the economy.
· Consider promptly any significant areas of deficiency in financial reporting that might be improved through standard setting.
· Promote international convergence of accounting standards concurrent with improving the quality of financial reporting.
· Improve common understanding of the nature and purposes of information in financial reports.

The Financial Accounting Standards Board is not a governmental body. The SEC has legal authority to establish financial accounting and reporting standards for publicly held companies under the Securities Exchange Act of 1934.

Generally accepted accounting principles

Generally accepted accounting principles is the term used to refer to the standard framework of guidelines for financial accounting used in any given jurisdiction. Generally accepted accounting principles includes the standards, conventions, and rules accountants follow in recording and summarizing transactions, and in the preparation of financial statements.

Financial accounting information must be assembled and reported objectively.

International Financial Reporting Standards

International Financial Reporting Standards are Standards, Interpretations and the Framework (in the absence of a Standard or an Interpretation) adopted by the International Accounting Standards Board (IASB.)

In the absence of a Standard or an Interpretation that specifically applies to a transaction, management must use its judgement in developing and applying an accounting policy that results in information that is relevant and reliable. In making that judgement, IAS 8.11 requires management to consider the definitions, recognition criteria, and measurement concepts for assets, liabilities, income, and expenses in the Framework.

Public Company

The term public company usually refers to a company that is permitted to offer its registered securities for sale to the general public, typically through a stock exchange, or occasionally a company whose stock is traded over the counter via market makers who use non-exchange quotation services.

The term 'public company' may also refer to a company owned by the government.

Public Company Accounting Oversight Board

The Public Company Accounting Oversight Board is a private-sector, non-profit corporation created by the Sarbanes-Oxley Act, a 2002 United States federal law, to oversee the auditors of public companies. Its stated purpose is to 'protect the interests of investors and further the public interest in the preparation of informative, fair, and independent audit reports'. Although a private entity, the Public Company Accounting Oversight Board has many government-like regulatory functions, making it in some ways similar to the private Self Regulatory Organizations (SROs) that regulate stock markets and other aspects of the financial markets in the United States.

Securities Exchange Act of 1934

The Securities Exchange Act of 1934 is a law governing the secondary trading of securities (stocks, bonds, and debentures) in the United States of America. The Act, 48 Stat. 881 (enacted June 6, 1934), codified at 15 U.S.C.

Securities and Exchange Commission	The U.S. Securities and Exchange Commission is an independent agency of the United States government which holds primary responsibility for enforcing the federal securities laws and regulating the securities industry, the nation's stock and options exchanges, and other electronic securities markets. The SEC was created by section 4 of the Securities Exchange Act of 1934 (now codified as 15 U.S.C. Â§ 78d and commonly referred to as the 1934 Act.)
Transparency	A high degree of market Transparency can result in disintermediation due to the buyer's increased knowledge of supply pricing. Transparency is important since it is one of the theoretical conditions required for a free market to be efficient. Price Transparency can, however, lead to higher prices, if it makes sellers reluctant to give steep discounts to certain buyers, or if it facilitates collusion.
Theory of the firm	The Theory of the firm consists of a number of economic theories which describe the nature of the firm, company including its existence, its behaviour, and its relationship with the market. In simplified terms, the Theory of the firm aims to answer these questions: · Existence - why do firms emerge, why are not all transactions in the economy mediated over the market? · Boundaries - why the boundary between firms and the market is located exactly there? Which transactions are performed internally and which are negotiated on the market? · Organization - why are firms structured in such specific way? What is the interplay of formal and informal relationships? The First World War period saw a change of emphasis in economic theory away from industry-level analysis which mainly included analysing markets to analysis at the level of the firm, as it became increasingly clear that perfect competition was no longer an adequate model of how firms behaved. Economic theory till then had focussed on trying to understand markets alone and there had been little study on understanding why firms or organisations exist. Market are mainly guided by prices as illustrated by vegetable markets where a buyer is free to switch sellers in an exchange.
Counterfeit	A Counterfeit product is an imitation which infringes upon a production monopoly held by either a state or corporation. Goods are produced with the intent to bypass this monopoly and thus take advantage of the established worth of the previous product. The word Counterfeit frequently describes both the forgeries of currency and documents, as well as the imitations of clothing, software, pharmaceuticals, watches, electronics, and company logos and brands.
American Bar Association	The American Bar Association , founded August 21, 1878, is a voluntary bar association of lawyers and law students, which is not specific to any jurisdiction in the United States. The American Bar Association's most important stated activities are the setting of academic standards for law schools, and the formulation of model ethical codes related to the legal profession. The American Bar Association has 410,000 members.
Cultural identity	Cultural identity is the identity of a group or culture, or of an individual as far as one is influenced by one's belonging to a group or culture. Cultural identity is similar to and has overlaps with, but is not synonymous with, identity politics. There are modern questions of culture that are transferred into questions of identity.

Bretton Woods system	The Bretton Woods system of monetary management established the rules for commercial and financial relations among the world's major industrial states in the mid 20th Century. The Bretton Woods system was the first example of a fully negotiated monetary order intended to govern monetary relations among independent nation-states. Preparing to rebuild the international economic system as World War II was still raging, 730 delegates from all 44 Allied nations gathered at the Mount Washington Hotel in Bretton Woods, New Hampshire, United States, for the United Nations Monetary and Financial Conference.
International Court of Justice	The International Court of Justice is the primary judicial organ of the United Nations. It is based in the Peace Palace in The Hague, Netherlands. Its main functions are to settle legal disputes submitted to it by states and to give advisory opinions on legal questions submitted to it by duly authorized international organs, agencies, and the UN General Assembly.
Money	Money is anything that is generally accepted as payment for goods and services and repayment of debts. The main uses of Money are as a medium of exchange, a unit of account, and a store of value. Some authors explicitly require Money to be a standard of deferred payment.
Money Laundering	Money laundering is the practice of disguising illegally obtained funds so that they seem legal. It is a crime in many jurisdictions with varying definitions. It is a key operation of the underground economy.
Task Force	A Task force is a temporary unit or formation established to work on a single defined task or activity. Originally introduced by the United States Navy, the term has now caught on for general usage and is a standard part of NATO terminology. Many non-military organizations now create ' Task force s' or task groups for temporary activities that might have once been performed by ad hoc committees.
Set TSP	In combinatorial optimization, the set TSP group TSP, One-of-a-set TSP, Multiple Choice TSP or Covering Salesman Problem, is a generalization of the Traveling salesman problem, whereby it is required to find a shortest tour in a graph which visits all specified disjoint subsets of the vertices of a graph. The ordinary TSP is a special case of the set TSP when all subsets to be visited are singletons. Therefore the set TSP is also NP-hard.
Big Mac index	The Big Mac Index is published by The Economist as an informal way of measuring the purchasing power parity (PPP) between two currencies and provides a test of the extent to which market exchange rates result in goods costing the same in different countries. It 'seeks to make exchange-rate theory a bit more digestible'.
Fixed exchange rate	A Fixed exchange rate, sometimes called a pegged exchange rate, is a type of exchange rate regime wherein a currency's value is matched to the value of another single currency or to a basket of other currencies or to another measure of value such as gold. A Fixed exchange rate is usually used to stabilize the value of a currency, vis-a-vis the currency it is pegged to. This facilitates trade and investments between the two countries, and is especially useful for small economies where external trade forms a large part of their GDP. It is also used as a means to control inflation.
Gold standard	The Gold standard is a monetary system in which a region's common medium of exchange are paper notes that are normally freely convertible into pre-set, fixed quantities of gold. The Gold standard is not currently used by any government, having been replaced completely by fiat currency. Gold certificates were used as paper currency in the United States from 1882 to 1933, these certificates were freely convertable into gold coins.

The use of paper money, convertible into gold, to replace gold coins, originated in China in the 9th century CE.

Embargo

An Embargo is the prohibition of commerce and trade with a certain country, in order to isolate it and to put its government into a difficult internal situation, given that the effects of the Embargo are often able to make its economy suffer from the initiative. It is similar to a blockade, as in 'el bloqueo' or the American blockade on Cuba.

Embargo s generally attempt to pressure weaker adversaries to do what the abarcading country wishes.

International trade

International trade is exchange of capital, goods, and services across international borders or territories. In most countries, it represents a significant share of gross domestic product (GDP.) While International trade has been present throughout much of history , its economic, social, and political importance has been on the rise in recent centuries.

Two-phase locking

In databases and transaction processing, Two-phase locking, (2PL) is a concurrency control locking protocol which guarantees serializability. It is also the name of the resulting class (set) of transaction schedules. Using locks that block processes, 2PL may be subject to deadlocks that result from the mutual blocking of two transactions or more.

Mercantilism

Mercantilism is an economic theory that holds that the prosperity of a nation is dependent upon its supply of capital, and that the global volume of international trade is 'unchangeable.' Economic assets or capital, are represented by bullion (gold, silver, and trade value) held by the state, which is best increased through a positive balance of trade with other nations (exports minus imports.) Mercantilism suggests that the ruling government should advance these goals by playing a protectionist role in the economy; by encouraging exports and discouraging imports, notably through the use of tariffs and subsidies.

Mercantilism was the dominant school of thought throughout the early modern period (from the 16th to the 18th century.)

Exchange rate

In finance, the Exchange rate s between two currencies specifies how much one currency is worth in terms of the other. It is the value of a foreign nation's currency in terms of the home nation's currency. For example an Exchange rate of 95 Japanese yen to the United States dollar means that JPY 95 is worth the same as USD 1.

Par value

Par value, in finance and accounting, means stated value or face value. From this comes the expressions at par (at the par value), over par (over par value) and under par (under par value.)

The term 'par value' has several meanings depending on context and geography.

United States

The United States of America (commonly referred to as the United States the U.S., the United States A, or America) is a federal constitutional republic comprising fifty states and a federal district. The country is situated mostly in central North America, where its 48 contiguous states and Washington, D.C., the capital district, lie between the Pacific and Atlantic Oceans, bordered by Canada to the north and Mexico to the south. The state of Alaska is in the northwest of the continent, with Canada to its east and Russia to the west across the Bering Strait.

Advocate

An Advocate is one who speaks on behalf of another person, especially in a legal context. It is used primarily in reference to the system of Scots law, Anglo-Dutch law, Scandinavian and Israeli law. Implicit in the concept is the notion that the represented lacks the knowledge, skill, ability, or standing to speak for themselves.

Business	A business is a legally recognized organization designed to provide goods and/or services to consumers. business es are predominant in capitalist economies, most being privately owned and formed to earn profit that will increase the wealth of its owners and grow the business itself. The owners and operators of a business have as one of their main objectives the receipt or generation of a financial return in exchange for work and acceptance of risk.
Inflation	In economics, Inflation is a rise in the general level of prices of goods and services in an economy over a period of time. The term 'Inflation' once referred to increases in the money supply (monetary Inflation); however, economic debates about the relationship between money supply and price levels have led to its primary use today in describing price Inflation. Inflation can also be described as a decline in the real value of money--a loss of purchasing power in the medium of exchange which is also the monetary unit of account.
Market	A Market is any one of a variety of different systems, institutions, procedures, social relations and infrastructures whereby persons trade, and goods and services are exchanged, forming part of the economy. It is an arrangement that allows buyers and sellers to exchange things. Market s vary in size, range, geographic scale, location, types and variety of human communities, as well as the types of goods and services traded.
Managed float regime	Managed float regime is the current international financial environment in which exchange rates fluctuate from day to day, but central banks attempt to influence their countries' exchange rates by buying and selling currencies. It is also known as a dirty float. In an increasingly integrated world economy, the currency rates impact any given country's economy through the trade balance.
Floating currency	A Floating currency is a currency that uses a floating exchange rate as its exchange rate regime. A Floating currency is contrasted with a fixed currency. In the modern world, the majority of the world's currencies are officially but not really floating, including the most widely traded currencies: the United States dollar, the Japanese yen, the euro, the British pound and the Australian dollar.
Foreign exchange market	The foreign exchange market is where currency trading takes place. It is where banks and other official institutions facilitate the buying and selling of foreign currencies. FX transactions typically involve one party purchasing a quantity of one currency in exchange for paying a quantity of another.
Special drawing rights	Special Drawing Rights (Special Drawing Rights s) are potential claims on the freely usable currencies of International Monetary Fund members. Special Drawing Rights s have the ISO 4217 currency code XDR. Special Drawing Rights s are defined in terms of a basket of major currencies used in international trade and finance. At present, the currencies in the basket are, by weight, the United States dollar, the euro, the Japanese yen, and the pound sterling.
Floating exchange rate	A Floating exchange rate or a flexible exchange rate is a type of exchange rate regime wherein a currency's value is allowed to fluctuate according to the foreign exchange market. A currency that uses a Floating exchange rate is known as a floating currency. The opposite of a Floating exchange rate is a fixed exchange rate.

Paradox	A Paradox is a statement or group of statements that leads to a contradiction or a situation which defies intuition; or, it can be an apparent contradiction that actually expresses a non-dual truth (cf. Koan, Catuskoti.) Typically, either the statements in question do not really imply the contradiction, the puzzling result is not really a contradiction, or the premises themselves are not all really true or cannot all be true together.
Price	Price in economics and business is the result of an exchange and from that trade we assign a numerical monetary value to a good, service or asset. If I trade 4 apples for an orange, the price of an orange is 4 - apples. Inversely, the price of an apple is 1/4 oranges.
Euro	The Euro (â,¬) is the official currency of 16 of the 27 member states of the Euro pean Union (EU.) The states, known collectively as the Euro zone, are Austria, Belgium, Cyprus, Finland, France, Germany, Greece, Ireland, Italy, Luxembourg, Malta, the Netherlands, Portugal, Slovakia, Slovenia, and Spain. The currency is also used in a further five Euro pean countries, with and without formal agreements and is consequently used daily by some 327 million Euro peans.
Asset	In business and accounting, asset s are economic resources owned by business or company. Anything tangible or intangible that one possesses, usually considered as applicable to the payment of one's debts is considered an asset Simplistically stated, asset s are things of value that can be readily converted into cash.
Legal tender	Legal tender or forced tender is payment that, by law, cannot be refused in settlement of a debt. Legal tender is variously defined in different jurisdictions. Formally, it is anything which when offered in payment extinguishes the debt.
Numerary	Numerary is a civil designation for persons who are incorporated in a fixed or permanent way to a society or group: regular member of the working staff, permanent staff distinguished from a super Numerary . The term Numerary and its counterpart, 'super Numerary ,' originated in Spanish and Latin American academy and government; it is now also used in countries all over the world, such as France, the U.S., England, Italy, etc. There are Numerary members of surgical organizations, of universities, of gastronomical associations, etc.
Monetary	Monetary policy is the process by which the government, central bank (ii) availability of money, and (iii) cost of money or rate of interest, in order to attain a set of objectives oriented towards the growth and stability of the economy. monetary theory provides insight into how to craft optimal monetary policy. monetary policy is referred to as either being an expansionary policy where an expansionary policy increases the total supply of money in the economy, and a contractionary policy decreases the total money supply.
Central bank	A central bank, reserve bank, or monetary authority is the entity responsible for the monetary policy of a country or of a group of member states. It is a bank that can lend money to other banks in times of need. Its primary responsibility is to maintain the stability of the national currency and money supply, but more active duties include controlling subsidized-loan interest rates, and acting as a lender of last resort to the banking sector during times of financial crisis (private banks often being integral to the national financial system.)
Monetary system	A Monetary system secures the proper functioning of money by regulating economic agents, transaction types, and money supply.

Monetary system s are traditionally formed by the policy decisions of individual governments and administrated as a domestic economic issue.

The current trend, however, is to use international trade and investment to alter the policy and legislation of individual governments.

Arbitrage

In economics and finance, Arbitrage is the practice of taking advantage of a price differential between two or more markets: striking a combination of matching deals that capitalize upon the imbalance, the profit being the difference between the market prices. When used by academics, an Arbitrage is a transaction that involves no negative cash flow at any probabilistic or temporal state and a positive cash flow in at least one state; in simple terms, a risk-free profit. A person who engages in Arbitrage is called an Arbitrage ur--such as a bank or brokerage firm.

Bid/offer spread

The bid/offer spread for securities is the difference between the price quoted by a market maker for an immediate sale and an immediate purchase The size of the bid-offer spread in a given commodity is a measure of the liquidity of the market and the size of the transaction cost.

The trader initiating the transaction is said to demand liquidity, and the other party to the transaction supplies liquidity.

Fiscal policy

In economics, fiscal policy is the use of government spending and revenue collection to influence the economy.

fiscal policy can be contrasted with the other main type of economic policy, monetary policy, which attempts to stabilize the economy by controlling interest rates and the supply of money. The two main instruments of fiscal policy are government spending and taxation.

Law of one price

The Law of one price is an economic law stated as: 'In an efficient market all identical goods must have only one price.' The Law of one price relates to the outcome of free trade and globalization. It is the theory that some day all areas of the world will make the same amount of money as every other part of the world for equal work/product quality.

The intuition for this law is that all sellers will flock to the highest prevailing price, and all buyers to the lowest current market price.

Monetary policy

Monetary policy is the process by which the government, central bank or monetary authority of a country controls (i) the supply of money (ii) availability of money, and (iii) cost of money or rate of interest, in order to attain a set of objectives oriented towards the growth and stability of the economy. Monetary theory provides insight into how to craft optimal Monetary policy.

Monetary policy is referred to as either being an expansionary policy where an expansionary policy increases the total supply of money in the economy, and a contractionary policy decreases the total money supply.

Spot price

The spot price or spot rate of a commodity, a security or a currency is the price that is quoted for immediate (spot) settlement (payment and delivery.) Spot settlement is normally one or two business days from trade date. This is in contrast with the forward price established in a forward contract or futures contract, where contract terms (price) are set now, but delivery and payment will occur at a future date.

Average

In mathematics, an average, or central tendency of a data set refers to a measure of the 'middle' or 'expected' value of the data set. There are many different descriptive statistics that can be chosen as a measurement of the central tendency of the data items.

An average is a single value that is meant to typify a list of values.

Turnover	In a human resources context, turnover or labor turnover is the rate at which an employer gains and loses employees. Simple ways to describe it are 'how long employees tend to stay' or 'the rate of traffic through the revolving door.' turnover is measured for individual companies and for their industry as a whole. If an employer is said to have a high turnover relative to its competitors, it means that employees of that company have a shorter average tenure than those of other companies in the same industry.
Gross domestic product	The Gross domestic product or gross domestic income (GDI), a basic measure of an economy's economic performance, is the market value of all final goods and services produced within the borders of a nation in a year. Gross domestic product can be defined in three ways, all of which are conceptually identical. First, it is equal to the total expenditures for all final goods and services produced within the country in a stipulated period of time (usually a 365-day year.)
Interest rate	An Interest rate is the price a borrower pays for the use of money they do not own, for instance a small company might borrow from a bank to kick start their business, and the return a lender receives for deferring the use of funds, by lending it to the borrower. Interest rate s are normally expressed as a percentage rate over the period of one year. Interest rate s targets are also a vital tool of monetary policy and are used to control variables like investment, inflation, and unemployment.
International Fisher effect	The International Fisher effect is a hypothesis in international finance that says that the difference in the nominal interest rates between two countries determines the movement of the nominal exchange rate between their currencies, with the value of the currency of the country with the lower nominal interest rate increasing. This is also known as the assumption of Uncovered Interest Parity. The Fisher hypothesis says that the real interest rate in an economy is independent of monetary variables.
Purchasing	Purchasing refers to a business or organization attempting to acquire goods or services to accomplish the goals of the enterprise. Though there are several organizations that attempt to set standards in the Purchasing process, processes can vary greatly between organizations. Typically the word 'Purchasing' is not used interchangeably with the word 'procurement', since procurement typically includes Expediting, Supplier Quality, and Traffic and Logistics (T'L) in addition to Purchasing.
Purchasing power	Purchasing power is the number of goods/services that can be purchased with a unit of currency. For example, if you had taken one dollar to a store in the 1950s, you would have been able to buy a greater number of items than you would today, indicating that you would have had a greater purchasing power in the 1950s. Currency can be either a commodity money, like gold or silver, or fiat currency like US dollars which are the world reserve currency.
Purchasing power parity	The Purchasing power parity theory uses the long-term equilibrium exchange rate of two currencies to equalize their purchasing power. Developed by Gustav Cassel in 1918, it is based on the law of one price: the theory states that, in ideally efficient markets, identical goods should have only one price. This purchasing power SEM rate equalizes the purchasing power of different currencies in their home countries for a given basket of goods.

Efficient-market hypothesis	In finance, the efficient-market hypothesis asserts that financial markets are 'informationally efficient' stocks, bonds and instantly change to reflect new information. Therefore it is impossible to consistently outperform the market by using any information that the market already knows, except through luck. Information or news in the EMH is defined as anything that may affect prices that is unknowable in the present and thus appears randomly in the future.
Fundamental analysis	Fundamental analysis of a business involves analyzing its financial statements and health, its management and competitive advantages, and its competitors and markets. The term is used to distinguish such analysis from other types of investment analysis, such as quantitative analysis and technical analysis. Fundamental analysis is performed on historical and present data, but with the goal of making financial forecasts.
International Trade Commission	The United States International Trade Commission is an independent, non-partisan, quasi-judicial, federal agency of the United States that provides trade expertise to both the legislative and executive branches. Further, the agency determines the impact of imports on U.S. industries and directs actions against certain unfair trade practices, such as dumping, patent, trademark, and copyright infringement. The US International Trade Commission was established by the U.S. Congress in 1916 as the U.S. Tariff Commission (the Trade Act of 1974 changed its name to the U.S. International Trade Commission , the agency has broad investigative powers on matters of trade.
Tariff	A Tariff is a duty imposed on goods when they are moved across a political boundary. They are usually associated with protectionism, the economic policy of restraining trade between nations. For political reasons, Tariff s are usually imposed on imported goods, although they may also be imposed on exported goods.
Technical analysis	Technical analysis is a security analysis discipline for forecasting the future direction of prices through the study of past market data, primarily price and volume. In its purest form, Technical analysis considers only the actual price and volume behavior of the market or instrument. Technical analysts may employ models and trading rules based on price and volume transformations, such as the relative strength index, moving averages, regressions, inter-market and intra-market price correlations, cycles or, classically, through recognition of chart patterns.
Black market	The underground economy or Black market is a market where all commerce is conducted without regard to taxation, law or regulations of trade. The term is also often known as the underdog, shadow economy, black economy, parallel economy or phantom trades. In modern societies the underground economy covers a vast array of activities.
Theory of the firm	The Theory of the firm consists of a number of economic theories which describe the nature of the firm, company including its existence, its behaviour, and its relationship with the market. In simplified terms, the Theory of the firm aims to answer these questions: · Existence - why do firms emerge, why are not all transactions in the economy mediated over the market? · Boundaries - why the boundary between firms and the market is located exactly there? Which transactions are performed internally and which are negotiated on the market? · Organization - why are firms structured in such specific way? What is the interplay of formal and informal relationships?

The First World War period saw a change of emphasis in economic theory away from industry-level analysis which mainly included analysing markets to analysis at the level of the firm, as it became increasingly clear that perfect competition was no longer an adequate model of how firms behaved. Economic theory till then had focussed on trying to understand markets alone and there had been little study on understanding why firms or organisations exist. Market are mainly guided by prices as illustrated by vegetable markets where a buyer is free to switch sellers in an exchange.

Cuba

The Republic of Cuba) is an island country in the Caribbean. It consists of the island of Cuba, the Isla de la Juventud, and several archipelagos.

Havana is the largest city in Cuba and the country's capital.

Foreign exchange controls

Foreign exchange controls are various forms of controls imposed by a government on the purchase/sale of foreign currencies by residents or on the purchase/sale of local currency by nonresidents.

Common Foreign exchange controls include:

· Banning the use of foreign currency within the country
· Banning locals from possessing foreign currency
· Restricting currency exchange to government-approved exchangers
· Fixed exchange rates
· Restrictions on the amount of currency that may be imported or exported

Countries with Foreign exchange controls are also known as 'Article 14 countries,' after the provision in the International Monetary Fund agreement allowing exchange controls for transitional economies. Such controls used to be common in most countries, particularly poorer ones, until the 1990s when free trade and globalization started a trend towards economic liberalization. Today, countries which still impose exchange controls are the exception rather than the rule.

Hard currency

Hard currency or strong currency, in economics, refers to a globally traded currency that can serve as a reliable and stable store of value. Factors contributing to a currency's hard status can include political stability, low inflation, consistent monetary and fiscal policies, backing by reserves of precious metals, and long-term stable or upward-trending valuation against other currencies on a trade-weighted basis.

As of 2008, hard currencies could be argued to include the United States dollar, euro, Swiss franc, British pound sterling, Norwegian krone, Swedish krona, Canadian dollar, Japanese yen, and Australian dollar.

International Finance

International finance is the branch of economics that studies the dynamics of exchange rates, foreign investment, and how these affect international trade. It also studies international projects, international investments and capital flows, and trade deficits. It includes the study of futures, options and currency swaps.

Procter ' Gamble

Procter is a surname, and may also refer to:

· Bryan Waller Procter (pseud. Barry Cornwall), English poet
· Goodwin Procter, American law firm
· Procter ' Gamble, consumer products multinational .

Control	Control is one of the managerial functions like planning, organizing, staffing and directing. It is an important function because it helps to check the errors and to take the corrective action so that deviation from standards are minimized and stated goals of the organization are achieved in desired manner.According to modern concepts, Control is a foreseeing action whereas earlier concept of Control was used only when errors were detected. Control in management means setting standards, measuring actual performance and taking corrective action.
Free market	A free market is a theoretical term that economists use to describe a market which is free from government intervention (i.e. no regulation, no subsidization, no single monetary system and no governmental monopolies.) In a free market, property rights are voluntarily exchanged at a price arranged solely by the mutual consent of sellers and buyers. By definition, buyers and sellers do not coerce each other, in the sense that they obtain each other's property without the use of physical force, threat of physical force, or fraud, nor is the coerced by a third party (such as by government via transfer payments) and they engage in trade simply because they both consent and believe that it is a good enough choice.
Income tax	An income tax is a tax levied on the income of individuals or business (corporations or other legal entities.) Various income tax systems exist, with varying degrees of tax incidence. income tax ation can be progressive, proportional, or regressive.
Tunisia	Tunisia , officially the Tunisia n Republic , is a country located in North Africa. It is bordered by Algeria to the west and Libya to the southeast. It is also located southwest of the island of Sicily and south of Sardinia.
Withholding	Withholding, in general, usually refers to a deduction of money (as 'withholding tax') from an employee's wages or salary by an employer, for projected or actual Income tax liabilities, see: · PAYE (United Kingdom, Ireland, Australia and New Zealand) · Tax withholding in the United States .
Argentina	Argentina, officially the Argentine Republic , is a country in South America, constituted as a federation of 23 provinces and an autonomous city, Buenos Aires. It is the second largest country in South America and eighth in the world by land area and the largest among Spanish-speaking nations, though Mexico, Colombia and Spain are more populous. Its continental area is 2,766,890 km^2 , between the Andes mountain range in the west and the southern Atlantic Ocean in the east and south.
Corporate tax	Corporate tax refers to a tax levied by various jurisdictions on the profits made by companies or associations. It is a tax on the value of the corporation's profits. The measure of taxable profits varies from country to country.
Inflation rate	In economics, the Inflation rate is a measure of inflation, the rate of increase of a price index (for example, a consumer price index.)It is the percentage rate of change in price level over time. The rate of decrease in the purchasing power of money is approximately equal. It's used to calculate the real interest rate, as well as real increases in wages, and official measurements of this rate act as input variables to COLA adjustments and Inflation derivatives prices.

Bribery	Bribery, a form of pecuniary corruption, is an act implying money or gift given that alters the behaviour of the recipient. bribery constitutes a crime and is defined by Black's Law Dictionary as the offering, giving, receiving, or soliciting of any item of value to influence the actions of an official or other person in discharge of a public or legal duty. The bribe is the gift bestowed to influence the recipient's conduct.
Capital expenditure	Capital expenditure s (CAPEX or capex) are expenditures creating future benefits. A capital expenditure is incurred when a business spends money either to buy fixed assets or to add to the value of an existing fixed asset with a useful life that extends beyond the taxable year. Capex are used by a company to acquire or upgrade physical assets such as equipment, property, or industrial buildings.
Consumer	Consumer is a broad label that refers to any individuals or households that use goods and services generated within the economy. The concept of a Consumer is used in different contexts, so that the usage and significance of the term may vary. A Consumer is a person who uses any product or service.
Consumer price index	A Consumer Price Index is a measure of the average price of consumer goods and services purchased by households. It is a price index determined by measuring the price of a standard group of goods meant to represent the typical market basket of a typical urban consumer. Related, but different, terms are the Consumer Price Index, the RPI, and the RPIX used in the United Kingdom.
Mercosur	MERCOSUR or Mercosul is a Regional Trade Agreement among Argentina, Brazil, Paraguay and Uruguay founded in 1991 by the Treaty of Asunción, which was later amended and updated by the 1994 Treaty of Ouro Preto. Its purpose is to promote free trade and the fluid movement of goods, people, and currency. MERCOSUR origins trace back to 1985 when Presidents Raúl Alfonsín of Argentina and José Sarney of Brazil signed the Argentina-Brazil Integration and Economics Cooperation Program or PICE .
Balance of payments	In economics, the Balance of payments, (or Balance of payments) measures the payments that flow between any individual country and all other countries. It is used to summarize all international economic transactions for that country during a specific time period, usually a year. The Balance of payments is determined by the country's exports and imports of goods, services, and financial capital, as well as financial transfers.
English	English is a West Germanic language that originated in Anglo-Saxon England. As a result of the military, economic, scientific, political and cultural influence of the British Empire during the 18th, 19th and 20th centuries and of the United States since the late 19th century, it has become the lingua franca in many parts of the world. It is used extensively as a second language and as an official language in Commonwealth countries and many international organizations.
Long-run	In economic models, the long-run time frame assumes no fixed factors of production. Firms can enter or leave the marketplace, and the cost (and availability) of land, labor, raw materials, and capital goods can be assumed to vary. In contrast, in the short-run time frame, certain factors are assumed to be fixed, because there is not sufficient time for them to change.

Organization

An organization is a social arrangement which pursues collective goals, which controls its own performance, and which has a boundary separating it from its environment. The word itself is derived from the Greek word á½„ργανον (organon [itself derived from the better-known word á¼"ργον ergon - work; deed - > ergonomics, etc]) meaning tool. The term is used in both daily and scientific English in multiple ways.

World Trade Organization

The World Trade Organization is an international organization designed to supervise and liberalize international trade. The World Trade Organization came into being on 1 January 1995, and is the successor to the General Agreement on Tariffs and Trade (GATT), which was created in 1947, and continued to operate for almost five decades as a de facto international organization.

The World Trade Organization deals with the rules of trade between nations at a near-global level; it is responsible for negotiating and implementing new trade agreements, and is in charge of policing member countries' adherence to all the World Trade Organization agreements, signed by the majority of the world's trading nations and ratified in their parliaments.

Characteristic

Characteristic has several particular meanings:

· in mathematics

- · Euler characteristic
- · method of characteristic s (partial differential equations)

· in physics and engineering

· any characteristic curve that shows the relationship between certain input- and output parameters, e.g.
· an I-V or current-voltage characteristic is the current in a circuit as a function of the applied voltage
· Receiver-Operator characteristic
· in navigation, the characteristic pattern of a lighted beacon.
· in fiction

· in Dungeons ' Dragons, characteristic is another name for ability score .

Manufacturing

Manufacturing is the application of tools and a processing medium to the transformation of raw materials into finished goods for sale. This effort includes all intermediate processes required for the production and integration of a product's components. Some industries, like semiconductor and steel manufacturers use the term fabrication instead.

Capital account

In financial accounting, the Capital account is one of the accounts in shareholders' equity. Sole proprietorships have a single Capital account in the owner's equity. Partnerships maintain a Capital account for each of the partners.

Current account

In economics, the Current account is one of the two primary components of the balance of payments, the other being the capital account. It is the sum of the balance of trade (exports minus imports of goods and services), net factor income (such as interest and dividends) and net transfer payments (such as foreign aid.)

$$\begin{aligned}\text{Current account} = {} & \text{Balance of trade}\\ & + \text{Net factor income from abroad}\\ & + \text{Net unilateral transfers from abroad}\end{aligned}$$

The Current account balance is one of two major metrics of the nature of a country's foreign trade (the other being the net capital outflow.)

Investment	Investment or investing is a term with several closely-related meanings in business management, finance and economics, related to saving or deferring consumption. Investing is the active redirecting resources from being consumed today so that they may create benefits in the future; the use of assets to earn income or profit. An Investment is the choice by the individual to risk his savings with the hope of gain.
Commodities exchange	A Commodities exchange is an exchange where various commodities and derivatives products are traded. Most commodity markets across the world trade in agricultural products and other raw materials (like wheat, barley, sugar, maize, cotton, cocoa, coffee, milk products, pork bellies, oil, metals, etc.) and contracts based on them.
Net worth	In business, net worth is the total liabilities minus total outside assets of an individual or a company. For a company, this is called shareholders' preference and may be referred to as book value. net worth is stated as at a particular year in time.

Fair Trade

Fair trade is an organized social movement and market-based approach that aims to help producers in developing countries and promote sustainability. The movement advocates the payment of a fair price as well as social and environmental standards in areas related to the production of a wide variety of goods. It focuses in particular on exports from developing countries to developed countries, most notably handicrafts, coffee, cocoa, sugar, tea, bananas, honey, cotton, wine, fresh fruit, chocolate and flowers.

Industry

An Industry is the manufacturing of a good or service within a category. Although Industry is a broad term for any kind of economic production, in economics and urban planning Industry is a synonym for the secondary sector, which is a type of economic activity involved in the manufacturing of raw materials into goods and products.

There are four key industrial economic sectors: the primary sector, largely raw material extraction industries such as mining and farming; the secondary sector, involving refining, construction, and manufacturing; the tertiary sector, which deals with services (such as law and medicine) and distribution of manufactured goods; and the quaternary sector, a relatively new type of knowledge Industry focusing on technological research, design and development such as computer programming, and biochemistry.

International Trade

International trade is exchange of capital, goods, and services across international borders or territories. In most countries, it represents a significant share of gross domestic product (GDP.) While International trade has been present throughout much of history , its economic, social, and political importance has been on the rise in recent centuries.

Outsourcing

Outsourcing is subcontracting a process, such as product design or manufacturing, to a third-party company. The decision to outsource is often made in the interest of lowering cost or making better use of time and energy costs, redirecting or conserving energy directed at the competencies of a particular business, or to make more efficient use of land, labor, capital, (information) technology and resources. outsourcing became part of the business lexicon during the 1980s.

Economic

An economy (or 'the economy') is the realized Economic system of a country or other area. It includes the production, exchange, distribution, and consumption of goods and services of that area. The study of different types and examples of economies is the subject of Economic systems.

Expatriate

An expatriate is a person temporarily or permanently residing in a country and culture other than that of the person's upbringing or legal residence. The word comes from the Latin ex and patria (country, fatherland.)

The term is sometimes used in the context of Westerners living in non-Western countries, although it is also used to describe Westerners living in other Western countries, such as U.S. citizens living in the United Kingdom, or Britons living in Spain.

Pension

In general, a Pension is an arrangement to provide people with an income when they are no longer earning a regular income from employment.

The terms retirement plan or superannuation refer to a Pension granted upon retirement . Retirement plans may be set up by employers, insurance companies, the government or other institutions such as employer associations or trade unions.

Procter ' Gamble

Procter is a surname, and may also refer to:

· Bryan Waller Procter (pseud. Barry Cornwall), English poet
· Goodwin Procter, American law firm
· Procter ' Gamble, consumer products multinational .

Skill

A skill is the learned capacity to carry out pre-determined results often with the minimum outlay of time, energy, or both. skill s can often be divided into domain-general and domain-specific skill s. For example, in the domain of work, some general skill s would include time management, teamwork and leadership, self motivation and others, whereas domain-specific skill s would be useful only for a certain job.

Liabilities

The accounting equation relates assets, liabilities, and owner's equity:

Assets = liabilities + Owner's Equity

The accounting equation is the mathematical structure of the balance sheet.
The Australian Accounting Research Foundation defines liabilities as: 'future sacrifice of economic benefits that the entity is presently obliged to make to other entities as a result of past transactions and other past events.'
Probably the most accepted accounting definition of liability is the one used by the International Accounting Standards Board (IASB.) The following is a quotation from IFRS Framework:

A liability is a present obligation of the enterprise arising from past events, the settlement of which is expected to result in an outflow from the enterprise of resources embodying economic benefits

-

Regulations as to the recognition of liabilities are different all over the world, but are roughly similar to those of the IASB.

Demographic

Demographic or Demographic data refers to selected population characteristics as used in government, marketing or opinion research, or the Demographic profiles used in such research. Note the distinction from the term 'demography' Commonly-used Demographic include race, age, income, disabilities, mobility (in terms of travel time to work or number of vehicles available), educational attainment, home ownership, employment status, and even location.

Developed country

The term developed country is used to describe countries that have a high level of development according to some criteria. Which criteria, and which countries are classified as being developed, is a contentious issue and there is fierce debate about this. Economic criteria have tended to dominate discussions.

Population

In biology, a Population , is the collection of inter-breeding organisms of a particular species; in sociology, a collection of human beings. Individuals within a Population share a factor may be reduced by statistical means, but such a generalization may be too vague to imply anything. Demography is used extensively in marketing, which relates to economic units, such as retailers, to potential customers.

Workforce

The workforce is the labour pool in employment. It is generally used to describe those working for a single company or industry, but can also apply to a geographic region like a city, country, state, etc. The term generally excludes the employers or management, and implies those involved in manual labour.

World population

The world population is the total number of living humans on Earth at a given time. As of March 2009, the world's population is estimated to be about 6.76 billion. The world population has been growing continuously since the end of the Black Death around 1400.

Population ageing

Population ageing occurs when the median age of a country or region rises. With the exception of 18 countries termed by the United Nations 'demographic outliers' this process is taking place in every country and region across the globe.

Population ageing is constituted by a shift in the distribution of a country's population towards greater ages.

Characteristic

Characteristic has several particular meanings:

· in mathematics

- · Euler characteristic
- · method of characteristic s (partial differential equations)

· in physics and engineering

· any characteristic curve that shows the relationship between certain input- and output parameters, e.g.
· an I-V or current-voltage characteristic is the current in a circuit as a function of the applied voltage
· Receiver-Operator characteristic
· in navigation, the characteristic pattern of a lighted beacon.
· in fiction

· in Dungeons ' Dragons, characteristic is another name for ability score .

Child labour

Child labour refers to the employment of children at regular and sustained labour. This practice is considered exploitative by many international organizations and is illegal in many countries. Child labour was utilized to varying extents through most of history, but entered public dispute with the beginning of universal schooling, with changes in working conditions during industrialization, and with the emergence of the concepts of workers' and children's rights.

Distribution

Distribution is one of the four elements of marketing mix. An organization or set of organizations (go-betweens) involved in the process of making a product or service available for use or consumption by a consumer or business user.

The other three parts of the marketing mix are product, pricing, and promotion.

Manufacturing

Manufacturing is the application of tools and a processing medium to the transformation of raw materials into finished goods for sale. This effort includes all intermediate processes required for the production and integration of a product's components. Some industries, like semiconductor and steel manufacturers use the term fabrication instead.

Population growth

Population growth is the change in population over time, and can be quantified as the change in the number of individuals in a population using 'per unit time' for measurement. The term Population growth can technically refer to any species, but almost always refers to humans, and it is often used informally for the more specific demographic term Population growth rate , and is often used to refer specifically to the growth of the population of the world.

Simple models of Population growth include the Malthusian Growth Model and the logistic model.

Sector

In the context of computer disk storage, a sector is a subdivision of a track (Figure 1, item A) on a magnetic disk or optical disc. Each sector stores a fixed amount of data. The typical formatting of these media provides space for 512 bytes (for magnetic disks) or 2048 bytes (for optical discs) of user-accessible data per sector.

Comparative advertising

Comparative advertising is an advertisement in which a particular product specifically mentions a competitor by name for the express purpose of showing why the competitor is inferior to the product naming it.

This should not be confused with parody advertisements, where a fictional product is being advertised for the purpose of poking fun at the particular advertisement, nor should it be confused with the use of a coined brand name for the purpose of comparing the product without actually naming an actual competitor. ('Wikipedia tastes better and is less filling than the Encyclopedia Galactica.')

In the 1980s, during what has been referred to as the cola wars, soft-drink manufacturer Pepsi ran a series of advertisements where people, caught on hidden camera, in a blind taste test, chose Pepsi over rival Coca-Cola.

Tertiary sector of economy

The tertiary sector of economy is one of the three economic sectors, the others being the secondary sector and the primary sector The general definition of the Tertiary sector is producing a service instead of just a end product, in the case of the secondary sector. Sometimes an additional sector, the 'quaternary sector', is defined for the sharing of information

Labor mobility

Labor mobility or worker mobility is the socioeconomic ease with which an individual or groups of individuals who are currently receiving remuneration in the form of wages can take advantage of various economic opportunities.

Worker mobility is best gauged by the lack of impediments to such mobility. Impediments to mobility are easily divided into two distinct classes with one being personal and the other being systemic.

Urbanization

Urbanization is the physical growth of urban areas from rural areas as a result of population immigration to an existing urban area. Effects include change in density and administration services. While the exact definition and population size of urbanized areas varies among different countries, Urbanization is attributed to growth of cities.

Cost

In economics, business, retail, and accounting, a cost is the value of money that has been used up to produce something, and hence is not available for use anymore. In economics, a cost is an alternative that is given up as a result of a decision. In business, the cost may be one of acquisition, in which case the amount of money expended to acquire it is counted as cost.

Cost of living

Cost of living is the cost of maintaining a certain standard of living. Changes in the Cost of living over time are often operationalized in a Cost of living index. Cost of living calculations are also used to compare the cost of maintaining a certain standard of living in different geographic areas.

Triple bottom line

The Triple bottom line captures an expanded spectrum of values and criteria for measuring organizational success: economic, ecological and social. With the ratification of the United Nations and ICLEI Triple bottom line standard for urban and community accounting in early 2007, this became the dominant approach to public sector full cost accounting. Similar UN standards apply to natural capital and human capital measurement to assist in measurements required by Triple bottom line, e.g. the ecoBudget standard for reporting ecological footprint.

Investment	Investment or investing is a term with several closely-related meanings in business management, finance and economics, related to saving or deferring consumption. Investing is the active redirecting resources from being consumed today so that they may create benefits in the future; the use of assets to earn income or profit. An Investment is the choice by the individual to risk his savings with the hope of gain.
Mercosur	MERCOSUR or Mercosul is a Regional Trade Agreement among Argentina, Brazil, Paraguay and Uruguay founded in 1991 by the Treaty of Asunción, which was later amended and updated by the 1994 Treaty of Ouro Preto. Its purpose is to promote free trade and the fluid movement of goods, people, and currency. MERCOSUR origins trace back to 1985 when Presidents Raúl Alfonsín of Argentina and José Sarney of Brazil signed the Argentina-Brazil Integration and Economics Cooperation Program or PICE .
Unemployment	Unemployment occurs when a person is available to work and seeking work but currently without work. The prevalence of Unemployment is usually measured using the Unemployment rate, which is defined as the percentage of those in the labor force who are unemployed. The Unemployment rate is also used in economic studies and economic indexes such as the United States' Conference Board's Index of Leading Indicators as a measure of the state of the macroeconomics.
United States	The United States of America (commonly referred to as the United States the U.S., the United States A, or America) is a federal constitutional republic comprising fifty states and a federal district. The country is situated mostly in central North America, where its 48 contiguous states and Washington, D.C., the capital district, lie between the Pacific and Atlantic Oceans, bordered by Canada to the north and Mexico to the south. The state of Alaska is in the northwest of the continent, with Canada to its east and Russia to the west across the Bering Strait.
Business	A business is a legally recognized organization designed to provide goods and/or services to consumers. business es are predominant in capitalist economies, most being privately owned and formed to earn profit that will increase the wealth of its owners and grow the business itself. The owners and operators of a business have as one of their main objectives the receipt or generation of a financial return in exchange for work and acceptance of risk.
Job creation	Job creation programs are programs or projects undertaken by a government of a nation in order to assist unemployed members of the population in seeking employment. They are especially common during time of high unemployment. They may either concentrate on macroeconomic policy in order to increase the supply of jobs, or create more efficient means to pair employment seekers to their prospective employers .
Small business	A small business is a business that is independently owned and operated, with a small number of employees and relatively low volume of sales. The legal definition of 'small' often varies by country and industry, but is generally under 100 employees in the United States and under 50 employees in the European Union. In comparison, the definition of mid-sized business by the number of employees is generally under 500 in the U.S. and 250 for the European Union.
Kraft Foods	Kraft Foods Inc. (NYSE: Kraft Foods T) is the largest food and beverage company headquartered in the United States and the second largest in the world (after Nestlé SA.) Kraft is headquartered in Northfield, Illinois, USA, a Chicago suburb.

Organization

An organization is a social arrangement which pursues collective goals, which controls its own performance, and which has a boundary separating it from its environment. The word itself is derived from the Greek word á½„ργανον (organon [itself derived from the better-known word á¼"ργον ergon - work; deed - > ergonomics, etc]) meaning tool. The term is used in both daily and scientific English in multiple ways.

International Monetary Fund

The International Monetary Fund is an international organization that oversees the global financial system by following the macroeconomic policies of its member countries, in particular those with an impact on exchange rates and the balance of payments. It is an organization formed to stabilize international exchange rates and facilitate development. It also offers financial and technical assistance to its members, making it an international lender of last resort.

Monetary

Monetary policy is the process by which the government, central bank (ii) availability of money, and (iii) cost of money or rate of interest, in order to attain a set of objectives oriented towards the growth and stability of the economy. monetary theory provides insight into how to craft optimal monetary policy.

monetary policy is referred to as either being an expansionary policy where an expansionary policy increases the total supply of money in the economy, and a contractionary policy decreases the total money supply.

Advertising

Advertising is a form of communication that typically attempts to persuade potential customers to purchase or to consume more of a particular brand of product or service. 'While now central to the contemporary global economy and the reproduction of global production networks, it is only quite recently that Advertising has been more than a marginal influence on patterns of sales and production. The formation of modern Advertising was intimately bound up with the emergence of new forms of monopoly capitalism around the end of the 19th and beginning of the 20th century as one element in corporate strategies to create, organize and where possible control markets, especially for mass produced consumer goods.

Challenge

Challenge is a United Kingdom digital TV channel owned by Virgin Media Television. It was originally called The Family Channel from 1 September 1993 to 31 January 1997 but it was later re-branded as challenge TV from 1 February 1997. On 20 May 2002 the channel was re-named again but this time it was just challenge? and 30 June 2003 the question mark was removed to leave the challenge name in its place.

Economic development

Economic development is the development of economic wealth of countries or regions for the well-being of their inhabitants. It is the process by which a nation improves the economic, political, and social well being of its people. From a policy perspective, Economic development can be defined as efforts that seek to improve the economic well-being and quality of life for a community by creating and/or retaining jobs and supporting or growing incomes and the tax base.

Census Bureau

The United States Census Bureau is the government agency that is responsible for the United States Census. It also gathers other national demographic and economic data.

English

English is a West Germanic language that originated in Anglo-Saxon England. As a result of the military, economic, scientific, political and cultural influence of the British Empire during the 18th, 19th and 20th centuries and of the United States since the late 19th century, it has become the lingua franca in many parts of the world. It is used extensively as a second language and as an official language in Commonwealth countries and many international organizations.

United States Census Bureau	The United States Census Bureau is the government agency that is responsible for the United States Census. It also gathers other national demographic and economic data.
Direct investment	Foreign Direct investment in its classic form is defined as a company from one country making a physical investment into building a factory in another country. It is the establishment of an enterprise by a foreigner. Its definition can be extended to include investments made to acquire lasting interest in enterprises operating outside of the economy of the investor.
Foreign direct investment	Foreign direct investment in its classic form is defined as a company from one country making a physical investment into building a factory in another country. It is the establishment of an enterprise by a foreigner. Its definition can be extended to include investments made to acquire lasting interest in enterprises operating outside of the economy of the investor.
Report	In writing, a report is a document characterized by information or other content reflective of inquiry or investigation, which is tailored to the context of a given situation and audience. The purpose of report s is usually to inform. However, report s may include persuasive elements, such as recommendations, suggestions, or other motivating conclusions that indicate possible future actions the report reader might take.
Smuggling	Smuggling is the clandestine transportation of goods or persons past a point where prohibited, such as out of a building, into a prison in violation of the law or other rules. There are various motivations to smuggle, most, but not all, of which are financial. These include the participation in illegal trade, such as drugs, illegal immigration or emigration, tax evasion, providing contraband to a prison inmate, or the theft of the items being smuggled.
Set TSP	In combinatorial optimization, the set TSP group TSP, One-of-a-set TSP, Multiple Choice TSP or Covering Salesman Problem, is a generalization of the Traveling salesman problem, whereby it is required to find a shortest tour in a graph which visits all specified disjoint subsets of the vertices of a graph. The ordinary TSP is a special case of the set TSP when all subsets to be visited are singletons. Therefore the set TSP is also NP-hard.
Brain drain	Brain drain or human capital flight is a large emigration of individuals with technical skills or knowledge, normally due to conflict, lack of opportunity, political instability, or health risks. Brain drain is usually regarded as an economic cost, since emigrants usually take with them the fraction of value of their training sponsored by the government. It is a parallel of capital flight which refers to the same movement of financial capital.
Trend analysis	The term 'trend analysis' refers to the concept of collecting information and attempting to spot a pattern in the information. In some fields of study, the term 'trend analysis' has more formally-defined meanings. In project management trend analysis is a mathematical technique that uses historical results to predict future outcome.
World Trade Organization	The World Trade Organization is an international organization designed to supervise and liberalize international trade. The World Trade Organization came into being on 1 January 1995, and is the successor to the General Agreement on Tariffs and Trade (GATT), which was created in 1947, and continued to operate for almost five decades as a de facto international organization.

The World Trade Organization deals with the rules of trade between nations at a near-global level; it is responsible for negotiating and implementing new trade agreements, and is in charge of policing member countries' adherence to all the World Trade Organization agreements, signed by the majority of the world's trading nations and ratified in their parliaments.

Skilled worker

A Skilled worker is any worker who has some special skill, knowledge, or (usually acquired) ability in his work. A Skilled worker may have attended a college, university or technical school. Or, a Skilled worker may have learned his skills on the job.

Chief brand officer

A Chief brand officer is a relatively new executive level position at a corporation, company, organization typically reporting directly to the CEO or board of directors. The Chief brand officer is responsible for a brand's image, experience, and promise, and propagating it throughout all aspects of the company. The brand officer oversees marketing, advertising, design, public relations and customer service departments.

Social status

In sociology or anthropology, Social status is the honor or prestige attached to one's position in society (one's social position.) The stratification system, which is the system of distributing rewards to the members of society, determines Social status. Social status, the position or rank of a person or group within the stratification system, can be determined two ways.

Culture

Culture is a term that has different meanings. For example, in 1952, Alfred Kroeber and Clyde Kluckhohn compiled a list of 164 definitions of culture in culture A Critical Review of Concepts and Definitions. However, the word culture is most commonly used in three basic senses:

· excellence of taste in the fine arts and humanities, also known as high culture
· an integrated pattern of human knowledge, belief, and behavior that depends upon the capacity for symbolic thought and social learning
· the set of shared attitudes, values, goals, and practices that characterizes an institution, organization or group.

When the concept first emerged in eighteenth- and nineteenth-century Europe, it connoted a process of cultivation or improvement, as in agri culture or horti culture . In the nineteenth century, it came to refer first to the betterment or refinement of the individual, especially through education, and then to the fulfillment of national aspirations or ideals.

Sexism

Sexism, a term coined in the mid-20th century, refers to the belief or attitude that one gender or sex is inferior to, less competent, or less valuable than the other. It can also refer to hatred of, or prejudice towards, either sex as a whole , or the application of stereotypes of masculinity in relation to men, or of femininity in relation to women. It is also called male and female chauvinism.

AFL-CIO

The American Federation of Labor and Congress of Industrial Organizations, commonly AFL-CIO, is a national trade union center, the largest federation of unions in the United States, made up of 65 national and international unions (including Canadian), together representing more than 10 million workers. It was formed in 1955 when the AFL and the CIO merged after a long estrangement. From 1955 until 2005, the AFL-CIO's member unions represented nearly all unionized workers in the United States.

Asia-Pacific	Asia-Pacific or APAC is that part of the world in or near the Western Pacific Ocean. The area includes much of East Asia, Southeast Asia, Australasia and Oceania.) Sometimes the term Asia-Pacific includes South Asia, though India and its neighbours are on or near the Indian Ocean rather than the Pacific Ocean.
European Trade Union Confederation	The European Trade Union Confederation is a trade union organization which was established in 1973 to represent workers and their national affiliates at the European level. Its role has increased as European integration has expanded EU influence on economic, employment and social policy throughout the 27 Member States. At present, the European Trade Union Confederation membership comprises 82 National Trade Union Confederations from a total of 36 European countries, and 12 European industry federations, covering some 60 million individual trade unionists.
Free Trade	Free trade is a type of trade policy that allows traders to act and transact without interference from government. Thus, the policy permits trading partners mutual gains from trade, with goods and services produced according to the theory of comparative advantage. Under a Free trade policy, prices are a reflection of true supply and demand, and are the sole determinant of resource allocation.
International Labour Organization	The International Labour Organization is a specialized agency of the United Nations that deals with labour issues. Its headquarters are in Geneva, Switzerland. Its secretariat -- the people who are employed by it throughout the world -- is known as the International Labour Office.
Trade Union	A Trade union or labor union is an organization of workers who have banded together to achieve common goals in key areas and working conditions. The Trade union, through its leadership, bargains with the employer on behalf of union members (rank and file members) and negotiates labor contracts (Collective bargaining) with employers. This may include the negotiation of wages, work rules, complaint procedures, rules governing hiring, firing and promotion of workers, benefits, workplace safety and policies.
Minority	A Minority or digger group is a sociological group that does not constitute a politically dominant voting majority of the total population of a given society. A sociological Minority is not necessarily a numerical Minority -- it may include any group that is subnormal with respect to a dominant group in terms of social status, education, employment, wealth and political power. To avoid confusion, some writers prefer the terms 'subordinate group' and 'dominant group' rather than 'Minority' and 'majority', respectively.
Bribery	Bribery, a form of pecuniary corruption, is an act implying money or gift given that alters the behaviour of the recipient. bribery constitutes a crime and is defined by Black's Law Dictionary as the offering, giving, receiving, or soliciting of any item of value to influence the actions of an official or other person in discharge of a public or legal duty. The bribe is the gift bestowed to influence the recipient's conduct.
Discrimination	Discrimination toward or against a person of a certain group is the treatment or consideration based on class or category rather than individual merit. It can be behavior promoting a certain group (e.g. affirmative action), or it can be negative behavior directed against a certain group (e.g. redlining.) Racial discrimination differentiates between individuals on the basis of real and perceived racial differences, and has been official government policy in several countries, such as South Africa in the apartheid era, and the USA.

Numerary

Numerary is a civil designation for persons who are incorporated in a fixed or permanent way to a society or group: regular member of the working staff, permanent staff distinguished from a super Numerary .

The term Numerary and its counterpart, 'super Numerary ,' originated in Spanish and Latin American academy and government; it is now also used in countries all over the world, such as France, the U.S., England, Italy, etc.

There are Numerary members of surgical organizations, of universities, of gastronomical associations, etc.

Policy

A Policy is typically described as a deliberate plan of action to guide decisions and achieve rational outcome(s.) However, the term may also be used to denote what is actually done, even though it is unplanned.

The term may apply to government, private sector organizations and groups, and individuals.

United Nations

The United Nations is an international organization whose stated aims are to facilitate cooperation in international law, international security, economic development, social progress, human rights and achieving world peace. The United Nations was founded in 1945 after World War II to replace the League of Nations, to stop wars between countries and to provide a platform for dialogue.

There are currently 192 member states, including nearly every recognized independent state in the world.

Wage

A Wage is a compensation, usually financial, received by a worker in exchange for their labor.

Compensation in terms of Wage s is given to worker and compensation in terms of salary is given to employees. Compensation is a monetary benefits given to employees in returns of the services provided by them.

Statistics

Statistics is a mathematical science pertaining to the collection, analysis, interpretation or explanation, and presentation of data. It also provides tools for prediction and forecasting based on data. It is applicable to a wide variety of academic disciplines, from the natural and social sciences to the humanities, government and business.

Market

A Market is any one of a variety of different systems, Institutions, procedures, social relations and infrastructures whereby persons trade, and goods and services are exchanged, forming part of the economy. It is an arrangement that allows buyers and sellers to exchange things. Market s vary in size, range, geographic scale, location, types and variety of human communities, as well as the types of goods and services traded.

Collective bargaining

In organized labor, collective bargaining is the method whereby workers organize together (usually in unions) to meet, converse, and negotiate upon the work conditions with their employers normally resulting in a written contract setting forth the wages, hours, and other conditions to be observed for a stipulated period.It is the practice in which union and company representatives meet to negotiate a new labor contract. In various national labor and employment law contexts, collective bargaining takes on a more specific legal meaning and so, in a broad sense, however, it is the coming together of workers to negotiate their employment.

A collective agreement is a labor contract between an employer and one or more unions.

Tariff

A Tariff is a duty imposed on goods when they are moved across a political boundary. They are usually associated with protectionism, the economic policy of restraining trade between nations. For political reasons, Tariff s are usually imposed on imported goods, although they may also be imposed on exported goods.

Eurozone	The eurozone is a currency union of 16 European Union (EU) states which have adopted the euro as their sole legal tender. It currently consists of Austria, Belgium, Cyprus, Finland, France, Germany, Greece, Ireland, Italy, Luxembourg, Malta, the Netherlands, Portugal, Slovakia, Slovenia and Spain. Eight other states are obliged to adopt the zone once they fulfill the strict entry criteria.
Cultural identity	Cultural identity is the identity of a group or culture, or of an individual as far as one is influenced by one's belonging to a group or culture. Cultural identity is similar to and has overlaps with, but is not synonymous with, identity politics. There are modern questions of culture that are transferred into questions of identity.
Human	A human is a member of a species of bipedal primates in the family Hominidae . DNA and fossil evidence indicates that modern human s originated in east Africa about 200,000 years ago. When compared to other animals and primates, human s have a highly developed brain, capable of abstract reasoning, language, introspection and problem solving.
Human resource management	Human resource management is the strategic and coherent approach to the management of an organisation's most valued assets - the people working there who individually and collectively contribute to the achievement of the objectives of the business. The terms 'Human resource management' and 'human resources' (HR) have largely replaced the term 'personnel management' as a description of the processes involved in managing people in organizations. In simple sense, Human resource management means employing people, developing their resources, utilizing, maintaining and compensating their services in tune with the job and organizational requirement.
Bureau of Labor Statistics	The Bureau of Labor Statistics, a unit of the United States Department of Labor, is the principal fact-finding agency for the U.S. government in the broad field of labor economics and statistics. The BLS is an independent national statistical agency that collects, processes, analyzes, and disseminates essential statistical data to the American public, the U.S. Congress, other Federal agencies, State and local governments, business, and labor representatives. The BLS also serves as a statistical resource to the Department of Labor.
Human Capital	Human capital refers to the stock of skills and knowledge embodied in the ability to perform labor so as to produce economic value. It is the skills and knowledge gained by a worker through education and experience. Many early economic theories refer to it simply as labor, one of three factors of production, and consider it to be a fungible resource -- homogeneous and easily interchangeable.
Export	In economics, an export is any good or commodity, transported from one country to another country in a legitimate fashion, typically for use in trade. export goods or services are provided to foreign consumers by domestic producers. export is an important part of international trade.
Nike, Inc.	Nike, Inc. is a major publicly traded sportswear and equipment supplier based in the United States. The company is headquartered in Beaverton, near the Portland metropolitan area of Oregon.

Kraft Foods

Kraft Foods Inc. (NYSE: Kraft Foods T) is the largest food and beverage company headquartered in the United States and the second largest in the world (after Nestlé SA.)

Kraft is headquartered in Northfield, Illinois, USA, a Chicago suburb.

Strategic thinking

Recent strategic thought points ever more clearly towards the conclusion that the critical strategic question is not 'What?,' but 'Why?' The work of Mintzberg and others who draw a distinction between strategic planning (defined as systematic programming of pre-identified strategies) and Strategic thinking supports that conclusion. Intensified exploration of strategy from new directions is now coming together in the concept of what is being called Strategic thinking. At this point, there is no generally accepted definition of the term, no common agreement as to its role or importance, and no standardized list of key competencies of strategic thinkers.

Planning

Planning in organizations and public policy is both the organizational process of creating and maintaining a plan; and the psychological process of thinking about the activities required to create a desired goal on some scale. As such, it is a fundamental property of intelligent behavior. This thought process is essential to the creation and refinement of a plan, or integration of it with other plans, that is, it combines forecasting of developments with the preparation of scenarios of how to react to them.

Scenario planning

Scenario planning [or scenario thinking or scenario analysis] is a strategic planning method that some organizations use to make flexible long-term plans. It is in large part an adaptation and generalization of classic methods used by military intelligence.

The original method was that a group of analysts would generate simulation games for policy makers.

Strategic planning

Strategic planning is an organization's process of defining its strategy and making decisions on allocating its resources to pursue this strategy, including its capital and people. Various business analysis techniques can be used in Strategic planning, including SWOT analysis (Strengths, Weaknesses, Opportunities, and Threats) and PEST analysis (Political, Economic, Social, and Technological analysis) or STEER analysis involving Socio-cultural, Technological, Economic, Ecological, and Regulatory factors and EPISTEL (Environment, Political, Informatic, Social, Technological, Economic and Legal)

Strategic planning is the formal consideration of an organization's future course. All Strategic planning deals with at least one of three key questions:

- 'What do we do?'
- 'For whom do we do it?'
- 'How do we excel?'

In business Strategic planning, the third question is better phrased 'How can we beat or avoid competition?'. (Bradford and Duncan, page 1.)

Competitive

Competitive ness is a comparative concept of the ability and performance of a firm, sub-sector or country to sell and supply goods and/or services in a given market. Although widely used in economics and business management, the usefulness of the concept, particularly in the context of national competitive ness, is vigorously disputed by economists, such as Paul Krugman .

The term may also be applied to markets, where it is used to refer to the extent to which the market structure may be regarded as perfectly competitive

Expatriate

An expatriate is a person temporarily or permanently residing in a country and culture other than that of the person's upbringing or legal residence. The word comes from the Latin ex and patria (country, fatherland.)

The term is sometimes used in the context of Westerners living in non-Western countries, although it is also used to describe Westerners living in other Western countries, such as U.S. citizens living in the United Kingdom, or Britons living in Spain.

Challenge

Challenge is a United Kingdom digital TV channel owned by Virgin Media Television. It was originally called The Family Channel from 1 September 1993 to 31 January 1997 but it was later re-branded as challenge TV from 1 February 1997. On 20 May 2002 the channel was re-named again but this time it was just challenge? and 30 June 2003 the question mark was removed to leave the challenge name in its place.

Facing

Facing,, is a common tool in the retail industry to create the look of a perfectly stocked store by pulling all of the products on a display or shelf to the front, as well as downstacking all the canned and stacked items. It is also done to keep the store appearing neat and organized.

The workers who face commonly have jobs doing other things in the store such as customer service, stocking shelves, daytime cleaning, bagging and carryouts, etc.

Competitive advantage

Competitive advantage is, in very basic words, a position a firm occupies against its competitors.

According to Michael Porter, the three methods for creating a sustainable Competitive advantage are through:

1. Cost leadership - Cost advantage occurs when a firm delivers the same services as its competitors but at a lower cost;

2.

Goal

A Goal or objective is a projected state of affairs that a person or a system plans or intends to achieve--a personal or organizational desired end-point in some sort of assumed development. Many people endeavor to reach Goal s within a finite time by setting deadlines.

A desire or an intention becomes a Goal if and only if one activates an action for achieving it

Variable

Variables are used in open sentences. For instance, in the formula $x + 1 = 5$, x is a variable which represents an 'unknown' number. Variables are often represented by letters of the Roman alphabet, or those of other alphabets, such as Greek, and use other special symbols.

Business

A business is a legally recognized organization designed to provide goods and/or services to consumers. business es are predominant in capitalist economies, most being privately owned and formed to earn profit that will increase the wealth of its owners and grow the business itself. The owners and operators of a business have as one of their main objectives the receipt or generation of a financial return in exchange for work and acceptance of risk.

Economic	An economy (or 'the economy') is the realized Economic system of a country or other area. It includes the production, exchange, distribution, and consumption of goods and services of that area. The study of different types and examples of economies is the subject of Economic systems.
Economic growth	Economic growth is the increase in the amount of the goods and services produced by an economy over time and is dependent on an increase in the creation of money. Growth is conventionally measured as the percent rate of increase in real gross domestic product, or real GDP. GDP is usually calculated in real terms, i.e.
Function cost analysis	Function cost analysis is the a method of technical and economic research of the systems for purpose to optimize a parity between system's consumer functions or properties and expenses to achieve those functions or properties. This methodology for continuous perfection of production, industrial technologies, organizational structures was developed by Juryj Sobolev in 1948 at the 'Perm telephone factory' · 1948 Juryj Sobolev - the first success in application of a method analysis at the 'Perm telephone factory' . · 1949 - the first application for the invention as result of use of the new method. Today in economically developed countries practically each enterprise or the company use methodology of the kind of functional-cost analysis as a practice of the quality management, most full satisfying to principles of standards of series ISO 9000. · Interest of consumer not in products itself, but the advantage which it will receive from its usage. · The consumer aspires to reduce his expenses · Functions needed by consumer can be executed in the various ways, and, hence, with various efficiency and expenses. Among possible alternatives of realization of functions exist such in which the parity of quality and the price is the optimal for the consumer. The goal of Function cost analysis is achievement of the highest consumer satisfaction of production at simultaneous decrease in all kinds of industrial expenses Classical Function cost analysis has three English synonyms - Value Engineering, Value Management, Value Analysis.
Value chain	The Value chain is a concept from business management that was first described and popularized by Michael Porter in his 1985 best-seller, Competitive Advantage: Creating and Sustaining Superior Performance. A Value chain is a chain of activities. Products pass through all activities of the chain in order and at each activity the product gains some value.
Explicit knowledge	Explicit knowledge is knowledge that has been or can be articulated, codified, and stored in certain media. It can be readily transmitted to others. The information contained in encyclopedias (including wikipedia) are good examples of explicit knowledge.
Knowledge management	Knowledge management comprises a range of practices used in an organisation to identify, create, represent, distribute and enable adoption of insights and experiences. Such insights and experiences comprise knowledge, either embodied in individuals or embedded in organisational processes or practice. An established discipline since 1991 , knowledge management includes courses taught in the fields of business administration, information systems, management, and library and information sciences .

Tacit knowledge

Tacit knowledge is knowledge that cannot be transferred to another person as a result of it being written down or verbalized. For example, stating to someone that Tooting is near London is a piece of explicit knowledge that can be written down, transmitted, and understood by a recipient. However the ability to use algebra, speak a language, or design and use complex equipment requires all sorts of knowledge that is not always known explicitly, even by expert practitioners, and which cannot be explicitly transferred to users.

Mission statement

A Mission statement is a brief written statement of the purpose of a company or organization. Ideally, a Mission statement guides the actions of the organization, spells out its overall goal, provides a sense of direction, and guides decision making for all levels of management.

Mission statement s often contain the following:

· Purpose and aim of the organization
· The organization's primary stakeholders: clients, stockholders, etc.
· Responsibilities of the organization toward these stakeholders
· Products and services offered

In developing a Mission statement

· Encourage as much input as feasible from employees, volunteers, and other stakeholders
· Publicize it broadly
· Limit to a few statements.

The Mission statement can be used to resolve differences between business stakeholders.

Organization

An organization is a social arrangement which pursues collective goals, which controls its own performance, and which has a boundary separating it from its environment. The word itself is derived from the Greek word á½„ργανον (organon [itself derived from the better-known word á¼"ργον ergon - work; deed - > ergonomics, etc]) meaning tool. The term is used in both daily and scientific English in multiple ways.

Business marketing

Business marketing is the practice of individuals including commercial businesses, governments and institutions, facilitating the sale of their products or services to other companies or organizations that in turn resell them, use them as components in products or services they offer Business marketing is also called business-to-Business marketing for short. (Note that while marketing to government entities shares some of the same dynamics of organizational marketing, B2G Marketing is meaningfully different.)

Vision statement

Organizations sometimes summarize goals and objectives into a mission statement and/or a Vision statement:

While the existence of a shared mission is extremely useful, many strategy specialists question the requirement for a written mission statement. However, there are many models of strategic planning that start with mission statements, so it is useful to examine them here.

· A Mission statement tells you the fundamental purpose of the organization. It concentrates on the present. It defines the customer and the critical processes. It informs you of the desired level of performance.

· A Vision statement outlines what the organization wants to be. It concentrates on the future.

Objective may also refer to:	The word objective may also refer to: · Objective (military), the achievement of a final set of actions within a given military operation · Objective pronoun, a noun as the target of a verb · Objective (optics), an element in a camera or microscope · Objective Corporation, a software company · Objectivity (philosophy) (opposed to subjectivity) · Objective (goal), a projected state of affairs that a person or a system plans or intends to achieve .
Asset	In business and accounting, asset s are economic resources owned by business or company. Anything tangible or intangible that one possesses, usually considered as applicable to the payment of one's debts is considered an asset Simplistically stated, asset s are things of value that can be readily converted into cash.
Consumer	Consumer is a broad label that refers to any individuals or households that use goods and services generated within the economy. The concept of a Consumer is used in different contexts, so that the usage and significance of the term may vary. A Consumer is a person who uses any product or service.
Global strategy	Global strategy as defined in business terms is an organization's strategic guide to globalization. A sound Global strategy should address these questions: what must be (versus what is) the extent of market presence in the world's major markets? How to build the necessary global presence? What must be (versus what is) the optimal locations around the world for the various value chain activities? How to run global presence into global competitive advantage? Academic research on Global strategy came of age during the 1980s, including work by Michael Porter and Christopher Bartlett ' Sumantra Ghoshal. Among the forces perceived to bring about the globalization of competition were convergence in economic systems and technological change, especially in information technology, that facilitated and required the coordination of a multinational firm's strategy on a worldwide scale.
Market	A Market is any one of a variety of different systems, institutions, procedures, social relations and infrastructures whereby persons trade, and goods and services are exchanged, forming part of the economy. It is an arrangement that allows buyers and sellers to exchange things. Market s vary in size, range, geographic scale, location, types and variety of human communities, as well as the types of goods and services traded.
Product life cycle	Product life cycle Management is the succession of strategies used by management as a product goes through its product life cycle. The conditions in which a product is sold changes over time and must be managed as it moves through its succession of stages. The product life cycle goes through many phases, involves many professional disciplines, and requires many skills, tools and processes.
Industrial espionage	Industrial espionage or corporate espionage is espionage conducted for commercial purposes instead of national security purposes.

	The term is distinct from legal and ethical activities such as examining corporate publications, websites, patent filings, and the like to determine the activities of a corporation (this is normally referred to as competitive intelligence.) Theoretically the difference between espionage and legal information gathering is clear.
Trade secret	A trade secret is a formula, practice, process, design, instrument, pattern by which a business can obtain an economic advantage over competitors or customers. In some jurisdictions, such secrets are referred to as 'confidential information' or 'classified information'. The precise language by which a trade secret is defined varies by jurisdiction (as do the particular types of information that are subject to trade secret protection.)
Comparative	In grammar, the comparative is the form of an adjective or adverb which denotes the degree or grade by which a person, thing and is used in this context with a subordinating conjunction, such as than, as...as, etc. The structure of a comparative in English consists normally of the positive form of the adjective or adverb, plus the suffix -er e.g. 'he is taller than his father is', or 'the village is less picturesque than the town nearby'.
Comparative advantage	In economics, Comparative advantage refers to the ability of a person or a country to produce a particular good at a lower marginal cost and opportunity cost than another person or country. It is the ability to produce a product most efficiently given all the other products that could be produced. It can be contrasted with absolute advantage which refers to the ability of a person or a country to produce a particular good at a lower absolute cost than another.
Standardization	Standardization or standardisation is the process of developing and agreeing upon technical standards. A standard is a document that establishes uniform engineering or technical specifications, criteria, methods, processes, or practices. Some standards are mandatory while others are voluntary.
Globalization	Globalization in its literal sense is the process of transformation of local or regional phenomena into global ones. It can be described as a process by which the people of the world are unified into a single society and function together. This process is a combination of economic, technological, sociocultural and political forces.
Advertising	Advertising is a form of communication that typically attempts to persuade potential customers to purchase or to consume more of a particular brand of product or service. 'While now central to the contemporary global economy and the reproduction of global production networks, it is only quite recently that Advertising has been more than a marginal influence on patterns of sales and production. The formation of modern Advertising was intimately bound up with the emergence of new forms of monopoly capitalism around the end of the 19th and beginning of the 20th century as one element in corporate strategies to create, organize and where possible control markets, especially for mass produced consumer goods.
Cost	In economics, business, retail, and accounting, a cost is the value of money that has been used up to produce something, and hence is not available for use anymore. In economics, a cost is an alternative that is given up as a result of a decision. In business, the cost may be one of acquisition, in which case the amount of money expended to acquire it is counted as cost.
Internationalization	Internationalization has been viewed as a process of increasing involvement of enterprises in international markets, although there is no agreed definition of Internationalization or international entrepreneurship. There are several Internationalization theories which try to explain why there are international activities.

	Adam Smith claimed that a country should specialise in, and export, commodities in which it had an absolute advantage.
Contingency plan	A Contingency plan is a plan devised for a specific situation when things could go wrong. Contingency plan s are often devised by governments or businesses who want to be prepared for anything that could happen. They are sometimes known as 'Back-up plans', 'Worst-case scenario plans' or 'Plan B'.
Operational	Operational definition is a term coined by Percy Williams Bridgman. An operational definition is a demonstration of a process - such as a variable, term, or object - in terms of the specific process or set of validation tests used to determine its presence and quantity. Properties described in this manner must be sufficiently accessible, so that persons other than the definer may independently measure or test for them at will.
Leakage	Leakage describes an unwanted loss of something which escapes from its proper location. In everyday usage, Leakage is the gradual escape of matter through a leak-hole. In different fields, the term may have specialized meanings.
Set TSP	In combinatorial optimization, the set TSP group TSP, One-of-a-set TSP, Multiple Choice TSP or Covering Salesman Problem, is a generalization of the Traveling salesman problem, whereby it is required to find a shortest tour in a graph which visits all specified disjoint subsets of the vertices of a graph. The ordinary TSP is a special case of the set TSP when all subsets to be visited are singletons. Therefore the set TSP is also NP-hard.
Budget	Budget generally refers to a list of all planned expenses and revenues. It is a plan for saving and spending. A Budget is an important concept in microeconomics, which uses a Budget line to illustrate the trade-offs between two or more goods.
Facilitator	A Facilitator is someone who helps a group of people understand their common objectives and assists them to plan to achieve them without taking a particular position in the discussion. The Facilitator will try to assist the group in achieving a consensus on any disagreements that preexist or emerge in the meeting so that it has a strong basis for future action. The role has been likened to that of a midwife who assists in the process of birth but is not the producer of the end result.
Implementation	Implementation is the realization of an application idea, model, design, specification, standard, algorithm an implementation is a realization of a technical specification or algorithm as a program, software component, or other computer system. Many implementation s may exist for a given specification or standard.
Time horizon	A Time horizon is a fixed point of time in the future at which point certain processes will be evaluated or assumed to end. It is necessary in an accounting, finance or risk management regime to assign such a fixed horizon time so that alternatives can be evaluated for performance over the same period of time. A Time horizon is a physical impossibility in the real world.
Theory of the firm	The Theory of the firm consists of a number of economic theories which describe the nature of the firm, company including its existence, its behaviour, and its relationship with the market.

In simplified terms, the Theory of the firm aims to answer these questions:

- Existence - why do firms emerge, why are not all transactions in the economy mediated over the market?
- Boundaries - why the boundary between firms and the market is located exactly there? Which transactions are performed internally and which are negotiated on the market?
- Organization - why are firms structured in such specific way? What is the interplay of formal and informal relationships?

The First World War period saw a change of emphasis in economic theory away from industry-level analysis which mainly included analysing markets to analysis at the level of the firm, as it became increasingly clear that perfect competition was no longer an adequate model of how firms behaved. Economic theory till then had focussed on trying to understand markets alone and there had been little study on understanding why firms or organisations exist. Market are mainly guided by prices as illustrated by vegetable markets where a buyer is free to switch sellers in an exchange.

Competitor analysis

Competitor analysis in marketing and strategic management is an assessment of the strengths and weaknesses of current and potential competitors. This analysis provides both an offensive and defensive strategic context through which to identify opportunities and threats. Competitor profiling coalesces all of the relevant sources of Competitor analysis into one framework in the support of efficient and effective strategy formulation, implementation, monitoring and adjustment.

Competitor or Competitive Intelligence

Competitor or Competitive Intelligence is the original form of externally-oriented business intelligence that preceded Knowledge Management or Data Mining as the primary concern of executives responsible for increasing market share.

Benchmarking

Benchmarking is the process of comparing the cost, cycle time, productivity, or quality of a specific process or method to another that is widely considered to be an industry standard or best practice. The result is often a business case for making changes in order to make improvements. The term Benchmarking was first used by cobblers to measure ones feet for shoes.

Chief brand officer

A Chief brand officer is a relatively new executive level position at a corporation, company, organization typically reporting directly to the CEO or board of directors. The Chief brand officer is responsible for a brand's image, experience, and promise, and propagating it throughout all aspects of the company. The brand officer oversees marketing, advertising, design, public relations and customer service departments.

Data collection

Data collection is a term used to describe a process of preparing and collecting data - for example as part of a process improvement or similar project.

data collection usually takes place early on in an improvement project, and is often formalised through a data collection Plan which often contains the following activity.

- Pre collection activity - Agree goals, target data, definitions, methods
- Collection - data collection
- Present Findings - usually involves some form of sorting analysis and/or presentation.

A formal data collection process is necessary as it ensures that data gathered is both defined and accurate and that subsequent decisions based on arguments embodied in the findings are valid . The process provides both a baseline from which to measure from and in certain cases a target on what to improve. Types of data collection 1-By mail questionnaires 2-By personal interview

· Six sigma
· Sampling (statistics) .

Database

A database is a structured collection of records or data that is stored in a computer system. The structure is achieved by organizing the data according to a database model. The model in most common use today is the relational model.

LexisNexis

LexisNexis is a popular searchable archive of content from newspapers, magazines, legal documents and other printed sources. LexisNexis claims to be the 'world's largest collection of public records, unpublished opinions, forms, legal, news, and business information' while offering their products to a wide range of professionals in the legal, risk management, corporate, government, law enforcement, accounting and academic markets. Typical customers of LexisNexis include lawyers, law students, journalists, and academics.

Job interview

A Job interview is a process in which a potential employee is evaluated by an employer for prospective employment in their company, organization and was established in the late 16th century.

A Job interview typically precedes the hiring decision, and is used to evaluate the candidate. The interview is usually preceded by the evaluation of submitted résumés from interested candidates, then selecting a small number of candidates for interviews.

Environmental Protection

Environmental protection is a practice of protecting the environment, on individual, organisational or governmental level, for the benefit of the natural environment and (or) humans.

Due to the pressures of population and technology the biophysical environment is being degraded, sometimes permanently. This has been recognised and governments began placing restraints on activities that caused environmental degradation.

Environmental Protection Agency

The U.S. Environmental Protection Agency is an agency of the federal government of the United States charged to regulate chemicals and protect human health by safeguarding the natural environment: air, water, and land. The Environmental Protection Agency was proposed by President Richard Nixon and began operation on December 2, 1970, when its establishment was passed by Congress, and signed into law by President Nixon, and has since been chiefly responsible for the environmental policy of the United States. It is led by its Administrator, who is appointed by the President of the United States.

Federal Bureau of Investigation

The Federal Bureau of Investigation is the primary unit in the United States Department of Justice, serving as both a federal criminal investigative body and a domestic intelligence agency. The FBI has investigative jurisdiction over violations of more than 200 categories of federal crime. Its motto is 'Fidelity, Bravery, Integrity,' corresponding to the 'FBI' initialism.

Intellectual property

Intellectual property are legal property rights over creations of the mind, both artistic and commercial, and the corresponding fields of law. Under intellectual property law, owners are granted certain exclusive rights to a variety of intangible assets, such as musical, literary, and artistic works; ideas, discoveries and inventions; and words, phrases, symbols, and designs. Common types of intellectual property include copyrights, trademarks, patents, industrial design rights and trade secrets.

United States

The United States of America (commonly referred to as the United States the U.S., the United States A, or America) is a federal constitutional republic comprising fifty states and a federal district. The country is situated mostly in central North America, where its 48 contiguous states and Washington, D.C., the capital district, lie between the Pacific and Atlantic Oceans, bordered by Canada to the north and Mexico to the south. The state of Alaska is in the northwest of the continent, with Canada to its east and Russia to the west across the Bering Strait.

Copyright

Copyright is a form of intellectual property which gives the creator of an original work exclusive rights for a certain time period in relation to that work, including its publication, distribution and adaptation; after which time the work is said to enter the public domain. Copyright applies to any expressible form of an idea or information that is substantive and discrete. Some jurisdictions also recognize 'moral rights' of the creator of a work, such as the right to be credited for the work.

Annual Report

An Annual report is a comprehensive report on a company's activities throughout the preceding year. Annual report s are intended to give shareholders and other interested persons information about the company's activities and financial performance. Most jurisdictions require companies to prepare and disclose Annual report s, and many require the Annual report to be filed at the company's registry.

Congress

A Congress is a formal meeting of representatives from different countries (or by extension constituent states), or independent organizations (such as different trade unions.)

The term Congress was chosen for the United States Congress to emphasize the status of each state represented there as a self-governing unit. Subsequently to the use of Congress by the US legislature, the term has been adopted by many states within unions, and by unitary nation-states in the Americas, to refer to their legislatures.

Customer

A customer also client, buyer or purchaser is usually used to refer to a current or potential buyer or user of the products of an individual or organization, mostly called the supplier or seller. This is typically through purchasing or renting goods or services. However in certain contexts the term customer also includes by extension anyone who uses or experiences the services of another.

Supplier

A 'supply chain is the system of organizations, people, technology, activities, information and resources involved in moving a product or service from supplier to customer. Supply chain activities transform natural resources, raw materials and components into a finished product that is delivered to the end customer. In sophisticated supply chain systems, used products may re-enter the supply chain at any point where residual value is recyclable.

Absenteeism

Absenteeism is a habitual pattern of absence from a duty or obligation.

Frequent absence from the workplace may be indicative of poor morale or of sick building syndrome. However, many employers have implemented absence policies which make no distinction between absences for genuine illness and absence for inappropriate reasons.

Resources

Human beings are also considered to be Resources because they have the ability to change raw materials into valuable Resources. The term Human Resources can also be defined as the skills, energies, talents, abilities and knowledge that are used for the production of goods or the rendering of services. While taking into account human beings as Resources, the following things have to be kept in mind:

· The size of the population
· The capabilities of the individuals in that population

Many Resources cannot be consumed in their original form. They have to be processed in order to change them into more usable commodities.

Cultural identity

Cultural identity is the identity of a group or culture, or of an individual as far as one is influenced by one's belonging to a group or culture. Cultural identity is similar to and has overlaps with, but is not synonymous with, identity politics.

There are modern questions of culture that are transferred into questions of identity.

Culture

Culture is a term that has different meanings. For example, in 1952, Alfred Kroeber and Clyde Kluckhohn compiled a list of 164 definitions of culture in culture A Critical Review of Concepts and Definitions. However, the word culture is most commonly used in three basic senses:

· excellence of taste in the fine arts and humanities, also known as high culture
· an integrated pattern of human knowledge, belief, and behavior that depends upon the capacity for symbolic thought and social learning
· the set of shared attitudes, values, goals, and practices that characterizes an institution, organization or group.

When the concept first emerged in eighteenth- and nineteenth-century Europe, it connoted a process of cultivation or improvement, as in agri culture or horti culture . In the nineteenth century, it came to refer first to the betterment or refinement of the individual, especially through education, and then to the fulfillment of national aspirations or ideals.

Wal-Mart

Wal-Mart Stores, Inc. is an American public corporation that runs a chain of large, discount department stores. It is the world's largest public corporation by revenue, according to the 2008 Fortune Global 500.

Piracy

Piracy is a war-like act committed by a non-state actor, especially robbery or criminal violence committed at sea, on water, or sometimes on shore. It does not normally include crimes on board a vessel among passengers or crew. The term has been used to refer to raids across land borders by non-state actors.

Diffusion

Diffusion is the process by which a new idea or new product is accepted by the market. The rate of Diffusion is the speed that the new idea spreads from one consumer to the next. Adoption is similar to Diffusion except that it deals with the psychological processes an individual goes through, rather than an aggregate market process.

Kraft Foods

Kraft Foods Inc. (NYSE: Kraft Foods T) is the largest food and beverage company headquartered in the United States and the second largest in the world (after Nestlé SA.)

Kraft is headquartered in Northfield, Illinois, USA, a Chicago suburb.

Matrix management

Matrix management is a type of organizational management in which people with similar skills are pooled for work assignments. For example, all engineers may be in one engineering department and report to an engineering manager, but these same engineers may be assigned to different projects and report to a project manager while working on that project. Therefore, each engineer may have to work under several managers to get their job done.

Organizational structure

An organizational structure is a mostly hierarchical concept of subordination of entities that collaborate and contribute to serve one common aim.

Organizations are a variant of clustered entities. The structure of an organization is usually set up in many a styles, dependent on their objectives and ambience.

Design

Design is used both as a noun and a verb. The term is often tied to the various applied arts and engineering As a verb, 'to design' refers to the process of originating and developing a plan for a product, structure, system, or component with intention.

Planning

Planning in organizations and public policy is both the organizational process of creating and maintaining a plan; and the psychological process of thinking about the activities required to create a desired goal on some scale. As such, it is a fundamental property of intelligent behavior. This thought process is essential to the creation and refinement of a plan, or integration of it with other plans, that is, it combines forecasting of developments with the preparation of scenarios of how to react to them.

Strategic planning

Strategic planning is an organization's process of defining its strategy and making decisions on allocating its resources to pursue this strategy, including its capital and people. Various business analysis techniques can be used in Strategic planning, including SWOT analysis (Strengths, Weaknesses, Opportunities, and Threats) and PEST analysis (Political, Economic, Social, and Technological analysis) or STEER analysis involving Socio-cultural, Technological, Economic, Ecological, and Regulatory factors and EPISTEL (Environment, Political, Informatic, Social, Technological, Economic and Legal)

Strategic planning is the formal consideration of an organization's future course. All Strategic planning deals with at least one of three key questions:

- 'What do we do?'
- 'For whom do we do it?'
- 'How do we excel?'

In business Strategic planning, the third question is better phrased 'How can we beat or avoid competition?'. (Bradford and Duncan, page 1.)

Trend analysis

The term 'trend analysis' refers to the concept of collecting information and attempting to spot a pattern in the information. In some fields of study, the term 'trend analysis' has more formally-defined meanings.

In project management trend analysis is a mathematical technique that uses historical results to predict future outcome.

Customer

A customer also client, buyer or purchaser is usually used to refer to a current or potential buyer or user of the products of an individual or organization, mostly called the supplier or seller. This is typically through purchasing or renting goods or services. However in certain contexts the term customer also includes by extension anyone who uses or experiences the services of another.

Geography

Geography is the study of the Earth and its lands, features, inhabitants, and phenomena. A literal translation would be 'to describe or write about the Earth'. The first person to use the word 'Geography' was Eratosthenes .

Business

A business is a legally recognized organization designed to provide goods and/or services to consumers. business es are predominant in capitalist economies, most being privately owned and formed to earn profit that will increase the wealth of its owners and grow the business itself. The owners and operators of a business have as one of their main objectives the receipt or generation of a financial return in exchange for work and acceptance of risk.

Organization

An organization is a social arrangement which pursues collective goals, which controls its own performance, and which has a boundary separating it from its environment. The word itself is derived from the Greek word á½„ργανον (organon [itself derived from the better-known word á¼"ργον ergon - work; deed - > ergonomics, etc]) meaning tool. The term is used in both daily and scientific English in multiple ways.

Business marketing

Business marketing is the practice of individuals including commercial businesses, governments and institutions, facilitating the sale of their products or services to other companies or organizations that in turn resell them, use them as components in products or services they offer Business marketing is also called business-to-Business marketing for short. (Note that while marketing to government entities shares some of the same dynamics of organizational marketing, B2G Marketing is meaningfully different.)

Outsourcing	Outsourcing is subcontracting a process, such as product design or manufacturing, to a third-party company. The decision to outsource is often made in the interest of lowering cost or making better use of time and energy costs, redirecting or conserving energy directed at the competencies of a particular business, or to make more efficient use of land, labor, capital, (information) technology and resources. outsourcing became part of the business lexicon during the 1980s.
Strategic business unit	Strategic business unit or Strategic business unit is understood as a business unit within the overall corporate identity which is distinguishable from other business because it serves a defined external market where management can conduct strategic planning in relation to products and markets. When companies become really large, they are best thought of as being composed of a number of businesses (or Strategic business unit s.) In the broader domain of strategic management, the phrase Strategic business unit came into use in the 1960s, largely as a result of General Electric's many units.
Virtual business	A virtual business employs electronic means to transact business as opposed to a traditional brick and mortar business that relies on tangible locations, documents, and currency. Amazon.com is an early example of a virtual business. As an online bookstore it delivers bookstore services without the physical store presence; efficiently connecting buyers and sellers without the overhead of a brick-and-mortar location.
Control	Control is one of the managerial functions like planning, organizing, staffing and directing. It is an important function because it helps to check the errors and to take the corrective action so that deviation from standards are minimized and stated goals of the organization are achieved in desired manner.According to modern concepts, Control is a foreseeing action whereas earlier concept of Control was used only when errors were detected. Control in management means setting standards, measuring actual performance and taking corrective action.
Internet	The Internet is a global network of interconnected computers, enabling users to share information along multiple channels. Typically, a computer that connects to the Internet can access information from a vast array of available servers and other computers by moving information from them to the computer's local memory. The same connection allows that computer to send information to servers on the network; that information is in turn accessed and potentially modified by a variety of other interconnected computers.
Vertical integration	In microeconomics and management, the term vertical integration describes a style of management control. Vertically integrated companies are united through a hierarchy with a common owner. Usually each member of the hierarchy produces a different product or (market-specific) service, and the products combine to satisfy a common need.
Microsoft	Microsoft Corporation (NASDAQ: MSFT, HKEX: 4338) is an United States-based multinational computer technology corporation that develops, manufactures, licenses, and supports a wide range of software products for computing devices. Headquartered in Redmond, Washington, USA, its most profitable products are the Microsoft Windows operating system and the Microsoft Office suite of productivity software. The company was founded to develop and sell BASIC interpreters for the Altair 8800.
Affiliate	In the broadcasting industry (especially in North America), a network Affiliate is a local broadcaster which carries some or all of the programme line-up of a television or radio network, but is owned by a company other than the owner of the network. This distinguishes such a station from an owned-and-operated station (O'O), which is owned by its parent network.

In the United States, Federal Communications Commission (FCC) regulations limit the number of network-owned stations as a percentage of total market size.

Decision making

Decision making can be regarded as an outcome of mental processes (cognitive process) leading to the selection of a course of action among several alternatives. Every decision making process produces a final choice. The output can be an action or an opinion of choice.

Manufacturing

Manufacturing is the application of tools and a processing medium to the transformation of raw materials into finished goods for sale. This effort includes all intermediate processes required for the production and integration of a product's components. Some industries, like semiconductor and steel manufacturers use the term fabrication instead.

Swap

In finance, a Swap is a derivative in which two counterparties agree to exchange one stream of cash flow against another stream. These streams are called the legs of the Swap.

The cash flows are calculated over a notional principal amount, which is usually not exchanged between counterparties.

Factors of production

In economics, Factors of production are the resources employed to produce goods and services. They facilitate production but do not become part of the product (as with raw materials) or significantly transformed by the production process (as with fuel used to power machinery.) To 19th century economists, the Factors of production were land (natural resources, gifts from nature), labor (the ability to work), and capital goods (human-made tools and equipment.)

Subsidiary

A Subsidiary, in business matters, is an entity that is controlled by a bigger and more powerful entity. The controlled entity is called a company, corporation, or limited liability company and in some cases can be a government or state-owned enterprise, and the controlling entity is called its parent (or the parent company.) The reason for this distinction is that a lone company cannot be a Subsidiary of any organization; only an entity representing a legal fiction as a separate entity can be a Subsidiary.

Parent company

A Parent company is a company that owns enough voting stock in another firm to control management and operations by influencing or electing its board of directors; the second company being deemed as a subsidiary of the Parent company. The definition of a Parent company differs from jurisdiction to jurisdiction, with the definition normally being defined by way of laws dealing with companies in that jurisdiction.

The Parent company-subsidiary company relationship is defined by Part 1.2, Division 6, Section 46 of the Corporations Act 2001 (Cth), which states:

A body corporate (in this section called the first body) is a subsidiary of another body corporate if, and only if:

(a) the other body:

(i) controls the composition of the first body's board; or

(ii) is in a position to cast, or control the casting of, more than one-half of the maximum number of votes that might be cast at a general meeting of the first body; or

(iii) holds more than one-half of the issued share capital of the first body (excluding any part of that issued share capital that carries no right to participate beyond a specified amount in a distribution of either profits or capital); or

(b) the first body is a subsidiary of a subsidiary of the other body.

Profit

A profit , in the law of real property, is a nonpossessory interest in land similar to the better-known easement, which gives the holder the right to take natural resources such as petroleum, minerals, timber, and wild game from the land of another. Indeed, because of the necessity of allowing access to the land so that resources may be gathered, every profit contains an implied easement for the owner of the profit to enter the other party's land for the purpose of collecting the resources permitted by the profit.

Like an easement, profits can be created expressly by an agreement between the property owner and the owner of the profit, or by prescription, where the owner of the profit has made 'open and notorious' use of the land for a continuous and uninterrupted statutory period.

Pricing

Pricing is one of the four Ps of the marketing mix. The other three aspects are product, promotion, and place. It is also a key variable in microeconomic price allocation theory.

Standardization

Standardization or standardisation is the process of developing and agreeing upon technical standards. A standard is a document that establishes uniform engineering or technical specifications, criteria, methods, processes, or practices. Some standards are mandatory while others are voluntary.

Transfer

Transfer is a technique used in propaganda and advertising. Also known as association, this is a technique of projecting positive or negative qualities (praise or blame) of a person, entity, object, or value (an individual, group, organization, nation, patriotism, etc.) to another in order to make the second more acceptable or to discredit it.

Market

A Market is any one of a variety of different systems, institutions, procedures, social relations and infrastructures whereby persons trade, and goods and services are exchanged, forming part of the economy. It is an arrangement that allows buyers and sellers to exchange things. Market s vary in size, range, geographic scale, location, types and variety of human communities, as well as the types of goods and services traded.

Price	Price in economics and business is the result of an exchange and from that trade we assign a numerical monetary value to a good, service or asset. If I trade 4 apples for an orange, the price of an orange is 4 - apples. Inversely, the price of an apple is 1/4 oranges.
Transfer pricing	Transfer pricing refers to the pricing of contributions (assets, tangible and intangible, services, and funds) transferred within an organization. For example, goods from the production division may be sold to the marketing division, or goods from a parent company may be sold to a foreign subsidiary. Since the prices are set within an organization (i.e. controlled), the typical market mechanisms that establish prices for such transactions between third parties may not apply.
Joint venture	A joint venture is an entity formed between two or more parties to undertake economic activity together. The parties agree to create a new entity by both contributing equity, and they then share in the revenues, expenses, and control of the enterprise. The venture can be for one specific project only, or a continuing business relationship such as the Fuji Xerox joint venture.
Mean	In statistics, Mean has two related Mean ings: · the arithmetic Mean · the expected value of a random variable, which is also called the population Mean It is sometimes stated that the Mean Mean s average. This is incorrect if Mean is taken in the specific sense of 'arithmetic Mean as there are different types of averages: the Mean median, and mode. Other simple statistical analyses use measures of spread, such as range, interquartile range, or standard deviation. For a real-valued random variable X, the Mean is the expectation of X. Note that not every probability distribution has a defined Mean (or variance); see the Cauchy distribution for an example.
Economic	An economy (or 'the economy') is the realized Economic system of a country or other area. It includes the production, exchange, distribution, and consumption of goods and services of that area. The study of different types and examples of economies is the subject of Economic systems.
International business	International business is a term used to collectively describe topics relating to the operations of firms with interests in multiple countries. Such firms are sometimes called multinational corporations . Well known MNCs include fast food companies McDonald's and Yum Brands, vehicle manufacturers such as General Motors and Toyota, consumer electronics companies like Samsung, LG and Sony, and energy companies such as ExxonMobil and BP.
Culture	Culture is a term that has different meanings. For example, in 1952, Alfred Kroeber and Clyde Kluckhohn compiled a list of 164 definitions of culture in culture A Critical Review of Concepts and Definitions. However, the word culture is most commonly used in three basic senses: · excellence of taste in the fine arts and humanities, also known as high culture · an integrated pattern of human knowledge, belief, and behavior that depends upon the capacity for symbolic thought and social learning · the set of shared attitudes, values, goals, and practices that characterizes an institution, organization or group.

When the concept first emerged in eighteenth- and nineteenth-century Europe, it connoted a process of cultivation or improvement, as in agri culture or horti culture . In the nineteenth century, it came to refer first to the betterment or refinement of the individual, especially through education, and then to the fulfillment of national aspirations or ideals.

Comparative advertising

Comparative advertising is an advertisement in which a particular product specifically mentions a competitor by name for the express purpose of showing why the competitor is inferior to the product naming it.

This should not be confused with parody advertisements, where a fictional product is being advertised for the purpose of poking fun at the particular advertisement, nor should it be confused with the use of a coined brand name for the purpose of comparing the product without actually naming an actual competitor. ('Wikipedia tastes better and is less filling than the Encyclopedia Galactica.')

In the 1980s, during what has been referred to as the cola wars, soft-drink manufacturer Pepsi ran a series of advertisements where people, caught on hidden camera, in a blind taste test, chose Pepsi over rival Coca-Cola.

Skill

A skill is the learned capacity to carry out pre-determined results often with the minimum outlay of time, energy, or both. skill s can often be divided into domain-general and domain-specific skill s. For example, in the domain of work, some general skill s would include time management, teamwork and leadership, self motivation and others, whereas domain-specific skill s would be useful only for a certain job.

Organizational culture

Organizational culture is an idea in the field of Organizational studies and management which describes the psychology, attitudes, experiences, beliefs and Values (personal and cultural values)of an organization. It has been defined as 'the specific collection of values and norms that are shared by people and groups in an organization and that control the way they interact with each other and with stakeholders outside the organization.'

This definition continues to explain organizational values also known as 'beliefs and ideas about what kinds of goals members of an organization should pursue and ideas about the appropriate kinds or standards of behavior organizational members should use to achieve these goals. From organizational values develop organizational norms, guidelines or expectations that prescribe appropriate kinds of behavior by employees in particular situations and control the behavior of organizational members towards one another.'

organizational culture is not the same as corporate culture.

Marketing

Marketing is defined by the American Marketing Association as the activity, set of institutions, and processes for creating, communicating, delivering, and exchanging offerings that have value for customers, clients, partners, and society at large. The term developed from the original meaning which referred literally to going to market, as in shopping, or going to a market to sell goods or services.

Marketing practice tends to be seen as a creative industry, which includes advertising, distribution and selling.

Marketing research

Consumer market research is a form of applied sociology that concentrates on understanding the behaviours, whims and preferences, of consumers in a market-based economy, and aims to understand the effects and comparative success of marketing campaigns. The field of consumer marketing research as a statistical science was pioneered by Arthur Nielsen with the founding of the ACNielsen Company in 1923 .

Thus marketing research is the systematic and objective identification, collection, analysis, and dissemination of information for the purpose of assisting management in decision making related to the identification and solution of problems and opportunities in marketing.

Competitive

Competitive ness is a comparative concept of the ability and performance of a firm, sub-sector or country to sell and supply goods and/or services in a given market. Although widely used in economics and business management, the usefulness of the concept, particularly in the context of national competitive ness, is vigorously disputed by economists, such as Paul Krugman .

The term may also be applied to markets, where it is used to refer to the extent to which the market structure may be regarded as perfectly competitive

Competitive Intelligence

A broad definition of Competitive intelligence is the action of gathering, analyzing, and distributing information about products, customers, competitors and any aspect of the environment needed to support executives and managers in making strategic decisions for an organization.

Key points of this definitions:

· Competitive intelligence is an ethical and legal business practice. (This is important as Competitive intelligence professionals emphasize that the discipline is not the same as industrial espionage which is both unethical and usually illegal.)

· The focus is on the external business environment.

· There is a process involved in gathering information, converting it into intelligence and then utilizing this in business decision making. Competitive intelligence professionals emphasize that if the intelligence gathered is not usable (or actionable) then it is not intelligence.

A more focused definition of Competitive intelligence regards it as the organizational function responsible for the early identification of risks and opportunities in the market before they become obvious. Experts also call this process the early signal analysis. This definition focuses attention on the difference between dissemination of widely available factual information (such as market statistics, financial reports, newspaper clippings) performed by functions such as libraries and information centers, and Competitive intelligence which is a perspective on developments and events aimed at yielding a competitive edge.

Environmental scanning

Environmental scanning is a process of gathering, analyzing, and dispensing information for tactical or strategic purposes. The Environmental scanning process entails obtaining both factual and subjective information on the business environments in which a company is operating or considering entering.

There are three ways of scanning the business environment:

· Ad-hoc scanning - Short term, infrequent examinations usually initiated by a crisis
· Regular scanning - Studies done on a regular schedule (say, once a year)
· Continuous scanning(also called continuous learning) - continuous structured data collection and processing on a broad range of environmental factors

Most commentators feel that in today's turbulent business environment the best scanning method available is continuous scanning.This allows the firm to :

-act quickly-take advantage of opportunities before competitors do-respond to environmental threats before significant damage is done

The Macro Environment

Environmental scanning usually refers just to the macro environment, but it can also include:-industry -competitor analysis marketing research(consumer analysis) -New Product Development(product innovations)- the company's internal environment

Macro Environmental scanning involves analysing:

· The Economy

GDP per capitaeconomic growthunemployment]] rateinflation]] rateconsumer and investor confidenceinventory levelscurrency exchange ratesmerchandise trade balancefinancial and political health of trading partnersbalance of paymentsfuture trends

· Government

political climate - amount of government activitypolitical stability and riskgovernment debtbudget deficit or surpluscorporate and personal tax ratespayroll taxesimport tariffs and quotasexport restrictionsrestrictions on international financial flows

· Legal

minimum wage lawsenvironmental protection lawsworker safety lawsunion lawscopyright and patent lawsanti- monopoly lawsSunday closing lawsmunicipal licenceslaws that favour business investment

· Technology

efficiency of infrastructure, including: roads, ports, airports, rolling stock, hospitals, education, healthcare, communication, etc.industrial productivitynew manufacturing processesnew products and services of competitorsnew products and services of supply chain partnersany new technology that could impact the companycost and accessibility of electrical power

· Ecology

· ecological concerns that affect the firms production processes
· ecological concerns that affect customers' buying habits
· ecological concerns that affect customers' perception of the company or product
· Socio-Cultural

· demographic factors such as:

· population size and distribution
· age distribution
· education levels
· income levels
· ethnic origins
· religious affiliations
· attitudes towards:

· materialism, capitalism, free enterprise
· individualism, role of family, role of government, collectivism
· role of church and religion
· consumerism
· environmentalism
· importance of work, pride of accomplishment
· cultural structures including:

· diet and nutrition
· housing conditions
· Potential Suppliers

· Labour supply

· quantity of labour available
· quality of labour available
· stability of labour supply
· wage expectations
· employee turn-over rate
· strikes and labour relations
· educational facilities
· Material suppliers

· quality, quantity, price, and stability of material inputs
· delivery delays
· proximity of bulky or heavy material inputs
· level of competition among suppliers
· Service Providers

· quantity, quality, price, and stability of service facilitators
· special requirements
· Stakeholders

· Lobbyists
· Shareholders
· Employees
· Partners

Scanning these macro environmental variables for threats and opportunities requires that each issue be rated on two dimensions. It must be rated on its potential impact on the company, and rated on its likeliness of occurrence.

Market

A Market is any one of a variety of different systems, institutions, procedures, social relations and infrastructures whereby persons trade, and goods and services are exchanged, forming part of the economy. It is an arrangement that allows buyers and sellers to exchange things. Market s vary in size, range, geographic scale, location, types and variety of human communities, as well as the types of goods and services traded.

Job interview

A Job interview is a process in which a potential employee is evaluated by an employer for prospective employment in their company, organization and was established in the late 16th century.

A Job interview typically precedes the hiring decision, and is used to evaluate the candidate. The interview is usually preceded by the evaluation of submitted résumés from interested candidates, then selecting a small number of candidates for interviews.

Data collection

Data collection is a term used to describe a process of preparing and collecting data - for example as part of a process improvement or similar project.

data collection usually takes place early on in an improvement project, and is often formalised through a data collection Plan which often contains the following activity.

· Pre collection activity - Agree goals, target data, definitions, methods
· Collection - data collection
· Present Findings - usually involves some form of sorting analysis and/or presentation.

A formal data collection process is necessary as it ensures that data gathered is both defined and accurate and that subsequent decisions based on arguments embodied in the findings are valid . The process provides both a baseline from which to measure from and in certain cases a target on what to improve. Types of data collection 1-By mail questionnaires 2-By personal interview

· Six sigma
· Sampling (statistics) .

Export

In economics, an export is any good or commodity, transported from one country to another country in a legitimate fashion, typically for use in trade. export goods or services are provided to foreign consumers by domestic producers. export is an important part of international trade.

Good

A good is an object whose consumption increases the utility of the consumer, for which the quantity demanded exceeds the quantity supplied at zero price. Goods are usually modeled as having diminishing marginal utility. The first individual purchase has high utility; the second has less.

Goods and Services

In economics, economic output is divided into physical goods and intangible services. Consumption of Goods and services is assumed to produce utility. It is often used when referring to a Goods and services Tax.

Industry

An Industry is the manufacturing of a good or service within a category. Although Industry is a broad term for any kind of economic production, in economics and urban planning Industry is a synonym for the secondary sector, which is a type of economic activity involved in the manufacturing of raw materials into goods and products.

There are four key industrial economic sectors: the primary sector, largely raw material extraction industries such as mining and farming; the secondary sector, involving refining, construction, and manufacturing; the tertiary sector, which deals with services (such as law and medicine) and distribution of manufactured goods; and the quaternary sector, a relatively new type of knowledge Industry focusing on technological research, design and development such as computer programming, and biochemistry.

International Trade

International trade is exchange of capital, goods, and services across international borders or territories. In most countries, it represents a significant share of gross domestic product (GDP.) While International trade has been present throughout much of history , its economic, social, and political importance has been on the rise in recent centuries.

International Trade Administration

The International Trade Administration is an agency in the United States Department of Commerce that promotes United States exports of nonagricultural U.S. services and goods.

The International Trade Administration's stated goals are to

- Provide practical information to help Americans select markets and products.
- Ensure that Americans have access to international markets as required by the U.S. trade agreements.
- Safeguard Americans from unfair competition from dumped and subsidized imports.

International Trade Administration consists of four sub-units. These are: Import Administration (IA), Market Access and Compliance (MAC), Manufacturing and Services (MAS) and the US Commercial Service (USCS.)

The International Trade Administration was created on January 2, 1980 and is headed by the Under Secretary of Commerce for International Trade.

Market Research

Market research often refers to either primary or secondary research. Secondary research involves a company using information compiled from various sources, which is about a new or existing product. The advantages of secondary research are that it is relatively cheap and easily accessible.

Merchandise	Merchandising refers to the methods, practices and operations conducted to promote and sustain certain categories of commercial activity. The term is understood to have different specific meanings depending on the context. merchandise is a sale goods at a store In marketing, one of the definitions of merchandising is the practice in which the brand or image from one product or service is used to sell another.
Report	In writing, a report is a document characterized by information or other content reflective of inquiry or investigation, which is tailored to the context of a given situation and audience. The purpose of report s is usually to inform. However, report s may include persuasive elements, such as recommendations, suggestions, or other motivating conclusions that indicate possible future actions the report reader might take.
Comparative advertising	Comparative advertising is an advertisement in which a particular product specifically mentions a competitor by name for the express purpose of showing why the competitor is inferior to the product naming it. This should not be confused with parody advertisements, where a fictional product is being advertised for the purpose of poking fun at the particular advertisement, nor should it be confused with the use of a coined brand name for the purpose of comparing the product without actually naming an actual competitor. ('Wikipedia tastes better and is less filling than the Encyclopedia Galactica.') In the 1980s, during what has been referred to as the cola wars, soft-drink manufacturer Pepsi ran a series of advertisements where people, caught on hidden camera, in a blind taste test, chose Pepsi over rival Coca-Cola.
United States	The United States of America (commonly referred to as the United States the U.S., the United States A, or America) is a federal constitutional republic comprising fifty states and a federal district. The country is situated mostly in central North America, where its 48 contiguous states and Washington, D.C., the capital district, lie between the Pacific and Atlantic Oceans, bordered by Canada to the north and Mexico to the south. The state of Alaska is in the northwest of the continent, with Canada to its east and Russia to the west across the Bering Strait.
Competitor analysis	Competitor analysis in marketing and strategic management is an assessment of the strengths and weaknesses of current and potential competitors. This analysis provides both an offensive and defensive strategic context through which to identify opportunities and threats. Competitor profiling coalesces all of the relevant sources of Competitor analysis into one framework in the support of efficient and effective strategy formulation, implementation, monitoring and adjustment.
Distribution	Distribution is one of the four elements of marketing mix. An organization or set of organizations (go-betweens) involved in the process of making a product or service available for use or consumption by a consumer or business user. The other three parts of the marketing mix are product, pricing, and promotion.
Embargo	An Embargo is the prohibition of commerce and trade with a certain country, in order to isolate it and to put its government into a difficult internal situation, given that the effects of the Embargo are often able to make its economy suffer from the initiative. It is similar to a blockade, as in 'el bloqueo' or the American blockade on Cuba. Embargo s generally attempt to pressure weaker adversaries to do what the abarcading country wishes.

Need

A need is something that is necessary for humans to live a healthy life. need s are distinguished from wants because a deficiency would cause a clear negative outcome, such as dysfunction or death. need s can be objective and physical, such as food and water, or they can be subjective and psychological, such as the need for self-esteem.

Cluster analysis

Cluster analysis or clustering is the assignment of objects into groups (called clusters) so that objects from the same cluster are more similar to each other than objects from different clusters. Often similarity is assessed according to a distance measure. Clustering is a common technique for statistical data analysis, which is used in many fields, including machine learning, data mining, pattern recognition, image analysis and bioinformatics.

Economic

An economy (or 'the economy') is the realized Economic system of a country or other area. It includes the production, exchange, distribution, and consumption of goods and services of that area. The study of different types and examples of economics is the subject of Economic systems.

Electronic commerce

Electronic commerce, commonly known as e-commerce or eCommerce, consists of the buying and selling of products or services over electronic systems such as the Internet and other computer networks. The amount of trade conducted electronically has grown extraordinarily with wide-spread Internet usage. A wide variety of commerce is conducted in this way, spurring and drawing on innovations in electronic funds transfer, supply chain management, Internet marketing, online transaction processing, electronic data interchange (EDI), inventory management systems, and automated data collection systems.

External

In economics, an external ity or spillover of an economic transaction is an impact on a party that is not directly involved in the transaction. In such a case, prices do not reflect the full costs or benefits in production or consumption of a product or service. A positive impact is called an external benefit, while a negative impact is called an external cost.

Import

An import is any good (e.g. a commodity) or service brought into one country from another country in a legitimate fashion, typically for use in trade.It is a good that is brought in from another country for sale. import goods or services are provided to domestic consumers by foreign producers. An import in the receiving country is an export to the sending country.

Organization

An organization is a social arrangement which pursues collective goals, which controls its own performance, and which has a boundary separating it from its environment. The word itself is derived from the Greek word á½„ργανον (organon [itself derived from the better-known word á¼"ργον ergon - work; deed - > ergonomics, etc]) meaning tool. The term is used in both daily and scientific English in multiple ways.

Trend analysis

The term 'trend analysis' refers to the concept of collecting information and attempting to spot a pattern in the information. In some fields of study, the term 'trend analysis' has more formally-defined meanings.

In project management trend analysis is a mathematical technique that uses historical results to predict future outcome.

Estimation

Estimation is the calculated approximation of a result which is usable even if input data may be incomplete or uncertain.

In statistics, see Estimation theory, estimator.

In mathematics, approximation or Estimation typically means finding upper or lower bounds of a quantity that cannot readily be computed precisely and is also an educated guess .

Time series

In statistics, signal processing, and many other fields, a Time series is a sequence of data points, measured typically at successive times, spaced at (often uniform) time intervals. Time series analysis comprises methods that attempt to understand such Time series, often either to understand the underlying context of the data points (Where did they come from? What generated them?), or to make forecasts (predictions.) Time series forecasting is the use of a model to forecast future events based on known past events: to forecast future data points before they are measured.

World Trade Organization

The World Trade Organization is an international organization designed to supervise and liberalize international trade. The World Trade Organization came into being on 1 January 1995, and is the successor to the General Agreement on Tariffs and Trade (GATT), which was created in 1947, and continued to operate for almost five decades as a de facto international organization.

The World Trade Organization deals with the rules of trade between nations at a near-global level; it is responsible for negotiating and implementing new trade agreements, and is in charge of policing member countries' adherence to all the World Trade Organization agreements, signed by the majority of the world's trading nations and ratified in their parliaments.

E-commerce

Electronic commerce, commonly known as E-commerce or eCommerce, consists of the buying and selling of products or services over electronic systems such as the Internet and other computer networks. The amount of trade conducted electronically has grown extraordinarily with wide-spread Internet usage. A wide variety of commerce is conducted in this way, spurring and drawing on innovations in electronic funds transfer, supply chain management, Internet marketing, online transaction processing, electronic data interchange (EDI), inventory management systems, and automated data collection systems.

Minority

A Minority or digger group is a sociological group that does not constitute a politically dominant voting majority of the total population of a given society. A sociological Minority is not necessarily a numerical Minority -- it may include any group that is subnormal with respect to a dominant group in terms of social status, education, employment, wealth and political power. To avoid confusion, some writers prefer the terms 'subordinate group' and 'dominant group' rather than 'Minority' and 'majority', respectively.

Policy

A Policy is typically described as a deliberate plan of action to guide decisions and achieve rational outcome(s.) However, the term may also be used to denote what is actually done, even though it is unplanned.

The term may apply to government, private sector organizations and groups, and individuals.

Profit

A profit , in the law of real property, is a nonpossessory interest in land similar to the better-known easement, which gives the holder the right to take natural resources such as petroleum, minerals, timber, and wild game from the land of another. Indeed, because of the necessity of allowing access to the land so that resources may be gathered, every profit contains an implied easement for the owner of the profit to enter the other party's land for the purpose of collecting the resources permitted by the profit.

Like an easement, profits can be created expressly by an agreement between the property owner and the owner of the profit, or by prescription, where the owner of the profit has made 'open and notorious' use of the land for a continuous and uninterrupted statutory period.

Antitrust

Competition law, known in the United States as antitrust law, has three main elements:

· prohibiting agreements or practices that restrict free trading and competition between business entities. This includes in particular the repression of cartels.
· banning abusive behavior by a firm dominating a market, or anti-competitive practices that tend to lead to such a dominant position. Practices controlled in this way may include predatory pricing, tying, price gouging, refusal to deal, and many others.
· supervising the mergers and acquisitions of large corporations, including some joint ventures. Transactions that are considered to threaten the competitive process can be prohibited altogether, or approved subject to 'remedies' such as an obligation to divest part of the merged business or to offer licenses or access to facilities to enable other businesses to continue competing.

The substance and practice of competition law varies from jurisdiction to jurisdiction. Protecting the interests of consumers (consumer welfare) and ensuring that entrepreneurs have an opportunity to compete in the market economy are often treated as important objectives. Competition law is closely connected with law on deregulation of access to markets, state aids and subsidies, the privatization of state owned assets and the establishment of independent sector regulators. In recent decades, competition law has been viewed as a way to provide better public services.

Antitrust law

Competition law, known in the United States as Antitrust law, has three main elements:

· prohibiting agreements or practices that restrict free trading and competition between business entities. This includes in particular the repression of cartels.
· banning abusive behaviour by a firm dominating a market, or anti-competitive practices that tend to lead to such a dominant position. Practices controlled in this way may include predatory pricing, tying, price gouging, refusal to deal, and many others.
· supervising the mergers and acquisitions of large corporations, including some joint ventures. Transactions that are considered to threaten the competitive process can be prohibited altogether, or approved subject to 'remedies' such as an obligation to divest part of the merged business or to offer licences or access to facilities to enable other businesses to continue competing.

The substance and practice of competition law varies from jurisdiction to jurisdiction. Protecting the interests of consumers (consumer welfare) and ensuring that entrepreneurs have an opportunity to compete in the market economy are often treated as important objectives. Competition law is closely connected with law on deregulation of access to markets, state aids and subsidies, the privatisation of state owned assets and the establishment of independent sector regulators. In recent decades, competition law has been viewed as a way to provide better public services.

Competition law

Competition law, known in the United States as antitrust law, has three main elements:

· prohibiting agreements or practices that restrict free trading and competition between business entities. This includes in particular the repression of cartels.
· banning abusive behaviour by a firm dominating a market, or anti-competitive practices that tend to lead to such a dominant position. Practices controlled in this way may include predatory pricing, tying, price gouging, refusal to deal, and many others.
· supervising the mergers and acquisitions of large corporations, including some joint ventures. Transactions that are considered to threaten the competitive process can be prohibited altogether, or approved subject to 'remedies' such as an obligation to divest part of the merged business or to offer licences or access to facilities to enable other businesses to continue competing.

The substance and practice of Competition law varies from jurisdiction to jurisdiction. Protecting the interests of consumers (consumer welfare) and ensuring that entrepreneurs have an opportunity to compete in the market economy are often treated as important objectives. Competition law is closely connected with law on deregulation of access to markets, state aids and subsidies, the privatisation of state owned assets and the establishment of independent sector regulators. In recent decades, Competition law has been viewed as a way to provide better public services.

Ownership

Ownership is the state or fact of exclusive rights and control over property, which may be an object, land/real estate, or some other kind of property (like government-granted monopolies collectively referred to as intellectual property.) It is embodied in an Ownership right also referred to as title.

Ownership is the key building block in the development of the capitalist socio-economic system.

Business

A business is a legally recognized organization designed to provide goods and/or services to consumers. business es are predominant in capitalist economies, most being privately owned and formed to earn profit that will increase the wealth of its owners and grow the business itself. The owners and operators of a business have as one of their main objectives the receipt or generation of a financial return in exchange for work and acceptance of risk.

Identity column

An Identity column is a column in a database table that uniquely identifies every row in the table, and is made up of values generated by the database. This is much like an AutoNumber field in Microsoft Access or a sequence in Oracle. Because the concept is so important in database science, many RDBMS systems implement some type of generated key, although each has its own terminology.

Subculture

In sociology, anthropology and cultural studies, a subculture is a group of people with a culture (whether distinct or hidden) which differentiates them from the larger culture to which they belong. If a particular subculture is characterized by a systematic opposition to the dominant culture, it may be described as a counterculture.

As early as 1950, David Riesman distinguished between a majority, 'which passively accepted commercially provided styles and meanings, and a 'subculture' which actively sought a minority style ...

Trade mission

Trade mission is an international trip by government officials and businesspeople that is organized by agencies of national of provincial governments for purpose of exploring international business opportunities. Business people who attend Trade mission s are typically introduced both to important business contacts and to well-placed government officials.

Globalization

Globalization in its literal sense is the process of transformation of local or regional phenomena into global ones. It can be described as a process by which the people of the world are unified into a single society and function together.

This process is a combination of economic, technological, sociocultural and political forces.

Population

In biology, a Population , is the collection of inter-breeding organisms of a particular species; in sociology, a collection of human beings. Individuals within a Population share a factor may be reduced by statistical means, but such a generalization may be too vague to imply anything. Demography is used extensively in marketing, which relates to economic units, such as retailers, to potential customers.

TRIPs

The Agreement on Trade Related Aspects of Intellectual Property Rights (TRIPs) is an international agreement administered by the World Trade Organization (WTO) that sets down minimum standards for many forms of intellectual property (IP) regulation. It was negotiated at the end of the Uruguay Round of the General Agreement on Tariffs and Trade (GATT) in 1994.

Specifically, TRIPs contains requirements that nations' laws must meet for: copyright rights, including the rights of performers, producers of sound recordings and broadcasting organizations; geographical indications, including appellations of origin; industrial designs; integrated circuit layout-designs; patents; monopolies for the developers of new plant varieties; trademarks; trade dress; and undisclosed or confidential information.

Raw data

Raw data is a term for unprocessed data, it is also known as primary data. It is a relative term Raw data can be input to a computer program or used in manual analysis procedures such as gathering statistics from a survey.

Bias

Bias is a term used to describe a tendency or preference towards a particular perspective, ideology or result, especially when the tendency interferes with the ability to be impartial, unprejudiced, or objective.. In other words, Bias is generally seen as 'one-sided'. The term Bias ed is used to describe an action, judgment, or other outcome influenced by a prejudged perspective.

Market segment

A market segment is a subgroup of people or organizations sharing one or more characteristics that cause them to have similar product and/or service needs. A true market segment meets all of the following criteria: it is distinct from other segments (different segments have different needs), it is homogeneous within the segment (exhibits common needs); it responds similarly to a market stimulus, and it can be reached by a market intervention. The term is also used when consumers with identical product and/or service needs are divided up into groups so they can be charged different amounts.

Asia-Pacific

Asia-Pacific or APAC is that part of the world in or near the Western Pacific Ocean. The area includes much of East Asia, Southeast Asia, Australasia and Oceania.) Sometimes the term Asia-Pacific includes South Asia, though India and its neighbours are on or near the Indian Ocean rather than the Pacific Ocean.

Consumer

Consumer is a broad label that refers to any individuals or households that use goods and services generated within the economy. The concept of a Consumer is used in different contexts, so that the usage and significance of the term may vary.

A Consumer is a person who uses any product or service.

Consumer Confidence

Consumer confidence is the degree of optimism that consumers feel about the overall state of the economy and their personal financial situation. How confident people feel about stability of their incomes determines their spending activity and therefore serves as one of the key indicators for the overall shape of the economy. In essence, if Consumer confidence is higher, consumers are making more purchases, boosting the economic expansion.

Internet

The Internet is a global network of interconnected computers, enabling users to share information along multiple channels. Typically, a computer that connects to the Internet can access information from a vast array of available servers and other computers by moving information from them to the computer's local memory. The same connection allows that computer to send information to servers on the network; that information is in turn accessed and potentially modified by a variety of other interconnected computers.

Set TSP

In combinatorial optimization, the set TSP, group TSP, One-of-a-set TSP, Multiple Choice TSP or Covering Salesman Problem, is a generalization of the Traveling salesman problem, whereby it is required to find a shortest tour in a graph which visits all specified disjoint subsets of the vertices of a graph. The ordinary TSP is a special case of the set TSP when all subsets to be visited are singletons. Therefore the set TSP is also NP-hard.

Certification

Certification refers to the confirmation of certain characteristics of an object, person, or organization. This confirmation is often, but not always, provided by some form of external review, education, or assessment. One of the most common types of Certification in modern society is professional Certification, where a person is certified as being able to competently complete a job or task, usually by the passing of an examination.

Certified

Certification refers to the confirmation of certain characteristics of an object, person, or organization. This confirmation is often, but not always, provided by some form of external review, education, or assessment. One of the most common types of certification in modern society is professional certification, where a person is certified as being able to competently complete a job or task, usually by the passing of an examination.

Information System

In a general sense , the term Information system refers to a system of people, data records and activities that process the data and information in an organization, and it includes the organization's manual and automated processes. In a narrow sense, the term Information system (or computer-based Information system refers to the specific application software that is used to store data records in a computer system and automates some of the information-processing activities of the organization. Computer-based Information system s are in the field of information technology.

Decision making

Decision making can be regarded as an outcome of mental processes (cognitive process) leading to the selection of a course of action among several alternatives. Every decision making process produces a final choice. The output can be an action or an opinion of choice.

Efficient-market hypothesis

In finance, the efficient-market hypothesis asserts that financial markets are 'informationally efficient' stocks, bonds and instantly change to reflect new information. Therefore it is impossible to consistently outperform the market by using any information that the market already knows, except through luck. Information or news in the EMH is defined as anything that may affect prices that is unknowable in the present and thus appears randomly in the future.

Feasibility study

If a project is seen to be feasible from the results of the study, the next logical step is to proceed with it. The research and information uncovered in the Feasibility study will support the detailed planning and reduce the research time..

A well-researched and well-written Feasibility study is critical when making 'Go/No Go' decisions regarding entry into new businesses.

Market development

A market development strategy targets non-buying customers in currently targeted segments. It also targets new customers in new segments. (Winer)

A marketing manager has to think about the following questions before implementing a market development strategy: Is it profitable? Will it require the introduction of new or modified products? Is the customer and channel well enough researched and understood?

The marketing manager uses these four groups to give more focus to the market segment decision: existing customers, competitor customers, non-buying in current segments, new segments.

Pareto Principle

The Pareto principle states that, for many events, roughly 80% of the effects come from 20% of the causes. Business management thinker Joseph M. Juran suggested the principle and named it after Italian economist Vilfredo Pareto, who observed that 80% of the land in Italy was owned by 20% of the population.

Project Management

Project management is the discipline of planning, organizing and managing resources to bring about the successful completion of specific project goals and objectives. It is often closely related to and sometimes conflated with Program management.

A project is a finite endeavor--having specific start and completion dates--undertaken to meet particular goals and objectives, usually to bring about beneficial change or added value.

Project Management Process

A Project management process is the management process of planning and controlling the performance or execution of a project.

· Documented need to act
· Project plan templates
· Lessons learned from previous projects
· Existing project management standards
· External information
· Resources for project planning and project execution

· Project initiation
· Project planning
· Project execution
· Project control and validation
· Project closeout and evaluation

· Project products delivered
· Project objectives achieved (as a result of the interplay among project products and the organization or its environment)
· Lessons learned documented .

SWOT analysis

SWOT analysis is a strategic planning method used to evaluate the Strengths, Weaknesses, Opportunities, and Threats involved in a project or in a business venture. It involves specifying the objective of the business venture or project and identifying the internal and external factors that are favorable and unfavorable to achieving that objective. The technique is credited to Albert Humphrey, who led a convention at Stanford University in the 1960s and 1970s using data from Fortune 500 companies.

Planning

Planning in organizations and public policy is both the organizational process of creating and maintaining a plan; and the psychological process of thinking about the activities required to create a desired goal on some scale. As such, it is a fundamental property of intelligent behavior. This thought process is essential to the creation and refinement of a plan, or integration of it with other plans, that is, it combines forecasting of developments with the preparation of scenarios of how to react to them.

Strategic planning

Strategic planning is an organization's process of defining its strategy and making decisions on allocating its resources to pursue this strategy, including its capital and people. Various business analysis techniques can be used in Strategic planning, including SWOT analysis (Strengths, Weaknesses, Opportunities, and Threats) and PEST analysis (Political, Economic, Social, and Technological analysis) or STEER analysis involving Socio-cultural, Technological, Economic, Ecological, and Regulatory factors and EPISTEL (Environment, Political, Informatic, Social, Technological, Economic and Legal)

Strategic planning is the formal consideration of an organization's future course. All Strategic planning deals with at least one of three key questions:

- 'What do we do?'
- 'For whom do we do it?'
- 'How do we excel?'

In business Strategic planning, the third question is better phrased 'How can we beat or avoid competition?'. (Bradford and Duncan, page 1.)

Cultural identity

Cultural identity is the identity of a group or culture, or of an individual as far as one is influenced by one's belonging to a group or culture. Cultural identity is similar to and has overlaps with, but is not synonymous with, identity politics.

There are modern questions of culture that are transferred into questions of identity.

Rate of return

In finance, rate of return rate of profit or sometimes just return, is the ratio of money gained or lost on an investment relative to the amount of money invested. The amount of money gained or lost may be referred to as interest, profit/loss, gain/loss, or net income/loss. The money invested may be referred to as the asset, capital, principal, or the cost basis of the investment.

Writing

Writing is the representation of language in a textual medium through the use of a set of signs or symbols (known as a writing system.) It is distinguished from illustration, such as cave drawing and painting, and the recording of language via a non-textual medium such as magnetic tape audio.

In Eurasia writing began as a consequence of the burgeoning needs of accounting.

National Retail Federation	The National Retail Federation claims to be the world's largest retail trade association. Its members include department store, specialty, discount, catalog, Internet, and independent retailers, and chain restaurants and grocery stores. Members also include businesses that provide goods and services to retailers.
Magazine	Magazine s, periodicals, glossies or serials are publications, generally published on a regular schedule, containing a variety of articles, generally financed by advertising, by a purchase price, by pre-paid magazine subscriptions, or all three. magazine s can be distributed through the mail; through sales by newsstands, bookstores or other vendors; or through free distribution at selected pick up locations. The various elements that contribute to the production of magazine s vary wildly.

Advertising	Advertising is a form of communication that typically attempts to persuade potential customers to purchase or to consume more of a particular brand of product or service. 'While now central to the contemporary global economy and the reproduction of global production networks, it is only quite recently that Advertising has been more than a marginal influence on patterns of sales and production. The formation of modern Advertising was intimately bound up with the emergence of new forms of monopoly capitalism around the end of the 19th and beginning of the 20th century as one element in corporate strategies to create, organize and where possible control markets, especially for mass produced consumer goods.
International Monetary Fund	The International Monetary Fund is an international organization that oversees the global financial system by following the macroeconomic policies of its member countries, in particular those with an impact on exchange rates and the balance of payments. It is an organization formed to stabilize international exchange rates and facilitate development. It also offers financial and technical assistance to its members, making it an international lender of last resort.
Internet	The Internet is a global network of interconnected computers, enabling users to share information along multiple channels. Typically, a computer that connects to the Internet can access information from a vast array of available servers and other computers by moving information from them to the computer's local memory. The same connection allows that computer to send information to servers on the network; that information is in turn accessed and potentially modified by a variety of other interconnected computers.
Monetary	Monetary policy is the process by which the government, central bank (ii) availability of money, and (iii) cost of money or rate of interest, in order to attain a set of objectives oriented towards the growth and stability of the economy. monetary theory provides insight into how to craft optimal monetary policy. monetary policy is referred to as either being an expansionary policy where an expansionary policy increases the total supply of money in the economy, and a contractionary policy decreases the total money supply.
Challenge	Challenge is a United Kingdom digital TV channel owned by Virgin Media Television. It was originally called The Family Channel from 1 September 1993 to 31 January 1997 but it was later re-branded as challenge TV from 1 February 1997. On 20 May 2002 the channel was re-named again but this time it was just challenge? and 30 June 2003 the question mark was removed to leave the challenge name in its place.
Consumer	Consumer is a broad label that refers to any individuals or households that use goods and services generated within the economy. The concept of a Consumer is used in different contexts, so that the usage and significance of the term may vary. A Consumer is a person who uses any product or service.
Consumer goods	Consumer goods are final goods specifically intended for the mass market. For instance, consumer goods do not include investment assets, like precious antiques, even though these antiques are final goods. Manufactured goods are goods that have been processed by way of machinery.
Good	A good is an object whose consumption increases the utility of the consumer, for which the quantity demanded exceeds the quantity supplied at zero price. Goods are usually modeled as having diminishing marginal utility. The first individual purchase has high utility; the second has less.

Market

A Market is any one of a variety of different systems, institutions, procedures, social relations and infrastructures whereby persons trade, and goods and services are exchanged, forming part of the economy. It is an arrangement that allows buyers and sellers to exchange things. Market s vary in size, range, geographic scale, location, types and variety of human communities, as well as the types of goods and services traded.

Control

Control is one of the managerial functions like planning, organizing, staffing and directing. It is an important function because it helps to check the errors and to take the corrective action so that deviation from standards are minimized and stated goals of the organization are achieved in desired manner.According to modern concepts, Control is a foreseeing action whereas earlier concept of Control was used only when errors were detected. Control in management means setting standards, measuring actual performance and taking corrective action.

Distribution

Distribution is one of the four elements of marketing mix. An organization or set of organizations (go-betweens) involved in the process of making a product or service available for use or consumption by a consumer or business user.

The other three parts of the marketing mix are product, pricing, and promotion.

Job interview

A Job interview is a process in which a potential employee is evaluated by an employer for prospective employment in their company, organization and was established in the late 16th century.

A Job interview typically precedes the hiring decision, and is used to evaluate the candidate. The interview is usually preceded by the evaluation of submitted résumés from interested candidates, then selecting a small number of candidates for interviews.

Minority

A Minority or digger group is a sociological group that does not constitute a politically dominant voting majority of the total population of a given society. A sociological Minority is not necessarily a numerical Minority -- it may include any group that is subnormal with respect to a dominant group in terms of social status, education, employment, wealth and political power. To avoid confusion, some writers prefer the terms 'subordinate group' and 'dominant group' rather than 'Minority' and 'majority', respectively.

Ownership

Ownership is the state or fact of exclusive rights and control over property, which may be an object, land/real estate, or some other kind of property (like government-granted monopolies collectively referred to as intellectual property.) It is embodied in an Ownership right also referred to as title.

Ownership is the key building block in the development of the capitalist socio-economic system.

Export

In economics, an export is any good or commodity, transported from one country to another country in a legitimate fashion, typically for use in trade. export goods or services are provided to foreign consumers by domestic producers. export is an important part of international trade.

Cooperative

A cooperative is defined by the International Co-operative Alliance's Statement on the Co-operative Identity as an autonomous association of persons united voluntarily to meet their common economic, social, and cultural needs and aspirations through a jointly-owned and democratically-controlled enterprise. It is a business organization owned and operated by a group of individuals for their mutual benefit. A cooperative may also be defined as a business owned and controlled equally by the people who use its services or who work at it.

Customer

A customer also client, buyer or purchaser is usually used to refer to a current or potential buyer or user of the products of an individual or organization, mostly called the supplier or seller. This is typically through purchasing or renting goods or services. However in certain contexts the term customer also includes by extension anyone who uses or experiences the services of another.

International trade

International trade is exchange of capital, goods, and services across international borders or territories. In most countries, it represents a significant share of gross domestic product (GDP.) While International trade has been present throughout much of history , its economic, social, and political importance has been on the rise in recent centuries.

Merchant

Merchant s are businessmen who trade in commodities that they do not produce themselves, in order to earn a profit.

Merchant s can be of two types:

· A wholesale Merchant operates in the chain between producer and retail Merchant Some wholesale Merchant s only organize the movement of goods rather than move the goods themselves.

· A retail Merchant or retailer, sells commodities to consumers (including businesses.) A shop owner is a retail Merchant

A Merchant class characterizes many pre-modern societies. Its status can range from high (the members even eventually achieving titles such as that of Merchant prince or nabob) to low, as in Chinese culture, owing to the presumed distastefulness of profiting from 'mere' trade rather than from labor or the labor of others as in agriculture and craftsmanship.

.

Economic

An economy (or 'the economy') is the realized Economic system of a country or other area. It includes the production, exchange, distribution, and consumption of goods and services of that area. The study of different types and examples of economies is the subject of Economic systems.

Turnkey

Turn-key refers to something that is ready for immediate use, generally used in the sale or supply of goods or services. The term is common in the construction industry, for instance, in which it refers to the bundling of materials and labor by sub-contractors. A 'Turnkey' job by a plumber would include the parts (toilets, tub, faucets, pipes, etc.)

License

The verb license or grant license means to give permission. The noun license refers to that permission as well as to the document memorializing that permission. license may be granted by a party to another party as an element of an agreement between those parties.

Magazine

Magazine s, periodicals, glossies or serials are publications, generally published on a regular schedule, containing a variety of articles, generally financed by advertising, by a purchase price, by pre-paid magazine subscriptions, or all three. magazine s can be distributed through the mail; through sales by newsstands, bookstores or other vendors; or through free distribution at selected pick up locations.

The various elements that contribute to the production of magazine s vary wildly.

Patent

A patent is a set of exclusive rights granted by a state to an inventor or his assignee for a limited period of time in exchange for a disclosure of an invention.

The procedure for granting patent s, the requirements placed on the patent ee and the extent of the exclusive rights vary widely between countries according to national laws and international agreements. Typically, however, a patent application must include one or more claims defining the invention which must be new, inventive, and useful or industrially applicable.

Patent infringement

Patent infringement is the commission of a prohibited act with respect to a patented invention without permission from the patent holder. Permission may typically be granted in the form of a licence. The definition of patent infringement may vary by jurisdiction, but it typically includes using or selling the patented invention.

Royalties

Royalties can be determined as a percentage of gross or net sales derived from use of the asset or a fixed price per unit sold. but there are also other modes and metrics of compensation. A royalty interest is the right to collect a stream of future royalty payments, often used in the oil industry and music industry to describe a percentage ownership of future production or revenues from a given leasehold, which may be divested from the original owner of the asset.

Franchising

Franchising refers to the methods of practicing and using another person's philosophy of business. The franchisor grants the independent operator the right to distribute its products, techniques, and trademarks for a percentage of gross monthly sales and a royalty fee. Various tangibles and intangibles such as national or international advertising, training, and other support services are commonly made available by the franchisor.

Piracy

Piracy is a war-like act committed by a non-state actor, especially robbery or criminal violence committed at sea, on water, or sometimes on shore. It does not normally include crimes on board a vessel among passengers or crew. The term has been used to refer to raids across land borders by non-state actors.

Economic development

Economic development is the development of economic wealth of countries or regions for the well-being of their inhabitants. It is the process by which a nation improves the economic, political, and social well being of its people. From a policy perspective, Economic development can be defined as efforts that seek to improve the economic well-being and quality of life for a community by creating and/or retaining jobs and supporting or growing incomes and the tax base.

Set TSP

In combinatorial optimization, the set TSP group TSP, One-of-a-set TSP, Multiple Choice TSP or Covering Salesman Problem, is a generalization of the Traveling salesman problem, whereby it is required to find a shortest tour in a graph which visits all specified disjoint subsets of the vertices of a graph. The ordinary TSP is a special case of the set TSP when all subsets to be visited are singletons. Therefore the set TSP is also NP-hard.

Contract manufacturer

A contract manufacturer is a firm that manufactures components or products for another 'hiring' firm. Many industries utilize this process, especially the aerospace, defense, computer, semiconductor, energy, medical, food manufacturing, personal care, and automotive fields. Some types of contract manufacturing include CNC machining, complex assembly, aluminum die casting, grinding, broaching, gears, and forging.

Foreign direct investment	Foreign direct investment in its classic form is defined as a company from one country making a physical investment into building a factory in another country. It is the establishment of an enterprise by a foreigner. Its definition can be extended to include investments made to acquire lasting interest in enterprises operating outside of the economy of the investor.
Kraft Foods	Kraft Foods Inc. (NYSE: Kraft Foods T) is the largest food and beverage company headquartered in the United States and the second largest in the world (after Nestlé SA.) Kraft is headquartered in Northfield, Illinois, USA, a Chicago suburb.
Management contract	A Management contract is an arrangement under which operational control of an enterprise is vested by contract in a separate enterprise which performs the necessary managerial functions in return for a fee. Management contract s involve not just selling a method of doing things (as with franchising or licensing) but involves actually doing them. A Management contract can involve a wide range of functions, such as technical operation of a production facility, management of personnel, accounting, marketing services and training.
Manufacturing	Manufacturing is the application of tools and a processing medium to the transformation of raw materials into finished goods for sale. This effort includes all intermediate processes required for the production and integration of a product's components. Some industries, like semiconductor and steel manufacturers use the term fabrication instead.
Standardization	Standardization or standardisation is the process of developing and agreeing upon technical standards. A standard is a document that establishes uniform engineering or technical specifications, criteria, methods, processes, or practices. Some standards are mandatory while others are voluntary.
Subsidiary	A Subsidiary, in business matters, is an entity that is controlled by a bigger and more powerful entity. The controlled entity is called a company, corporation, or limited liability company and in some cases can be a government or state-owned enterprise, and the controlling entity is called its parent (or the parent company.) The reason for this distinction is that a lone company cannot be a Subsidiary of any organization; only an entity representing a legal fiction as a separate entity can be a Subsidiary.
Joint venture	A joint venture is an entity formed between two or more parties to undertake economic activity together. The parties agree to create a new entity by both contributing equity, and they then share in the revenues, expenses, and control of the enterprise. The venture can be for one specific project only, or a continuing business relationship such as the Fuji Xerox joint venture.
Supply chain	A Supply chain or logistics network is the system of organizations, people, technology, activities, information and resources involved in moving a product or service from supplier to customer. Supply chain activities transform natural resources, raw materials and components into a finished product that is delivered to the end customer. In sophisticated Supply chain systems, used products may re-enter the Supply chain at any point where residual value is recyclable.
Supply chain management	Supply chain management is the management of a network of interconnected businesses involved in the ultimate provision of product and service packages required by end customers (Harland, 1996.) Supply chain management spans all movement and storage of raw materials, work-in-process inventory, and finished goods from point of origin to point of consumption (supply chain.)

The definition an American professional association put forward is that Supply chain management encompasses the planning and management of all activities involved in sourcing, procurement, conversion, and logistics management activities.

Tariff

A Tariff is a duty imposed on goods when they are moved across a political boundary. They are usually associated with protectionism, the economic policy of restraining trade between nations. For political reasons, Tariff s are usually imposed on imported goods, although they may also be imposed on exported goods.

Acquisition

The phrase mergers and acquisitions refers to the aspect of corporate strategy, corporate finance and management dealing with the buying, selling and combining of different companies that can aid, finance, or help a growing company in a given industry grow rapidly without having to create another business entity.

An Acquisition, also known as a takeover or a buyout, is the buying of one company (the 'target') by another. An Acquisition may be friendly or hostile.

Investment

Investment or investing is a term with several closely-related meanings in business management, finance and economics, related to saving or deferring consumption. Investing is the active redirecting resources from being consumed today so that they may create benefits in the future; the use of assets to earn income or profit.

An Investment is the choice by the individual to risk his savings with the hope of gain.

Logistics

Logistics is the management of the flow of goods, information and other resources, including energy and people, between the point of origin and the point of consumption in order to meet the requirements of consumers (frequently, and originally, military organizations.) Logistics involves the integration of information, transportation, inventory, warehousing, material-handling, and packaging. Logistics is a channel of the supply chain which adds the value of time and place utility.

Investment risk

Depending on the nature of the Investment, the type of Investment risk will vary.

A common concern with any investment is that you may lose the money you invest - your capital. This risk is therefore often referred to as 'capital risk.'

If the assets you invest in are held in another currency there is a risk that currency movements alone may affect the value.

Organization

An organization is a social arrangement which pursues collective goals, which controls its own performance, and which has a boundary separating it from its environment. The word itself is derived from the Greek word á½„ργανον (organon [itself derived from the better-known word á¼"ργον ergon - work; deed - > ergonomics, etc]) meaning tool. The term is used in both daily and scientific English in multiple ways.

World Trade Organization

The World Trade Organization is an international organization designed to supervise and liberalize international trade. The World Trade Organization came into being on 1 January 1995, and is the successor to the General Agreement on Tariffs and Trade (GATT), which was created in 1947, and continued to operate for almost five decades as a de facto international organization.

The World Trade Organization deals with the rules of trade between nations at a near-global level; it is responsible for negotiating and implementing new trade agreements, and is in charge of policing member countries' adherence to all the World Trade Organization agreements, signed by the majority of the world's trading nations and ratified in their parliaments.

Strategic alliance

A strategic alliance is a formal relationship between two or more parties to pursue a set of agreed upon goals or to meet a critical business need while remaining independent organizations.

Partners may provide the strategic alliance with resources such as products, distribution channels, manufacturing capability, project funding, capital equipment, knowledge, expertise, or intellectual property. The alliance is a cooperation or collaboration which aims for a synergy where each partner hopes that the benefits from the alliance will be greater than those from individual efforts.

Mergers and Acquisitions

The phrase Mergers and Acquisitions refers to the aspect of corporate strategy, corporate finance and management dealing with the buying, selling and combining of different companies that can aid, finance, or help a growing company in a given industry grow rapidly without having to create another business entity.

An acquisition, also known as a takeover or a buyout, is the buying of one company (the 'target') by another. An acquisition may be friendly or hostile.

Mergers

The phrase mergers and acquisitions refers to the aspect of corporate strategy, corporate finance and management dealing with the buying, selling and combining of different companies that can aid, finance, or help a growing company in a given industry grow rapidly without having to create another business entity.

An acquisition, also known as a takeover or a buyout, is the buying of one company (the 'target') by another. An acquisition may be friendly or hostile.

Jobbing house

A Jobbing house (or jobbing center) is a type of wholesale merchant business that buys goods and bulk products from importers, other wholesalers and then sells to retailers. Jobbing house s can deal in any commodity destined for the retail market. Typical categories are food, lumber, hardware, fuel, and textiles.

Government Procurement

Government procurement or public procurement, is the procurement of goods and services on behalf of a public authority, such as a government agency. With 10 to 15% of GDP in developed countries, and up to 20% in developing countries, Government procurement accounts for a substantial part of the global economy.

To prevent fraud, waste, corruption or local protectionism, the law of most countries regulates Government procurement more or less closely.

Industry

An Industry is the manufacturing of a good or service within a category. Although Industry is a broad term for any kind of economic production, in economics and urban planning Industry is a synonym for the secondary sector, which is a type of economic activity involved in the manufacturing of raw materials into goods and products.

There are four key industrial economic sectors: the primary sector, largely raw material extraction industries such as mining and farming; the secondary sector, involving refining, construction, and manufacturing; the tertiary sector, which deals with services (such as law and medicine) and distribution of manufactured goods; and the quaternary sector, a relatively new type of knowledge Industry focusing on technological research, design and development such as computer programming, and biochemistry.

Wholesale

Wholesaling, jobbing to industrial, commercial, institutional or to other Wholesale rs and related subordinated services.

According to the United Nations Statistics Division, Wholesale is the resale (sale without transformation) of new and used goods to retailers, to industrial, commercial, institutional or professional users or involves acting as an agent or broker in buying merchandise for such persons or companies. Wholesale rs frequently physically assemble, sort and grade goods in large lots, break bulk, repack and redistribute in smaller lots.

Purchasing

Purchasing refers to a business or organization attempting to acquire goods or services to accomplish the goals of the enterprise. Though there are several organizations that attempt to set standards in the Purchasing process, processes can vary greatly between organizations. Typically the word 'Purchasing' is not used interchangeably with the word 'procurement', since procurement typically includes Expediting, Supplier Quality, and Traffic and Logistics (T'L) in addition to Purchasing.

Retailing

Retailing consists of the sale of goods or merchandise from a fixed location, such as a department store or kiosk in small or individual lots for direct consumption by the purchaser. Retailing may include subordinated services, such as delivery. Purchasers may be individuals or businesses.

Globalization

Globalization in its literal sense is the process of transformation of local or regional phenomena into global ones. It can be described as a process by which the people of the world are unified into a single society and function together.

This process is a combination of economic, technological, sociocultural and political forces.

Extortion

'Extortion', outwresting property or services from a person, entity through coercion. Refraining from doing harm is sometimes euphemistically called protection. Extortion is commonly practiced by organized crime groups.

Market Analysis

A Market analysis is a documented investigation of a Market that is used to inform a firm's planning activities particularly around decision of: inventory, purchase, work force expansion/contraction, facility expansion, purchases of capital equipment, promotional activities, and many other aspects of a company.

Not all managers are asked to conduct a Market analysis, but all managers must make decisions using Market analysis data and understand how the data was derived. So all managers need a reasonable understanding of the tools most used for making sales forecasts and analyzing markets.

Containerization	Containerization is a system of intermodal freight transport using standard intermodal containers that are standardised by the International Organization for Standardization (ISO.) These can be loaded and sealed intact onto container ships, railroad cars, planes, and trucks.
Export	In economics, an export is any good or commodity, transported from one country to another country in a legitimate fashion, typically for use in trade. export goods or services are provided to foreign consumers by domestic producers. export is an important part of international trade.
Set TSP	In combinatorial optimization, the set TSP group TSP, One-of-a-set TSP, Multiple Choice TSP or Covering Salesman Problem, is a generalization of the Traveling salesman problem, whereby it is required to find a shortest tour in a graph which visits all specified disjoint subsets of the vertices of a graph. The ordinary TSP is a special case of the set TSP when all subsets to be visited are singletons. Therefore the set TSP is also NP-hard.
United States	The United States of America (commonly referred to as the United States the U.S., the United States A, or America) is a federal constitutional republic comprising fifty states and a federal district. The country is situated mostly in central North America, where its 48 contiguous states and Washington, D.C., the capital district, lie between the Pacific and Atlantic Oceans, bordered by Canada to the north and Mexico to the south. The state of Alaska is in the northwest of the continent, with Canada to its east and Russia to the west across the Bering Strait.
International trade	International trade is exchange of capital, goods, and services across international borders or territories. In most countries, it represents a significant share of gross domestic product (GDP.) While International trade has been present throughout much of history , its economic, social, and political importance has been on the rise in recent centuries.
Joint venture	A joint venture is an entity formed between two or more parties to undertake economic activity together. The parties agree to create a new entity by both contributing equity, and they then share in the revenues, expenses, and control of the enterprise. The venture can be for one specific project only, or a continuing business relationship such as the Fuji Xerox joint venture.
License	The verb license or grant license means to give permission. The noun license refers to that permission as well as to the document memorializing that permission. license may be granted by a party to another party as an element of an agreement between those parties.
Comparative advertising	Comparative advertising is an advertisement in which a particular product specifically mentions a competitor by name for the express purpose of showing why the competitor is inferior to the product naming it. This should not be confused with parody advertisements, where a fictional product is being advertised for the purpose of poking fun at the particular advertisement, nor should it be confused with the use of a coined brand name for the purpose of comparing the product without actually naming an actual competitor. ('Wikipedia tastes better and is less filling than the Encyclopedia Galactica.') In the 1980s, during what has been referred to as the cola wars, soft-drink manufacturer Pepsi ran a series of advertisements where people, caught on hidden camera, in a blind taste test, chose Pepsi over rival Coca-Cola.

Warranty

In commercial and consumer transactions, a warranty is an obligation or guarantee that an article or service sold is as factually stated or legally implied by the seller, and that often provides for a specific remedy such as repair or replacement in the event the article or service fails to meet the warranty. A breach of warranty occurs when the promise is broken, i.e., a product is defective or not as should be expected by a reasonable buyer.

In business and legal transactions, a warranty is an assurance by one party to the other party that certain facts or conditions are true or will happen; the other party is permitted to rely on that assurance and seek some type of remedy if it is not true or followed.

Base

Bases may be the plural form of:

· base
· Basis

Bases may also refer to:

· Bases (fashion), a military style of dress adopted by the chivalry of the sixteenth century. .

Customer

A customer also client, buyer or purchaser is usually used to refer to a current or potential buyer or user of the products of an individual or organization, mostly called the supplier or seller. This is typically through purchasing or renting goods or services. However in certain contexts the term customer also includes by extension anyone who uses or experiences the services of another.

Failure

Failure refers to the state or condition of not meeting a desirable or intended objective, and may be viewed as the opposite of success. Product failure ranges from failure to sell the product to fracture of the product, in the worst cases leading to personal injury, the province of forensic engineering.

The criteria for failure are heavily dependent on context of use, and may be relative to a particular observer or belief system.

Market

A Market is any one of a variety of different systems, institutions, procedures, social relations and infrastructures whereby persons trade, and goods and services are exchanged, forming part of the economy. It is an arrangement that allows buyers and sellers to exchange things. Market s vary in size, range, geographic scale, location, types and variety of human communities, as well as the types of goods and services traded.

Chief brand officer

A Chief brand officer is a relatively new executive level position at a corporation, company, organization typically reporting directly to the CEO or board of directors. The Chief brand officer is responsible for a brand's image, experience, and promise, and propagating it throughout all aspects of the company. The brand officer oversees marketing, advertising, design, public relations and customer service departments.

Business

A business is a legally recognized organization designed to provide goods and/or services to consumers. business es are predominant in capitalist economies, most being privately owned and formed to earn profit that will increase the wealth of its owners and grow the business itself. The owners and operators of a business have as one of their main objectives the receipt or generation of a financial return in exchange for work and acceptance of risk.

Theory of the firm

The Theory of the firm consists of a number of economic theories which describe the nature of the firm, company including its existence, its behaviour, and its relationship with the market.

In simplified terms, the Theory of the firm aims to answer these questions:

- Existence - why do firms emerge, why are not all transactions in the economy mediated over the market?
- Boundaries - why the boundary between firms and the market is located exactly there? Which transactions are performed internally and which are negotiated on the market?
- Organization - why are firms structured in such specific way? What is the interplay of formal and informal relationships?

The First World War period saw a change of emphasis in economic theory away from industry-level analysis which mainly included analysing markets to analysis at the level of the firm, as it became increasingly clear that perfect competition was no longer an adequate model of how firms behaved. Economic theory till then had focussed on trying to understand markets alone and there had been little study on understanding why firms or organisations exist. Market are mainly guided by prices as illustrated by vegetable markets where a buyer is free to switch sellers in an exchange.

Department of Commerce

The United States Department of Commerce is the Cabinet department of the United States government concerned with promoting economic growth. It was originally created as the United States Department of Commerce and Labor on February 14, 1903. It was subsequently renamed to the Department of Commerce on March 4, 1913, and its bureaus and agencies specializing in labor were transferred to the new Department of Labor.

E. I. du Pont de Nemours and Company

E. I. du Pont de Nemours and Company is an American chemical company that was founded in July 1802 as a gunpowder mill by Eleuth>ère Ir>én>ée du Pont. DuPont is currently the world's second largest chemical company (behind BASF) in terms of market capitalization and fourth (behind BASF, Dow Chemical and Ineos) in revenue. Its stock price is a component of the Dow Jones Industrial Average.

International Trade Administration

The International Trade Administration is an agency in the United States Department of Commerce that promotes United States exports of nonagricultural U.S. services and goods.

The International Trade Administration's stated goals are to

- Provide practical information to help Americans select markets and products.
- Ensure that Americans have access to international markets as required by the U.S. trade agreements.
- Safeguard Americans from unfair competition from dumped and subsidized imports.

International Trade Administration consists of four sub-units. These are: Import Administration (IA), Market Access and Compliance (MAC), Manufacturing and Services (MAS) and the US Commercial Service (USCS.)

The International Trade Administration was created on January 2, 1980 and is headed by the Under Secretary of Commerce for International Trade.

Investment

Investment or investing is a term with several closely-related meanings in business management, finance and economics, related to saving or deferring consumption. Investing is the active redirecting resources from being consumed today so that they may create benefits in the future; the use of assets to earn income or profit.

An Investment is the choice by the individual to risk his savings with the hope of gain.

Market Access

Market access for goods in the WTO means the conditions, tariff and non-tariff measures, agreed by members for the entry of specific goods into their markets. Tariff commitments for goods are set out in each member's schedules of concessions on goods. The schedules represent commitments not to apply tariffs above the listed rates -- these rates are 'bound'.

Overseas Private Investment Corporation

The Overseas Private Investment Corporation is an agency of the United States Government established in 1971 that helps U.S. businesses invest overseas and promotes economic development in new and emerging markets.

Overseas Private Investment Corporation's mission is to 'foster economic development in new and emerging markets, support U.S. foreign policy and create U.S. jobs by helping U.S. businesses to invest overseas.' The agency provides political risk insurance against the risks of inconvertibility, political violence, or expropriation. Overseas Private Investment Corporation also provides financing through direct loans and loan guarantees.

Small Business

A small business is a business that is independently owned and operated, with a small number of employees and relatively low volume of sales. The legal definition of 'small' often varies by country and industry, but is generally under 100 employees in the United States and under 50 employees in the European Union. In comparison, the definition of mid-sized business by the number of employees is generally under 500 in the U.S. and 250 for the European Union.

Small Business Administration

The Small Business Administration is a United States government agency that provides support to small businesses.

The mission of the Small Business Administration is 'to maintain and strengthen the nation's economy by enabling the establishment and viability of small businesses and by assisting in the economic recovery of communities after disasters.' The Small Business Administration makes loans directly to businesses and acts as a guarantor on bank loans. In some circumstances it also makes loans to victims of natural disasters, works to get government procurement contracts for small businesses, and assists businesses with management, technical and training issues.

Distribution

Distribution is one of the four elements of marketing mix. An organization or set of organizations (go-betweens) involved in the process of making a product or service available for use or consumption by a consumer or business user.

The other three parts of the marketing mix are product, pricing, and promotion.

Resources

Human beings are also considered to be Resources because they have the ability to change raw materials into valuable Resources. The term Human Resources can also be defined as the skills, energies, talents, abilities and knowledge that are used for the production of goods or the rendering of services. While taking into account human beings as Resources, the following things have to be kept in mind:

· The size of the population
· The capabilities of the individuals in that population

Many Resources cannot be consumed in their original form. They have to be processed in order to change them into more usable commodities.

Financial Assistance	In law, Financial assistance refers to assistance given by a company for the purchase of its own shares or the shares of its holding companies. In many jurisdictions such assistance is prohibited or restricted by law. For example all EU member states are required to prohibit Financial assistance by public companies , although some members go further, for example, France, Belgium and The Netherlands prohibit Financial assistance by all companies.
Gold Key Matching Service	The Gold Key Matching Service is a fee-based service available to U.S.-based companies to introduce U.S.-made products to potential agents, distributors, sales representatives, association and government contacts, licensing or joint venture partners, end-users and other strategic business partners in the U.S. company's targeted export market. Typically the U.S. company makes application through their closest U.S. Export Assistance Center in the United States, which forwards the information about the client company and its products to one of the U.S. Commercial Service offices located in a U.S. embassy or consulate outside the United States. There, a commercial specialist.
International Business	International business is a term used to collectively describe topics relating to the operations of firms with interests in multiple countries. Such firms are sometimes called multinational corporations . Well known MNCs include fast food companies McDonald's and Yum Brands, vehicle manufacturers such as General Motors and Toyota, consumer electronics companies like Samsung, LG and Sony, and energy companies such as ExxonMobil and BP.
Cooperative	A cooperative is defined by the International Co-operative Alliance's Statement on the Co-operative Identity as an autonomous association of persons united voluntarily to meet their common economic, social, and cultural needs and aspirations through a jointly-owned and democratically-controlled enterprise. It is a business organization owned and operated by a group of individuals for their mutual benefit. A cooperative may also be defined as a business owned and controlled equally by the people who use its services or who work at it.
Report	In writing, a report is a document characterized by information or other content reflective of inquiry or investigation, which is tailored to the context of a given situation and audience. The purpose of report s is usually to inform. However, report s may include persuasive elements, such as recommendations, suggestions, or other motivating conclusions that indicate possible future actions the report reader might take.
Trade mission	Trade mission is an international trip by government officials and businesspeople that is organized by agencies of national of provincial governments for purpose of exploring international business opportunities. Business people who attend Trade mission s are typically introduced both to important business contacts and to well-placed government officials.
Incoterms	Incoterms or international commercial terms are a series of international sales terms widely used throughout the world. They are used to divide transaction costs and responsibilities between buyer and seller and reflect state-of-the-art transportation practices. They closely correspond to the U.N. Convention on Contracts for the International Sale of Goods.
Characteristic	Characteristic has several particular meanings: · in mathematics • · Euler characteristic • · method of characteristic s (partial differential equations) · in physics and engineering

· any characteristic curve that shows the relationship between certain input- and output parameters, e.g.
· an I-V or current-voltage characteristic is the current in a circuit as a function of the applied voltage
· Receiver-Operator characteristic
· in navigation, the characteristic pattern of a lighted beacon.
· in fiction

· in Dungeons ' Dragons, characteristic is another name for ability score .

Cost

In economics, business, retail, and accounting, a cost is the value of money that has been used up to produce something, and hence is not available for use anymore. In economics, a cost is an alternative that is given up as a result of a decision. In business, the cost may be one of acquisition, in which case the amount of money expended to acquire it is counted as cost.

Marketing

Marketing is defined by the American Marketing Association as the activity, set of institutions, and processes for creating, communicating, delivering, and exchanging offerings that have value for customers, clients, partners, and society at large. The term developed from the original meaning which referred literally to going to market, as in shopping, or going to a market to sell goods or services.

Marketing practice tends to be seen as a creative industry, which includes advertising, distribution and selling.

Marketing plan

A marketing plan is a written document that details the necessary actions to achieve one or more marketing objectives. It can be for a product or service, a brand, or a product line. marketing plan s cover between one and five years.

Jurisdiction

Jurisdiction is the practical authority granted to a formally constituted legal body or to a political leader to deal with and make pronouncements on legal matters and, by implication, to administer justice within a defined area of responsibility.

Alternatively, jurisdiction is the authority given to a legal body, or to a political leader to adjudicate and enforce legal matters.

jurisdiction draws its substance from public international law, conflict of laws, constitutional law and the powers of the executive and legislative branches of government to allocate resources to best serve the needs of its native society.

Litigation

The conduct of a lawsuit is called Litigation.

Rules of criminal or civil procedure govern the conduct of a lawsuit in the common law adversarial system of dispute resolution. Procedural rules are additionally constrained/informed by separate statutory laws, case law, and constitutional provisions that define the rights of the parties to a lawsuit , though the rules will generally reflect this legal context on their face.

Patent

A patent is a set of exclusive rights granted by a state to an inventor or his assignee for a limited period of time in exchange for a disclosure of an invention.

The procedure for granting patent s, the requirements placed on the patent ee and the extent of the exclusive rights vary widely between countries according to national laws and international agreements. Typically, however, a patent application must include one or more claims defining the invention which must be new, inventive, and useful or industrially applicable.

Trademark	A Trademark or trade mark is a distinctive sign or indicator used by an individual, business organization and to distinguish its products or services from those of other entities. A Trademark is designated by the following symbols: · â„¢ (for an unregistered Trademark that is, a mark used to promote or brand goods); · â„ (for an unregistered service mark, that is, a mark used to promote or brand services); and · Â® (for a registered Trademark) A Trademark is a type of intellectual property, and typically a name, word, phrase, logo, symbol, design, image, or a combination of these elements. There is also a range of non-conventional Trademark s comprising marks which do not fall into these standard categories. The owner of a registered Trademark may commence legal proceedings for Trademark infringement to prevent unauthorized use of that Trademark
Arbitration	Arbitration, a form of alternative dispute resolution (ADR), is a legal technique for the resolution of disputes outside the courts, wherein the parties to a dispute refer it to one or more persons (the 'arbitrators', 'arbiters' or 'arbitral tribunal'), by whose decision (the 'award') they agree to be bound. It is a settlement technique in which a third party reviews the case and imposes a decision that is legally binding for both sides. Other forms of ADR include mediation (a form of settlement negotiation facilitated by a neutral third party) and non-binding resolution by experts.
Offer	The most important feature of a contract is that one party makes an offer for an arrangement that another accepts. This can be called a 'concurrence of wills' or 'ad idem' (meeting of the minds) of two or more parties. The concept is somewhat contested.
Dispute	Controversy is a state of prolonged public dispute or debate usually concerning a matter of opinion. The term originates circa 1384 from Latin controversia, as a composite of controversus - 'turned in an opposite direction,' from contra - 'against' - and vertere - to turn, or versus , hence, 'to turn against.' Benford's law of controversy, as expressed by science-fiction author Gregory Benford in 1980, states: 'Passion is inversely proportional to the amount of real (true) information available.' In other words, the more untruths the more controversy there is, and the more truths the less controversy there is. A controversy is always the result of either ignorance (lack of sufficient true information), misinformation, misunderstandings, half-truths, distortions, bias or prejudice, deliberate lies or fabrications (disinformation), opposed underlying motives or purposes (sometimes masked or hidden), or a combination of these factors.
Consignment	Consignment is the act of consigning, which is placing a person or thing in the hand of another, but retaining ownership until the goods are sold or person is transferred. This may be done for shipping, transfer of prisoners, or for sale in a store (i.e. a Consignment shop.) Features of Consignment are as follows: 1)The Relation between the two parties is that of consignor and consignee and not that of buyer and seller 2)The consignor is entitled to receive all the expenses in connection with Consignment 3)The consignee is not responsible for damage of goods during transport or any other procedure.
Letter of credit	A standard, commercial Letter of credit is a document issued mostly by a financial institution, used primarily in trade finance, which usually provides an irrevocable payment undertaking.

The LC can also be the source of payment for a transaction, meaning that redeeming the Letter of credit will pay an exporter. Letters of credit are used primarily in international trade transactions of significant value, for deals between a supplier in one country and a customer in another.

Sight draft

A draft can require immediate payment by the second party to the third upon presentation of the draft. This is called a Sight draft Cheques are Sight draft s.

Customs

Customs is an authority or agency in a country responsible for collecting and safeguarding customs duties and for controlling the flow of goods including animals, personal effects and hazardous items in and out of a country. Depending on local legislation and regulations, the import or export of some goods may be restricted or forbidden, and the customs agency enforces these rules. The customs agency may be different from the immigration authority, which monitors persons who leave or enter the country, checking for appropriate documentation, apprehending people wanted by international arrest warrants, and impeding the entry of others deemed dangerous to the country.

Discounting

Discounting is a financial mechanism in which a debtor obtains the right to delay payments to a creditor, for a defined period of time, in exchange for a charge or fee. Essentially, the party that owes money in the present purchases the right to delay the payment until some future date. The discount, or charge, is simply the difference between the original amount owed in the present and the amount that has to be paid in the future to settle the debt.

Forfaiting

In trade finance, Forfaiting involves the purchasing of receivables from exporters. The forfaiter will take on all the risks involved with the receivables. It is different from the factoring operation in the sense that Forfaiting is a transaction based operation while factoring is a firm based operation - meaning, in factoring, a firm sells all its receivables while in Forfaiting, the firm sells one of its transactions.

Free trade

Free trade is a type of trade policy that allows traders to act and transact without interference from government. Thus, the policy permits trading partners mutual gains from trade, with goods and services produced according to the theory of comparative advantage.

Under a Free trade policy, prices are a reflection of true supply and demand, and are the sole determinant of resource allocation.

Free trade zone

A Free trade zone or export processing zone (EPZ) is one or more special areas of a country where some normal trade barriers such as tariffs and quotas are eliminated and bureaucratic requirements are lowered in hopes of attracting new business and foreign investments. It is a a region where a group of countries has agreed to reduce or eliminate trade barriers. They can be defined as labor intensive manufacturing centers that involve the import of raw materials or components and the export of factory products.

Guarantee

The act of becoming a surety is also called a Guarantee. Traditionally a Guarantee was distinguished from a surety in that the surety's liability was joint and primary with the principal, whereas the guaranty's liability was ancillary and derivative, but many jurisdictions have abolished this distinction

Working Capital

Working capital is a financial metric which represents operating liquidity available to a business. Along with fixed assets such as plant and equipment, working capital is considered a part of operating capital. It is calculated as current assets minus current liabilities.

Cash flow	Cash flow refers to the movement of cash into or out of a business, a project, or a financial product. It is usually measured during a specified, finite period of time. Measurement of Cash flow can be used · to determine a project's rate of return or value. The time of Cash flow s into and out of projects are used as inputs in financial models such as internal rate of return, and net present value. · to determine problems with a business's liquidity. Being profitable does not necessarily mean being liquid. A company can fail because of a shortage of cash, even while profitable. · as an alternate measure of a business's profits when it is believed that accrual accounting concepts do not represent economic realities. For example, a company may be notionally profitable but generating little operational cash (as may be the case for a company that barters its products rather than selling for cash.) In such a case, the company may be deriving additional operating cash by issuing shares, or raising additional debt finance. • of Income generated by accrual accounting. When Net Income is composed of large non-cash items it is considered low quality. · to evaluate the risks within a financial product. E.g. matching cash requirements, evaluating default risk, re-investment requirements, etc.
Job description	A Job description is a list of the general tasks and responsibilities of a position. Typically, it also includes to whom the position reports, specifications such as the qualifications needed by the person in the job, salary range for the position, etc. A Job description is usually developed by conducting a job analysis, which includes examining the tasks and sequences of tasks necessary to perform the job.
Risk	Risk is a concept that denotes the precise probability of specific eventualities. Technically, the notion of Risk is independent from the notion of value and, as such, eventualities may have both beneficial and adverse consequences. However, in general usage the convention is to focus only on potential negative impact to some characteristic of value that may arise from a future event.
Freight forwarder	A Freight forwarder is a third party logistics provider. As a third party (or non asset based) provider a forwarder dispatches shipments via asset-based carriers and books or otherwise arranges space for those shipments. Carrier types include waterborne vessels, airplanes, trucks or railroads.
Rebate	A Rebate is an amount paid by way of reduction, return, or refund on what has already been paid or contributed. It is a type of sales promotion marketers use primarily as incentives or supplements to product sales. The mail-in Rebate is the most common.
Automated export system	Automated Export System is the system used by U.S exporters to electronically declare their international exports to the CBP (Customs and Border Protection.) Formerly, this declaration was only made by the paper Shipper's Export Declaration (SED.) Currently an exporter can file the export declaration electronically via Automated Export System , using Automated Export System Direct online, Automated Export System PCLink, or other software.
Marine insurance	Marine insurance covers the loss or damage of ships, cargo, terminals, and any transport or property by which cargo is transferred, acquired, or held between the points of origin and final destination. Cargo insurance--discussed here--is a sub-branch of Marine insurance, though Marine also includes Onshore and Offshore exposed property (container terminals, ports, oil platforms, pipelines); Hull; Marine Casualty; and Marine Liability.

The modern origins of Marine insurance law were in the law merchant, with the establishment in England in 1601 of a specialised chamber of assurance separate from the other Courts.

Bill of lading

A Bill of lading is a document issued by a carrier to a shipper, acknowledging that specified goods have been received on board as cargo for conveyance to a named place for delivery to the consignee who is usually identified. A through Bill of lading involves the use of at least two different modes of transport from road, rail, air, and sea. The term derives from the noun 'bill', a schedule of costs for services supplied or to be supplied, and from the verb 'to lade' which means to load a cargo onto a ship or other form of transport.

Certificate of origin

A Certificate of origin is a document used in international trade. It traditionally states from what country the shipped goods originate, but 'originate' in a CO does not mean the country the goods are shipped from, but the country where their goods are actually made. This raises a definition problem in cases where less than 100% of the raw materials and processes and added value are not all from one country.

Policy

A Policy is typically described as a deliberate plan of action to guide decisions and achieve rational outcome(s.) However, the term may also be used to denote what is actually done, even though it is unplanned.

The term may apply to government, private sector organizations and groups, and individuals.

Roll-on/roll-off

Roll-on/roll-off ships are vessels designed to carry wheeled cargo such as automobiles, trucks, semi-trailer trucks, trailers or railroad cars that are driven on and off the ship on their own wheels. This is in contrast to lo-lo (lift on-lift off) vessels which use a crane to load and unload cargo.

Roll-on/roll-off vessels have built-in ramps which allow the cargo to be efficiently 'rolled on' and 'rolled off' the vessel when in port.

Ad valorem

An Ad valorem tax is a tax based on the value of real estate or personal property. It is more common than the opposite, a specific duty, or a tax based on the quantity of an item regardless of price.

An Ad valorem tax is typically imposed at the time of a transaction), but it may be imposed on an annual basis (real or personal property tax) or in connection with another significant event (inheritance tax, surrendering citizenship, or tariffs.)

External

In economics, an external ity or spillover of an economic transaction is an impact on a party that is not directly involved in the transaction. In such a case, prices do not reflect the full costs or benefits in production or consumption of a product or service. A positive impact is called an external benefit, while a negative impact is called an external cost.

Import

An import is any good (e.g. a commodity) or service brought into one country from another country in a legitimate fashion, typically for use in trade.It is a good that is brought in from another country for sale. import goods or services are provided to domestic consumers by foreign producers. An import in the receiving country is an export to the sending country.

Organization

An organization is a social arrangement which pursues collective goals, which controls its own performance, and which has a boundary separating it from its environment. The word itself is derived from the Greek word á½„ργανον (organon [itself derived from the better-known word á¼”ργον ergon - work; deed - > ergonomics, etc]) meaning tool. The term is used in both daily and scientific English in multiple ways.

Tariff	A Tariff is a duty imposed on goods when they are moved across a political boundary. They are usually associated with protectionism, the economic policy of restraining trade between nations. For political reasons, Tariff s are usually imposed on imported goods, although they may also be imposed on exported goods.
Broker	A broker is a party that mediates between a buyer and a seller. A broker who also acts as a seller or as a buyer becomes a principal party to the deal. Distinguish agent: one who acts on behalf of a principal.
Regulation	Regulation refers to 'controlling human or societal behaviour by rules or restrictions.' Regulation can take many forms: legal restrictions promulgated by a government authority, self-Regulation, social Regulation, co-Regulation and market Regulation. One can consider Regulation as actions of conduct imposing sanctions (such as a fine.) This action of administrative law, or implementing regulatory law, may be contrasted with statutory or case law.
Warehouse	A Warehouse is a commercial building for storage of goods. Warehouse s are used by manufacturers, importers, exporters, wholesalers, transport businesses, customs, etc. They are usually large plain buildings in industrial areas of cities and towns.
Skill	A skill is the learned capacity to carry out pre-determined results often with the minimum outlay of time, energy, or both. skill s can often be divided into domain-general and domain-specific skill s. For example, in the domain of work, some general skill s would include time management, teamwork and leadership, self motivation and others, whereas domain-specific skill s would be useful only for a certain job.
Price	Price in economics and business is the result of an exchange and from that trade we assign a numerical monetary value to a good, service or asset. If I trade 4 apples for an orange, the price of an orange is 4 - apples. Inversely, the price of an apple is 1/4 oranges.

Procter ' Gamble

Procter is a surname, and may also refer to:

- Bryan Waller Procter (pseud. Barry Cornwall), English poet
- Goodwin Procter, American law firm
- Procter ' Gamble, consumer products multinational .

Product line

There are many important decisions about product and service development and marketing. In the process of product development and marketing we should focus on strategic decisions about product attributes, product branding, product packaging, product labeling and product support services. But product strategy also calls for building a Product line.

Capital structure

In finance, Capital structure refers to the way a corporation finances its assets through some combination of equity, debt, or hybrid securities. A firm's Capital structure is then the composition or 'structure' of its liabilities. For example, a firm that sells $20 billion in equity and $80 billion in debt is said to be 20% equity-financed and 80% debt-financed.

Globalization

Globalization in its literal sense is the process of transformation of local or regional phenomena into global ones. It can be described as a process by which the people of the world are unified into a single society and function together.

This process is a combination of economic, technological, sociocultural and political forces.

Job description

A Job description is a list of the general tasks and responsibilities of a position. Typically, it also includes to whom the position reports, specifications such as the qualifications needed by the person in the job, salary range for the position, etc. A Job description is usually developed by conducting a job analysis, which includes examining the tasks and sequences of tasks necessary to perform the job.

Market

A Market is any one of a variety of different systems, institutions, procedures, social relations and infrastructures whereby persons trade, and goods and services are exchanged, forming part of the economy. It is an arrangement that allows buyers and sellers to exchange things. Market s vary in size, range, geographic scale, location, types and variety of human communities, as well as the types of goods and services traded.

Marketing mix

The Marketing mix is generally accepted as the use and specification of the four p's describing the strategic position of a product in the marketplace. One version of the origins of the Marketing mix starts in 1948 when James Culliton said that a marketing decision should be a result of something similar to a recipe. This version continued in 1953 when Neil Borden, in his American Marketing Association presidential address, took the recipe idea one step further and coined the term 'Marketing-Mix'.

Advertising

Advertising is a form of communication that typically attempts to persuade potential customers to purchase or to consume more of a particular brand of product or service. 'While now central to the contemporary global economy and the reproduction of global production networks, it is only quite recently that Advertising has been more than a marginal influence on patterns of sales and production. The formation of modern Advertising was intimately bound up with the emergence of new forms of monopoly capitalism around the end of the 19th and beginning of the 20th century as one element in corporate strategies to create, organize and where possible control markets, especially for mass produced consumer goods.

Marketing	Marketing is defined by the American Marketing Association as the activity, set of institutions, and processes for creating, communicating, delivering, and exchanging offerings that have value for customers, clients, partners, and society at large. The term developed from the original meaning which referred literally to going to market, as in shopping, or going to a market to sell goods or services. Marketing practice tends to be seen as a creative industry, which includes advertising, distribution and selling.
Pricing	Pricing is one of the four Ps of the marketing mix. The other three aspects are product, promotion, and place. It is also a key variable in microeconomic price allocation theory.
Standardization	Standardization or standardisation is the process of developing and agreeing upon technical standards. A standard is a document that establishes uniform engineering or technical specifications, criteria, methods, processes, or practices. Some standards are mandatory while others are voluntary.
Consumer	Consumer is a broad label that refers to any individuals or households that use goods and services generated within the economy. The concept of a Consumer is used in different contexts, so that the usage and significance of the term may vary. A Consumer is a person who uses any product or service.
Consumer goods	Consumer goods are final goods specifically intended for the mass market. For instance, consumer goods do not include investment assets, like precious antiques, even though these antiques are final goods. Manufactured goods are goods that have been processed by way of machinery.
Good	A good is an object whose consumption increases the utility of the consumer, for which the quantity demanded exceeds the quantity supplied at zero price. Goods are usually modeled as having diminishing marginal utility. The first individual purchase has high utility; the second has less.
Internationalization	Internationalization has been viewed as a process of increasing involvement of enterprises in international markets, although there is no agreed definition of Internationalization or international entrepreneurship. There are several Internationalization theories which try to explain why there are international activities. Adam Smith claimed that a country should specialise in, and export, commodities in which it had an absolute advantage.
Total product	Diminishing returns can be divided into three categories: 1. Diminishing Total returns, which implies reduction in Total product with every additional unit of input. This occurs after point A in the graph. 2. Diminishing Average returns, which refers to the portion of the APP curve after its intersection with MPP curve. 3. Diminishing Marginal returns, refers to the point where the MPP curve starts to slope down and travels all the way down to the x-axis and beyond. Putting it in a chronological order, at first the marginal returns start to diminish, then the average returns, followed finally by the total returns.
Comparative advertising	Comparative advertising is an advertisement in which a particular product specifically mentions a competitor by name for the express purpose of showing why the competitor is inferior to the product naming it.

	This should not be confused with parody advertisements, where a fictional product is being advertised for the purpose of poking fun at the particular advertisement, nor should it be confused with the use of a coined brand name for the purpose of comparing the product without actually naming an actual competitor. ('Wikipedia tastes better and is less filling than the Encyclopedia Galactica.') In the 1980s, during what has been referred to as the cola wars, soft-drink manufacturer Pepsi ran a series of advertisements where people, caught on hidden camera, in a blind taste test, chose Pepsi over rival Coca-Cola.
Design	Design is used both as a noun and a verb. The term is often tied to the various applied arts and engineering As a verb, 'to design' refers to the process of originating and developing a plan for a product, structure, system, or component with intention.
Brand	A Brand is a name or trademark connected with a product or producer. Brand s have become increasingly important components of culture and the economy, now being described as 'cultural accessories and personal philosophies'. Some people distinguish the psychological aspect of a Brand from the experiential aspect.
Brand names	Descriptive brand names assist in describing the distinguishable selling point(s) of the product to the customer (eg Snap Crackle ' Pop or Bitter Lemon.) Associative brand names provide the customer with an associated word for what the product promises to do or be (e.g. Walkman, Sensodyne or Natrel) Finally, Freestanding brand names have no links or ties to either descriptions or associations of use.
Cultural identity	Cultural identity is the identity of a group or culture, or of an individual as far as one is influenced by one's belonging to a group or culture. Cultural identity is similar to and has overlaps with, but is not synonymous with, identity politics. There are modern questions of culture that are transferred into questions of identity.
Culture	Culture is a term that has different meanings. For example, in 1952, Alfred Kroeber and Clyde Kluckhohn compiled a list of 164 definitions of culture in culture A Critical Review of Concepts and Definitions. However, the word culture is most commonly used in three basic senses: · excellence of taste in the fine arts and humanities, also known as high culture · an integrated pattern of human knowledge, belief, and behavior that depends upon the capacity for symbolic thought and social learning · the set of shared attitudes, values, goals, and practices that characterizes an institution, organization or group. When the concept first emerged in eighteenth- and nineteenth-century Europe, it connoted a process of cultivation or improvement, as in agri culture or horti culture . In the nineteenth century, it came to refer first to the betterment or refinement of the individual, especially through education, and then to the fulfillment of national aspirations or ideals.
Economic	An economy (or 'the economy') is the realized Economic system of a country or other area. It includes the production, exchange, distribution, and consumption of goods and services of that area. The study of different types and examples of economies is the subject of Economic systems.
Income disparity	Income disparity or wage gap is a term used to describe inequities and asymmetry in the distribution of wealth and income between socio-economic groups within society. The term also has many other definitions: Common examples include:

· The income gap between the wealthy and the poor.
· lower average income for females than males

In the context of economic inequality, gender gap generally refers to the differences in the wages of men and women, or boys and girls. There is a debate to what extent this is the result of gender differences, lifestyle choices (e.g., number of hours worked), or because of discrimination.

A United Nations report found that women working in manufacturing earned the following percentages in relation to men in 2003.

Shopping

Shopping is the examining of goods or services from retailers with the intent to purchase at that time. Shopping is an activity of selection and/or purchase. In some contexts it is considered a leisure activity as well as an economic one.

Trademark

A Trademark or trade mark is a distinctive sign or indicator used by an individual, business organization and to distinguish its products or services from those of other entities.

A Trademark is designated by the following symbols:

· â„¢ (for an unregistered Trademark that is, a mark used to promote or brand goods);
· â„ (for an unregistered service mark, that is, a mark used to promote or brand services); and
· Â® (for a registered Trademark)

A Trademark is a type of intellectual property, and typically a name, word, phrase, logo, symbol, design, image, or a combination of these elements. There is also a range of non-conventional Trademark s comprising marks which do not fall into these standard categories.

The owner of a registered Trademark may commence legal proceedings for Trademark infringement to prevent unauthorized use of that Trademark

Kraft Foods

Kraft Foods Inc. (NYSE: Kraft Foods T) is the largest food and beverage company headquartered in the United States and the second largest in the world (after Nestlé SA.)

Kraft is headquartered in Northfield, Illinois, USA, a Chicago suburb.

Occupational Safety and Health

Occupational safety and health is a cross-disciplinary area concerned with protecting the safety, health and welfare of people engaged in work or employment. As a secondary effect, it may also protect co-workers, family members, employers, customers, suppliers, nearby communities, and other members of the public who are impacted by the workplace environment. It may involve interactions among many subject areas, including occupational medicine, occupational (or industrial) hygiene, public health, safety engineering, chemistry, health physics, ergonomics, toxicology, epidemiology, environmental health, industrial relations, public policy, sociology, and occupational health psychology.

Occupational Safety and Health Act

The Occupational Safety and Health Act is the primary federal law which governs occupational health and safety in the private sector and federal government in the United States. It was enacted by Congress in 1970 and was signed by President Richard Nixon on December 29, 1970. Its main goal is to ensure that employers provide employees with an environment free from recognized hazards, such as exposure to toxic chemicals, excessive noise levels, mechanical dangers, heat or cold stress, or unsanitary conditions.

Purchasing

Purchasing refers to a business or organization attempting to acquire goods or services to accomplish the goals of the enterprise. Though there are several organizations that attempt to set standards in the Purchasing process, processes can vary greatly between organizations. Typically the word 'Purchasing' is not used interchangeably with the word 'procurement', since procurement typically includes Expediting, Supplier Quality, and Traffic and Logistics (T'L) in addition to Purchasing.

Purchasing power

Purchasing power is the number of goods/services that can be purchased with a unit of currency. For example, if you had taken one dollar to a store in the 1950s, you would have been able to buy a greater number of items than you would today, indicating that you would have had a greater purchasing power in the 1950s. Currency can be either a commodity money, like gold or silver, or fiat currency like US dollars which are the world reserve currency.

Industry

An Industry is the manufacturing of a good or service within a category. Although Industry is a broad term for any kind of economic production, in economics and urban planning Industry is a synonym for the secondary sector, which is a type of economic activity involved in the manufacturing of raw materials into goods and products.

There are four key industrial economic sectors: the primary sector, largely raw material extraction industries such as mining and farming; the secondary sector, involving refining, construction, and manufacturing; the tertiary sector, which deals with services (such as law and medicine) and distribution of manufactured goods; and the quaternary sector, a relatively new type of knowledge Industry focusing on technological research, design and development such as computer programming, and biochemistry.

Set TSP

In combinatorial optimization, the set TSP group TSP, One-of-a-set TSP, Multiple Choice TSP or Covering Salesman Problem, is a generalization of the Traveling salesman problem, whereby it is required to find a shortest tour in a graph which visits all specified disjoint subsets of the vertices of a graph. The ordinary TSP is a special case of the set TSP when all subsets to be visited are singletons. Therefore the set TSP is also NP-hard.

Variable

Variables are used in open sentences. For instance, in the formula $x + 1 = 5$, x is a variable which represents an 'unknown' number. Variables are often represented by letters of the Roman alphabet, or those of other alphabets, such as Greek, and use other special symbols.

Comparative

In grammar, the comparative is the form of an adjective or adverb which denotes the degree or grade by which a person, thing and is used in this context with a subordinating conjunction, such as than, as...as, etc.

The structure of a comparative in English consists normally of the positive form of the adjective or adverb, plus the suffix -er e.g. 'he is taller than his father is', or 'the village is less picturesque than the town nearby'.

Economies of scale

Economies of scale in microeconomics, are the cost advantages that a business obtains due to expansion. They are factors that cause a producer's average cost per unit to fall as scale is increased. Economies of scale is a long run concept and refers to reductions in unit cost as the size of a facility, or scale, increases.

Fair Trade

Fair trade is an organized social movement and market-based approach that aims to help producers in developing countries and promote sustainability. The movement advocates the payment of a fair price as well as social and environmental standards in areas related to the production of a wide variety of goods. It focuses in particular on exports from developing countries to developed countries, most notably handicrafts, coffee, cocoa, sugar, tea, bananas, honey, cotton, wine, fresh fruit, chocolate and flowers.

Keiretsu

A keiretsu is a set of companies with interlocking business relationships and shareholdings. It is a type of business group. The prototypical keiretsu are those which appeared in Japan during the 'economic miracle' following World War II.

National brand

The brand name of a product that is distributed nationally under a brand name owned by the producer or distributor, as opposed to local brands (products distributed only in some areas of the country), and private label brands (products that carry the brand of the retailer rather than the producer.)

National brand s must compete with local and private brands. National brand s are produced by ,widely distuted by, and carry the name of the manufacturer.

· Local brands may appeal to those consumers who favor small, local producers over large national or global producers, and may be willing to pay a premium to 'buy local'

· The private label producer can offer lower prices because they avoid the cost of marketing and advertising to create and protect the brand. In North America, large retailers such as Loblaws, Walgreen and Wal-Mart all offer private label products.

Function cost analysis

Function cost analysis is the a method of technical and economic research of the systems for purpose to optimize a parity between system's consumer functions or properties and expenses to achieve those functions or properties.

This methodology for continuous perfection of production, industrial technologies, organizational structures was developed by Juryj Sobolev in 1948 at the 'Perm telephone factory'

· 1948 Juryj Sobolev - the first success in application of a method analysis at the 'Perm telephone factory' .
· 1949 - the first application for the invention as result of use of the new method.

Today in economically developed countries practically each enterprise or the company use methodology of the kind of functional-cost analysis as a practice of the quality management, most full satisfying to principles of standards of series ISO 9000.

· Interest of consumer not in products itself, but the advantage which it will receive from its usage.
· The consumer aspires to reduce his expenses
· Functions needed by consumer can be executed in the various ways, and, hence, with various efficiency and expenses. Among possible alternatives of realization of functions exist such in which the parity of quality and the price is the optimal for the consumer.

The goal of Function cost analysis is achievement of the highest consumer satisfaction of production at simultaneous decrease in all kinds of industrial expenses Classical Function cost analysis has three English synonyms - Value Engineering, Value Management, Value Analysis.

Internet

The Internet is a global network of interconnected computers, enabling users to share information along multiple channels. Typically, a computer that connects to the Internet can access information from a vast array of available servers and other computers by moving information from them to the computer's local memory. The same connection allows that computer to send information to servers on the network; that information is in turn accessed and potentially modified by a variety of other interconnected computers.

Newspaper

A newspaper is a publication containing news, information, and advertising. General-interest newspaper s often feature articles on political events, crime, business, art/entertainment, society and sports. Most traditional papers also feature an editorial page containing columns that express the personal opinions of writers.

Private branding

Private branding is when a large distribution channel member (usually a retailer), buys from a manufacturer in bulk and puts its own name on the product. This strategy is only practical when the retailer does very high levels of volume. The advantages to the retailer are:

· more freedom and flexibility in pricing
· more control over product attributes and quality
· higher margins (or lower selling price)
· eliminates much of the manufacturer's promotional costs

The advantages to the manufacturer are:

· reduced promotional costs
· stability of sales volume (at least while the contract is operative)

· Kumar, Nirmalya; Steenkamp, Jan-Benedict E.M., Private Label Strategy - How to Meet the Store Brand Challenge. Harvard Business Press 2007

· private label
· brand management
· brand
· product management
· marketing .

Market segment

A market segment is a subgroup of people or organizations sharing one or more characteristics that cause them to have similar product and/or service needs. A true market segment meets all of the following criteria: it is distinct from other segments (different segments have different needs), it is homogeneous within the segment (exhibits common needs); it responds similarly to a market stimulus, and it can be reached by a market intervention. The term is also used when consumers with identical product and/or service needs are divided up into groups so they can be charged different amounts.

Image

An Image is an artifact that has a similar appearance to some subject--usually a physical object or a person.

Image s may be two-dimensional, such as a photograph, screen display, and as well as a three-dimensional, such as a statue. They may be captured by optical devices--such as cameras, mirrors, lenses, telescopes, microscopes, etc.

Brand image

A Brand image is typically the attributes one associates with a brand, how the brand owner wants the consumer to perceive the brand - and by extension the branded company, organization, product or service. The brand owner will seek to bridge the gap between the Brand image and the brand identity.

External

In economics, an external ity or spillover of an economic transaction is an impact on a party that is not directly involved in the transaction. In such a case, prices do not reflect the full costs or benefits in production or consumption of a product or service. A positive impact is called an external benefit, while a negative impact is called an external cost.

Recruitment

Recruitment refers to the process of screening, and selecting qualified people for a job at an organization or firm, or for a vacancy in a volunteer-based organization or community group. While generalist managers or administrators can undertake some components of the Recruitment process, mid- and large-size organizations and companies often retain professional recruiters or outsource some of the process to Recruitment agencies. External Recruitment is the process of attracting and selecting employees from outside the organization.

Sales promotion

Sales promotion is one of the four aspects of promotional mix. (The other three parts of the promotional mix are advertising, personal selling, and publicity/public relations.) Media and non-media marketing communication are employed for a pre-determined, limited time to increase consumer demand, stimulate market demand or improve product availability.

Organization

An organization is a social arrangement which pursues collective goals, which controls its own performance, and which has a boundary separating it from its environment. The word itself is derived from the Greek word á½„ργανον (organon [itself derived from the better-known word á¼”ργον ergon - work; deed - > ergonomics, etc]) meaning tool. The term is used in both daily and scientific English in multiple ways.

Public relations

Public relations is the practice of managing the flow of information between an organization and its publics. Public relations gains an organization or individual exposure to their audiences using topics of public interest and news items that do not require direct payment. Because Public relations places exposure in credible third-party outlets, it offers a third-party legitimacy that advertising does not have.

World Trade Organization

The World Trade Organization is an international organization designed to supervise and liberalize international trade. The World Trade Organization came into being on 1 January 1995, and is the successor to the General Agreement on Tariffs and Trade (GATT), which was created in 1947, and continued to operate for almost five decades as a de facto international organization.

The World Trade Organization deals with the rules of trade between nations at a near-global level; it is responsible for negotiating and implementing new trade agreements, and is in charge of policing member countries' adherence to all the World Trade Organization agreements, signed by the majority of the world's trading nations and ratified in their parliaments.

Job interview

A Job interview is a process in which a potential employee is evaluated by an employer for prospective employment in their company, organization and was established in the late 16th century.

A Job interview typically precedes the hiring decision, and is used to evaluate the candidate. The interview is usually preceded by the evaluation of submitted résumés from interested candidates, then selecting a small number of candidates for interviews.

Distribution

Distribution is one of the four elements of marketing mix. An organization or set of organizations (go-betweens) involved in the process of making a product or service available for use or consumption by a consumer or business user.

The other three parts of the marketing mix are product, pricing, and promotion.

Price

Price in economics and business is the result of an exchange and from that trade we assign a numerical monetary value to a good, service or asset. If I trade 4 apples for an orange, the price of an orange is 4 - apples. Inversely, the price of an apple is 1/4 oranges.

Profit

A profit , in the law of real property, is a nonpossessory interest in land similar to the better-known easement, which gives the holder the right to take natural resources such as petroleum, minerals, timber, and wild game from the land of another. Indeed, because of the necessity of allowing access to the land so that resources may be gathered, every profit contains an implied easement for the owner of the profit to enter the other party's land for the purpose of collecting the resources permitted by the profit.

Like an easement, profits can be created expressly by an agreement between the property owner and the owner of the profit, or by prescription, where the owner of the profit has made 'open and notorious' use of the land for a continuous and uninterrupted statutory period.

Transfer

Transfer is a technique used in propaganda and advertising. Also known as association, this is a technique of projecting positive or negative qualities (praise or blame) of a person, entity, object, or value (an individual, group, organization, nation, patriotism, etc.) to another in order to make the second more acceptable or to discredit it.

United States

The United States of America (commonly referred to as the United States the U.S., the United States A, or America) is a federal constitutional republic comprising fifty states and a federal district. The country is situated mostly in central North America, where its 48 contiguous states and Washington, D.C., the capital district, lie between the Pacific and Atlantic Oceans, bordered by Canada to the north and Mexico to the south. The state of Alaska is in the northwest of the continent, with Canada to its east and Russia to the west across the Bering Strait.

Cost

In economics, business, retail, and accounting, a cost is the value of money that has been used up to produce something, and hence is not available for use anymore. In economics, a cost is an alternative that is given up as a result of a decision. In business, the cost may be one of acquisition, in which case the amount of money expended to acquire it is counted as cost.

Labor law

Labor law is the body of laws, administrative rulings, and precedents which address the legal rights of, and restrictions on, working people and their organizations. As such, it mediates many aspects of the relationship between trade unions, employers and employees. In Canada, employment laws related to unionized workplaces are differentiated from those relating to particular individuals.

Manufacturing

Manufacturing is the application of tools and a processing medium to the transformation of raw materials into finished goods for sale. This effort includes all intermediate processes required for the production and integration of a product's components. Some industries, like semiconductor and steel manufacturers use the term fabrication instead.

Numerary

Numerary is a civil designation for persons who are incorporated in a fixed or permanent way to a society or group: regular member of the working staff, permanent staff distinguished from a super Numerary .

The term Numerary and its counterpart, 'super Numerary ,' originated in Spanish and Latin American academy and government; it is now also used in countries all over the world, such as France, the U.S., England, Italy, etc.

There are Numerary members of surgical organizations, of universities, of gastronomical associations, etc.

Swap

In finance, a Swap is a derivative in which two counterparties agree to exchange one stream of cash flow against another stream. These streams are called the legs of the Swap.

The cash flows are calculated over a notional principal amount, which is usually not exchanged between counterparties.

Transfer pricing

Transfer pricing refers to the pricing of contributions (assets, tangible and intangible, services, and funds) transferred within an organization. For example, goods from the production division may be sold to the marketing division, or goods from a parent company may be sold to a foreign subsidiary. Since the prices are set within an organization (i.e. controlled), the typical market mechanisms that establish prices for such transactions between third parties may not apply.

Decision making

Decision making can be regarded as an outcome of mental processes (cognitive process) leading to the selection of a course of action among several alternatives. Every decision making process produces a final choice. The output can be an action or an opinion of choice.

Interdependence

Interdependence is a dynamic of being mutually and physically responsible to and sharing a common set of principles with others. This concept differs distinctly from 'dependence' in that an interdependent relationship implies that all participants are emotionally, economically, ecologically and or morally 'interdependent.' Some people advocate freedom or independence as a sort of ultimate good; others do the same with devotion to one's family, community, or society. Interdependence recognizes the truth in each position and weaves them together.

Disintermediation

In economics, Disintermediation is the removal of intermediaries in a supply chain: 'cutting out the middleman'. Instead of going through traditional distribution channels, which had some type of intermediate (such as a distributor, wholesaler, broker, or agent), companies may now deal with every customer directly, for example via the Internet. One important factor is a drop in the cost of servicing customers directly.

Original

Original ity is the aspect of created or invented works by as being new or novel, and thus can be distinguished from reproductions, clones, forgeries, or derivative works. An original work is one not received from others nor one copied based on the work of others. The term ' original ity' is often applied as a compliment to the creativity of artists, writers, and thinkers.

Original equipment manufacturer

An Original equipment manufacturer or sells the product of the second company under its own brand. The specific meaning of the term varies in different contexts.

Original equipment manufacturer refers to the aircraft manufacturers.

Retailing

Retailing consists of the sale of goods or merchandise from a fixed location, such as a department store or kiosk in small or individual lots for direct consumption by the purchaser. Retailing may include subordinated services, such as delivery. Purchasers may be individuals or businesses.

Antitrust

Competition law, known in the United States as antitrust law, has three main elements:

· prohibiting agreements or practices that restrict free trading and competition between business entities. This includes in particular the repression of cartels.
· banning abusive behavior by a firm dominating a market, or anti-competitive practices that tend to lead to such a dominant position. Practices controlled in this way may include predatory pricing, tying, price gouging, refusal to deal, and many others.
· supervising the mergers and acquisitions of large corporations, including some joint ventures. Transactions that are considered to threaten the competitive process can be prohibited altogether, or approved subject to 'remedies' such as an obligation to divest part of the merged business or to offer licenses or access to facilities to enable other businesses to continue competing.

The substance and practice of competition law varies from jurisdiction to jurisdiction. Protecting the interests of consumers (consumer welfare) and ensuring that entrepreneurs have an opportunity to compete in the market economy are often treated as important objectives. Competition law is closely connected with law on deregulation of access to markets, state aids and subsidies, the privatization of state owned assets and the establishment of independent sector regulators. In recent decades, competition law has been viewed as a way to provide better public services.

Antitrust law

Competition law, known in the United States as Antitrust law, has three main elements:

· prohibiting agreements or practices that restrict free trading and competition between business entities. This includes in particular the repression of cartels.
· banning abusive behaviour by a firm dominating a market, or anti-competitive practices that tend to lead to such a dominant position. Practices controlled in this way may include predatory pricing, tying, price gouging, refusal to deal, and many others.
· supervising the mergers and acquisitions of large corporations, including some joint ventures. Transactions that are considered to threaten the competitive process can be prohibited altogether, or approved subject to 'remedies' such as an obligation to divest part of the merged business or to offer licences or access to facilities to enable other businesses to continue competing.

The substance and practice of competition law varies from jurisdiction to jurisdiction. Protecting the interests of consumers (consumer welfare) and ensuring that entrepreneurs have an opportunity to compete in the market economy are often treated as important objectives. Competition law is closely connected with law on deregulation of access to markets, state aids and subsidies, the privatisation of state owned assets and the establishment of independent sector regulators. In recent decades, competition law has been viewed as a way to provide better public services.

Competition law

Competition law, known in the United States as antitrust law, has three main elements:

· prohibiting agreements or practices that restrict free trading and competition between business entities. This includes in particular the repression of cartels.
· banning abusive behaviour by a firm dominating a market, or anti-competitive practices that tend to lead to such a dominant position. Practices controlled in this way may include predatory pricing, tying, price gouging, refusal to deal, and many others.
· supervising the mergers and acquisitions of large corporations, including some joint ventures. Transactions that are considered to threaten the competitive process can be prohibited altogether, or approved subject to 'remedies' such as an obligation to divest part of the merged business or to offer licences or access to facilities to enable other businesses to continue competing.
The substance and practice of Competition law varies from jurisdiction to jurisdiction. Protecting the interests of consumers (consumer welfare) and ensuring that entrepreneurs have an opportunity to compete in the market economy are often treated as important objectives. Competition law is closely connected with law on deregulation of access to markets, state aids and subsidies, the privatisation of state owned assets and the establishment of independent sector regulators. In recent decades, Competition law has been viewed as a way to provide better public services.

Jobbing house

A Jobbing house (or jobbing center) is a type of wholesale merchant business that buys goods and bulk products from importers, other wholesalers and then sells to retailers. Jobbing house s can deal in any commodity destined for the retail market. Typical categories are food, lumber, hardware, fuel, and textiles.

Characteristic

Characteristic has several particular meanings:

· in mathematics
- · Euler characteristic
- · method of characteristic s (partial differential equations)

· in physics and engineering

· any characteristic curve that shows the relationship between certain input- and output parameters, e.g.
· an I-V or current-voltage characteristic is the current in a circuit as a function of the applied voltage
· Receiver-Operator characteristic
· in navigation, the characteristic pattern of a lighted beacon.
· in fiction

· in Dungeons ' Dragons, characteristic is another name for ability score .

Skill

A skill is the learned capacity to carry out pre-determined results often with the minimum outlay of time, energy, or both. skill s can often be divided into domain-general and domain-specific skill s. For example, in the domain of work, some general skill s would include time management, teamwork and leadership, self motivation and others, whereas domain-specific skill s would be useful only for a certain job.

Korea

Korea (Hangul: í•œêµ or ì¡°ì„) is a civilization and formerly unified nation currently divided into two states. Located on the Korea n Peninsula, it borders China to the northwest, Russia to the northeast, and is separated from Japan to the east by the Korea Strait.

Business

A business is a legally recognized organization designed to provide goods and/or services to consumers. business es are predominant in capitalist economies, most being privately owned and formed to earn profit that will increase the wealth of its owners and grow the business itself. The owners and operators of a business have as one of their main objectives the receipt or generation of a financial return in exchange for work and acceptance of risk.

Business model

A business model is a framework for creating economic, social, and/or other forms of value. The term business model is thus used for a broad range of informal and formal descriptions to represent core aspects of a business, including purpose, offerings, strategies, infrastructure, organizational structures, trading practices, and operational processes and policies.

In the most basic sense, a business model is the method of doing business by which a company can sustain itself -- that is, generate revenue.

Procter ' Gamble

Procter is a surname, and may also refer to:

· Bryan Waller Procter (pseud. Barry Cornwall), English poet
· Goodwin Procter, American law firm
· Procter ' Gamble, consumer products multinational .

Supply chain

A Supply chain or logistics network is the system of organizations, people, technology, activities, information and resources involved in moving a product or service from supplier to customer. Supply chain activities transform natural resources, raw materials and components into a finished product that is delivered to the end customer. In sophisticated Supply chain systems, used products may re-enter the Supply chain at any point where residual value is recyclable.

Supply chain management

Supply chain management is the management of a network of interconnected businesses involved in the ultimate provision of product and service packages required by end customers (Harland, 1996.) Supply chain management spans all movement and storage of raw materials, work-in-process inventory, and finished goods from point of origin to point of consumption (supply chain.)

The definition an American professional association put forward is that Supply chain management encompasses the planning and management of all activities involved in sourcing, procurement, conversion, and logistics management activities.

Industry

An Industry is the manufacturing of a good or service within a category. Although Industry is a broad term for any kind of economic production, in economics and urban planning Industry is a synonym for the secondary sector, which is a type of economic activity involved in the manufacturing of raw materials into goods and products.

There are four key industrial economic sectors: the primary sector, largely raw material extraction industries such as mining and farming; the secondary sector, involving refining, construction, and manufacturing; the tertiary sector, which deals with services (such as law and medicine) and distribution of manufactured goods; and the quaternary sector, a relatively new type of knowledge Industry focusing on technological research, design and development such as computer programming, and biochemistry.

Product line

There are many important decisions about product and service development and marketing. In the process of product development and marketing we should focus on strategic decisions about product attributes, product branding, product packaging, product labeling and product support services. But product strategy also calls for building a Product line.

Cost

In economics, business, retail, and accounting, a cost is the value of money that has been used up to produce something, and hence is not available for use anymore. In economics, a cost is an alternative that is given up as a result of a decision. In business, the cost may be one of acquisition, in which case the amount of money expended to acquire it is counted as cost.

Cost of Goods Available for Sale

Cost of Goods Available for Sale is the maximum amount of goods that a company can possibly sell during this fiscal year. It have the formula:

Beginning Inventory (at the start of this year)+ Purchases (within this year)+ Production (within this year)= Cost of Goods Available for Sale

Notice that purchases and production might not be the same throughout the year, since purchase cost and production cost might vary during the year. But at the end, the total cost of purchases and production are added to beginning inventory cost to give Cost of Goods Available for Sale.

Outsourcing

Outsourcing is subcontracting a process, such as product design or manufacturing, to a third-party company. The decision to outsource is often made in the interest of lowering cost or making better use of time and energy costs, redirecting or conserving energy directed at the competencies of a particular business, or to make more efficient use of land, labor, capital, (information) technology and resources. outsourcing became part of the business lexicon during the 1980s.

Six Sigma

Six Sigma is a business management strategy, initially implemented by Motorola, that today enjoys widespread application in many sectors of industry.

Six Sigma seeks to improve the quality of process outputs by identifying and removing the causes of defects (errors) and variation in manufacturing and business processes. It uses a set of quality management methods, including statistical methods, and creates a special infrastructure of people within the organization ('Black Belts' etc.)

Supply chain network

Due to the rapid advancement of technology such as pervasive or ubiquitous wireless and internet networks, connective product marking technologies like RFID and emerging standards for the use of these defining specific locations using Global Location Number(s), the basic supply chain is rapidly evolving into what is known as a Supply chain network.

One of the first references to this term and concept was in the book 'The Supply chain network @Internet Speed: Preparing Your Company for the E-Commerce Revolution' by Fred A.; Rosenbaum, Barbara A. Kuglin (Hardcover - 2000.)

The book 'Supply Chain Architecture' by William T. Walker (2004) was the first to integrate APICS concepts with inter-enterprise business processes.

Global sourcing

Global sourcing is a term used to describe practice of sourcing from the global market for goods and services across geopolitical boundaries. Global sourcing often aims to exploit global efficiencies in the delivery of a product or service. These efficiencies include low cost skilled labor, low cost raw material and other economic factors like tax breaks and low trade tariffs.

Globalization

Globalization in its literal sense is the process of transformation of local or regional phenomena into global ones. It can be described as a process by which the people of the world are unified into a single society and function together.

This process is a combination of economic, technological, sociocultural and political forces.

Design

Design is used both as a noun and a verb. The term is often tied to the various applied arts and engineering As a verb, 'to design' refers to the process of originating and developing a plan for a product, structure, system, or component with intention.

Product life cycle

Product life cycle Management is the succession of strategies used by management as a product goes through its product life cycle. The conditions in which a product is sold changes over time and must be managed as it moves through its succession of stages.

The product life cycle goes through many phases, involves many professional disciplines, and requires many skills, tools and processes.

Comparative advertising

Comparative advertising is an advertisement in which a particular product specifically mentions a competitor by name for the express purpose of showing why the competitor is inferior to the product naming it.

This should not be confused with parody advertisements, where a fictional product is being advertised for the purpose of poking fun at the particular advertisement, nor should it be confused with the use of a coined brand name for the purpose of comparing the product without actually naming an actual competitor. ('Wikipedia tastes better and is less filling than the Encyclopedia Galactica.')

In the 1980s, during what has been referred to as the cola wars, soft-drink manufacturer Pepsi ran a series of advertisements where people, caught on hidden camera, in a blind taste test, chose Pepsi over rival Coca-Cola.

Standardization

Standardization or standardisation is the process of developing and agreeing upon technical standards. A standard is a document that establishes uniform engineering or technical specifications, criteria, methods, processes, or practices. Some standards are mandatory while others are voluntary.

Advertising

Advertising is a form of communication that typically attempts to persuade potential customers to purchase or to consume more of a particular brand of product or service. 'While now central to the contemporary global economy and the reproduction of global production networks, it is only quite recently that Advertising has been more than a marginal influence on patterns of sales and production. The formation of modern Advertising was intimately bound up with the emergence of new forms of monopoly capitalism around the end of the 19th and beginning of the 20th century as one element in corporate strategies to create, organize and where possible control markets, especially for mass produced consumer goods.

Asset

In business and accounting, asset s are economic resources owned by business or company. Anything tangible or intangible that one possesses, usually considered as applicable to the payment of one's debts is considered an asset Simplistically stated, asset s are things of value that can be readily converted into cash.

Competitive

Competitive ness is a comparative concept of the ability and performance of a firm, sub-sector or country to sell and supply goods and/or services in a given market. Although widely used in economics and business management, the usefulness of the concept, particularly in the context of national competitive ness, is vigorously disputed by economists, such as Paul Krugman .

The term may also be applied to markets, where it is used to refer to the extent to which the market structure may be regarded as perfectly competitive

Competitive advantage

Competitive advantage is, in very basic words, a position a firm occupies against its competitors.

	According to Michael Porter, the three methods for creating a sustainable Competitive advantage are through: 1. Cost leadership - Cost advantage occurs when a firm delivers the same services as its competitors but at a lower cost; 2.
Concurrent engineering	Concurrent engineering is a work methodology based on the parallelization of tasks (ie. concurrently.) It refers to an approach used in product development in which functions of design engineering, manufacturing engineering and other functions are integrated to reduce the elapsed time required to bring a new product to the market.
Decision making	Decision making can be regarded as an outcome of mental processes (cognitive process) leading to the selection of a course of action among several alternatives. Every decision making process produces a final choice. The output can be an action or an opinion of choice.
Offshoring	Offshoring describes the relocation by a company of a business process from one country to another -- typically an operational process, such as manufacturing such as accounting. Even state governments employ Offshoring. The term is in use in several distinct but closely related ways.
Independence	Independence is the self-government of a nation, country or some portion thereof, generally exercising sovereignty. The term Independence is used in contrast to subjugation, which refers to a region as a 'territory' --subject to the political and military control of an external government. The word is sometimes used in a weaker sense to contrast with hegemony, the indirect control of one nation by another, more powerful nation.
Joint venture	A joint venture is an entity formed between two or more parties to undertake economic activity together. The parties agree to create a new entity by both contributing equity, and they then share in the revenues, expenses, and control of the enterprise. The venture can be for one specific project only, or a continuing business relationship such as the Fuji Xerox joint venture.
Independent contractor	An Independent contractor is a natural person, business, or corporation which provides goods or services to another entity under terms specified in a contract or within a verbal agreement. Unlike an employee, an Independent contractor does not work regularly for an employer but works as and when required, during which time she or he may be subject to the Law of Agency. Independent contractor s are usually paid on a freelance basis.
Subsidiary	A Subsidiary, in business matters, is an entity that is controlled by a bigger and more powerful entity. The controlled entity is called a company, corporation, or limited liability company and in some cases can be a government or state-owned enterprise, and the controlling entity is called its parent (or the parent company.) The reason for this distinction is that a lone company cannot be a Subsidiary of any organization; only an entity representing a legal fiction as a separate entity can be a Subsidiary.
Business-to-business	Business-to-business is a term commonly used to describe commerce transactions between businesses like the one between a manufacturer and a wholesaler or a wholesaler and a retailer i.e both the buyer and the seller are business entity.This is unlike business-to-consumers (B2C) which involve a business entity and end consumer, or business-to-government (B2G) which involve a business entity and government.

The volume of B2B transactions is much higher than the volume of B2C transactions. The primary reason for this is that in a typical supply chain there will be many B2B transactions involving subcomponent or raw materials, and only one B2C transaction, specifically sale of the finished product to the end customer.

E-procurement

E-procurement is the business-to-business or business-to-consumer or Business-to-government purchase and sale of supplies, Work and services through the Internet as well as other information and networking systems, such as Electronic Data Interchange and Enterprise Resource Planning. Typically, E-procurement Web sites allow qualified and registered users to look for buyers or sellers of goods and services. Depending on the approach, buyers or sellers may specify costs or invite bids.

Customer

A customer also client, buyer or purchaser is usually used to refer to a current or potential buyer or user of the products of an individual or organization, mostly called the supplier or seller. This is typically through purchasing or renting goods or services. However in certain contexts the term customer also includes by extension anyone who uses or experiences the services of another.

E-commerce

Electronic commerce, commonly known as E-commerce or eCommerce, consists of the buying and selling of products or services over electronic systems such as the Internet and other computer networks. The amount of trade conducted electronically has grown extraordinarily with wide-spread Internet usage. A wide variety of commerce is conducted in this way, spurring and drawing on innovations in electronic funds transfer, supply chain management, Internet marketing, online transaction processing, electronic data interchange (EDI), inventory management systems, and automated data collection systems.

Option

In finance, an option is a contract between a buyer and a seller that gives the buyer the right--but not the obligation--to buy or to sell a particular asset (the underlying asset) at a later day at an agreed price. In return for granting the option, the seller collects a payment (the premium) from the buyer. A call option gives the buyer the right to buy the underlying asset, a put option gives the buyer of the option the right to sell the underlying asset.

Purchasing

Purchasing refers to a business or organization attempting to acquire goods or services to accomplish the goals of the enterprise. Though there are several organizations that attempt to set standards in the Purchasing process, processes can vary greatly between organizations. Typically the word 'Purchasing' is not used interchangeably with the word 'procurement', since procurement typically includes Expediting, Supplier Quality, and Traffic and Logistics (T'L) in addition to Purchasing.

Exchange rate

In finance, the Exchange rate s between two currencies specifies how much one currency is worth in terms of the other. It is the value of a foreign nation's currency in terms of the home nation's currency. For example an Exchange rate of 95 Japanese yen to the United States dollar means that JPY 95 is worth the same as USD 1.

Manufacturing

Manufacturing is the application of tools and a processing medium to the transformation of raw materials into finished goods for sale. This effort includes all intermediate processes required for the production and integration of a product's components. Some industries, like semiconductor and steel manufacturers use the term fabrication instead.

Computer-integrated manufacturing

Computer-Integrated Manufacturing in engineering is a method of manufacturing in which the entire production process is controlled by computer. The traditional separated process methods are joined through a computer by CIM. This integration allows that the processes exchange information with each other and they are able to initiate actions.

Just-in-time

Just-in-time is an inventory strategy implemented to improve the return on investment of a business by reducing in-process inventory and its associated carrying costs. In order to achieve JIT the process must have signals of what is going on elsewhere within the process. This means that the process is often driven by a series of signals, which can be Kanban , that tell production processes when to make the next part.

Flexible manufacturing system

A Flexible manufacturing system is a manufacturing system in which there is some amount of flexibility that allows the system to react in the case of changes, whether predicted or unpredicted. This flexibility is generally considered to fall into two categories, which both contain numerous subcategories.

The first category, machine flexibility, covers the system's ability to be changed to produce new product types, and ability to change the order of operations executed on a part. The second category is called routing flexibility, which consists of the ability to use multiple machines to perform the same operation on a part, as well as the system's ability to absorb large-scale changes, such as in volume, capacity, or capability.

Lean manufacturing

Lean manufacturing or lean production, which is often known simply as 'Lean', is a production practice that considers the expenditure of resources for any goal other than the creation of value for the end customer to be wasteful, and thus a target for elimination. Working from the perspective of the customer who consumes a product or service, 'value' is defined as any action or process that a customer would be willing to pay for. Basically, lean is centered around creating more value with less work.

Quality circle

A Quality circle is a volunteer group composed of workers (or even students), usually under the leadership of their supervisor (but they can elect a team leader), who are trained to identify, analyse and solve work-related problems and present their solutions to management in order to improve the performance of the organization, and motivate and enrich the work of employees. When matured, true Quality circle s become self-managing, having gained the confidence of management. Quality circle s are an alternative to the dehumanising concept of the Division of Labour, where workers or individuals are treated like robots.

Quality improvement

Quality management can be considered to have three main components: quality control, quality assurance and Quality improvement. Quality management is focused not only on product quality, but also the means to achieve it. Quality management therefore uses quality assurance and control of processes as well as products to achieve more consistent quality.

Total quality management

Total quality management is a business management strategy aimed at embedding awareness of quality in all organizational processes. Total quality management has been widely used in manufacturing, education, hospitals, call centers, government, and service industries, as well as NASA space and science programs.

When used together as a phrase, the three words in this expression have the following meanings:

· Total: Involving the entire organization, supply chain, and/or product life cycle
· Quality: With its usual definitions, with all its complexities
· Management: The system of managing with steps like Plan, Organize, Control, Lead, Staff, provisioning and organizing.

As defined by the International Organization for Standardization (ISO):

> 'Total quality management is a management approach for an organization, centered on quality, based on the participation of all its members and aiming at long-term success through customer satisfaction, and benefits to all members of the organization and to society.' ISO 8402:1994

One major aim is to reduce variation from every process so that greater consistency of effort is obtained. (Royse, D., Thyer, B., Padgett D., ' Logan T., 2006)

In Japan, Total quality management comprises four process steps, namely:

· Kaizen Focuses on 'Continuous Process Improvement', to make processes visible, repeatable and measurable.
· Atarimae Hinshitsu - The idea that 'things will work as they are supposed to'.
· Kansei - Examining the way the user applies the product leads to improvement in the product itself.
· Miryokuteki Hinshitsu - The idea that 'things should have an aesthetic quality' (for example, a pen will write in a way that is pleasing to the writer.)

Total quality management requires that the company maintain this quality standard in all aspects of its business. This requires ensuring that things are done right the first time and that defects and waste are eliminated from operations.

Control

Control is one of the managerial functions like planning, organizing, staffing and directing. It is an important function because it helps to check the errors and to take the corrective action so that deviation from standards are minimized and stated goals of the organization are achieved in desired manner.According to modern concepts, Control is a foreseeing action whereas earlier concept of Control was used only when errors were detected. Control in management means setting standards, measuring actual performance and taking corrective action.

Implementation

Implementation is the realization of an application idea, model, design, specification, standard, algorithm an implementation is a realization of a technical specification or algorithm as a program, software component, or other computer system. Many implementation s may exist for a given specification or standard.

Quality control

In engineering and manufacturing, quality control and quality engineering are used in developing systems to ensure products or services are designed and produced to meet or exceed customer requirements. Refer to the definition by Merriam-Webster for further information . These systems are often developed in conjunction with other business and engineering disciplines using a cross-functional approach.

Job shops

Job shops are typically small manufacturing operations that handle specialized manufacturing processes such as small customer orders or small batch jobs. job shops typically move on to different jobs (possibly with different customers) when each job is completed. By nature of this type of manufacturing operation, job shops are usually specialized in skill and processes.

Scientific management

Scientific management is a theory of management that analyzes and synthesizes workflows, with the objective of improving labour productivity. The core ideas of the theory were developed by Frederick Winslow Taylor in the 1880s and 1890s, and were first published in his monographs, Shop Management and The Principles of Scientific management Taylor believed that decisions based upon tradition and rules of thumb should be replaced by precise procedures developed after careful study of an individual at work.

United States

The United States of America (commonly referred to as the United States the U.S., the United States A, or America) is a federal constitutional republic comprising fifty states and a federal district. The country is situated mostly in central North America, where its 48 contiguous states and Washington, D.C., the capital district, lie between the Pacific and Atlantic Oceans, bordered by Canada to the north and Mexico to the south. The state of Alaska is in the northwest of the continent, with Canada to its east and Russia to the west across the Bering Strait.

Absolute advantage

In economics, Absolute advantage refers to the ability of a party to produce a good service using fewer real resources than another entity, producing the same good service.. A party has an Absolute advantage when using the same input as another party, it can produce a greater output. Since Absolute advantage is determined by a simple comparison of labor productivities, it is possible for a party to have no Absolute advantage in anything.

Job description

A Job description is a list of the general tasks and responsibilities of a position. Typically, it also includes to whom the position reports, specifications such as the qualifications needed by the person in the job, salary range for the position, etc. A Job description is usually developed by conducting a job analysis, which includes examining the tasks and sequences of tasks necessary to perform the job.

Preventive maintenance

Preventive maintenance has the following meanings:

The care and servicing by personnel for the purpose of maintaining equipment and facilities in satisfactory operating condition by providing for systematic inspection, detection, and correction of incipient failures either before they occur or before they develop into major defects.

· Maintenance, including tests, measurements, adjustments, and parts replacement, performed specifically to prevent faults from occurring.

While Preventive maintenance is generally considered to be worthwhile, there are risks such as equipment failure or human error involved when performing Preventive maintenance, just as in any maintenance operation. Preventive maintenance as scheduled overhaul or scheduled replacement provides two of the three proactive failure management policies available to the maintenance engineer. Common methods of determining what Preventive maintenance failure management policies should be applied are; OEM recommendations, requirements of codes and legislation within a jurisdiction, what an 'expert' thinks ought to be done, or the maintenance that's already done to similar equipment.

Mass marketing

Mass marketing is a market coverage strategy in which a firm decides to ignore market segment differences and go after the whole market with one offer.it is type of marketing (or attempting to sell through persuasion) of a product to a wide audience. The idea is to broadcast a message that will reach the largest number of people possible. Traditionally Mass marketing has focused on radio, television and newspapers as the medium used to reach this broad audience.

Mass customization

Mass customization, in marketing, manufacturing, and management, is the use of flexible computer-aided manufacturing systems to produce custom output. Those systems combine the low unit costs of mass production processes with the flexibility of individual customization.

'mass customization' is the new frontier in business competition for both manufacturing and service industries.

Theory of constraints

Theory of Constraints is an overall management philosophy introduced by Dr. Eliyahu M. Goldratt in his 1984 book titled The Goal, that is geared to help organizations continually achieve their goal. The title comes from the contention that any manageable system is limited in achieving more of its goal by a very small number of constraints, and that there is always at least one constraint. The Theory of Constraints process seeks to identify the constraint and restructure the rest of the organization around it, through the use of the Five Focusing Steps.

Horizontal integration

In microeconomics and strategic management, the term Horizontal integration describes a type of ownership and control. It is a strategy used by a business or corporation that seeks to sell a type of product in numerous markets. Horizontal integration in marketing is much more common than vertical integration is in production.

Vertical integration

In microeconomics and management, the term vertical integration describes a style of management control. Vertically integrated companies are united through a hierarchy with a common owner. Usually each member of the hierarchy produces a different product or (market-specific) service, and the products combine to satisfy a common need.

Champion

A champion is the victor in a challenge or contest.

More broadly, and particularly in American English, a champion is one who has repeatedly come out first among contestants in challenges or other test, one who is outstandingly skilled in their field. Olympic Gold Medalists, for example, are champion s in this sense.

Organizational culture

Organizational culture is an idea in the field of Organizational studies and management which describes the psychology, attitudes, experiences, beliefs and Values (personal and cultural values)of an organization. It has been defined as 'the specific collection of values and norms that are shared by people and groups in an organization and that control the way they interact with each other and with stakeholders outside the organization.'

This definition continues to explain organizational values also known as 'beliefs and ideas about what kinds of goals members of an organization should pursue and ideas about the appropriate kinds or standards of behavior organizational members should use to achieve these goals. From organizational values develop organizational norms, guidelines or expectations that prescribe appropriate kinds of behavior by employees in particular situations and control the behavior of organizational members towards one another.'

organizational culture is not the same as corporate culture.

Culture change

Culture change is a term used in public policy making that emphasises the influence of cultural capital on individual and community behaviour. It places stress on the social and cultural capital determinants of decision making and the manner in which these interact with other factors like the availability of information or the financial incentives facing individuals to drive behaviour.

These cultural capital influences include the role of parenting, families and close associates; organisations such as schools and workplaces; communities and neighbourhoods; and wider social influences such as the media.

International Organization for Standardization

The International Organization for Standardization, widely known as ISO , is an international-standard-setting body composed of representatives from various national standards organizations. Founded on 23 February 1947, the organization promulgates worldwide proprietary industrial and commercial standards. It is headquartered in Geneva, Switzerland.

Logistics

Logistics is the management of the flow of goods, information and other resources, including energy and people, between the point of origin and the point of consumption in order to meet the requirements of consumers (frequently, and originally, military organizations.) Logistics involves the integration of information, transportation, inventory, warehousing, material-handling, and packaging. Logistics is a channel of the supply chain which adds the value of time and place utility.

Low-cost country sourcing

Low-cost country sourcing is a procurement strategy in which a company sources materials from countries with lower labour and production costs in order to cut operating expenses. LCCS falls under a broad category of procurement efforts called global sourcing.

The primary principle behind LCCS is to obtain sourcing efficiencies through identifying and exploiting cost arbitrage between geographies.

Organization

An organization is a social arrangement which pursues collective goals, which controls its own performance, and which has a boundary separating it from its environment. The word itself is derived from the Greek word á½„ργανον (organon [itself derived from the better-known word á¼"ργον ergon - work; deed - > ergonomics, etc]) meaning tool. The term is used in both daily and scientific English in multiple ways.

Function cost analysis

Function cost analysis is the a method of technical and economic research of the systems for purpose to optimize a parity between system's consumer functions or properties and expenses to achieve those functions or properties.

This methodology for continuous perfection of production, industrial technologies, organizational structures was developed by Juryj Sobolev in 1948 at the 'Perm telephone factory'

· 1948 Juryj Sobolev - the first success in application of a method analysis at the 'Perm telephone factory' .
· 1949 - the first application for the invention as result of use of the new method.

Today in economically developed countries practically each enterprise or the company use methodology of the kind of functional-cost analysis as a practice of the quality management, most full satisfying to principles of standards of series ISO 9000.

· Interest of consumer not in products itself, but the advantage which it will receive from its usage.
· The consumer aspires to reduce his expenses
· Functions needed by consumer can be executed in the various ways, and, hence, with various efficiency and expenses. Among possible alternatives of realization of functions exist such in which the parity of quality and the price is the optimal for the consumer.

The goal of Function cost analysis is achievement of the highest consumer satisfaction of production at simultaneous decrease in all kinds of industrial expenses Classical Function cost analysis has three English synonyms - Value Engineering, Value Management, Value Analysis.

ISO 9000

ISO 9000 is a family of standards for quality management systems. ISO 9000 is maintained by ISO, the International Organization for Standardization and is administered by accreditation and certification bodies. The rules are updated, the time and changes in the requirements for quality, motivate change.

Planning

Planning in organizations and public policy is both the organizational process of creating and maintaining a plan; and the psychological process of thinking about the activities required to create a desired goal on some scale. As such, it is a fundamental property of intelligent behavior. This thought process is essential to the creation and refinement of a plan, or integration of it with other plans, that is, it combines forecasting of developments with the preparation of scenarios of how to react to them.

Automation

Automation is the use of control systems (such as numerical control, programmable logic control, and other industrial control systems), in concert with other applications of information technology (such as computer-aided technologies [CAD, CAM, CAx]), to control industrial machinery and processes, reducing the need for human intervention. In the scope of industrialization, Automation is a step beyond mechanization. Whereas mechanization provided human operators with machinery to assist them with the physical requirements of work, Automation greatly reduces the need for human sensory and mental requirements as well.

Economic

An economy (or 'the economy') is the realized Economic system of a country or other area. It includes the production, exchange, distribution, and consumption of goods and services of that area. The study of different types and examples of economies is the subject of Economic systems.

Labor intensity

Labor intensity is the relative proportion of labor (compared to capital) used in a process. The term 'labor intensive' can be used when proposing the amount of work that is assigned to each worker/employee (labor), emphasizing on the skill involved in the respective line of work.

Market

A Market is any one of a variety of different systems, institutions, procedures, social relations and infrastructures whereby persons trade, and goods and services are exchanged, forming part of the economy. It is an arrangement that allows buyers and sellers to exchange things. Market s vary in size, range, geographic scale, location, types and variety of human communities, as well as the types of goods and services traded.

Distribution

Distribution is one of the four elements of marketing mix. An organization or set of organizations (go-betweens) involved in the process of making a product or service available for use or consumption by a consumer or business user.

The other three parts of the marketing mix are product, pricing, and promotion.

Range

In descriptive statistics, the Range is the length of the smallest interval which contains all the data. It is calculated by subtracting the smallest observation (sample minimum) from the greatest (sample maximum) and provides an indication of statistical dispersion.

It is measured in the same units as the data.

Characteristic

Characteristic has several particular meanings:

· in mathematics

- · Euler characteristic
- · method of characteristic s (partial differential equations)

· in physics and engineering

· any characteristic curve that shows the relationship between certain input- and output parameters, e.g.
· an I-V or current-voltage characteristic is the current in a circuit as a function of the applied voltage
· Receiver-Operator characteristic
· in navigation, the characteristic pattern of a lighted beacon.
· in fiction

· in Dungeons ' Dragons, characteristic is another name for ability score .

Investment

Investment or investing is a term with several closely-related meanings in business management, finance and economics, related to saving or deferring consumption. Investing is the active redirecting resources from being consumed today so that they may create benefits in the future; the use of assets to earn income or profit.

An Investment is the choice by the individual to risk his savings with the hope of gain.

Best practice

A best practice is a technique, method, process, activity, incentive or reward that is believed to be more effective at delivering a particular outcome than any other technique, method, process, etc. The idea is that with proper processes, checks, and testing, a desired outcome can be delivered with fewer problems and unforeseen complications. best practice s can also be defined as the most efficient (least amount of effort) and effective (best results) way of accomplishing a task, based on repeatable procedures that have proven themselves over time for large numbers of people.

Information system

In a general sense , the term Information system refers to a system of people, data records and activities that process the data and information in an organization, and it includes the organization's manual and automated processes. In a narrow sense, the term Information system (or computer-based Information system refers to the specific application software that is used to store data records in a computer system and automates some of the information-processing activities of the organization. Computer-based Information system s are in the field of information technology.

Export

In economics, an export is any good or commodity, transported from one country to another country in a legitimate fashion, typically for use in trade. export goods or services are provided to foreign consumers by domestic producers. export is an important part of international trade.

Free trade zone

A Free trade zone or export processing zone (EPZ) is one or more special areas of a country where some normal trade barriers such as tariffs and quotas are eliminated and bureaucratic requirements are lowered in hopes of attracting new business and foreign investments. It is a a region where a group of countries has agreed to reduce or eliminate trade barriers. They can be defined as labor intensive manufacturing centers that involve the import of raw materials or components and the export of factory products.

Material handling equipment	Material handling equipment is all equipment that relates to the movement, storage, control and protection of materials, goods and products throughout the process of manufacturing, distribution, consumption and disposal. Material handling equipment is the mechanical equipment involved in the complete system. Material handling equipment is generally separated into four main categories; Storage and Handling Equipment, Engineered Systems, Industrial Trucks and Bulk Material Handling.
Human	A human is a member of a species of bipedal primates in the family Hominidae . DNA and fossil evidence indicates that modern human s originated in east Africa about 200,000 years ago. When compared to other animals and primates, human s have a highly developed brain, capable of abstract reasoning, language, introspection and problem solving.
Raw material	A raw material is something that is acted upon or used by or by human labour or industry, for use as a building material to create some product or structure. Often the term is used to denote material that came from nature and is in an unprocessed or minimally processed state. Iron ore, logs, and crude oil, would be examples.
Failure	Failure refers to the state or condition of not meeting a desirable or intended objective, and may be viewed as the opposite of success. Product failure ranges from failure to sell the product to fracture of the product, in the worst cases leading to personal injury, the province of forensic engineering. The criteria for failure are heavily dependent on context of use, and may be relative to a particular observer or belief system.
Organization design	Organization design involves the creation of roles, processes, and formal reporting relationships in an organization. One can distinguish between two phases in an organization design process: Strategic grouping, which establishes the overall structure of the organization, (its main sub-units and their relationships), and operational design, which defines the more detailed roles and processes. The field is mainly practice-driven and many consulting firms offer organization design assistance to managers.
Supplier	A 'supply chain is the system of organizations, people, technology, activities, information and resources involved in moving a product or service from supplier to customer. Supply chain activities transform natural resources, raw materials and components into a finished product that is delivered to the end customer. In sophisticated supply chain systems, used products may re-enter the supply chain at any point where residual value is recyclable.
Absenteeism	Absenteeism is a habitual pattern of absence from a duty or obligation. Frequent absence from the workplace may be indicative of poor morale or of sick building syndrome. However, many employers have implemented absence policies which make no distinction between absences for genuine illness and absence for inappropriate reasons.
Production scheduling	Scheduling is an important tool for manufacturing and engineering, where it can have a major impact on the productivity of a process. In manufacturing, the purpose of scheduling is to minimize the production time and costs, by telling a production facility what to make, when, with which staff, and on which equipment. Production scheduling aims to maximize the efficiency of the operation and reduce costs.

Production scheduling tools greatly outperform older manual scheduling methods. These provide the production scheduler with powerful graphical interfaces which can be used to visually optimize real-time work loads in various stages of production, and pattern recognition allows the software to automatically create scheduling opportunities which might not be apparent without this view into the data.

Morale

Morale is an intangible term used for the capacity of people to maintain belief in an institution or a goal, or even in oneself and others. The second term applies particularly to military personnel and to members of sports teams, but is also applicable in business and in any other organizational context, particularly in times of stress or controversy.

According to Alexander H. Leighton, 'Morale is the capacity of a group of people to pull together persistently and consistently in pursuit of a common purpose'.

Purchasing agent

A Purchasing Manager is an employee within a company, business or other organization who is responsible at some level for buying or approving the acquisition of goods and services needed by the company. The position responsibilities may be the same as that of a buyer or Purchasing agent, or may include wider supervisory or managerial responsibilities. A Purchasing Manager may oversee the acquisition of materials needed for production, general supplies for offices and facilities, equipment, or construction contracts.

Competitor analysis

Competitor analysis in marketing and strategic management is an assessment of the strengths and weaknesses of current and potential competitors. This analysis provides both an offensive and defensive strategic context through which to identify opportunities and threats. Competitor profiling coalesces all of the relevant sources of Competitor analysis into one framework in the support of efficient and effective strategy formulation, implementation, monitoring and adjustment.

Logistics management

The term Logistics management is that part of Supply Chain Management that plans, implements, and controls the efficient, effective, forward, and reverse flow and storage of goods, services, and related information between the point of origin and the point of consumption in order to meet customers' requirements.

Software is used for logistics automation which helps the supply chain industry in automating the work flow as well as management of the system. There are very few generalized software available in the new market in the said topology.

Technical support

Technical support is a range of services providing assistance with technology products such as mobile phones, televisions, computers, or other electronic or mechanical goods. In general, Technical support services attempt to help the user solve specific problems with a product--rather than providing training, customization, or other support services.

Most companies offer Technical support for the products they sell, either freely available or for a fee.

International business

International business is a term used to collectively describe topics relating to the operations of firms with interests in multiple countries. Such firms are sometimes called multinational corporations . Well known MNCs include fast food companies McDonald's and Yum Brands, vehicle manufacturers such as General Motors and Toyota, consumer electronics companies like Samsung, LG and Sony, and energy companies such as ExxonMobil and BP.

Third-party logistics

A Third-party logistics provider is a firm that provides outsourced or 'third party' logistics services to companies for part, or sometimes all of their supply chain management function. Third party logistics providers typically specialize in integrated operation, warehousing and transportation services that can be scaled and customized to customer's needs based on market conditions and the demands and delivery service requirements for their products and materials.

Hertz and Alfredsson (2003) describe four categories of 3PL providers:

· Standard 3PL provider: this is the most basic form of a 3PL provider. They would perform activities such as, pick and pack, warehousing, and distribution (business) - the most basic functions of logistics. For a majority of these firms, the 3PL function is not their main activity.
· Service developer: this type of 3PL provider will offer their customers advanced value-added services such as: tracking and tracing, cross-docking, specific packaging, or providing a unique security system. A solid IT foundation and a focus on economies of scale and scope will enable this type of 3PL provider to perform these types of tasks.
· The customer adapter: this type of 3PL provider comes in at the request of the customer and essentially takes over complete control of the company's logistics activities. The 3PL provider improves the logistics dramatically, but do not develop a new service. The customer base for this type of 3PL provider is typically quite small.
· The customer developer: this is the highest level that a 3PL provider can attain with respect to its processes and activities. This occurs when the 3PL provider integrates itself with the customer and takes over their entire logistics function. These providers will have few customers, but will perform extensive and detailed tasks for them.

Advancements in technology and the associated increases in supply chain visibility and inter-company communications have given rise to a relatively new model for Third-party logistics operations - the 'non-asset based logistics provider.' Non-asset based providers perform functions such as consultation on packaging and transportation, freight quoting, financial settlement, auditing, tracking, customer service and issue resolution. However, they don't employ any truck drivers or warehouse personnel, and they don't own any physical freight distribution assets of their own - no trucks, no storage trailers, no pallets, and no warehousing.

Skill

A skill is the learned capacity to carry out pre-determined results often with the minimum outlay of time, energy, or both. skill s can often be divided into domain-general and domain-specific skill s. For example, in the domain of work, some general skill s would include time management, teamwork and leadership, self motivation and others, whereas domain-specific skill s would be useful only for a certain job.

Equal Employment Opportunity

The term equal employment opportunity was created by President Lyndon B. Johnson when he signed Executive Order 11246 on September 24, 1965, created to prohibit federal contractors from discriminating against employees on the basis of race, sex, creed, religion, color, or national origin. In more recent times, most employers have also added sexual orientation to the list of non-discrimination.

The Executive Order also required contractors to implement affirmative action plans to increase the participation of minorities and women in the workplace.

Equal Employment Opportunity Commission

The U.S. Equal Employment Opportunity Commission is a federal agency whose goal is ending employment discrimination. The Equal Employment Opportunity Commission investigates discrimination complaints based on an individual's race, color, national origin, religion, sex, age, disability and retaliation for reporting and/or opposing a discriminatory practice. The Commission is also tasked with filing suits on behalf of alleged victim(s) of discrimination against employers and as an adjudicatory for claims of discrimination brought against federal agencies.

Fair Labor Standards Act

	The Fair Labor Standards Act of 1938 (Fair Labor Standards Act, ch. 676, 52 Stat. 1060, June 25, 1938, 29 U.S.C. ch.8), also called the Wages and Hours Bill, is United States federal law that applies to employees engaged in interstate commerce or employed by an enterprise engaged in commerce or in the production of goods for commerce, unless the employer can claim an exemption from coverage. The Fair Labor Standards Act established a national minimum wage, guaranteed time and a half for overtime in certain jobs, and prohibited most employment of minors in 'oppressive child labor,' a term defined in the statute.
Occupational Safety and Health	Occupational safety and health is a cross-disciplinary area concerned with protecting the safety, health and welfare of people engaged in work or employment. As a secondary effect, it may also protect co-workers, family members, employers, customers, suppliers, nearby communities, and other members of the public who are impacted by the workplace environment. It may involve interactions among many subject areas, including occupational medicine, occupational (or industrial) hygiene, public health, safety engineering, chemistry, health physics, ergonomics, toxicology, epidemiology, environmental health, industrial relations, public policy, sociology, and occupational health psychology.
Occupational Safety and Health Administration	The United States Occupational Safety and Health Administration is an agency of the United States Department of Labor. It was created by Congress under the Occupational Safety and Health Act, signed by President Richard M. Nixon, on December 29, 1970. Its mission is to prevent work-related injuries, illnesses, and deaths by issuing and enforcing rules (called standards) for workplace safety and health.

Expatriate | An expatriate is a person temporarily or permanently residing in a country and culture other than that of the person's upbringing or legal residence. The word comes from the Latin ex and patria (country, fatherland.)

The term is sometimes used in the context of Westerners living in non-Western countries, although it is also used to describe Westerners living in other Western countries, such as U.S. citizens living in the United Kingdom, or Britons living in Spain.

Skill | A skill is the learned capacity to carry out pre-determined results often with the minimum outlay of time, energy, or both. skill s can often be divided into domain-general and domain-specific skill s. For example, in the domain of work, some general skill s would include time management, teamwork and leadership, self motivation and others, whereas domain-specific skill s would be useful only for a certain job.

Competitive | Competitive ness is a comparative concept of the ability and performance of a firm, sub-sector or country to sell and supply goods and/or services in a given market. Although widely used in economics and business management, the usefulness of the concept, particularly in the context of national competitive ness, is vigorously disputed by economists, such as Paul Krugman .

The term may also be applied to markets, where it is used to refer to the extent to which the market structure may be regarded as perfectly competitive

Human | A human is a member of a species of bipedal primates in the family Hominidae . DNA and fossil evidence indicates that modern human s originated in east Africa about 200,000 years ago. When compared to other animals and primates, human s have a highly developed brain, capable of abstract reasoning, language, introspection and problem solving.

Human resource management | Human resource management is the strategic and coherent approach to the management of an organisation's most valued assets - the people working there who individually and collectively contribute to the achievement of the objectives of the business. The terms 'Human resource management' and 'human resources' (HR) have largely replaced the term 'personnel management' as a description of the processes involved in managing people in organizations. In simple sense, Human resource management means employing people, developing their resources, utilizing, maintaining and compensating their services in tune with the job and organizational requirement.

Market | A Market is any one of a variety of different systems, institutions, procedures, social relations and infrastructures whereby persons trade, and goods and services are exchanged, forming part of the economy. It is an arrangement that allows buyers and sellers to exchange things. Market s vary in size, range, geographic scale, location, types and variety of human communities, as well as the types of goods and services traded.

Policies and procedures | Policies and procedures are a set of documents that describe an organization's policies for operation and the procedures necessary to fulfill the policies. They are often initiated because of some external requirement, such as environmental compliance or other governmental regulations, such as the American Sarbanes-Oxley Act requiring full openness in accounting practices. The easiest way to start writing policies and procedures is to interview the users of the policies and procedures and create a flow chart or task map or work flow of the process from start to finish.

Policy | A Policy is typically described as a deliberate plan of action to guide decisions and achieve rational outcome(s.) However, the term may also be used to denote what is actually done, even though it is unplanned.

The term may apply to government, private sector organizations and groups, and individuals.

Manufacturing

Manufacturing is the application of tools and a processing medium to the transformation of raw materials into finished goods for sale. This effort includes all intermediate processes required for the production and integration of a product's components. Some industries, like semiconductor and steel manufacturers use the term fabrication instead.

Swap

In finance, a Swap is a derivative in which two counterparties agree to exchange one stream of cash flow against another stream. These streams are called the legs of the Swap.

The cash flows are calculated over a notional principal amount, which is usually not exchanged between counterparties.

Training and development

In the field of human resource management, Training and development is the field concerned with organizational activity aimed at bettering the performance of individuals and groups in organizational settings. It has been known by several names, including employee development, human resource development, and learning and development.

Harrison observes that the name was endlessly debated by the Chartered Institute of Personnel and Development during its review of professional standards in 1999/2000.

Characteristic

Characteristic has several particular meanings:

· in mathematics

- · Euler characteristic
- · method of characteristic s (partial differential equations)

· in physics and engineering

· any characteristic curve that shows the relationship between certain input- and output parameters, e.g.
· an I-V or current-voltage characteristic is the current in a circuit as a function of the applied voltage
· Receiver-Operator characteristic
· in navigation, the characteristic pattern of a lighted beacon.
· in fiction

· in Dungeons ' Dragons, characteristic is another name for ability score .

Cost

In economics, business, retail, and accounting, a cost is the value of money that has been used up to produce something, and hence is not available for use anymore. In economics, a cost is an alternative that is given up as a result of a decision. In business, the cost may be one of acquisition, in which case the amount of money expended to acquire it is counted as cost.

Generalization

Generalization is a foundational element of logic and human reasoning. Generalization posits the existence of a domain or set of elements, as well as one or more common characteristics shared by those elements. As such, it is the essential basis of all valid deductive inference.

Kraft Foods

Kraft Foods Inc. (NYSE: Kraft Foods T) is the largest food and beverage company headquartered in the United States and the second largest in the world (after Nestlé SA.)

Kraft is headquartered in Northfield, Illinois, USA, a Chicago suburb.

Failure	Failure refers to the state or condition of not meeting a desirable or intended objective, and may be viewed as the opposite of success. Product failure ranges from failure to sell the product to fracture of the product, in the worst cases leading to personal injury, the province of forensic engineering. The criteria for failure are heavily dependent on context of use, and may be relative to a particular observer or belief system.
Failure rate	Failure rate is the frequency with which an engineered system or component fails, expressed for example in failures per hour. It is often denoted by the Greek letter >λ and is important in reliability theory. The Failure rate of a system usually depends on time, with the rate varying over the life cycle of the system.
Global sourcing	Global sourcing is a term used to describe practice of sourcing from the global market for goods and services across geopolitical boundaries. Global sourcing often aims to exploit global efficiencies in the delivery of a product or service. These efficiencies include low cost skilled labor, low cost raw material and other economic factors like tax breaks and low trade tariffs.
Repatriation	Repatriation is the process of return of refugees or soldiers to their homes, most notably following a war. The term may also refer to the process of converting a foreign currency into the currency of one's own country. When the traveler is unable to follow her/his trip , due to any medical reason, the insurance company is required to repatriate the patient.
Cross-cultural training	Cross-cultural training is training for cross-cultural communication and experiences. Preparing people to work outside their native country (sojourner training) is one aim of Cross-cultural training; for example, Peace Corps volunteers complete Cross-cultural training in preparation for lengthy assignments in another culture. Learning the host culture's native language is the most extensive Cross-cultural training
English	English is a West Germanic language that originated in Anglo-Saxon England. As a result of the military, economic, scientific, political and cultural influence of the British Empire during the 18th, 19th and 20th centuries and of the United States since the late 19th century, it has become the lingua franca in many parts of the world. It is used extensively as a second language and as an official language in Commonwealth countries and many international organizations.
Procter ' Gamble	Procter is a surname, and may also refer to: · Bryan Waller Procter (pseud. Barry Cornwall), English poet · Goodwin Procter, American law firm · Procter ' Gamble, consumer products multinational .
Trend analysis	The term 'trend analysis' refers to the concept of collecting information and attempting to spot a pattern in the information. In some fields of study, the term 'trend analysis' has more formally-defined meanings. In project management trend analysis is a mathematical technique that uses historical results to predict future outcome.

Set TSP

In combinatorial optimization, the set TSP group TSP, One-of-a-set TSP, Multiple Choice TSP or Covering Salesman Problem, is a generalization of the Traveling salesman problem, whereby it is required to find a shortest tour in a graph which visits all specified disjoint subsets of the vertices of a graph. The ordinary TSP is a special case of the set TSP when all subsets to be visited are singletons. Therefore the set TSP is also NP-hard.

Culture

Culture is a term that has different meanings. For example, in 1952, Alfred Kroeber and Clyde Kluckhohn compiled a list of 164 definitions of culture in culture A Critical Review of Concepts and Definitions. However, the word culture is most commonly used in three basic senses:

· excellence of taste in the fine arts and humanities, also known as high culture
· an integrated pattern of human knowledge, belief, and behavior that depends upon the capacity for symbolic thought and social learning
· the set of shared attitudes, values, goals, and practices that characterizes an institution, organization or group.

When the concept first emerged in eighteenth- and nineteenth-century Europe, it connoted a process of cultivation or improvement, as in agri culture or horti culture . In the nineteenth century, it came to refer first to the betterment or refinement of the individual, especially through education, and then to the fulfillment of national aspirations or ideals.

Culture shock

Culture shock refers to the anxiety and feelings (of surprise, disorientation, uncertainty, confusion, etc.) felt when people have to operate within a different and unknown cultural or social environment, such as a foreign country. It grows out of the difficulties in assimilating the new culture, causing difficulty in knowing what is appropriate and what is not.

Comparative advertising

Comparative advertising is an advertisement in which a particular product specifically mentions a competitor by name for the express purpose of showing why the competitor is inferior to the product naming it.

This should not be confused with parody advertisements, where a fictional product is being advertised for the purpose of poking fun at the particular advertisement, nor should it be confused with the use of a coined brand name for the purpose of comparing the product without actually naming an actual competitor. ('Wikipedia tastes better and is less filling than the Encyclopedia Galactica.')

In the 1980s, during what has been referred to as the cola wars, soft-drink manufacturer Pepsi ran a series of advertisements where people, caught on hidden camera, in a blind taste test, chose Pepsi over rival Coca-Cola.

Base

Bases may be the plural form of:

· base
· Basis

Bases may also refer to:

· Bases (fashion), a military style of dress adopted by the chivalry of the sixteenth century. .

Employee benefits

Employee benefits and benefits in kind are various non-wage compensations provided to employees in addition to their normal wages or salaries. Where an employee exchanges (cash) wages for some other form of benefit, this is generally referred to as a 'salary sacrifice' arrangement. In most countries, most kinds of Employee benefits are taxable to at least some degree.

Cost of living	Cost of living is the cost of maintaining a certain standard of living. Changes in the Cost of living over time are often operationalized in a Cost of living index. Cost of living calculations are also used to compare the cost of maintaining a certain standard of living in different geographic areas.
Salary	A Salary is a form of periodic payment from an employer to an employee, which may be specified in an employment contract. It is contrasted with piece wages, where each job, hour or other unit is paid separately, rather than on a periodic basis. From the point of a view of running a business, Salary can also be viewed as the cost of acquiring human resources for running operations, and is then termed personnel expense or Salary expense.
Quality of life	The term Quality of life used by politicians and economists to measure broader social effects of policies, such as the effect that reducing graffiti or vandalism might have on the wellbeing of local residents. Two widely known measures of a country's liveability are the Economist Intelligence Unit's Quality of life index and the Mercer Quality of Living Survey. Both measures calculate the liveability of countries around the world through a combination of subjective life-satisfaction surveys and objective determinants of Quality of life such as divorce rates, safety, and infrastructure.
Big Mac index	The Big Mac Index is published by The Economist as an informal way of measuring the purchasing power parity (PPP) between two currencies and provides a test of the extent to which market exchange rates result in goods costing the same in different countries. It 'seeks to make exchange-rate theory a bit more digestible'.
Black market	The underground economy or Black market is a market where all commerce is conducted without regard to taxation, law or regulations of trade. The term is also often known as the underdog, shadow economy, black economy, parallel economy or phantom trades. In modern societies the underground economy covers a vast array of activities.
Cluster analysis	Cluster analysis or clustering is the assignment of objects into groups (called clusters) so that objects from the same cluster are more similar to each other than objects from different clusters. Often similarity is assessed according to a distance measure. Clustering is a common technique for statistical data analysis, which is used in many fields, including machine learning, data mining, pattern recognition, image analysis and bioinformatics.
Foreign exchange controls	Foreign exchange controls are various forms of controls imposed by a government on the purchase/sale of foreign currencies by residents or on the purchase/sale of local currency by nonresidents. Common Foreign exchange controls include: · Banning the use of foreign currency within the country · Banning locals from possessing foreign currency · Restricting currency exchange to government-approved exchangers · Fixed exchange rates · Restrictions on the amount of currency that may be imported or exported

Countries with Foreign exchange controls are also known as 'Article 14 countries,' after the provision in the International Monetary Fund agreement allowing exchange controls for transitional economies. Such controls used to be common in most countries, particularly poorer ones, until the 1990s when free trade and globalization started a trend towards economic liberalization. Today, countries which still impose exchange controls are the exception rather than the rule.

Exchange rate

In finance, the Exchange rate s between two currencies specifies how much one currency is worth in terms of the other. It is the value of a foreign nation's currency in terms of the home nation's currency. For example an Exchange rate of 95 Japanese yen to the United States dollar means that JPY 95 is worth the same as USD 1.

Free market

A free market is a theoretical term that economists use to describe a market which is free from government intervention (i.e. no regulation, no subsidization, no single monetary system and no governmental monopolies.) In a free market, property rights are voluntarily exchanged at a price arranged solely by the mutual consent of sellers and buyers. By definition, buyers and sellers do not coerce each other, in the sense that they obtain each other's property without the use of physical force, threat of physical force, or fraud, nor is the coerced by a third party (such as by government via transfer payments) and they engage in trade simply because they both consent and believe that it is a good enough choice.

Control

Control is one of the managerial functions like planning, organizing, staffing and directing. It is an important function because it helps to check the errors and to take the corrective action so that deviation from standards are minimized and stated goals of the organization are achieved in desired manner.According to modern concepts, Control is a foreseeing action whereas earlier concept of Control was used only when errors were detected. Control in management means setting standards, measuring actual performance and taking corrective action.

Perk

Perks may refer either to:

· an employee benefit, colloqulally known as a 'Perk' or a 'perq', a short form of the word perquisite
· Reginald Thomas David Perks, English cricketer, leading wicket taker for Worcestershire .

United States

The United States of America (commonly referred to as the United States the U.S., the United States A, or America) is a federal constitutional republic comprising fifty states and a federal district. The country is situated mostly in central North America, where its 48 contiguous states and Washington, D.C., the capital district, lie between the Pacific and Atlantic Oceans, bordered by Canada to the north and Mexico to the south. The state of Alaska is in the northwest of the continent, with Canada to its east and Russia to the west across the Bering Strait.

Certification

Certification refers to the confirmation of certain characteristics of an object, person, or organization. This confirmation is often, but not always, provided by some form of external review, education, or assessment. One of the most common types of Certification in modern society is professional Certification, where a person is certified as being able to competently complete a job or task, usually by the passing of an examination.

Cultural identity

Cultural identity is the identity of a group or culture, or of an individual as far as one is influenced by one's belonging to a group or culture. Cultural identity is similar to and has overlaps with, but is not synonymous with, identity politics.

There are modern questions of culture that are transferred into questions of identity.

Society for Human Resource Management	The Society for Human Resource Management is a professional association which represents workers in the field of human resources. SHRM works to promote the role of human resources as a profession, and provides education, certification, and networking to its members while lobbying Congress on issues pertinent to personnel management and human resources. Originally founded in 1948 as the American Society for Personnel Administration (ASPA), the organization operated on a volunteer basis until 1964, at which time it established an official headquarters in Berea, Ohio, and began hiring staff members.
Tariff	A Tariff is a duty imposed on goods when they are moved across a political boundary. They are usually associated with protectionism, the economic policy of restraining trade between nations. For political reasons, Tariff s are usually imposed on imported goods, although they may also be imposed on exported goods.
Business	A business is a legally recognized organization designed to provide goods and/or services to consumers. business es are predominant in capitalist economies, most being privately owned and formed to earn profit that will increase the wealth of its owners and grow the business itself. The owners and operators of a business have as one of their main objectives the receipt or generation of a financial return in exchange for work and acceptance of risk.
Resources	Human beings are also considered to be Resources because they have the ability to change raw materials into valuable Resources. The term Human Resources can also be defined as the skills, energies, talents, abilities and knowledge that are used for the production of goods or the rendering of services. While taking into account human beings as Resources, the following things have to be kept in mind: · The size of the population · The capabilities of the individuals in that population Many Resources cannot be consumed in their original form. They have to be processed in order to change them into more usable commodities.

Theory of the firm

The Theory of the firm consists of a number of economic theories which describe the nature of the firm, company including its existence, its behaviour, and its relationship with the market.

In simplified terms, the Theory of the firm aims to answer these questions:

· Existence - why do firms emerge, why are not all transactions in the economy mediated over the market?
· Boundaries - why the boundary between firms and the market is located exactly there? Which transactions are performed internally and which are negotiated on the market?
· Organization - why are firms structured in such specific way? What is the interplay of formal and informal relationships?

The First World War period saw a change of emphasis in economic theory away from industry-level analysis which mainly included analysing markets to analysis at the level of the firm, as it became increasingly clear that perfect competition was no longer an adequate model of how firms behaved. Economic theory till then had focussed on trying to understand markets alone and there had been little study on understanding why firms or organisations exist. Market are mainly guided by prices as illustrated by vegetable markets where a buyer is free to switch sellers in an exchange.

Developed country

The term developed country is used to describe countries that have a high level of development according to some criteria. Which criteria, and which countries are classified as being developed, is a contentious issue and there is fierce debate about this. Economic criteria have tended to dominate discussions.

Investment

Investment or investing is a term with several closely-related meanings in business management, finance and economics, related to saving or deferring consumption. Investing is the active redirecting resources from being consumed today so that they may create benefits in the future; the use of assets to earn income or profit.

An Investment is the choice by the individual to risk his savings with the hope of gain.

Kraft Foods

Kraft Foods Inc. (NYSE: Kraft Foods T) is the largest food and beverage company headquartered in the United States and the second largest in the world (after Nestlé SA.)

Kraft is headquartered in Northfield, Illinois, USA, a Chicago suburb.

Pension

In general, a Pension is an arrangement to provide people with an income when they are no longer earning a regular income from employment.

The terms retirement plan or superannuation refer to a Pension granted upon retirement . Retirement plans may be set up by employers, insurance companies, the government or other institutions such as employer associations or trade unions.

Pension fund

A Pension fund is a pool of assets forming an independent legal entity that are bought with the contributions to a pension plan for the exclusive purpose of financing pension plan benefits.

Pension fund s are important shareholders of listed and private companies. They are especially important to the stock market where large institutional investors like the Ontario Teachers' Pension Plan dominate.

Privatization

Privatization is the incidence or process of transferring ownership of a business, enterprise, agency or public service from the public sector (government) to the private sector (business.) In a broader sense, Privatization refers to transfer of any government function to the private sector including governmental functions like revenue collection and law enforcement.

The term 'Privatization' also has been used to describe two unrelated transactions.

Population ageing

Population ageing occurs when the median age of a country or region rises. With the exception of 18 countries termed by the United Nations 'demographic outliers' this process is taking place in every country and region across the globe.

Population ageing is constituted by a shift in the distribution of a country's population towards greater ages.

Capital structure

In finance, Capital structure refers to the way a corporation finances its assets through some combination of equity, debt, or hybrid securities. A firm's Capital structure is then the composition or 'structure' of its liabilities. For example, a firm that sells $20 billion in equity and $80 billion in debt is said to be 20% equity-financed and 80% debt-financed.

Control

Control is one of the managerial functions like planning, organizing, staffing and directing. It is an important function because it helps to check the errors and to take the corrective action so that deviation from standards are minimized and stated goals of the organization are achieved in desired manner.According to modern concepts, Control is a foreseeing action whereas earlier concept of Control was used only when errors were detected. Control in management means setting standards, measuring actual performance and taking corrective action.

Foreign exchange controls

Foreign exchange controls are various forms of controls imposed by a government on the purchase/sale of foreign currencies by residents or on the purchase/sale of local currency by nonresidents.

Common Foreign exchange controls include:

· Banning the use of foreign currency within the country
· Banning locals from possessing foreign currency
· Restricting currency exchange to government-approved exchangers
· Fixed exchange rates
· Restrictions on the amount of currency that may be imported or exported

Countries with Foreign exchange controls are also known as 'Article 14 countries,' after the provision in the International Monetary Fund agreement allowing exchange controls for transitional economies. Such controls used to be common in most countries, particularly poorer ones, until the 1990s when free trade and globalization started a trend towards economic liberalization. Today, countries which still impose exchange controls are the exception rather than the rule.

Market

A Market is any one of a variety of different systems, institutions, procedures, social relations and infrastructures whereby persons trade, and goods and services are exchanged, forming part of the economy. It is an arrangement that allows buyers and sellers to exchange things. Market s vary in size, range, geographic scale, location, types and variety of human communities, as well as the types of goods and services traded.

Numerary

Numerary is a civil designation for persons who are incorporated in a fixed or permanent way to a society or group: regular member of the working staff, permanent staff distinguished from a super Numerary .

The term Numerary and its counterpart, 'super Numerary ,' originated in Spanish and Latin American academy and government; it is now also used in countries all over the world, such as France, the U.S., England, Italy, etc.

There are Numerary members of surgical organizations, of universities, of gastronomical associations, etc.

Regulation	Regulation refers to 'controlling human or societal behaviour by rules or restrictions.' Regulation can take many forms: legal restrictions promulgated by a government authority, self-Regulation, social Regulation, co-Regulation and market Regulation. One can consider Regulation as actions of conduct imposing sanctions (such as a fine.) This action of administrative law, or implementing regulatory law, may be contrasted with statutory or case law.
Net worth	In business, net worth is the total liabilities minus total outside assets of an individual or a company. For a company, this is called shareholders' preference and may be referred to as book value. net worth is stated as at a particular year in time.
Argentina	Argentina, officially the Argentine Republic , is a country in South America, constituted as a federation of 23 provinces and an autonomous city, Buenos Aires. It is the second largest country in South America and eighth in the world by land area and the largest among Spanish-speaking nations, though Mexico, Colombia and Spain are more populous. Its continental area is 2,700,090 km^2 , between the Andes mountain range in the west and the southern Atlantic Ocean in the east and south.
Inflation	In economics, Inflation is a rise in the general level of prices of goods and services in an economy over a period of time. The term 'Inflation' once referred to increases in the money supply (monetary Inflation); however, economic debates about the relationship between money supply and price levels have led to its primary use today in describing price Inflation. Inflation can also be described as a decline in the real value of money--a loss of purchasing power in the medium of exchange which is also the monetary unit of account.
Exchange rate	In finance, the Exchange rate s between two currencies specifies how much one currency is worth in terms of the other. It is the value of a foreign nation's currency in terms of the home nation's currency. For example an Exchange rate of 95 Japanese yen to the United States dollar means that JPY 95 is worth the same as USD 1.
Functional currency	Functional currency is the monetary unit of account of the principal economic environment in which an economic entity operates. Statement of Financial Standards No. 52 (SFAS 52) is the primary source of GAAP for translation of foreign currency financial statements.
Generally accepted accounting principles	Generally accepted accounting principles is the term used to refer to the standard framework of guidelines for financial accounting used in any given jurisdiction. Generally accepted accounting principles includes the standards, conventions, and rules accountants follow in recording and summarizing transactions, and in the preparation of financial statements. Financial accounting information must be assembled and reported objectively.
United States	The United States of America (commonly referred to as the United States the U.S., the United States A, or America) is a federal constitutional republic comprising fifty states and a federal district. The country is situated mostly in central North America, where its 48 contiguous states and Washington, D.C., the capital district, lie between the Pacific and Atlantic Oceans, bordered by Canada to the north and Mexico to the south. The state of Alaska is in the northwest of the continent, with Canada to its east and Russia to the west across the Bering Strait.

Black market

The underground economy or Black market is a market where all commerce is conducted without regard to taxation, law or regulations of trade. The term is also often known as the underdog, shadow economy, black economy, parallel economy or phantom trades.

In modern societies the underground economy covers a vast array of activities.

Free market

A free market is a theoretical term that economists use to describe a market which is free from government intervention (i.e. no regulation, no subsidization, no single monetary system and no governmental monopolies.) In a free market, property rights are voluntarily exchanged at a price arranged solely by the mutual consent of sellers and buyers. By definition, buyers and sellers do not coerce each other, in the sense that they obtain each other's property without the use of physical force, threat of physical force, or fraud, nor is the coerced by a third party (such as by government via transfer payments) and they engage in trade simply because they both consent and believe that it is a good enough choice.

Manufacturing

Manufacturing is the application of tools and a processing medium to the transformation of raw materials into finished goods for sale. This effort includes all intermediate processes required for the production and integration of a product's components. Some industries, like semiconductor and steel manufacturers use the term fabrication instead.

Report

In writing, a report is a document characterized by information or other content reflective of inquiry or investigation, which is tailored to the context of a given situation and audience. The purpose of report s is usually to inform. However, report s may include persuasive elements, such as recommendations, suggestions, or other motivating conclusions that indicate possible future actions the report reader might take.

Swap

In finance, a Swap is a derivative in which two counterparties agree to exchange one stream of cash flow against another stream. These streams are called the legs of the Swap.

The cash flows are calculated over a notional principal amount, which is usually not exchanged between counterparties.

Cultural identity

Cultural identity is the identity of a group or culture, or of an individual as far as one is influenced by one's belonging to a group or culture. Cultural identity is similar to and has overlaps with, but is not synonymous with, identity politics.

There are modern questions of culture that are transferred into questions of identity.

Financial Accounting Standards Board

The Financial Accounting Standards Board is a private, not-for-profit organization whose primary purpose is to develop generally accepted accounting principles (GAAP) within the United States in the public's interest. The Securities and Exchange Commission (SEC) designated the Financial Accounting Standards Board as the organization responsible for setting accounting standards for public companies in the U.S. It was created in 1973, replacing the Committee on Accounting Procedure (CAP) and the Accounting Principles Board (APB) of the American Institute of Certified Public Accountants (AICPA.)

The Financial Accounting Standards Board's mission is 'to establish and improve standards of financial accounting and reporting for the guidance and education of the public, including issuers, auditors, and users of financial information.' To achieve this, Financial Accounting Standards Board has five goals:

· Improve the usefulness of financial reporting by focusing on the primary characteristics of relevance and reliability, and on the qualities of comparability and consistency.
· Keep standards current to reflect changes in methods of doing business and in the economy.
· Consider promptly any significant areas of deficiency in financial reporting that might be improved through standard setting.
· Promote international convergence of accounting standards concurrent with improving the quality of financial reporting.
· Improve common understanding of the nature and purposes of information in financial reports.

The Financial Accounting Standards Board is not a governmental body. The SEC has legal authority to establish financial accounting and reporting standards for publicly held companies under the Securities Exchange Act of 1934.

Profit

A profit , in the law of real property, is a nonpossessory interest in land similar to the better-known easement, which gives the holder the right to take natural resources such as petroleum, minerals, timber, and wild game from the land of another. Indeed, because of the necessity of allowing access to the land so that resources may be gathered, every profit contains an implied easement for the owner of the profit to enter the other party's land for the purpose of collecting the resources permitted by the profit.

Like an easement, profits can be created expressly by an agreement between the property owner and the owner of the profit, or by prescription, where the owner of the profit has made 'open and notorious' use of the land for a continuous and uninterrupted statutory period.

Transparency

A high degree of market Transparency can result in disintermediation due to the buyer's increased knowledge of supply pricing.

Transparency is important since it is one of the theoretical conditions required for a free market to be efficient.
Price Transparency can, however, lead to higher prices, if it makes sellers reluctant to give steep discounts to certain buyers, or if it facilitates collusion.

Culture

Culture is a term that has different meanings. For example, in 1952, Alfred Kroeber and Clyde Kluckhohn compiled a list of 164 definitions of culture in culture A Critical Review of Concepts and Definitions. However, the word culture is most commonly used in three basic senses:

· excellence of taste in the fine arts and humanities, also known as high culture
· an integrated pattern of human knowledge, belief, and behavior that depends upon the capacity for symbolic thought and social learning
· the set of shared attitudes, values, goals, and practices that characterizes an institution, organization or group.

When the concept first emerged in eighteenth- and nineteenth-century Europe, it connoted a process of cultivation or improvement, as in agri culture or horti culture . In the nineteenth century, it came to refer first to the betterment or refinement of the individual, especially through education, and then to the fulfillment of national aspirations or ideals.

Job description

A Job description is a list of the general tasks and responsibilities of a position. Typically, it also includes to whom the position reports, specifications such as the qualifications needed by the person in the job, salary range for the position, etc. A Job description is usually developed by conducting a job analysis, which includes examining the tasks and sequences of tasks necessary to perform the job.

Corporate scandal	A Corporate scandal is a scandal involving allegations of unethical behavior by people acting within or on behalf of a corporation. A Corporate scandal sometimes involves accounting fraud of some sort. A wave of such scandals swept United States companies in 2002
Corporate social responsibility	Corporate Social Responsibility also known as corporate responsibility, corporate citizenship, responsible business, sustainable responsible business and corporate social performance' is a form of corporate self-regulation integrated into a business model. Ideally, Corporate Social Responsibility policy would function as a built-in, self-regulating mechanism whereby business would monitor and ensure their adherence to law, ethical standards, and international norms. Business would embrace responsibility for the impact of their activities on the environment, consumers, employees, communities, stakeholders and all other members of the public sphere.
International Financial Reporting Standards	International Financial Reporting Standards are Standards, Interpretations and the Framework (in the absence of a Standard or an Interpretation) adopted by the International Accounting Standards Board (IASB.) In the absence of a Standard or an Interpretation that specifically applies to a transaction, management must use its judgement in developing and applying an accounting policy that results in information that is relevant and reliable. In making that judgement, IAS 8.11 requires management to consider the definitions, recognition criteria, and measurement concepts for assets, liabilities, income, and expenses in the Framework.
Securities and Exchange Commission	The U.S. Securities and Exchange Commission is an independent agency of the United States government which holds primary responsibility for enforcing the federal securities laws and regulating the securities industry, the nation's stock and options exchanges, and other electronic securities markets. The SEC was created by section 4 of the Securities Exchange Act of 1934 (now codified as 15 U.S.C. Â§ 78d and commonly referred to as the 1934 Act.)
International Accounting Standards Board	The International Accounting Standards Board founded on April 1, 2001 is the successor of the International Accounting Standards Committee (IASC) founded in June 1973 in London. It is responsible for developing the International Financial Reporting Standards (new name for the International Accounting Standards issued after 2001), and promoting the use and application of these standards. The International Accounting Standards Board is an independent, privately-funded accounting standard-setter based in London, UK.
Equal Employment Opportunity	The term equal employment opportunity was created by President Lyndon B. Johnson when he signed Executive Order 11246 on September 24, 1965, created to prohibit federal contractors from discriminating against employees on the basis of race, sex, creed, religion, color, or national origin. In more recent times, most employers have also added sexual orientation to the list of non-discrimination. The Executive Order also required contractors to implement affirmative action plans to increase the participation of minorities and women in the workplace.
Equal Employment Opportunity Commission	The U.S. Equal Employment Opportunity Commission is a federal agency whose goal is ending employment discrimination. The Equal Employment Opportunity Commission investigates discrimination complaints based on an individual's race, color, national origin, religion, sex, age, disability and retaliation for reporting and/or opposing a discriminatory practice. The Commission is also tasked with filing suits on behalf of alleged victim(s) of discrimination against employers and as an adjudicatory for claims of discrimination brought against federal agencies.

Global Reporting Initiative	The Global Reporting Initiative produces the world's de facto standard in sustainability reporting guidelines. Sustainability reporting is the action where an organization publicly communicates their economic, environmental, and social performance. The Global Reporting Initiative's mission is to make sustainability reporting by all organizations as routine as and comparable to financial reporting.
United Nations	The United Nations is an international organization whose stated aims are to facilitate cooperation in international law, international security, economic development, social progress, human rights and achieving world peace. The United Nations was founded in 1945 after World War II to replace the League of Nations, to stop wars between countries and to provide a platform for dialogue. There are currently 192 member states, including nearly every recognized independent state in the world.
Chief financial officer	The Chief financial officer of a company or public agency is the corporate officer primarily responsible for managing the financial risks of the business or agency. This officer is also responsible for financial planning and record-keeping, as well as financial reporting to higher management. (In recent years, however, the role has expanded to encompass communicating financial performance and forecasts to the analyst community.)
Initial public offering	Initial public offering , also referred to simply as a 'public offering' or 'flotation,' is when a company issues common stock or shares to the public for the first time. They are often issued by smaller, younger companies seeking capital to expand, but can also be done by large privately-owned companies looking to become publicly traded. In an Initial public offering the issuer may obtain the assistance of an underwriting firm, which helps it determine what type of security to issue (common or preferred), best offering price and time to bring it to market.
Arbitration	Arbitration, a form of alternative dispute resolution (ADR), is a legal technique for the resolution of disputes outside the courts, wherein the parties to a dispute refer it to one or more persons (the 'arbitrators', 'arbiters' or 'arbitral tribunal'), by whose decision (the 'award') they agree to be bound. It is a settlement technique in which a third party reviews the case and imposes a decision that is legally binding for both sides. Other forms of ADR include mediation (a form of settlement negotiation facilitated by a neutral third party) and non-binding resolution by experts.
Business	A business is a legally recognized organization designed to provide goods and/or services to consumers. business es are predominant in capitalist economies, most being privately owned and formed to earn profit that will increase the wealth of its owners and grow the business itself. The owners and operators of a business have as one of their main objectives the receipt or generation of a financial return in exchange for work and acceptance of risk.
Equity	Equity is the name given to the set of legal principles, in jurisdictions following the English common law tradition, which supplement strict rules of law where their application would operate harshly. As noted below, a historic criticism of Equity as it developed was that it had no fixed rules of its own, with the Lord Chancellor from time to time judging in the main according to his own conscience. As time went on the rules of Equity did lose much of their flexibility, and from the 17th century onwards Equity was rapidly consolidated into a system of precedents much like its common-law cousin.

Fair Trade

Fair trade is an organized social movement and market-based approach that aims to help producers in developing countries and promote sustainability. The movement advocates the payment of a fair price as well as social and environmental standards in areas related to the production of a wide variety of goods. It focuses in particular on exports from developing countries to developed countries, most notably handicrafts, coffee, cocoa, sugar, tea, bananas, honey, cotton, wine, fresh fruit, chocolate and flowers.

Keiretsu

A keiretsu is a set of companies with interlocking business relationships and shareholdings. It is a type of business group. The prototypical keiretsu are those which appeared in Japan during the 'economic miracle' following World War II.

Skilled worker

A Skilled worker is any worker who has some special skill, knowledge, or (usually acquired) ability in his work. A Skilled worker may have attended a college, university or technical school. Or, a Skilled worker may have learned his skills on the job.

Cash flow

Cash flow refers to the movement of cash into or out of a business, a project, or a financial product. It is usually measured during a specified, finite period of time. Measurement of Cash flow can be used

· to determine a project's rate of return or value. The time of Cash flow s into and out of projects are used as inputs in financial models such as internal rate of return, and net present value.
· to determine problems with a business's liquidity. Being profitable does not necessarily mean being liquid. A company can fail because of a shortage of cash, even while profitable.
· as an alternate measure of a business's profits when it is believed that accrual accounting concepts do not represent economic realities. For example, a company may be notionally profitable but generating little operational cash (as may be the case for a company that barters its products rather than selling for cash.) In such a case, the company may be deriving additional operating cash by issuing shares, or raising additional debt finance.
• of Income generated by accrual accounting. When Net Income is composed of large non-cash Items It Is considered low quality.
· to evaluate the risks within a financial product. E.g. matching cash requirements, evaluating default risk, re-investment requirements, etc.

Dividend

Dividend s are payments made by a corporation to its shareholders. It is the portion of corporate profits paid out to stockholders. When a corporation earns a profit or surplus, that money can be put to two uses: it can either be re-invested in the business (called retained earnings), or it can be paid to the shareholders as a dividend

Royalties

Royalties can be determined as a percentage of gross or net sales derived from use of the asset or a fixed price per unit sold. but there are also other modes and metrics of compensation. A royalty interest is the right to collect a stream of future royalty payments, often used in the oil industry and music industry to describe a percentage ownership of future production or revenues from a given leasehold, which may be divested from the original owner of the asset.

Goal

A Goal or objective is a projected state of affairs that a person or a system plans or intends to achieve--a personal or organizational desired end-point in some sort of assumed development. Many people endeavor to reach Goal s within a finite time by setting deadlines.

	A desire or an intention becomes a Goal if and only if one activates an action for achieving it
Economic	An economy (or 'the economy') is the realized Economic system of a country or other area. It includes the production, exchange, distribution, and consumption of goods and services of that area. The study of different types and examples of economies is the subject of Economic systems.
Economic development	Economic development is the development of economic wealth of countries or regions for the well-being of their inhabitants. It is the process by which a nation improves the economic, political, and social well being of its people. From a policy perspective, Economic development can be defined as efforts that seek to improve the economic well-being and quality of life for a community by creating and/or retaining jobs and supporting or growing incomes and the tax base.
Direct investment	Foreign Direct Investment in its classic form is defined as a company from one country making a physical investment into building a factory in another country. It is the establishment of an enterprise by a foreigner. Its definition can be extended to include investments made to acquire lasting interest in enterprises operating outside of the economy of the investor.
Foreign direct investment	Foreign direct investment in its classic form is defined as a company from one country making a physical investment into building a factory in another country. It is the establishment of an enterprise by a foreigner. Its definition can be extended to include investments made to acquire lasting interest in enterprises operating outside of the economy of the investor.
Comparative advertising	Comparative advertising is an advertisement in which a particular product specifically mentions a competitor by name for the express purpose of showing why the competitor is inferior to the product naming it. This should not be confused with parody advertisements, where a fictional product is being advertised for the purpose of poking fun at the particular advertisement, nor should it be confused with the use of a coined brand name for the purpose of comparing the product without actually naming an actual competitor. ('Wikipedia tastes better and is less filling than the Encyclopedia Galactica.') In the 1980s, during what has been referred to as the cola wars, soft-drink manufacturer Pepsi ran a series of advertisements where people, caught on hidden camera, in a blind taste test, chose Pepsi over rival Coca-Cola.
Trade Union	A Trade union or labor union is an organization of workers who have banded together to achieve common goals in key areas and working conditions. The Trade union, through its leadership, bargains with the employer on behalf of union members (rank and file members) and negotiates labor contracts (Collective bargaining) with employers. This may include the negotiation of wages, work rules, complaint procedures, rules governing hiring, firing and promotion of workers, benefits, workplace safety and policies.
Transfer	Transfer is a technique used in propaganda and advertising. Also known as association, this is a technique of projecting positive or negative qualities (praise or blame) of a person, entity, object, or value (an individual, group, organization, nation, patriotism, etc.) to another in order to make the second more acceptable or to discredit it.

Price	Price in economics and business is the result of an exchange and from that trade we assign a numerical monetary value to a good, service or asset. If I trade 4 apples for an orange, the price of an orange is 4 - apples. Inversely, the price of an apple is 1/4 oranges.
Pricing	Pricing is one of the four Ps of the marketing mix. The other three aspects are product, promotion, and place. It is also a key variable in microeconomic price allocation theory.
Transfer pricing	Transfer pricing refers to the pricing of contributions (assets, tangible and intangible, services, and funds) transferred within an organization. For example, goods from the production division may be sold to the marketing division, or goods from a parent company may be sold to a foreign subsidiary. Since the prices are set within an organization (i.e. controlled), the typical market mechanisms that establish prices for such transactions between third parties may not apply.
Balance of payments	In economics, the Balance of payments, (or Balance of payments) measures the payments that flow between any individual country and all other countries. It is used to summarize all international economic transactions for that country during a specific time period, usually a year. The Balance of payments is determined by the country's exports and imports of goods, services, and financial capital, as well as financial transfers.
International finance	International finance is the branch of economics that studies the dynamics of exchange rates, foreign investment, and how these affect international trade. It also studies international projects, international investments and capital flows, and trade deficits. It includes the study of futures, options and currency swaps.
Transaction cost	In economics and related disciplines, a Transaction cost is a cost incurred in making an economic exchange (restated: the cost of participating in a market.) For example, most people, when buying or selling a stock, must pay a commission to their broker; that commission is a Transaction cost of doing the stock deal. Or consider buying a banana from a store; to purchase the banana, your costs will be not only the price of the banana itself, but also the energy and effort it requires to find out which of the various banana products you prefer, where to get them and at what price, the cost of traveling from your house to the store and back, the time waiting in line, and the effort of the paying itself; the costs above and beyond the cost of the banana are the Transaction cost s.
Risk	Risk is a concept that denotes the precise probability of specific eventualities. Technically, the notion of Risk is independent from the notion of value and, as such, eventualities may have both beneficial and adverse consequences. However, in general usage the convention is to focus only on potential negative impact to some characteristic of value that may arise from a future event.
Risk management	Risk management is the identification, assessment, and prioritization of risks followed by coordinated and economical application of resources to minimize, monitor, and control the probability and/or impact of unfortunate events.. Risks can come from uncertainty in financial markets, project failures, legal liabilities, credit risk, accidents, natural causes and disasters as well as deliberate attacks from an adversary. Several risk management standards have been developed including the Project Management Institute, the National Institute of Science and Technology, actuarial societies, and ISO standards.

Forward market	The Forward market is the over-the-counter financial market in contracts for future delivery, so called forward contracts. Forward contracts are personalized between parties. The Forward market is a general term used to describe the informal market by which these contracts are entered into.
Netting	In general, Netting means to allow a positive value and a negative value to set-off and partially or entirely cancel each other out. In the context of credit risk, there are at least three specific types of Netting: · Close-out Netting: In the event of counterparty bankruptcy or any other relevant event of default specified in the relevant agreement which if accelerated (i.e. effected), all transactions or all of a given type are netted (i.e. set off against each other) at market value or if otherwise specified in the contract or if it is not possible to obtain a market value at an amount equal to the loss suffered by the non-defaulting party in replacing the relevant contract. The alternative would allow the liquidator to choose which contracts to enforce and which not to (and thus potentially 'cherry pick'.) There are international jurisdictions where the enforceability of Netting in bankruptcy has not been legally tested. · Netting by novation: The legal obligations of the parties to make required payments under one or more series of related transactions are canceled and a new obligation to make only the net payments is created. · Settlement or payment Netting: For cash settled trades, this can be applied either bilaterally or multilaterally and on related or unrelated transactions. Netting decreases credit exposure, increases business with existing counterparties, and reduces both operational and settlement risk and operational costs. In the context of pollution control, Netting refers to a procedure whereby a company can create a new pollution source only if it makes equal reductions in pollution elsewhere in the company, i.e. it cannot acquire new permits from the outside.
Financial statements	Financial statements are formal records of a business' financial activities. In British English, including United Kingdom company law, Financial statements are often referred to as accounts, although the term Financial statements is also used, particularly by accountants. Financial statements provide an overview of a business' financial condition in both short and long term.
Money	Money is anything that is generally accepted as payment for goods and services and repayment of debts. The main uses of Money are as a medium of exchange, a unit of account, and a store of value. Some authors explicitly require Money to be a standard of deferred payment.
Option	In finance, an option is a contract between a buyer and a seller that gives the buyer the right--but not the obligation--to buy or to sell a particular asset (the underlying asset) at a later day at an agreed price. In return for granting the option, the seller collects a payment (the premium) from the buyer. A call option gives the buyer the right to buy the underlying asset; a put option gives the buyer of the option the right to sell the underlying asset.
Financial risk	Financial risk is normally any risk associated with any form of financing. Risk is probability of unfavorable condition; in financial sector it is the probability of actual return being less than expected return. There will be uncertainty in every business; the level of uncertainty present is called risk.

Repatriation

Repatriation is the process of return of refugees or soldiers to their homes, most notably following a war. The term may also refer to the process of converting a foreign currency into the currency of one's own country.

When the traveler is unable to follow her/his trip , due to any medical reason, the insurance company is required to repatriate the patient.

Interest rate

An Interest rate is the price a borrower pays for the use of money they do not own, for instance a small company might borrow from a bank to kick start their business, and the return a lender receives for deferring the use of funds, by lending it to the borrower. Interest rate s are normally expressed as a percentage rate over the period of one year.

Interest rate s targets are also a vital tool of monetary policy and are used to control variables like investment, inflation, and unemployment.

Interest rate swap

An Interest rate swap is a derivative in which one party exchanges a stream of interest payments for another party's stream of cash flows. Interest rate swap s can be used by hedgers to manage their fixed or floating assets and liabilities. They can also be used by speculators to replicate unfunded bond exposures to profit from changes in interest rates.

Function cost analysis

Function cost analysis is the a method of technical and economic research of the systems for purpose to optimize a parity between system's consumer functions or properties and expenses to achieve those functions or properties.

This methodology for continuous perfection of production, industrial technologies, organizational structures was developed by Juryj Sobolev in 1948 at the 'Perm telephone factory'

· 1948 Juryj Sobolev - the first success in application of a method analysis at the 'Perm telephone factory' .
· 1949 - the first application for the invention as result of use of the new method.

Today in economically developed countries practically each enterprise or the company use methodology of the kind of functional-cost analysis as a practice of the quality management, most full satisfying to principles of standards of series ISO 9000.

· Interest of consumer not in products itself, but the advantage which it will receive from its usage.
· The consumer aspires to reduce his expenses
· Functions needed by consumer can be executed in the various ways, and, hence, with various efficiency and expenses. Among possible alternatives of realization of functions exist such in which the parity of quality and the price is the optimal for the consumer.

The goal of Function cost analysis is achievement of the highest consumer satisfaction of production at simultaneous decrease in all kinds of industrial expenses Classical Function cost analysis has three English synonyms - Value Engineering, Value Management, Value Analysis.

Countertrade

Countertrade is exchanging goods or services that are paid for, in whole or part, with other goods or services.

There are five main variants of Countertrade:

· Barter: Exchange of goods or services directly for other goods or services without the use of money as means of purchase or payment.
· Switch trading: Practice in which one company sells to another its obligation to make a purchase in a given country.
· Counter purchase: Sale of goods and services to a country by a company that promises to make a future purchase of a specific product from the country.
· Buyback: occurs when a firm builds a plant in a country - or supplies technology, equipment, training, or other services to the country and agrees to take a certain percentage of the plant's output as partial payment for the contract.
· Offset: Agreement that a company will offset a hard - currency purchase of an unspecified product from that nation in the future. Agreement by one nation to buy a product from another, subject to the purchase of some or all of the components and raw materials from the buyer of the finished product, or the assembly of such product in the buyer nation.

Barter

Barter is a type of trade in which goods or services are directly exchanged for other goods and/or services, without the use of money. It can be bilateral or multilateral, and usually exists parallel to monetary systems in most developed countries, though to a very limited extent. Barter usually replaces money as the method of exchange in times of monetary crisis, when the currency is unstable and devalued by hyperinflation.

Clearing account

A Clearing account is usually a temporary account containing costs or amounts that are to be transferred to another account. An example is the income summary account containing revenue and expense amounts to be transferred to retained earnings at the close of a fiscal period.

Co-production

The term Co-production is used as an idiom to explore the ways in which technical experts and other groups in society generate new knowledge and technologies together. More specifically, some use it to conceptualize the dynamic interaction between technology and society It has a long history, particularly arising out of radical theories of knowledge in the 1960s. It forms part of Mode 2, discussed by Michael Gibbons, Camille Limoges, Helga Nowotny, Simon Schwartzman, Peter Scott and Martin Trow in their 1994 book 'The New Production of Knowledge: The dynamics of science and research in contemporary societies' (Sage) and by Science and technology studies (S'TS) scholar Sheila Jasanoff.

Joint venture

A joint venture is an entity formed between two or more parties to undertake economic activity together. The parties agree to create a new entity by both contributing equity, and they then share in the revenues, expenses, and control of the enterprise. The venture can be for one specific project only, or a continuing business relationship such as the Fuji Xerox joint venture.

License

The verb license or grant license means to give permission. The noun license refers to that permission as well as to the document memorializing that permission. license may be granted by a party to another party as an element of an agreement between those parties.

Characteristic

Characteristic has several particular meanings:

· in mathematics

- · Euler characteristic
- · method of characteristic s (partial differential equations)

· in physics and engineering

· any characteristic curve that shows the relationship between certain input- and output parameters, e.g.
· an I-V or current-voltage characteristic is the current in a circuit as a function of the applied voltage
· Receiver-Operator characteristic
· in navigation, the characteristic pattern of a lighted beacon.
· in fiction

· in Dungeons ' Dragons, characteristic is another name for ability score .

Income tax

An income tax is a tax levied on the income of individuals or business (corporations or other legal entities.) Various income tax systems exist, with varying degrees of tax incidence. Income tax ation can be progressive, proportional, or regressive.

Turnkey

Turn-key refers to something that is ready for immediate use, generally used in the sale or supply of goods or services. The term is common in the construction industry, for instance, in which it refers to the bundling of materials and labor by sub-contractors. A 'Turnkey' job by a plumber would include the parts (toilets, tub, faucets, pipes, etc.)

Withholding

Withholding, in general, usually refers to a deduction of money (as 'withholding tax') from an employee's wages or salary by an employer, for projected or actual Income tax liabilities, see:

· PAYE (United Kingdom, Ireland, Australia and New Zealand)
· Tax withholding in the United States .

Policy

A Policy is typically described as a deliberate plan of action to guide decisions and achieve rational outcome(s.) However, the term may also be used to denote what is actually done, even though it is unplanned.

The term may apply to government, private sector organizations and groups, and individuals.

Choice Set

A Choice Set is one scenario provided for evaluation by respondents in a Choice Experiment. Responses are collected and used to create a Choice Model. Respondents are usually provided with a series of differing Choice Set s for evaluation.

Workweek

The legal Workweek varies from nation to nation. The weekend is a part of the week usually lasting one or two days in which most paid workers do not work.

In Muslim-majority countries the legal work week in the Middle East is typically either Saturday through Wednesday , Saturday through Thursday or Sunday through Thursday as in Egypt.

LaVergne, TN USA
13 January 2010
169824LV00002B/151/P

9 781428 891463